MAGICAL HOUSE PROTECTION

Magical House Protection

The Archaeology of Counter-Witchcraft

Brian Hoggard

berghahn
NEW YORK · OXFORD
www.berghahnbooks.com

First published in 2019 by
Berghahn Books
www.berghahnbooks.com

Library of Congress Cataloging-in-Publication Data
Names: Hoggard, Brian, author.
Title: Magical house protection : the archaeology of counter-witchcraft /
Brian Hoggard.
Description: First Edition. | New York : Berghahn Books, 2019. | Includes
bibliographical references and indexes.
Identifiers: LCCN 2019003734 (print) | LCCN 2019009463 (ebook) | ISBN
9781789202069 (ebook) | ISBN 9781789202052 (hardback : alk. paper)
Subjects: LCSH: Protection magic. | Houses--Miscellanea. | Magic. |
Witchcraft.
Classification: LCC BF1623.P75 (ebook) | LCC BF1623.P75 H64 2019 (print) |
DDC 133.4/30941--dc23
LC record available at https://lccn.loc.gov/2019003734

British Library Cataloguing in Publication Data
A catalogue record for this book is available from the British Library

ISBN 978-1-78920-205-2 hardback
ISBN 978-1-80073-021-2 paperback
ISBN 978-1-78920-206-9 ebook

Contents

◉ Illustrations

Acknowledgements

Over the years many people have taken the time to contact me with information about objects or to share their own hard won research. Some people have helped just by being supportive during difficult times. There is every chance I have forgotten to mention someone in the list below who was helpful or otherwise informative since I began this project back in 1999 and to those people I promise a mention in the second edition. To the following people I owe many thanks for generosity of spirit and a willingness to exchange information in an otherwise shark-infested academic world:

Dr Alan Massey, Dr Janet Pennington, June Swann MBE, Jeremy Harte, John Billingsley, Jennie Cobban, Jason Semmens, Matthew Slocombe and all at the Society for the Protection of Ancient Buildings, The Vernacular Architecture Group, Buket Akgün, Daniela Àvido, Dr Riley Auge, Linda Hall, Patricia Winzar, James Wright, Simon Walker, Marko Manninen, Timothy Easton, Dr David Gaimster, Alan Abbey, Jon Hughett, Linda Wilson, Christopher Binding, Simon Lisney, Chris Manning, Dr Ian Evans, Professor Marshall Becker, Sonja Hukantaival, Adina Hulubaş, Professor Ronald Hutton, Rainer Atzbach, Nicolas Vernot, Ric Kemp, Matthew Champion, Andy Bentham, Ivan Bunn, Simon Walker, Ioana Repciuc, Alison Fearn, Walter Wheeler, Marc Robben and Alyssa Conary.

I have always tried my best to help people who are interested in the subject and who ask me for material too. I am proud to have shared all of my USA material about horse skulls and witch-bottles with Chris Manning and several others many years ago. Special thanks must go to Dr Riley Auge who gave a lecture on my behalf in the USA and who persuaded me to attend the Medieval Congress in Kalamazoo in May 2008, which was such a fun time.

I would also like to thank all of those curatorial staff and archaeologists who took the time to reply to my huge postal survey way back in 1999. You provided the foundation for this book.

Preface

Hidden within the fabric of buildings all over the world, waiting to be exposed by demolition, renovation or repair, there remains the evidence of magical house protection. These objects and animals were secretly tucked away to act as a layer of protection against all manner of supernatural dangers. Some of these ideas persist, with many examples from the twentieth century on record. In addition to objects like shoes, cats, bottles and horse skulls, people would also conceal written charms and inscribe markings designed to invoke the protection of the Virgin Mary or to distract the attention of evil spirits.

Some of these practices can be clearly traced back to medieval times and for others we only have substantial amounts of evidence from the seventeenth century onwards. Part of the reason for this is simply down to the quantity of buildings from the period which have survived, another part will be due to the survival of the materials over time. Marks on stone would normally be far more durable than a piece of paper tucked between beams or a cat wedged in a roof space.

The advent of the printing press and the dissemination of frightening tales regarding witchcraft likely raised awareness and fears, leading to the popularisation of counter-witchcraft practices such as these. Clearly the period of the witch trials, which varies in different countries but broadly occurred between the sixteenth and eighteenth centuries, also had an impact on the need for personal spiritual protection.

The fairly arbitrary divide between the work of archaeologists and historians means that in the history of witchcraft there has only been the occasional nod towards this physical evidence. This is mainly due to the fact that, with the exception of witch-bottles, there is no contemporary written evidence for these practices. It is quite striking how absent this mass of physical evidence regarding people's beliefs about witchcraft and the supernatural is from the large body of work which is out there about the history of witchcraft. What we tend to see in those books (but not all) is a concentration on trial records where elite beliefs about witchcraft are imposed upon accused and accusers, producing a distorted account of supposed witchcraft, often based on false accusations in the first place. It is all fascinating to read about but, essentially, the witch trials may teach us a lot but they are not necessarily the best place to look for information about what ordinary people thought about witchcraft.

This subject area fell into the gaps between the disciplines of history and archaeology with historians not wanting to address artefacts for which there were no records (except for witch-bottles) and archaeologists (with a few notable exceptions) not treating these objects seriously when found in otherwise very interesting standing buildings. I have spoken to many archaeologists who have told me anecdotes of finding bottles, shoes and cats which did not find their way into archives or dig reports.

The other issue which has always affected this topic is that the main finders of the artefacts are builders who are not always in the best situation to record and report the objects they find. Many objects end up in the builder's skip or for sale on the black market. To their credit, however, a large number of objects they encounter do find their way into local museums where it then depends on the diligence of the member of staff and their collections policy as to whether the finds are properly accessioned and interpreted. One independent museum I visited had a box of old shoes and fragments of bellarmines which people had brought in, but they had not recorded the address of the properties, their context within the building or even the name of the finder. Most museums are professional of course and uphold good standards in this regard but that case was not entirely unusual.

The objects which are the subject of this book are not generally mentioned in any primary or secondary material regarding witchcraft and yet they are extremely numerous, widespread and testify tangibly to the beliefs people held. Here we can see the beliefs of these people whose voices are usually not heard laid bare in physical form through these artefacts.

These objects testify to people's acute fears regarding witchcraft and other supernatural dangers. They are the actual counter-spells which were created in an everyday battle with perceived forces of evil which, it was believed, existed all around them. That people turned to these methods so readily shows that the church alone was unable to provide the kind of protection people felt they needed and also that belief in the supernatural was a normal part of their existence. Indeed, we often find these artefacts and symbols in churches too so people clearly thought that even churches were vulnerable.

The most popular locations to conceal objects within buildings are usually at portals such as the hearth, the threshold and also voids or dead spaces. This suggests that people believed it was possible for dark forces to travel through the landscape and attack them in their homes. Whether these forces were emanations from a witch in the form of a spell, a witch's familiar pestering their property, an actual witch flying in spirit or a combination of all of those is difficult to tell. Additional sources of danger could be ghosts, fairies and demons. People went to great lengths to ensure their homes and property were protected, highlighting the fact that these beliefs and fears were visceral and, as far as they were concerned, literally terrifying.

The pioneer of research in this area was Ralph Merrifield whose 1987 *Archaeology of Ritual and Magic* led to this book. He had published many papers from the 1950s onwards which examined witch-bottles, written charms and other objects. In his work he also drew on the research of Britain's foremost expert on historic footwear, June Swann, who had begun researching the area of concealed shoes at around the same time as he began his work. Margaret Howard's paper on dried cats also received a mention. Merrifield had a network of correspondents including Jennie Cobban, Janet Pennington and Timothy Easton who have all made significant contributions to this field over the years. Easton, in particular, pioneered the study of protective marks, an area not covered by Merrifield.

Against that backdrop my own research began in 1999 with a huge survey of museums and archaeological establishments in the UK. The raw data that came in from that survey, and the numerous reports submitted to the Apotropaios website each week from all over the world, have contributed to the largest database of objects of this type. This research has also featured in TV programmes in the UK on Sky Discovery, Channel 4, BBC2, and ABC Australia, and on several radio stations; there have also been features in national newspapers. Each time some new research is published there is an upsurge in reports, as indeed will probably occur on the publication of this work.

People who discover these objects, from whatever background, normally experience great curiosity about the objects and get in touch for advice about how to deal with this new element to their home's history and heritage. Some become incredibly superstitious about the objects and can become very fearful of the consequences of it leaving the building for analysis. It is really quite remarkable the extent to which people can experience a deep-rooted emotional response when these discoveries are made. At times they seem to make an almost visceral connection with the motivations and fears and of those who initially concealed them. This was the case with a witch-bottle discovered in Suffolk where the owner requested a ceremonial re-interment of the bottle beneath the hearth which involved myself and some local nuns. Part of this was filmed for an episode of BBC2's *History Detectives* back in 2007.

Another example of these emerging feelings upon discovering a formerly concealed object was reported in 2001 from Curry Rivel in Somerset. The correspondent reported via email:

> About 40 years ago my grandfather found sealed behind the jamb of the front door the leg of a wooden toy, with painted stocking. They left it out for a few days, when, it is claimed, the atmosphere of the house became disturbed, strange noises were heard etc. As soon as my grandfather replaced it and resealed it, calm returned. However, as my grandmother was decidedly fanciful I remain fairly sceptical about the claimed effects.

The study of concealed objects is gaining in popularity and there are now people working on it in various areas: in the USA (Walter Wheeler, Patrick Donmoyer, Professor Marshall Becker, Dr Riley Auge and Chris Manning); in Australia (Dr Ian Evans); in Romania (Adina Hulubaş); in France (Nicholas Vernot); in Finland (Sonja Hukantaival); and in the world of speleology, where Linda Wilson and Chris Binding have been making amazing discoveries in caves (mainly in Somerset at present).

In the UK a whole host of people have begun engaging in regional research and a few have started to conduct national surveys very similar to the one I carried out in 1999 and which led to this book. One of the most interesting recent developments is the English Medieval Graffiti Survey established by Matt Champion. It has spawned a host of enthusiasts who now find and record graffiti and share their photos and thoughts via the Survey's social media output. A large portion of the marks reported are of the building protection type so there is now a bigger body of evidence than ever from all parts of England and beyond.

The evidence is telling us that counter-witchcraft, house protection and good luck charms which were inserted into and carved onto buildings were spread through global trade and travel. It also tells us that people generally believed in supernatural forces of all kinds and were prepared to expend considerable time and effort in order to alleviate their fears regarding them. These practices continued well into the twentieth century and in some areas continue to this day. Despite the lack of written sources, enough finds are emerging for the true purpose of these objects to become evident.

This book is divided into two parts: the first deals with the context and principal find types in this subject area, the second focuses on some case studies and includes a gazetteer of discoveries from Britain. When I first began this research back in 1999 the first task was to survey a representative sample of the museums and archaeological units across the UK. This took the form of a postal survey with a list of questions asking the establishment to describe what kind of objects they held which may fall into the house protection category. The response was quite good and I established a database of finds from all parts of the UK. Since that time people have been reporting objects to me following lectures I have given, in response to press releases and articles, following TV appearances and by searching for the topic online and discovering my website. The reports have become more international over the years with the global spread of internet usage.

At the time of writing I have been studying this subject area for some twenty years and this book represents an attempt to distil what I have learned into hard copy. The theories presented in this book are the best I have at this point in time; as new discoveries continue to emerge and more new scholars enter the field, I am sure they will be challenged and modified – perhaps even by myself.

PART I

CONTEXT AND DISCUSSION OF PRINCIPAL FIND TYPES

⁖●⁖ Chapter 1

Folklore, Witchcraft, Religion

If we are to understand the reasons behind many of the practices described in this book, it is important to try to imagine some of the ways in which the world was experienced in the past. For example, in pre-Reformation England the experience of church was very different to the one which people might have today. Folklore was much more than just a curiosity written in a book; it could have a tangible effect on one's interaction with the landscape. The period of the witch trials, although manifesting at slightly different times and in different ways across Europe and America, had a huge impact on people's sense of vulnerability and awareness of supernatural dangers. It is a simple point but the absence of noise and distractions from vehicles and technology should also be noted, as should the absence of electric light. When considering the meanings of these finds, it is important to attempt to imagine something of the sensory world in which they were used.

The Church

If we imagine a visit to a church service in pre-Reformation England, we are entering a foreign land as far as comparisons to a modern church service are concerned. Firstly, the service would be conducted in Latin, a language which the congregation would not understand (with rare exceptions). In fact, it is likely that the serving priest would not understand the Latin either as many learned their services by rote, although of course some, a minority, were Latin scholars and understood every word.

Services were conducted behind the rood screen which separated the nave from the chancel. This was a large latticed screen which enabled the assembled to see the Catholic ritual being conducted but kept them apart from it. On top of the screen was the rood itself, normally a large figure of Christ on judgement day with images of doom – skulls and other bones – strewn around his feet. Jesus was quite a formidable presence in these churches.

The walls of the church would probably have been far more colourful than the plain and austere décor which we normally see today in English churches. There may have been images of hell with demons devouring human souls, the devil himself would sometimes be portrayed, and the carved corbels often showed grotesque figures. These images reinforced the idea that you would be judged and could go to hell if you did not live according to the rules of the church.

Add to this atmosphere a liberal use of pungent incense and many candles and it could be said that we are witnessing an elaborate and eerie ritual, partially concealed behind a screen with what must have seemed like an ancient magical language being spoken. Little of what happened actually informed those present about what was going on and there was certainly very little attempt to educate. When asked who Jesus was, people had been known to guess that maybe he was God's uncle, illustrating a very poor understanding of what now seem to be very basic Christian concepts.

Within the church there also may have been shrines for a variety of saints, or possibly a nearby holy well which would also be regarded as a sacred place. There would almost always be a part of the church dedicated to the Virgin Mary, the most loved and popular of the Christian figures.

When we look at this experience from the outside, this experience could be described as entering a temple full of foreboding images, witnessing a magical ritual which invokes the presence of the temple's chief deity, having the opportunity to make offerings or pray to a variety of lesser deities, catching up with friends and neighbours. The church appears to have been a place where you could tap into this range of Christian forces, while also reminding you of the vulnerability of your soul in a rather negative way by filling your mind with images of doom, demons and gargoyles.

Throughout the period of the Reformation and the dissolution of the monasteries in England, many changes occurred in churches but for many people it seems these were changes for the worse: the whitewashing of church walls to cover up images, the stripping out of rood screens, and the installation of plain altar tables. Many shrines for saints were removed, lady chapels torn down, stained glass broken, statuary defaced. Anderson states that 'The iconoclasts fell with particular fury upon images of the Madonna; carvings were burnt or smashed and a few of the thousands of windows in which she must once have been represented remain intact' (Anderson 1971: 129). Despite this many people clung on to the reverence of the Virgin Mary in particular. Of the range of Christian figures available, hers was the most kind, nurturing, protecting and forgiving, and although many images of her were no longer present in churches her presence in Bible stories was still very strong.

Folklore and Fairies

Folklore also played a very important role in the everyday interactions with the landscape, people and things. People made predictions about the weather and other outcomes based on the movements or appearances of certain creatures such as birds and fish. Failure to observe tiny rites in everyday contacts with people could be seen as harbingers of bad luck. There was and is a huge range of superstitions which helped people to understand the at times haphazard and random nature of human life. Many of these practices and observations are detailed in *Religion and the Decline of Magic* by Keith Thomas (Thomas 1971).

One of the more full-bodied areas of folklore was the belief in the fairy folk. Firstly, we must put aside Victorian notions of fairies and images such as those presented in the Cottingley Fairies photographs and in Disney movies like *Peter Pan*. In those depictions fairies are very small winged magical creatures capable, in some cases, of granting wishes.

The fairies of old were believed to be another race of beings, not too dissimilar to us, who existed in a parallel world which intersected with ours at certain points in the landscape. These points were usually fairy hills which, from the descriptions, appear to be ancient barrows. A famous account of fairy lore was written by the seventeenth-century Scottish priest Robert Kirk. He tells of some very convoluted methods for seeing fairies, including the following: 'put his foot on the Seer's foot, and [then] the Seer's hand is put on the inquirer's head, who is [then] to look over the wizard's [seer's] right shoulder'. Other much more detailed methods, such as looking backwards between your legs, are also explained (Stewart 1990: 33).

If you accidentally built across a fairy path or damaged one of their hills, you could find yourself in a lot of trouble and possibly end up being 'elf shot'. This is where the fairies shoot you with their magical arrows causing you to become lame, or worse. Evidence of elf-shot could be found in the shape of prehistoric flint arrowheads which occasionally turn up on the ground thanks to our Neolithic ancestors. Fairy beliefs are still very strong in some countries, notably Iceland and Ireland.

There is such a huge range of folkloric practices that it is very difficult to summarise. Some customs relate to particular days or dates, some are in response to events in nature, and others concern birth, marriage and death. Often these end up becoming incorporated into church practice which can create confusion. Some customs, such as ancient threshold customs which can be seen all around the ancient world, appear to be born out of a basic human instinct to protect and mark out zones for different kinds of behaviour. This instinct feeds directly into the content of this book.

Witchcraft

Of course, one of the most prevalent fears in the past was of witchcraft. This in part stemmed from the reliance of communities on the cunning folk, or wise men and women. These individuals provided many different services which could not be found elsewhere. They often had herbal or other healing knowledge and in addition could provide more arcane services. These cunning folk are really the 'white witches' of our past, although many were actually slightly 'grey'.

The services they provided included thief detection, love magic, help in identifying future partners, fortune telling and in the case of some, more nefarious services. They also tended to be expert in all matters of folklore. One of their roles – which came from their diagnosis of the cause of people's problems – was witch detection. If someone had become lame or unwell, this may be due to a known and treatable condition, or it may be due to witchcraft. If the latter was the cause, then a range of cures were on offer, including many of the objects detailed in this book, but most notably witch-bottles.

Cunning folk generally charged for their services or bartered for them. They also tended to have specialisms, so people sometimes travelled quite far to benefit from a specific skill. The role they provided in their communities was pivotal and they held high status. George Gifford, writing in 1597, complained that his parishioners went to the cunning man 'as if they were his god'.

It is clear then that these cunning folk were a tremendously important part of society and were generally regarded as a force for good. It follows, however, that if people could use magic for good then they could also use it to cause harm, or 'maleficium' as it was known. There was a general belief in the existence of harmful witches, and suspicion could fall upon anyone whose behaviour transgressed 'normal' thresholds. People could be accused of witchcraft by children who may have misinterpreted their actions, or because someone witnessed them performing an act of witchcraft. From trial records, it would seem that acts of witchcraft included anything from wishing someone ill, with a harsh stare and a mumbled curse, to ritual acts performed with a coven on a hilltop.

In order to accuse someone of witchcraft, it was normally necessary to have a reason, rather than just a vague suspicion. If someone became unexpectedly unwell, experienced sudden pain in a limb, or was troubled with livestock deaths or crops repeatedly failing, then this might be diagnosed as having been caused by witchcraft. The diagnosis may have come from the general consensus of the victim's neighbours, or be the outcome of a consultation with the local cunning person. People commissioned written charms from their local cunning folk for exactly this reason and were often also advised to boil up or bury witch-bottles.

These fears were widespread and were made even more so by the advent of popular printed material during the seventeenth century. A large number of pamphlets told terrifying tales of witchcraft and the Devil. Although literacy levels were fairly low during that period, people would often gather together to hear someone read them aloud. Those present could then tell others what they had heard and the contents of these pamphlets thus found a wide circulation. In this way, what had been fairly straightforward, popular notions of the supernatural became intermingled with ideas from the elite regarding theology and cosmology.

The way in which the law dealt with witchcraft varied, depending on the country. In England the law placed the onus on the accuser to prove that a witch had caused harm using witchcraft. There were stiff penalties for false accusations and providing proof that you had suffered harm through witchcraft was not a simple thing to do. The legal elite at this time were, however, inclined to believe in witchcraft and had their own theories concerning witchcraft and the agency of the Devil, so it was necessary only for the accuser to provide proof that some harm had been caused in a way which accorded with these notions. If someone was convicted of causing harm using witchcraft in England, they could be sent to the gallows. They would only be burned in England if they were found guilty of an additional offence for which burning was normally the punishment. For example, if a woman was convicted of killing her husband using witchcraft, this would be regarded as petty treason, the punishment for which was burning.

Elsewhere the law simply required evidence that the witch had some sort of pact with the Devil. This could be in the form of an actual written pact, which were somewhat dubiously produced to convict witches in France, or in the form of witness testimony. From our modern perspective, it is tragic that so many were burned, lynched and hanged for witchcraft, a crime which most people today would think is actually impossible to commit.

All these factors contributed to an environment where supernatural forces were considered real and ever present. There was a strong belief that certain people could mediate these forces. Priests could channel something of the power of God, cunning folk could harness magical forces (mostly) for good, and, it was felt, dark witches could utilise these forces to cause harm, or 'maleficium'.

In Britain beliefs such as these persisted in rural areas until well into the twentieth century. William Paynter wrote extensively about witchcraft beliefs in Cornwall during his own lifetime in his book, published posthumously by Jason Semmens who recognised the value of his testimony. In it he described sticking a pig's heart with pins to remove witchcraft, and discussed the power of the evil eye, fairies, written charms and herbal remedies (Paynter 2016). It is clear from this work that these practices continued in an unbroken thread from the earliest examples to almost the present day. It would not be surprising to find these beliefs and practices surviving in pockets in various parts of the world.

For these reasons it was necessary to be aware of the measures which could be taken to repel, trap, divert or confuse these harmful energies which may seek one out. Some of these measures would be undertaken by carpenters, builders and thatchers as part of the construction process, not unlike installing a burglar alarm or top-of-the-range locks. People would often take advantage of changes to buildings to add new layers of protection, and the construction methods sometimes left certain voids open as a receptacle for further measures. The home's occupants also took action. For example, shoes and other objects were often deposited on ledges within the chimney breast or behind the fireback. If it was believed that someone had been bewitched, a visit the local cunning man or woman may be deemed necessary to take specific action such as commissioning a written charm or creating a witch-bottle. It was also possible to scratch or engrave marks onto the surfaces inside a building.

When we consider the objects and marks found in buildings today, as described in this book, it is important that we keep in mind the environment in which they were created.

Chapter 2

WITCH-BOTTLES

Witch-bottles are unusual in the context of counter-witchcraft objects in that they were written about in pamphlets and books during the seventeenth century and later. Other practices and objects which we have substantial evidence for, such as concealed shoes, animal remains and protection marks, are curiously absent from the literature of the period, suggesting a level of secrecy about those practices.

This chapter will begin by looking at the seventeenth-century written evidence about witch-bottles, before discussing the different types of bottles, and providing some case studies. It will also explore the contents and locations of the bottles and finish with an exploration of their usage and what this might tell us about past perceptions of the supernatural.

Before launching into the chapter proper, some points about the general difficulties involved in this topic should be made. Witch-bottles, like other apotropaic objects, were deliberately concealed so it is only when buildings are demolished or repaired, or when archaeologists excavate building sites that they come to light. In the case of demolitions and repairs, the likely finders are builders who often dispose of these objects because they do not know what they are. Sometimes the opposite is true, and they are destroyed for superstitious reasons. This means that only very few get reported to www.apotropaios.co.uk or to a local museum or archaeology unit. The amount that could be found is also limited by the number of buildings that survive from any given period. Suffice to say, the number dealt with in this chapter is likely to be only a tiny portion of the total number which were concealed.

Some questions have been raised about the terminology applied to these finds. At the Hidden Charms conference in April 2016 in Norwich, Annie Thwaite delivered a paper called 'The Urinary Experiment'. In this paper the term 'witch-bottles' was questioned as not being an accurate name for these bottles; Thwaite argued instead that at the time the creation of one of these bottles was considered a scientific cure for illness caused by witchcraft. She had conducted meticulous background research and uncovered references to these bottles not previously noted in the field. Even if we ignore the archaeological evidence and restrict ourselves to the contemporary literature, we can see that these bottles were created as a specific remedy to being bewitched and this remedy worked with the perceived magical forces at the time. I therefore have no problem referring to these bottles as witch-bottles, but Thwaite's paper has certainly raised some interesting points.

Written Evidence

Ralph Merrifield in his *Archaeology of Ritual and Magic* cited four early modern documents in his work on witch-bottles: Joseph Blagrave's *Astrological Practice of Physick* (1671), Joseph Glanvil's *Sadducismus Triumphatus* (1681), Increase Mather's *An Essay for the Recording of Illustrious Providences* (1684) and Cotton Mather's *Late Memorable Providences* (1691) which all contain references to the practice of creating a counter-witchcraft bottle.

The reference in Blagrave's work appears in a section on 'experimental Rules, whereby to afflict the Witch, causing the evil to return back upon them'. He describes the practice as follows:

> Another way is stop the urine of the Patient, close up in a bottle, and put into it three nails, pins or needles, with a little white Salt, keeping the urine always warm: if you let it remain long in the bottle, it will endanger the witches life: for I have found by experience that they will be grievously tormented making their water with great difficulty, if any at all, and the more if the Moon be in Scorpio in Square or Opposition to his Significator, when its done.

His reasoning for the success of the operation is as follows: 'The reason ... is because there is part of the vital spirit of the Witch in it, for such is the subttlety of the Devil, that he will not suffer the Witch to infuse any poysonous matter into the body of man or beast, without some of the Witches blood mingled with it' (Blagrave 1671). Clearly Blagrave is prescribing a method of turning the witches power back upon them using the sympathetic link between the witch and victim. The detail of placing pins in the bottle is affirmed by a later author who mentions similar contents. The idea was supposedly that the bottle represented the witch's bladder and that inserting pins and the victim's urine into the bottle would cause intense pain in that region to the witch, forcing them to lift whatever spell it was believed they had placed on the victim.

Cotton Mather described the contents of a witch-bottle in his 1691 work, *Late Memorable Providences*, as 'Nails, Pins, and such Instruments … as carry a shew of Torture with them' (Mather 1691). Joseph Glanvil relates a tale of witchcraft which mentions witch-bottles. He speaks of a woman whose health had been languishing and a travelling cunning man's diagnosis that the cause of her malady was a 'dead Spright'. He recommended that her husband 'take a Bottle, and put his Wife's Urine into it, together with Pins and Needles and Nails, and Cork them up, and set the Bottle to the Fire, but be sure the Cork be fast in it, that it fly not out'. The inevitable result was that the cork flew off with a loud bang and showered the contents everywhere. When they next saw the man, he recommended burying the bottle instead, at which point the wife's health began to improve.

> But there came a Woman from a town some miles off to their house, with a lamentable outcry, that they had killed her Husband … But at last they understood by her that her Husband was a Wizard and had bewitched this Man's Wife, and that this counter-practice prescribed by the Old Man, which saved the Man's Wife from languishment, was the death of that Wizard that had bewitched her. (Glanvil 1681: 205–208)

Jason Semmens, in his article 'The Usage of Witch-Bottles and Apotropaic Charms in Cornwall', also cites an early description of the making of a witch-bottle. Instructions for making one were given to a pregnant woman in 1701 in St Merryn by a local conjuror. The description is here quoted from Semmens' article:

> For Thamson Leverton on Saturday next being the 17th of this Instant September any time that day take about a pint of your owne Urine and make it almost scalding hot then Emtie it into a stone Jugg with a narrow Mouth then put into it so Much white Salt as you can take up with the Thumb and two forefingers of your lift hand and three new nails with their points down wards, their points being first made very sharp then stop the mouth of the Jugg very close with a piece of Tough cley and bind a piece of Leather firm over the stop then put the Jugg into warm Embers and keep him there 9 or 10 days and nights following so that it go not stone cold all that mean time day nor night and your private Enemies will never after have any power upon you either in Body or Goods, So be it. (Semmens 2000: 25–30)

These early mentions of creating a counter-spell using a bottle are fascinating and all broadly give the same set of instructions about how to exploit the sympathetic link between the witch and her or his victim via an easily obtainable body fluid, urine. They instruct the victim to heat the urine with a mixture of salt and sharp objects until the pain this inflicts upon the witch becomes so great that they will be forced to make amends with their target.

Owen Davies, in his *Witchcraft, Magic and Culture 1736–1951*, has traced other later examples of the use of witch-bottles. During a case of spirit possession in Bristol in 1762, a local cunning woman was consulted who confirmed that witchcraft was responsible for the fits, visions, voices and other manifestations that were suffered by the daughters of Richard Giles, an innkeeper. Her recommendation was to boil a witch-bottle, and it is reported that the daughters recovered once this was done. Another example of the boiling of a witch-bottle proved fatal in 1804 when the cunning man John Hepworth of Bradford experimented with boiling an iron witch-bottle which exploded, killing his client (Davies 1999b: 218). In earlier times it is more likely that the cork or bung would have simply exploded outwards, showering its contents in whichever direction the bottle was pointing.

It is important to note that the bottles described in the texts above would not generally have been concealed in buildings; if the boiling of the bottle was successful, it is likely that the bottle was then discarded. All the actual examples of witch-bottles discussed in this book have been recovered from concealed contexts and have had a different treatment to the ones mentioned in those texts. The accounts only refer to the bottles being buried or concealed if heating them had been deemed unsuccessful; as all the examples reported to me were of buried or concealed bottles, this suggests that the process of heating the bottles did not work very well and that the practice of burying bottles was widespread and well known. It is my contention that this became the normal way to treat a witch-bottle.

The Bottles

At the time of writing 294 examples of concealed bottles were recorded in the files of the author; these came to light via a survey conducted from 1999 to 2001 and through later accounts reported to www.apotropaios.co.uk. Until the mid-eighteenth century, the most popular form of bottle was a type of German stoneware, but glass bottles were also concealed with similar contents.

The glazed stoneware bottles, known colloquially as 'bellarmines' (Gaimster 1997) – the technical term is Bartmann stoneware – come in various sizes and all have a large round 'belly'. Most of these bottles have a small mask portraying a bearded individual of menacing appearance which has been placed onto the neck of the bottle, making them anthropomorphic in appearance. This mask takes the form of a clay tablet pressed into a mould and fixed to the bottle before firing. They usually also have a medallion on the belly of the bottle which includes armorial devices or a striking pattern, sometimes related to their location of origin and sometimes also showing their date of manufacture. Occasionally these bottles have a symbol on their 'belly' resembling a daisy wheel. These bottles were initially imported in large quantities from the Rhineland in Germany but later Dutch examples began to appear and English manufacturers began to produce copies for mass production (Allan 1983: 37–45). The colloquial name of these stoneware bottles, 'bellarmines', appears to have evolved around tales of Cardinal Bellarmine who was hostile to Protestants in the volumes he wrote on heresy in the late sixteenth century; the satire arises from a comparison between the mean face on the bottles and the perceived nature of the Cardinal. By 1700 the peak of importation of stoneware drinking vessels had ended and glass was becoming more commonplace. Into the eighteenth century the use of glass bottles as witch-bottles became more usual, and into the nineteenth and twentieth centuries we find a mixture of glass and earthenware.

Figure 2.1 Suffolk witch-bottle prior to re-burial. © Brian Hoggard.

M.R. Holmes investigated the origins and naming of these bottles in his 1950 article for the *Antiquaries Journal*. In his article he traced the evolution of the mask from the richly carved German examples found on tankards in the Rhineland, on which he comments, 'The beard is square, the face well formed and not without dignity' (Holmes 1950: 173–179). The English examples lack the same attention to detail and are usually found on bottles and jugs, not tankards. The expression on the mask in England is variously cheerful, neutral and aggressive. Holmes developed a type series broadly categorising the bottles in which he demonstrated the way in which the mask apparently had a reverse evolution from the neat and precise German examples to no mask at all. His type series ranged from Type I, the German examples, to Type IX, where the mask had become very simple. He completed his evolution with examples from the Fulham factory during the short period when similar bottles were manufactured in England which bore no mask at all, but which were otherwise very similar. Holmes' type series has been surpassed by the work of David Gaimster, but has still been used by many archaeologists over the years as a convenient way of categorising these bottles.

The highly durable nature of stoneware meant the bottles could be re-used many times and had a very long life; it therefore follows that it is not always possible to be sure when they were concealed. Their anthropomorphic appearance, with the face of a wild bearded man on the neck and the large, round belly, would almost certainly have made people gravitate towards choosing them for magical purposes. Some of these stoneware bottles also bear patterns with spoked wheel forms, resembling the daisy wheel symbol in some ways, which may have been another reason for using them. The glass bottles, which were increasingly used later on, range in type from onion bottles and steeple bottles to small glass phials and jars, but earthenware also crops up.

Of the 97 bottles which have been positively identified as bellarmines, only 39 have been firmly dated. In many cases the dates are very approximate and vague. In 13 examples the date of the seventeenth century was given. More detailed information was offered on 12 bottles which were described as Holmes type IX, placing them rather broadly in the late seventeenth century, and 7 were described as Holmes type VIII, placing them somewhere in the region of 1664–1688. One bottle was described as originating in the mid-seventeenth century and some bottles were stamped with their date of manufacture. 2 of these were from 1600 and one example of each of the following occurs: 1620, 1680, 1699 and 1700. Although the known dates for the bottles are very incomplete, there does appear to be a distinct bias towards the latter half of the seventeenth century, suggesting an increase in the practice or a greater survival of vernacular architecture from this period. Broadly speaking, these bottles appear to have been used as counter-witchcraft devices from the mid-seventeenth century onwards. This seems to indicate that their use as witch-bottles slightly pre-dates their appearance in known texts. This is significant as the concealed and buried bottles have slightly different contents and more specific siting within the building than the ones which occur in the texts.

Of the 294 discoveries of concealed bottles that have been reported to me, just over a third have been positively identified as being of the bellarmine type; the rest are glass or earthenware. A small portion have been reported as witch-bottles by the museum or archaeological unit that holds them, but full details have not been supplied regarding the bottle type. These numbers are growing all the time as awareness of the topic increases.

Distribution

In the earliest period the distribution and extent of bellarmine witch-bottles shows a distinct bias towards the south-east of England and parts of the south coast. This very closely matches those places which imported the largest quantity of stoneware from the Low Countries. The distribution map contained in John Allan's 1983 article on the post-medieval trade in ceramics (Allan 1983) clearly correlates, with a map showing the distribution of bellarmine witch-bottles. Allan states that the East Anglian ports specialised in trade with Holland which would explain the large number of finds in Norfolk and Suffolk. However, he also points out that imports into London in the last third of the sixteenth century accounted for 75 per cent of all imported stoneware into England. These goods were redistributed on ships along the English coast. The two principal ports which received redistributed stoneware from London were Colchester and Ipswich, both of which served areas with a high density of bellarmine witch-bottles. Allan states that overland transport was eight or ten times more expensive than transport by sea. However, local trade in small quantities did not pose the same problems as bulk orders of up to and over 1000 bottles at a time, as was common in the London ports (Allan 1983), hence the redistribution of bottles into the catchment area of principal towns and sometimes beyond.

There is a strong correlation between the distribution of bellarmines and the distribution of witch-bottles when compared to Allan's map of the redistribution of the bottles. The survey undertaken for this project did not reveal any examples of bellarmine witch-bottles further north than Leeds, yet clearly the trade in stoneware vessels did reach this far. The practice, therefore, had clear geographical limits within which the bellarmine bottle was considered the most appropriate vessel for that practice during its peak of high-volume importing and manufacture – approximately 1550 to 1700. This is particularly evidenced by the relatively small numbers of these bottles found in a folk magic context at significant distances away from the nearest port. In terms of distribution, therefore, it can be concluded that (based on the evidence available) there appears to be a strong bias towards areas served principally by sea but also river ports in some cases. As time moved forward and the transport network improved, there was much less of a clear pattern in the distribution of witch-bottles.

Later, glass witch-bottles in the shape of small phials, bottles and occasionally jars can be found in all parts of Britain, but still mainly in England. A possible example was found in Australia (Evans 2010: 100) and Professor Marshall Becker and Chris Manning detail many examples which have been found in America (Manning 2014: 53–58). A fine example of a bellarmine witch-bottle was found in in 2012 on the site of Beaux [Bow] Lane House, Mercer's Street, Dublin, and anecdotally others have been found in Ireland. This practice does not appear to have taken hold in Europe despite this being the place where bellarmine bottles were made, so it does appear to be an English invention.

Contents

51 bellarmine witch-bottles were found with contents, in varying states of decay. The contents are striking in their general similarities, with few variations. Even where the contents appear to differ from the norm, there has usually been a clear attempt to find substitutes for unavailable items. 44 contained iron nails and pins. Inside two examples were the tine of a rake, one contained red dust, one contained rust and one other contained a mass of metal. Assuming that these last five were also iron, a total of 49 of the bellarmines with contents contained iron. Iron was not the only metal present within the bottles, however. Six bottles contained bronze pins in addition to iron nails or pins, and of the four containing what is described as brass pins, only one did not also contain iron. It must be stated that bronze and brass have the same ingredients in different quantities, so identification of the pins as bronze or brass is sometimes unreliable. Assuming this is the case, a total of 10 have a

bronze/brass alloy and, as already stated, only in one example did this alloy exist without iron also being present. In one bottle bent silver pins were discovered and in one other traces of copper were found.

One aspect not mentioned in the seventeenth-century texts about witch-bottles but for which there is ample evidence from the bottles themselves is the process of bending the pins or nails. In virtually all cases where pins or nails have been found in bottles they have been deliberately bent prior to inclusion in the bottle. It seems that this was done to ritually 'kill' the pins, activating a ghost pin which would be effective against spiritual enemies coming into contact with the bottle. Dr Alan Massey has demonstrated that in several bottles these pins were often bent all together in one movement, perhaps by holding them in a vice or bending around a rod using grips of some kind (Massey 2017: 55–67). In these cases this proves that this was a deliberate act and that the bent pins and nails were not just found from old bits of timber or other sources, although there is no reason why found pins or nails could not also have been used.

The idea of deliberately 'killing' the pins and nails hinges on the perception of an invisible supernatural or spirit world which includes the dead, magical forces and perhaps divine forces. Dr Massey has also noted chips to the neck or rim of several of the bottles which he thinks may be evidence of the bottles being deliberately damaged for a similar reason. This ritual killing of objects has been seen since prehistory with votive offerings to river gods being the obvious example.

Aside from the act of bending the pins and nails, the metal content of the bottles fully supports the primary source evidence from Blagrave, Mather and Glanvil that the bottles were intended to contain pins or nails. The other recommended ingredient, according to the recipe described by these early modern authors, was urine. In an early study of Suffolk witch-bottles, a total of nine bottles tested positive for the previous presence of urine using a basic phosphate test (Smedley, Owles and Paulsen 1964–1966: 88–93). Although the basic phosphate test is not regarded as an entirely reliable test for the presence of urine, the smells associated with these bottles and the strong literary evidence for this part of the recipe suggest that these results are correct. Many of the bottles were reported to have let out a 'hiss' or 'pop' when they were opened, indicating that some kind of liquid had been present. It seems likely that a great many of these bottles did once contain urine and, indeed, this has been borne out when a serious analysis of the contents has been undertaken, such as that conducted by Dr Alan Massey who has had the opportunity to analyse the residues and liquid from several bottles. He also had the opportunity to open a previously unopened bottle from Greenwich in laboratory conditions (Massey 2017: 13–31). Several bottles reported as witch-bottles, where the finder was able to describe a typical find spot and contents, had subsequently been cleaned out by the finder rendering any future analysis of the bottles almost futile.

Contents other than metal or body fluids included thorns, found in three bottles, only one of which did not also contain pins or nails. These were sometimes an addition to the pins or, as in the latter example, a substitute for pins. All these items fit nicely with Cotton Mather's statement: 'Nails, Pins, and such Instruments ... as carry a shew of Torture with them'. In addition, one example contained tree bark, one contained a fragment of wood, and one contained a small number of blades of grass. These three may all constitute organic alternatives or additions to the principle of including objects with sharp points.

Other organic objects found in the bottles include bones. Five of the bottles contained bones of small animals such as voles and rats. In only two of these cases were bones found in addition to pins or nails, suggesting that small sharp bones were also seen as being an important ingredient which could, if necessary, be used in place of pins or nails.

Other contents follow common themes but these objects do not appear to have been part of any published recipe in the early modern documents relating to these bellarmines. In 13 of the bottles human hair has been found. Human nail parings have been also found in several bottles. Dr Massey has been able to examine, photograph and place under powerful microscopes these items, to reveal the presence of several nits (Massey 2017: 46–47).

The urine, hair and nail parings were clearly included to incorporate more of the personal body signature inside a bottle with an anthropomorphic appearance. Further to this, two bottles contained small human figures. One was described as containing dolls and another, more doubtful because of decay, described as containing an effigy. Another item which appears to serve this purpose is the piece of fabric cut into the shape of a heart and stuck with pins, which has been found in five examples. In another example fabric was found which was badly degraded and whose form was not clear. A finder reported on 'a twist of something' existing in the neck of one bottle which was subsequently thrown away.

Half of all bellarmine bottles were found either beneath the hearth stone or within the construct of an inglenook fireplace. This was by far the most common location for witch-bottles of the bellarmine type to be positioned within the building, based on currently available evidence. The next most common location was beneath the floor, and a similar number were found concealed beneath the threshold, either the door-step or immediately adjacent. An unusual group of five bottles were discovered in a stone-lined culvert in central London; this only con-stitutes one incident but distorts the figures slightly. Four bottles were discovered in or beneath walls. Gardens have yielded three examples so far but these may have been the former locations of other properties. One example was found in river mud, one in a ditch and one in open countryside. Many bottles are discovered inverted in the ground too; this may be to keep the bung moist and thereby retain a good seal to the bottle.

Non bellarmine witch-bottles show similar contents and locations but these later bottle have a broader distribution and, as we move into the twentieth century, a wider variety of contents as it seems the interpretation of the counter-spell was being modified over time. Some bottles were used for other kinds of spells too. Some of the unusual items found within the bottles include written charms, small bones, frog skin, seaweed, stones, masses of lead, insects and in one case small lizards. Those dating from the seventeenth century are still pre-dominately found in the south-east of England but later ones appear in Wales, Scotland, Yorkshire and Guernsey and can turn up anywhere. The locations within the building of these later bottles was recorded in 53 of the examples: 16 were found in or near the hearth, 13 under the floorboards, 14 in walls, five outside buildings, one in a ceiling, two in a roof and two with dead bodies.

Some Examples of Witch-Bottles

The aim here is to present a sample of the bottles from different periods and regions in order to get a sense of the variety of reports which come in. As will be seen, the early bottles are all of a similar type but as we move through time the materials, contents and usage vary increasingly. It also appears that there is a remnant of the witch-bottle practice alive in the building industry today.

The Greenwich Bottle (Seventeenth Century)

In 2004 a bellarmine bottle was discovered about 1.5m below the ground in Greenwich. The discoverers of the bottle found that the bottle made a splashing and rattling sound when shaken so knew that there was something of interest within. I recommended that Dr Alan Massey should have the opportunity to examine it. As a Doctor of Chemistry with access to laboratory facilities at Loughborough University, he is well equipped to analyse the murky contents of a witch-bottle. His analysis of this bottle is the single most detailed and comprehensive analysis of any witch-bottle undertaken thus far, so detailed in fact, that he even recorded the growth of vivianite crystals in the leg socket of a head louse (Massey 2017: 48).

He arranged for an x-ray to be taken of the bottle which showed a clear mass of small pins or nails in the neck and a few larger nails in the belly of the bottle. This mass of corroded pins in the neck is not uncommon in bellarmine witch-bottles as they were often inverted when concealed, causing the material to coalesce at the neck. These masses expand as they rust and can cause cracking which did happen to this bottle. One bottle exploded due to an expanding rusty mass in Liverpool Museum in 1954 (Massey 2017: 3).

The x-ray did not reveal the presence of any liquid so a CT scan was arranged at Liverpool University which showed that there was a body of liquid which almost half filled the bottle. This liquid was tested initially using nuclear magnetic resonance and later using a combination of gas chromatography and mass spectrometry which revealed categorically that this was urine which had degraded over time.

When the contents were extracted it was shown that the bottle contained 12 iron nails, eight brass pins, locks of hair, a piece of leather pierced by a nail, and fingernail parings. Several examples of pieces of fabric in the shape of a heart which have been pierced by nails or pins have been found inside witch-bottles, so it is possible that this piece of leather was fashioned to represent a heart.

One of the distinguishing features of this bottle is that it is proven to have had a quantity of sulphur inside it, determined by the presence of iron sulphide which was widely present inside the bottle (Massey 2017: 13–15).

The bottle itself is consistent with other examples from the late seventeenth century and is currently held at the Exhibition Centre at the Old Royal Naval College in Greenwich.

Gravesend Bottle (Seventeenth Century)

This example was pulled from the mud of the Thames in 1962 from near West Street in Gravesend during excavations for foundations. It is of the bellarmine type and was reported as being around 9 inches high, badly misshapen and, when found, was stopped with a solid lead plug. The bottle was found to contain 600 grams of material of which 420 grams were iron nails. There were also many bits of

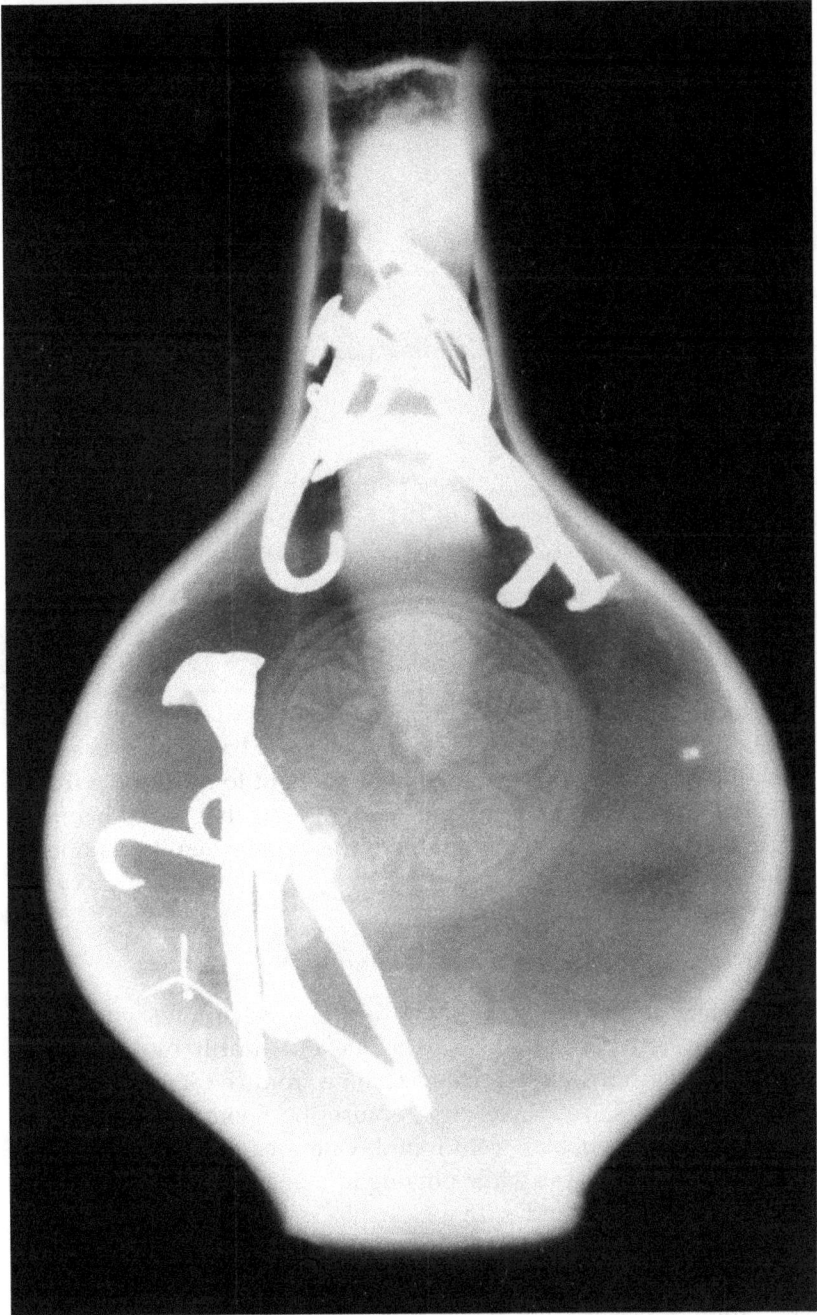

Figure 2.2 Greenwich bottle x-ray. Reproduced with permission of Dr Alan Massey.

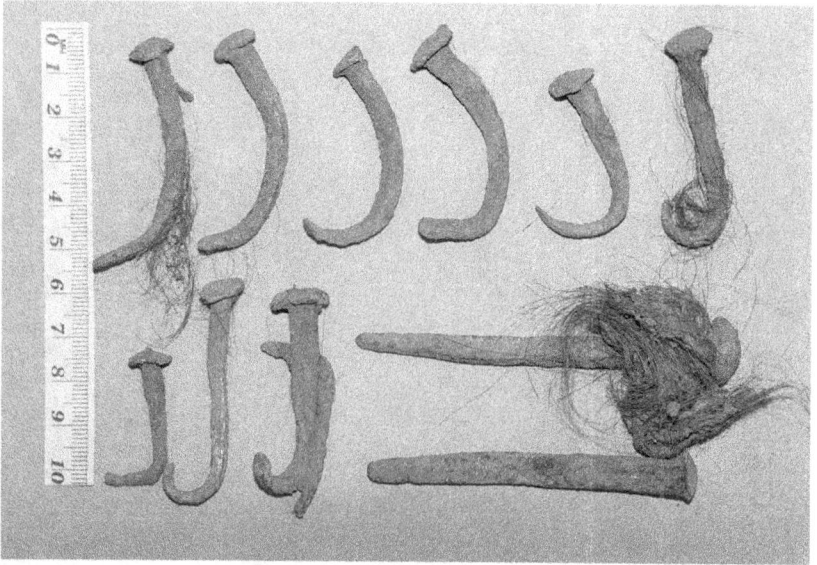

Figure 2.3 Nails and hair from Greenwich Bottle. Reproduced with permission of Dr Alan Massey.

wire, hundreds of brass pins and fragments of lead. Also present were stones, pieces of bone, wood, grass, dirt, a lock of hair, a glass bead and a small diamond shaped gilt ornament, thought to have come from a belt. The corrosion present on the nails suggests that liquid had been present within the bottle though there was none when it was opened (Tilley 1965: 252–54).

Felmersham Bottle (Late Seventeenth Century)

At a cottage in Felmersham, Bedfordshire, a bellarmine witch-bottle was discovered beneath the site of the old hearth by builders in late 2001. The house is estimated to date from the late seventeenth century. The tiles were taken up because the floors were damp and beneath the dirt, cobbles were found. One area of the floor did not have cobbles and it was while digging in this area that the bottle was discovered, inverted and with a clear blockage in its neck (excepting a small hole).

The bottle was discovered at around the same level as the cobbles. The builders washed the bottle and almost certainly destroyed the liquid evidence it contained. I collected the bottle in November 2001 and within a week took it to Dr Alan Massey in Loughborough for analysis of its contents. A large lock of dark hair was discovered in addition to a congealed mass of nails and pins.

It was then decided to consult Dr David Gaimster, the foremost expert on German stoneware, who considered the bottle to have been produced in the mid to third quarter of the seventeenth century.

The builder who found the bottle and his friends eventually sold the item on ebay despite our arranging for a local museum to purchase it from them; its current whereabouts are unknown.

Loughton Bottle (Late Seventeenth/Early Eighteenth Century)

In the grave of a young adult at All Saints Church, Loughton, Buckinghamshire, a late seventeenth- or early eighteenth-century glass steeple bottle was discovered lying between the left humerus and upper chest. The bottle contained several copper pins and a number of pins were also stuck into the cork. The bottle contained liquid which may be urine, although no analysis has yet taken place on this substance. The author of the report into the bottle, David Bonner, noted that witch-bottles are unusual in this context (Bonner 1994). Based on currently available records for witch-bottles, it seems that this is the only case of one being discovered in a coffin although several other bottles have been found buried in churchyards (Davies 1999a: 89). Despite the fact that the location for concealing the bottle is apparently unusual, it may have occurred more frequently than excavations have so far revealed where it was believed that death was caused by witchcraft. The contents of the bottle adhere to the usual formula of pins and urine and presumably the bottle was placed in the coffin as a form of counter-witchcraft to perhaps help protect the body and soul in death or to exact revenge on the perpetrator of the witchcraft which was thought to have led to his death.

Holywell Priory Bottle (Early Eighteenth Century)

During excavations at Holywell Priory in London, a bellarmine witch-bottle was found. It is thought to date from the late seventeenth century but according to the archaeologist, the context indicated that it was concealed beneath the brick floor some time between 1700 and 1740. The bottle contained many bent pins (Lewis 2010: 253–54).

Coopersale Bottles (Eighteenth Century)

Three witch-bottles were discovered at a house in the district of Coopersale, near Epping in Essex. As part of renovations to the fireplace to restore it to its original size, material was being chipped away from the surface and at some point a whole section of plaster fell away revealing the first two bottles. They were discovered side by side, set into plaster within the structure of the hearth and adjacent to a former rear entry into the house. The bottles were accidentally broken on discovery which meant that any liquid contents were lost. Photographs of the bottles were sent for analysis to Matthew Slocombe who thought them to be late eighteenth century in date. Although the bottles had broken and the contents had ended up being mixed in with rubble, there were some traces of liquid and some hairs still visible by the time they were inspected. The owners of the house decided that they would put a glass panel across the parts of the bottles that remained in the hearth to preserve what was left and make a feature of it in their home.

Later work revealed a further bottle, apparently intact, further up the structure of the hearth and evidently sealed into the hearth in the same way. This bottle is entirely complete and clearly had something inside, but the home owners wished for it to remain in-situ rather than be disturbed.

A local did some further research into the house and discovered that in the second half of the eighteenth century the lady of the house died of a long lingering illness; apparently the owner of the house was grief

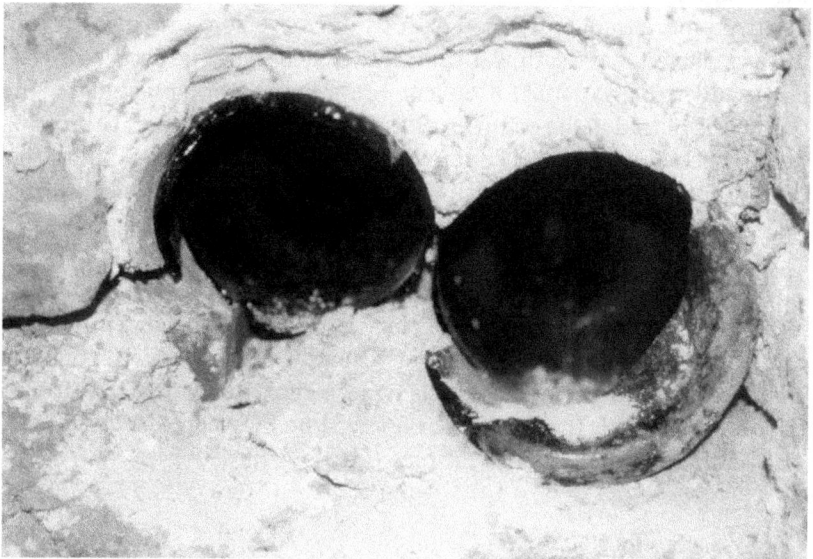

Figure 2.4 Two glass bottles found in a hearth surround, Coopersale, Essex. © Brian Hoggard.

stricken and sealed the house with all furnishings intact. The house was only reopened in the early nineteenth century and was quite an attraction when it was, thanks to the tragic story associated with it. It may be that the bottles were placed in the house because the owner believed his wife was bewitched.

Staplehurst Bottle (Late Eighteenth/Early Nineteenth Century)

A late example of a stoneware witch-bottle dating to the late eighteenth or early nineteenth century was discovered under the hearth of a farm in Staplehurst, Kent. When the bottle was found, it contained nails and pieces of wood (Tilley 1965: 252–56). This example demonstrates the custom of burying the bottle by the hearth and also shows the addition of material (the wood) not described in the early modern documents about witch-bottles. It is difficult to comment on the inclusion of wood in this case as no precise details about it were provided; however, in other examples small sharp pieces of wood were included and it seems that this was to inflict more harm on the witch, in addition to the pins and nails.

Ogden Bottle (Nineteenth Century)

Kai Roberts reported this unusual bottle via e-mail in December 2011. The bottle was discovered at Lane Head Farm near Ogden, near Halifax sometime around 1975. It was found beneath the doorstep of a nineteenth-century outdoor toilet which stood next to the east wing of the house before it was demolished to make way for a modern extension.

The jar is roughly 12 inches tall and 7 inches wide. It is described as earthenware with a very basic glaze, probably of local origin, and the neck was broken at the top. Inside, there was apparently some sludge when it was discovered and two figurines, both about 5 to 6 inches tall. They are made of some sort of very fine clay and are hollow, and neither shows any obvious signs of being male or female. Kai wondered if the bottle might have been intended to cause harm rather than repel it, or possibly be a love charms due to the presence of two figures.

Otley Bottle (1840s)

When this bottle first came to light in the chimney of a seventeenth-century house in Otley, it was assumed it would be fairly early in date. However, the type of earthenware was in use until recent times and fragments of modern red brick in the same area as the bottle suggested a later date than first anticipated. When emptied it was found to contain some pins (several bent) and nails and some dark, dusty material.

Pershore Phials (Nineteenth Century)

In Pershore, Worcestershire, two small glass phials were discovered along with three child's shoes and a collection of toys. The group was discovered behind the hearth on the ground floor, and were dated to the mid-nineteenth century. The phials contained wheat husks and the research of Dr Alan Massey showed that they may also have contained some pine resin. This is possibly residue connected with the production of pine beer which was once commonplace. The use of small glass phials became relatively common in the late eighteenth century and through to the nineteenth century. Shoes are perhaps the most commonly encountered of apotropaic objects and often had an association with the hearth. The idea with this collection of objects appears to have been to bring together the shoes, bottles and toys to serve as a decoy for any bad influences that might wish to attack the home via the chimney.

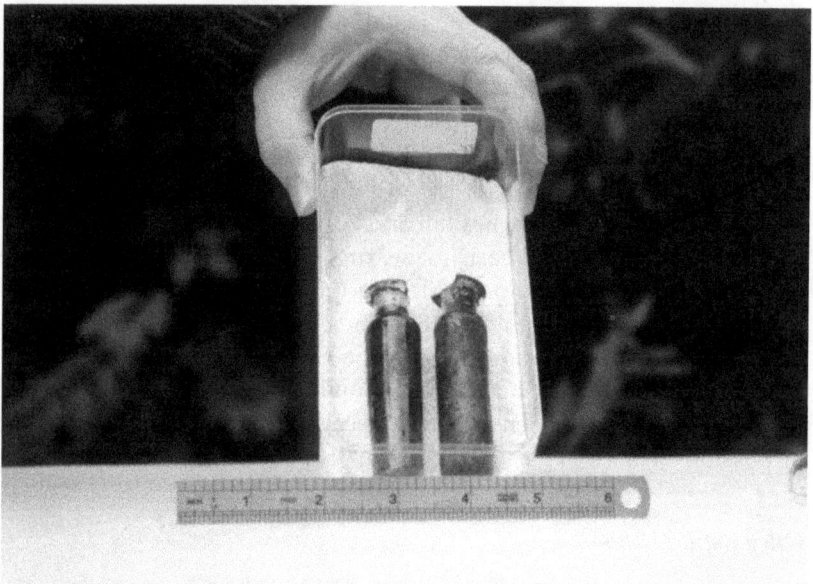

Figure 2.5 Two phials found with toys and shoes behind a hearth, Pershore, Worcestershire. © Brian Hoggard.

Wembley Bottle (Early Twentieth Century)

A much more recent example of a witch-bottle was discovered at St Augustine's Church, Wembley Park. The bottle contained a liquid, possibly just water, and a small pottery figurine. The figurine resembled the modern stereotype of the witch and it is possible that this 1906 deposit under a concrete floor was a modern re-interpretation of the witch-bottle (Merrifield 1987: 182).

Inclusion of Bottles in Modern Building Practices

There are several other examples of the use of bottles in magic and of concealed bottles even into the twentieth century. Jeffrey Patton related a family story to me by e-mail in September 2000 concerning witchcraft beliefs in a north Devon village. He was intrigued and surprised that such beliefs persisted and were considered normal. The story is worth quoting in full:

> My mother-in-law has told us the tale about the farm where my wife's grandfather was brought up and the farm above it. My wife's forebears in the lower farm were going through a bad patch – plague of fleas, sick stock, diseased crops etc. They naturally assumed, as one does around here, that someone was witching them. The old lady in the farm above was the prime suspect as she was known to have powers – inherited. They decided to contact a white witch to put things right and one had been recommended in Exeter. They rang him and he told them to come down to Exeter on the train where he would meet them at the station to get the details. One exciting bit of detail given by my mother-in-law was that when they asked how they would know him, her just said that he would know them when they got off the train.
>
> He told them to put some water (the word she used) into a jar and put it in the chimney corner. The lid of the jar had to be tightly sealed. Devon farmhouses have large chimneys with the grate in the centre and are often large enough to have seats in sometimes. He said that within twenty four hours the person who was witching them would have to come to them for the jar as they would not be able to pass water. They would then be released from the witching when the jar was handed over. I asked if the old lady came for the jar to which mother in law answered – 'Oh Yes! She was in a hell of a state'. She promised that nothing like that would ever happen again. However, the families did not speak to each other for about thirty or forty years. One day my wife's grandfather was having difficulty in lambing a sheep and he sent someone over to the other family for help, which was given. They were quite surprised how normal the other chap (the old lady's son) was and from then on

they started speaking again. I think the witching took place about 1910 and my mother in law was born in 1920 so it was quite fresh in people's minds when she was a little girl, which was when she was told what had happened.

This example and the example from Otley both demonstrate that there was still an active tradition of using witch-bottles well into the early twentieth century. The last one in particular contains an echo of the boiling of bottles referred to in the earliest texts.

In March 2010 Gary from Snoqualmie, Washington, USA got in touch to report the discovery of a remarkable number of bottles from within a dividing wall in their duplex. During remodelling of the property, they found over 100 bottles hanging on wires; some wires had two, some six bottles hanging on them. Investigation showed that the wall was completely original to the first phase of building in 1919.

From Sherburn-in-Elmet, North Yorkshire, a correspondent reported the following tradition to me in October 2002:

Reading about witch bottles on your site reminded me of two houses in the village I grew up, which had milk bottles cemented into the eaves. My friend lived in one of these and told me that if the bottles were ever damaged in any way, something bad would happen to the house. What's interesting about this is that these two houses were built as recently as the 1950's.

Another modern example of a bottle was from Wiltshire. In June 2007 it was reported as follows:

I have just had the front of my house painted during which it was necessary to cut back a clematis covering the front porch. This revealed the bottom end of a glass bottle immediately beneath the ridge tile at the apex of the gable. The house is only 27 years old, yet I wonder whether this is a modern example of a 'Witch Bottle' or simply a Wiltshire/rural building tradition.

Many modern witches have reported to me that they use witch-bottles. The contents in some cases are identical to those of early witch-bottles and in others they are very different, with iron filings and herbs used in one example or menses in another. The use is also different as they are used primarily by witches as protection against either non-specific negative energies of various kinds or other witches. Attempts to trace the source of the modern version of witch-bottles has proved unsuccessful but they appear to be widely used in the modern pagan witchcraft community and fuse old and new ideas about magic.

Bottles to Protect Livestock

Two bottles so far appear to have been created specifically to protect livestock.

In Dorset, between the parishes of Langton Matravers and Worth Matravers. a beautiful little glass bottle dating to the mid-eighteenth century was discovered beneath a wall. The bottle had a peculiar characteristic in that when it is first picked up the contents feel solid but after a short time they begin to feel like a viscous fluid. National Trust archaeologist Nancy Grace kindly allowed Dr Massey to analyse it; he discovered that it contained a mixture of beef tallow and spring water. It would seem likely in this case that part of a diseased animal, probably perceived to be bewitched, was placed inside the bottle with water which perhaps came from a nearby holy or healing well. The bottle seemed to be acting as a decoy or trap for any further malicious forces aimed at the animals and was presumably placed in between the target and the likely source of danger.

Another example from Rutland was of the bellarmine type, found beneath the hearth of a cottage. Dr Massey's analysis of the contents revealed the presence of horse urine and horse fat, suggesting an attempt to protect valuable horses (Massey 2017: 20).

Usage and Meanings

The written evidence cited at the beginning of this chapter gave a clear description of the intended use for witch-bottles. They were specifically used to cause pain to a witch, exploiting the sympathetic link between a witch and her or his victim. The bottle symbolised the witch's bladder and into it the victim would put their own urine, pins, nails or anything else with a 'shew of torture' about it. This would then be heated on a fire, causing excruciating pain to the witch who would then be forced to coming knocking on the victim's door begging for the heating to stop, in return for which they could negotiate a release from whatever malign influence the witch had cast onto them. If this failed, the advice was to bury the bottle and, as we have seen, a great many buried bottles have already been discovered and presumably many more are yet to be found under floors and in walls.

The texts do not mention the following elements which are often found in buried witch-bottles: the ritual 'killing' of the pins or nails before inclusion in the bottle and possibly also the deliberate damaging of the bottle, both done to render the bottle and contents active on a more spiritual plane; and the inclusion of hair and nail parings, not specifically mentioned in the texts.

In 2001 I was contacted by Jack Montgomery who was working as a librarian at Western Kentucky University in the USA. He told me that during the 1970s he did extensive fieldwork with traditional healers and shamanic practitioners in the rural areas of South Carolina as part of his research on regional folk religious practices. His description of the principle behind witch-bottles as he found them bears some similarities to my own interpretation of buried witch-bottles:

> I did encounter the use of 'witch bottles' in the German-American and Afro-American communities. Their principle uses were twofold: first they were used as a 'trap' or 'snare' for an evil spirit or the spirit of an evil person. Usually, some 'lure' was used to draw in the spirit and then the bottle would be capped and sealed with wax. It was considered important for the bottle to contain some physical element of the person (hair, nail clippings, etc). The bottle, once sealed, was kept in a secret place by the 'root-doctor' or 'Powwow'. I once was shown a bottle reputed to be over 100 years old that contained a very evil spirit. It was surprisingly cold to the touch even though kept on the shelf of a hot closet. I declined to open it when asked.

The effort that went into burying or concealing these bottles was often very significant. No doubt some were buried with minimum effort but there are many examples where bottles are found buried deeply below flagstones in front of the hearth. This level of effort is a testament to the strength of belief that people had in the efficacy of this practice and also to the belief that whatever bad fortune befell them was caused by witchcraft. The frequency of concealments in front of the hearth also points to the belief that this vulnerable opening in the home was perceived as being the principle point of entry for any bad energies or spells that might be aimed at someone.

The location of witch-bottles within the building is also important. Of those which had their location recorded, half were found beneath or within the hearth; this was by far the most common location for the bottles overall. The next most common location of the bottles was under the floor, followed by the threshold, in or beneath walls; the remainder were found in various locations outside of known buildings, including a group found in a stone-lined culvert in London (as mentioned above).

The hearth appears to have been a focal point for many of the artefacts which have been discovered concealed in buildings. The hearth was always open to the sky and it was also the place where the whole family would gather in winter in order to keep warm. R.W. Brunskill described the hearth thus in his *Traditional Buildings of Britain*: 'It is impossible to exaggerate the significance of the hearth in the design of vernacular houses ... it has been suggested that the house began as a shelter for fire and that it was fire that made the house sacred' (Brunskill 1992: 110). The hearth was a point of vulnerability for those who believed that dangerous creatures including the witch, were abroad at night, and as such needed to be protected.

The apparent popularity of the hearth as a good place to bury a witch-bottle raises interesting questions about their purpose. If the practice was to follow the seventeenth-century texts precisely, it should not have mattered exactly where the bottle was buried because the spell was thought to work via the sympathetic link between the witch and her or his intended victim. Yet the evidence shows that half of all bottles were concealed in or near the hearth, with another 10 per cent at thresholds, indicating that the person doing the work wanted to protect those areas specifically. It seems likely, therefore, that the burial of a witch-bottle by the hearth or threshold may not always have been as a specific retaliatory act against the witch but may also have served a more general protective purpose. In support of this, the hearth or threshold is a popular location for other house protection methods such as shoes.

Also, if the creation of a witch-bottle was a specifically retaliatory counter-spell, then it seems strange that so many bottles remained buried or concealed. This could have been either because it was too much effort to remove them or because there was a belief that the bottles would continue to have a protective function beyond whatever events caused them to be created in the first place.

It seems likely, therefore, that people began to make and conceal witch-bottles as a general part of their spiritual defences in the home in anticipation of needing to ward off negative forces. It is also possible that people may have begun to use witch-bottles more as spirit traps instead of as bladder torturing devices.

If people believed that the hearth needed to be protected in particular as it is always open to the sky, then this clearly implies that something would come down it. Here it can be imagined that an actual body of energy of some kind had been projected from the witch and was airborne, aimed at its potential target and following the scent of its intended victim. Upon entering the chimney, it would smell its victim and plunge downwards to attack, only to discover it had been fooled and was now trapped inside the belly of a tiny, urine-filled humanoid (the bellarmine) and skewered by the ghosts of dead pins, nails and thorns. In this way the bottle acted as a spirit trap, similar to the way in which concealed shoes may have worked but with more powerful consequences.

Conclusions

Witch-bottles appear to have originated in England around the middle of the seventeenth century at a time when bellarmine bottles were being imported in huge numbers from the continent. Initially this particular type of bottle seems to have been the specified vessel for this counter-spell, chosen for its anthropomorphic appearance which made it perfect for magical practice. So it is not entirely surprising that there is a close link between distribution maps for these bottles and evidence of the practice. As production of glass bottles increased during the eighteenth century and imports of stoneware fell, a natural shift towards using glass bottles as witch-bottles took place. By this time the practice began to be much more widely distributed throughout England and glass bottles could be obtained almost anywhere.

Seventeenth-century texts are quite clear that witch-bottles should be made using urine and sharp objects and that they should be heated to inflict pain upon the witch. The idea was that this would compel the witch to do a deal which would 'unbewitch' their victim. It was suggested that should the heating process not produce the required results, then the victim should bury the bottle and it is this evidence that archaeologists and builders occasionally find.

The material evidence strongly suggests that magical, or witchcraft, forces were perceived as very real, in a similar way to how we now think of electricity or perhaps wi-fi. These forces were powerful but invisible and experts in their use could manipulate them for good or ill. It was of critical importance to put in place decoys and traps containing the essence of the house occupants in case an attack was ever directed at one's home.

Buried witch-bottles are different in several respects from the bottles which were described in the texts and which needed to be 'boiled up'. The hair and nail parings, the specific location for their burial, the bent pins – all these things form a significant part of the evidence yet there is no mention of them. Nor is there any mention of the cloth hearts stuck with thorns and pins. The evidence suggests that these buried bottles were deployed in a very different way to those which were boiled. These buried ones were mostly placed at the hearth, in between the source of danger and its target, they were anthropomorphic (at least the early bellarmines were), and they contained urine, hair and nail parings, 'dead' pins and nails and sometimes an effigy or cloth heart. The harmful spell or energy would lunge for the decoy person and be impaled or trapped within the bottle. Witch-bottles formed a potent part of the line of defence in a person's home alongside other measures which are described in this volume.

Note

Some passages in this chapter were first published in Hoggard. 2016a. 'Witch-Bottles: Their Contents, Contexts and Uses', in R. Hutton (ed.), *Physical Evidence for Ritual Acts, Sorcery and Witchcraft in Christian Britain – A Feeling for Magic*. Basingstoke: Palgrave, pp. 91–105.

⚬●⚬ Chapter 3

CONCEALED SHOES

Shoes are the most commonly encountered of all the concealed objects. The pioneer of the study into the subject, June Swann, while curator of the Boot and Shoe Collection at Northampton Central Museum, recognised that shoes were being brought in from contexts where they were being deliberately hidden. As a result, she set up the Concealed Shoes Index at the museum and it currently has records of over 2000 examples. Although this is a huge number of records, it is likely to be only a tiny portion of those which have actually been found. A casual chat with any builder working on historic properties will likely reveal a fairly large number of anecdotal accounts of the discovery of shoes, usually not reported to Northampton. I saw a small collection of shoes held in an independent museum in Gloucestershire for which there were no records of date of discovery, address or location within building. That small collection alone would have added another eleven shoes to the records but the successive curators were not aware of the significance of the shoes or what to do with them.

The examples in the Concealed Shoes Index are primarily from Britain, but the Index holds records from as far away as Canada and Australia. The date range of the finds is interesting and appears to be proportionally related to surviving buildings from the period concerned, until the twentieth century when the practice appears to have gone into decline. The earliest examples in the index date from the thirteenth century. When Fiona Pitt produced a breakdown of the figures in 1997, the results showed that there are around fifty examples for the period before 1600, around 200 for 1600–1699, approximately 270 for 1700–1799, around 500 for 1800–1899, and around 50 for 1900 and later (when the records appear to decline) (Pitt 1997: 5). The decline in the twentieth century may be due to there being no need to

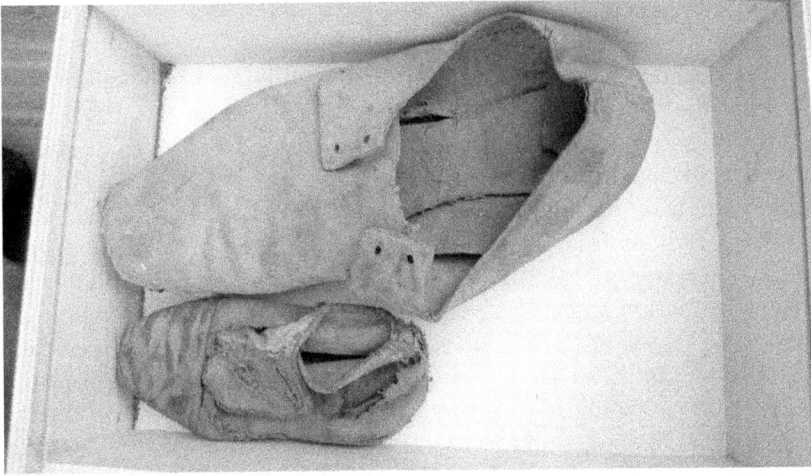

Figure 3.1 Two shoes discovered at a property in Haw Bridge, Gloucestershire. © Brian Hoggard.

investigate chimneys and other house structures of this period because they are still in good repair. Most of the finds have been discovered during demolition work or alterations to buildings and are usually discarded as rubbish. Around a quarter of shoes are found in chimneys, usually on a ledge within the chimney; others are found in roof spaces, in walls and under floors. Shoes can be discovered in large groups and sometimes with other artefacts. 11 per cent are pairs of shoes but they are usually found singly. 40 per cent of shoes belonged to children, with the others broadly split between men and women (Swann 1996: 59–62).

The most common places to find concealed shoes are in chimneys and walls, under floorboards and in roofs but they can also be found around doors, windows and staircases. Denise Dixon-Smith suggested that 'One reason for hiding shoes in chimneys and around doors may have been because these were "openings" where evil spirits could enter the home, and the shoe – as a good luck symbol – should warn them off' (Dixon-Smith 1990).

Ralph Merrifield suggests that the practice may have derived from one of England's unofficial saints, John Schorn of North Marston, Buckinghamshire (died 1313). He was alleged to have performed the remarkable feat of conjuring the devil into his boot. This legend, Merrifield continues, may have resulted in shoes being seen as some kind of spirit trap, which might explain many of the locations in which they are found (Merrifield 1987: 134). Schorn's legend is also thought to have led to the creation of the jack-in-the-box, in French called a *'diable en boîte'* (literally 'boxed devil').

John Schorn's legend became very well-known and ultimately became the second most popular pilgrimage in the country. It was generating so much money that it was appropriated by the Crown and moved to Windsor in the second half of the fifteenth century. His was a tremendously popular pilgrimage route from his death in 1313 until the mid-16th century. There were several designs of pilgrim badges depicting Schorn holding a boot with a devil or demon's head popping out of it, the inference being clearly that he had trapped it inside the boot. The association with him and casting the devil into a boot, while understandable given the imagery associated with him, was apparently not the real meaning of those images. It seems he was reputed to have had special healing skills in curing the 'ague', or fever, and also for complaints relating to the feet, so it could be that he was casting the devil out of someone's boot, thereby curing them.

Richard Marks describes the area of the church in North Marston where Schorn's shrine would have been; there was a small recess which probably 'housed the relic of the boot from which the devil was miraculously conjured' and that another recess had 'every appearance of being designed for the insertion of the pilgrim's foot with the hope of effecting a cure for gout'. It is likely that Schorn's remains must have been very close by (Marks 2002: 192–94).

It is difficult to assess the numbers of people who would have seen this image, but it certainly would have been carried to all parts of the British Isles and beyond over a period of 250 years. Schorn's image was not only encountered on pilgrim badges; paintings of him still exist in Devon on screens at Alphington, Hennock and Wolborough churches, and in Norfolk and Suffolk at Cawston, Gateley, Suffield and Sudbury (Marks 2002: 202–204). There would probably have been a good deal more of these paintings and other images elsewhere prior to the dissolution of the monasteries and the activities of iconoclasts. These widely seen images and pilgrim badges would have conveyed the impression that it was possible to capture the devil or other harmful forces in a boot or shoe. It seems highly likely that this is the source of the practice of concealing shoes for reasons of protection in the fabric of buildings. If it is not the source, it certainly hugely popularised knowledge of the association between footwear and spirit traps.

In Troston Church, Suffolk, there is a graffito on the wall of the chancel arch, on the south side, which depicts a shoe outline and the face of a demon (Champion 2014: 247). This is not particularly far from the churches at Gately, Cawston and Suffield in Norfolk where there

Figure 3.2 Image of unofficial Saint, John Schorn, from Sudbury, Suffolk.
© Brian Hoggard.

are excellent images of John Schorn pictured with a demon popping out of a boot. These are probably the last meagre survivals of what was once the very popular cult of John Schorn.

Further to beliefs concerning shoes, Reginald Scot mentions that spitting on the shoes is a way of protecting against witchcraft. There are other theories about how the practice of concealing shoes developed.

There appears to be a link between shoes and fertility. For example, Roy Palmer in *The Folklore of Hereford and Worcester* cites a very recent account from Broadwas-on-Teme where in 1960 a midwife refused to allow a young woman to remove her shoes until her child was born (Palmer 1992: 87). Merrifield notes the old rhyme, 'there was an old woman who lived in a shoe' as being further evidence of the connection with fertility and states that in Lancashire women used to try on the shoes of women who had just given birth in order to try and conceive (Merrifield 1987: 134). This seems to relate to the personal nature of shoes and is reminiscent of the old Native American practice of enemies walking in one another's shoes in order to empathise more deeply – in this case to hopefully 'catch' something of the new mother. E. and M.A. Radford in the *Encyclopedia of Superstitions* recite an old method for young ladies to dream of their future partners. It involved pinning their garters to a wall and arranging their shoes in the form of a 'T' and singing a short rhyme (Radford and Radford 1961: 169). Further, it is possible that many children's shoes, particularly when found in isolation, were concealed in the vicinity of the master bedroom as aids to fertility. There is also the possibility that these shoes were kept as keepsakes in the same way that some people keep a child's first booties.

One other explanation to consider is that, with infant mortality being so high in the past, these children's shoes are private memorials to children who have passed away. For example, during the restoration of a sixteenth-century cottage in Wooburn Green, Buckinghamshire, a small zinc plate was discovered in the floor of one of the bedrooms. Upon lifting the plate a small shoe was discovered beneath which has since been dated to 1867. The finder is sure that this had belonged to a small girl because he had experienced clear visions of a young girl in this part of the house.

June Swann suggests that this is probably a male practice owing to the fact that the shoes need to be concealed during building, and thinks that it may be a symbolic substitute for ancient practices related to making sacrifices at the foundations of new buildings (Swann 1997: 2). Clearly some examples were concealed during building which would confirm that point of view; however, it seems clear to me that many of

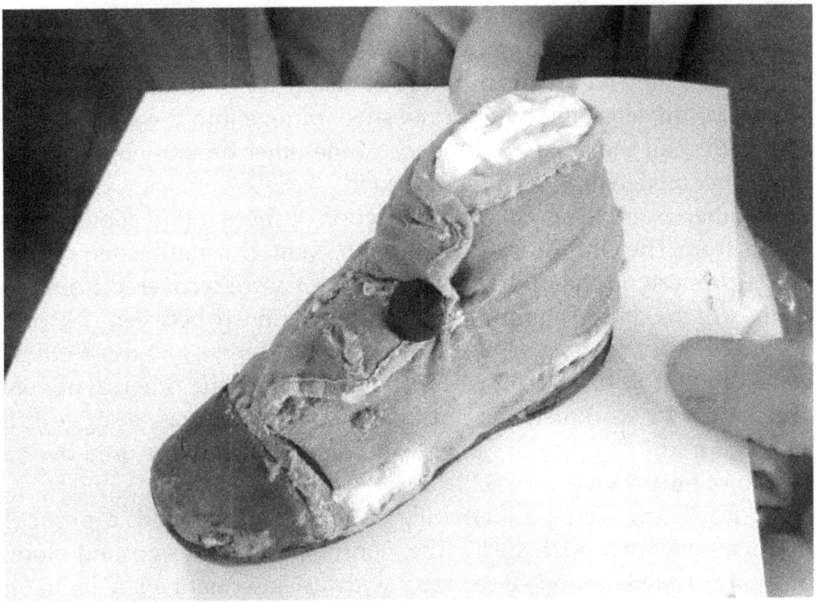

Figure 3.3 Child's shoe recovered from beneath a zinc plate, Wooburn Green. © Brian Hoggard.

the shoes found on ledges within chimneys or even beneath floorboards could easily have been placed there by the occupants.

Timothy Easton has shown that many of the places where shoes were concealed could be accessed by the occupants and has termed them 'spiritual middens'. He used the term to describe large collections of broken household objects and personal possessions which have been deposited into voids created by the insertion of brick chimney stacks into older buildings (Easton 1997). He describes these collections of objects as acting like a lightning conductor.

These masses of objects frequently contain shoes, as in the example at Sittingbourne in Kent where, during demolition of a pub called The Plough, a huge number of shoes and other material was recovered from eight different assemblages within the building. Sittingbourne Heritage Museum now holds this huge collection in cabinets specifically acquired to house them all. The Plough was originally built in a couple of phases in the second half of the seventeenth century and many of the finds came from voids created by the boxing in of the chimney stack with lathe and plaster panels and from locations beneath the floor. The finds included footwear, garments, glass and hats ranging in date from the seventeenth to the twentieth centuries (Abbey 2010).

My interpretation of spiritual middens would suggest that the role of the shoes in these assemblages is that, due to their uniqueness to the wearer, they would act as a lure or decoy for the malevolent force which would sense its target in the shoe, plunge into the void and be trapped on all the spikes and edges of the other broken objects, with their jagged edges and splinters of wood.

Another example of a sizeable collection of shoes found at one property is from The Old Vicarage, Upchurch, Kent. During the demolition of the property in the mid-1970s, eight shoes were recovered from the vicinity of the central chimney stack dating variously between 1740 and 1820. Three of the shoes were ladies' walking slippers and three others were thought to have belonged to male children; the other two were taken away by workmen and not examined. The date range suggests a spiritual midden where different shoes were added to the void over a period of time (Moad 1976: 110–12).

At Rockview Cottage, Bettyhill, Caithness in Scotland, a number of shoes were found beneath the floorboards on the ground floor. Two more were found associated with an interment of a lamb in one of the walls surrounding the property too. In addition, some cases of socks stuffed with thistle heads were deliberately concealed in chimneys; one was found in the eighteenth-century farm at the Mull of Galloway.

In the 1970s a pile of old boots and shoes were found beneath stairs at a seventeenth-century farmhouse on the Rhiwlas estate just a mile or so north-east of Bala in the old county of Merioneth, Wales. The staircase was not original and was thought to be no more 200 years old of the time of writing. The footwear was sent for analysis to June Swann who dated the boots to the 1860s–1870s.

At a property in the High Street, Thornbury, north of Bristol, a hoard of shoes was found, possibly from the late 1800s, in a timber-framed building thought to date from the sixteenth century.

An article from 1985 reported the discovery of 17 boots and shoes from a thatched cottage on the border between Suffolk and Cambridgeshire. The owner discovered them while excavating the bricked-up inglenook fireplace there. Although the cottage dated from the mid-sixteenth century, the footwear all dated from the second half of the nineteenth century suggesting they had been concealed during the installation of a bread oven. The finds apparently represented an entire family group with footwear belonging to men, women and children included (Brendan 1985: 10).

At Ightham Mote in Kent, 11 boots and shoes were discovered coming from several different contexts and dates. One group was discovered beneath an attic staircase and dated from the 1620s (Brooks 2000: 66–67).

At a cottage called Gelli Iago, Nant Gwynant in Snowdonia, over 100 concealed shoes were found in 2010. This property belongs to the National Trust. The shoes were apparently hidden 'under a fireplace' and are Victorian, though the cottage dates from the seventeenth century.

Two adult shoes were discovered during renovation work on the fireplace at the Green Hill pub in Linton, Cambridgeshire. The shoes were considered to date from the seventeenth century (*Cambridge Evening News* 1979: 26).

Bari Hooper describes the discovery of a hoard of nineteenth-century shoes during roof repairs at the Coach and Horses pub in Wicken Bonhunt, Essex. They comprised five children's boots, a lady's boot and a lady's wooden patten with leather straps (Hooper 1989: 22–23).

Concealed shoes were reported from Lochgoilhead in Argyll and Bute. Craig Ross reported on this in December 2012:

> I'm a joiner and doing a farmhouse renovation in the Lochgoilhead area of Scotland in Argyll and Bute. I have recently found shoes under the floorboards of the attic space of the house. They are a mix of children's shoes with laces and green/gold eyelets. Men's shoes with iron nails on the sole. Also found were baby shoes and clogs. It probably amounts to 12 pairs all in. I found them all in the one area, under the floor boards in the attic, underneath the partition wall between the farmhouse and the barn which backs onto it. The barn dates to at least 1840 with the farm house having been built onto the side at a later date, although still Victorian.

Nick Platt reported the following discovery of shoes in December 2012:

> I am restoring an old house dating from around 1500 in Domfront, Bass-Normandie (61700) and have found a collection of shoes buried at the top of the rear wall between a doorway and small hatch access to the exterior. The stone rear wall had two wall plates about 2′ 6″ apart at this point. The shoes were buried in a mix of earth, sand and lime mortar that hadn't quite gone off. They are of several sizes, made of leather and looked more like slip-ons or slippers. There are men's, women's and children's shoes. Alas they have been moved from their original position but only by a few inches or so as the area had to be cleaned up prior to removal of a staircase and the reopening of the window/hatchway. They will be reburied (possibly with one of my own and a note) as the work progresses.

Another French example comes from Saint-Benoît du Sault where six shoes or fragments were found in different parts of a barn. These included three baby's shoes, a child's boot and two adult shoes, all dating to the second half of the nineteenth century (Montembault 2005: 31–33).

Two examples of concealed shoes were discovered in the Liedberg Palace in Korschenbroich, Germany. One group of eight shoes, which were all well-worn but of a high-status type, were apparently recovered from a wall twelve metres high and date from the early eighteenth century. Another two shoes dating from the nineteenth century were recovered from another wall. This is a good example of the practice persisting over time in a high-status environment (*The Local de* 2010).

Rainer Atzbach noted a large assemblage of material including shoes which came from between the floors of three houses in Reichsstadt Kempten (Allgäu), Germany. The footwear that came from one of the houses dated mainly from the fifteenth and sixteenth centuries.

At Causeway House, Northumberland, a child's right clog sole was found during repairs to the thatch. The clog is likely to have been made during the nineteenth century. Other items including garments were recovered from the thatch (Emery, Warner and Pearson 1990: 135–37).

In February 2007 Shomik Mukherjee reported:

> one weekend I found myself among the medieval ruins of Sijilmassa, one of the most historically important northern termini for the trans-Saharan trade route from West Africa. It was here that I discovered that a boundary wall has been constructed so as to encompass the most central of the ruins remaining visible above ground. By sheer chance, I observed that a shoe (one only, ostensibly formerly belonging to a child) had been incorporated into the fabric of the wall: the wall itself appears to have been very hastily constructed, with minimal time and resources; and the shoe was thus clearly visible protruding from the side. I mention the crude nature of the wall's construction; and indeed it would be very easy to assume that the wall itself constitutes one of the original ruins (especially in that locality, where the Saharan sands render ruins and modern housing alike a uniform beige); but I am told by an authority at the University of al-Akhawayn that the wall is in fact of twentieth century provenance. As to the reason for the shoe's presence, we can for now only speculate.

Bruce Sidebotham emailed a report in August 2006:

> Back in 1990 my wife and I with three kids moved into a house in Indonesia. The address was Jalan Batang Lembang No. 22, Padang, Sumatera Barat, Indonesia. Above the ceiling tiles near the center of the house I found a wicker basket with one man's shoe, one women's shoe, one baby's shoe, and one child's shoe. The shoes were of high quality leather. Having been subjected to the extreme attic environment beneath a tin roof all of the polish and color was gone and the leather was extremely dry and cracked. We presumed that the basket and shoes were part of a magic charm and burned them. It was very difficult to get them

to burn and they never did really catch fire, but sort of slowly melted to ash the way that charcoal does in a barbecue.

A concealed shoe was found in Blackburn, Lancashire. Correspondent Matt Rishton reported his discovery in October 2011:

Hi there I read the article on hidden shoes on the apotropaios website with great interest having just recently found one in my house. It was a ladies strappy sandal high heel appearing like it came from the seventies and had the look of a prop from the film the omen which creeped me out a bit. It was nailed to the underside of the main roofing joist in the attic and I had seen it before but paid it no mind thinking of it as a builders prank. Only when it struck me as particularly odd did I ever inspect it closely. Just the other week I removed it but kept it in the garage just in case. No significant change has occurred but I think I will return it anyway. There are also a pair of lucky horseshoes nailed to the back fence so I can only presume a former occupant must have been superstitious. The house is a suburban semi in Blackburn Lancashire and was built in 1965 I believe. So this would be one of the later examples of this habit.

An interesting case from Geddinge Farm near Sheperdswell in Kent was reported in 2011 which brings together the two aspects of fertility and protection. An old child's shoe was found on a ledge up the chimney. My correspondent told me in August 2011:

We are about to move into an old family house and when looking around tonight I found an old child's shoe on a ledge in the chimney, I'd like to make it a special feature perhaps putting it in a frame to protect it and house it on the ledge, but is the tradition that I hide it and never speak of it, to leave it to protect the house and family, I'd so love to think it would bring fertility ... any suggestions and what's the traditional thing to do.

She later added:

I will take a photo and send it to you, the shoe was found about 50 years ago by the father of a friend of my other half, they had the house and grew up in it as children, oddly the friend dropped by just before Christmas and when we showed him around he went to the fireplace and pulled out the shoe he knew it would still be there, I hadn't mentioned it!!! he said his dad found it when they uncovered the fireplace years ago and placed a note by it ... that note is still there asking that the shoe was not removed as it protects the families from evil spirits.
    I think I will leave the shoe alone, although I'd like to preserve it.

An interesting report from Susan Moy in January 2002 reveals the ongoing practice of concealing shoes with a Romanian couple living in Chicago, Illinois: 'The Romanian couple have been doing the maintenance for the last twelve years on this apartment building ... When the worn out shoes wedged under the stairways and empty air fresher were thrown out, they went CRAZY! Now, I know why'. Shoes are still being concealed in Devon according to Isabelle Kenny who related the following anecdote in May 2002: 'When we built our new house in 1989, the builders persuaded us to put shoes belonging to our small children & coins in the chimney breast, behind the cement! So superstition still rules at least in rural Devon'.

There are cases where it was deemed necessary to place only a representation of a shoe in the building rather than an actual shoe. Clearly in these cases some memory of the practice persisted but without the full understanding of the original concept. So for example Tom Murison reported to me in September 2017 the discovery of a piece of leather in the shape of a shoe outline from above the front door lintel of an 1846 shoemaker's house in Oakville, Ontario. Another example was reported by Melanie Greenwood in December 2011, describing a tiny wooden clog which was discovered under the rafters next to the chimney stack at a cottage in Silver Street, Wrington, North Somerset. It is a remarkable little clog with a decoration resembling a hash-tag on it and the word 'ANVERS' carved into the wood. ANVERS is the Belgian way of spelling Antwerp so this was clearly a little souvenir clog which has been used in the same way as a concealed shoe.

Shoes have been concealed in Britain from the fourteenth century right up until the twenty-first century. The practise occurs in the USA, Canada, throughout Europe, North Africa, Indonesia, Australia and New Zealand. In the earliest period there seems to be an undeniable connection with the imagery associated with John Schorn. These images were very widespread and illustrate the devil being trapped in a boot. One of the fundamental issues that has come out of studying this topic is that people believed that evil forces were real and that they could attack you, particularly via the chimney which was always open to the sky. The legend and imagery associated with John Schorn provided one very simple idea to try and negate that danger. The practice of concealing footwear in and around hearths, voids and roof spaces has worked its way into folk belief since then.

It is clear that there are also times when children's shoes in particular were concealed for reasons of fertility and bereavement. Infant mortality has been terribly high at times so it is hardly surprising that methods of enhancing fertility and of diverting evil away from children were a preoccupation for many people. Therefore, there are times when the discovery of a child's shoe from beneath the floorboards of a master bedroom triggers sad thoughts, and there are times when the discovery of a family group of shoes from behind a fireplace signals the fears a community had concerning witchcraft.

◦●◦ Chapter 4

DRIED CATS

Dried cats are commonly encountered by people working on historic buildings in Britain and Ireland but examples have also been discovered in the USA, Canada, Europe and Australia. Ralph Merrifield referred to dried cats in his work of 1987 (Merrifield 1987: 123) but Margaret Howard was the first to properly address the topic in her 1951 article, 'Dried Cats' (Howard 1951: 149–51).

These cats are found in roof spaces, under floors, between lath and plaster panels and occasionally in sealed cavities where they have been intentionally interred. Sometimes they are found posed as if hunting, with an accompanying mouse or rat. Examples of the latter require a certain amount of wire-work to keep the cat in position, something which we find at times where cats have been attached to joists, beams or posts. In these cases, significant time and effort would have gone into preparing and positioning the animal. Hidden away in a dry place, these animals dry out very gradually, leading some people to refer to them as mummified cats. The hair usually falls out of the animal as it dries, leading to a very shrivelled appearance which can be very disconcerting, particularly if one is discovered by someone who is entirely unprepared.

Many individuals, when asked, ridicule the suggestion that the animals were intentionally placed in the building, preferring to believe that they crawled into a tight space and became trapped or crawled away to die. While this is distinctly possible, it does not account for many examples where the cats have clearly been sealed into places or fixed into position. In some cases, it is difficult to tell if the animal has been purposely concealed but it is worth noting that the smell of any animal which dies in a house is usually sufficiently bad to suspect that few accidentally trapped animals would have been left if it were possible to remove them.

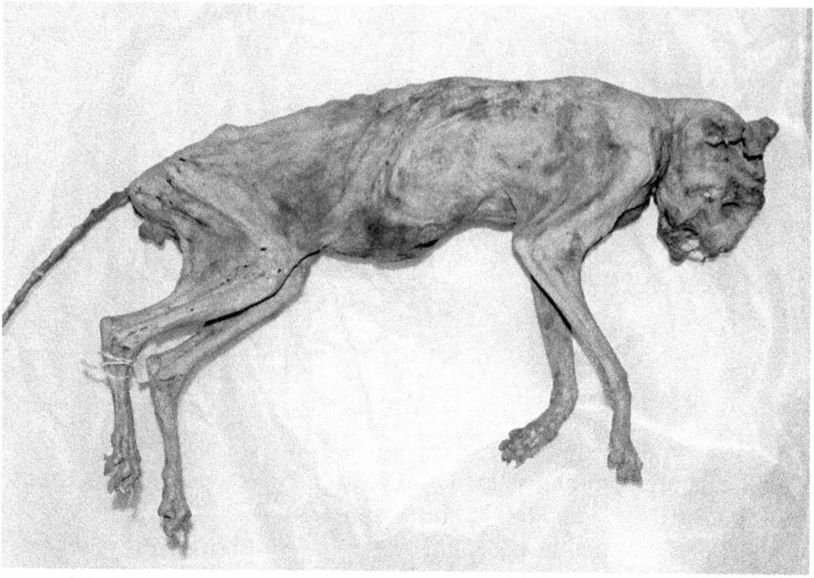

Figure 4.1 Dried cat from Newport, Wales. Reproduced with permission of Newport Museum and Art Gallery.

There are three main theories put forward as to why cats are concealed in buildings and two of them were outlined by Margaret Howard in her 1951 article. She explored both the foundation sacrifice idea and also the possible practical function of vermin scares. The conclusion to her paper combines both ideas: 'The evidence at present available thus suggests that, generally speaking, the cat was first immured for utilitarian reasons, but, having become an object of superstition, it came to be used as a luck-bringer or building sacrifice and also as a protector against magic or pestilence' (Howard 1951: 151).

A small percentage of the cats (roughly 6 per cent) discovered so far were posed as if they were hunting, as at Christchurch Cathedral in Dublin or at the Castle of Saint-Germain en Laye in France (de Somer 2003: 7). These are the examples cited as evidence that the cats were set up as vermin scares. Rats in particular are more likely to eat a dead cat than run away from it however fierce it looks and it certainly would not take them very long to realise that the tableau posed no threat. In the event that an individual chose to experiment with using dead cats as vermin scares, it seems likely that the practice would be a short-lived one and soon overtaken by the idea that live cats do the job far more effectively. If, as is argued later in this chapter, the cats were intended to act on a more spiritual or ethereal level, then a vicious looking cat frozen in time might act almost like a gargoyle or guardian, warning away spiritual foes such as the witch's familiar. If the spirit of the animal emerged and began to attack or fight the intruder, then a fairly potent example of counter-witchcraft can be seen.

The idea of foundation sacrifices was also discussed in Howard's paper as the less probable of the two theories. The evidence put forward is that of the ancient tradition of foundation sacrifices to appease the land and local gods (Howard 1951: 151). It has also been suggested by several people during the course of this research, including none other than author Terry Pratchett (RIP), that the sacrifice is to the building itself – to give it a life so that it will not take one later through some kind of tragic accident. This practice is extremely ancient and it does seem likely that there is some link between the practice of concealing cats in buildings and foundation sacrifices. John Sheehan's in-depth study of a dried cat found at Ennis Friary in Co. Clare, Ireland, came to the conclusion that it 'appears to have been the subject of a seventeenth-century reduced form of foundation sacrifice' (Sheehan 1990: 64–68). This theory certainly has some appeal and provides continuity with ancient evidence of foundation sacrifice, although foundation sacrifices are usually associated with the ground (whereas cats are normally found within the building structure) and in known examples connected with horse skulls there is often some ritual involved.

Howard also discusses the bad treatment that cats received in the Middle Ages through their association with witchcraft and the devil. Black cats were variously tortured, whipped and burned according to a variety of folk customs throughout Europe as there was a perceived association with the devil. In England, where there was a strong belief in the witch's familiar, the cat could be seen as the agent of the witch. Of course it could also be seen as a friendly animal playing a useful role in people's lives.

The way in which cats are perceived provides an alternative theory which may be presented purely out of an observation of cats and comparison with other finds. It is certain that witch-bottles and the other finds mentioned were concealed as forms of house protection. The locations within the house in which cats are found compares well with the other finds – they have been found concealed most commonly in walls, but also under floors and in roofs. As a result of their nocturnal habits, relative independence, distinctive eyes and lightning reflexes, cats can be viewed as mysterious creatures, which no doubt helped to foster their popular association with witchcraft and the devil in the Middle Ages. Cats also perform a role which is helpful to humans in terms of catching vermin and being, at times, charming companions. A combination of these perceptions, along with the belief that a cat could become a servant of some kind (like a familiar), could easily explain why it may have been hoped that a dead cat concealed in a building would continue its vermin catching role on a more spiritual plane of existence. It may also have been hoped that the cat could ward off evil spirits and the familiar of the witch, and it seems that however the practice began, this was one of its perceived functions in more recent centuries.

A dried cat and rat were discovered in thatch at Pilton, Northamptonshire, when the house was demolished in 1890. The cat is said to have been pegged down with wooden pegs (Howard 1951: 151). It is unlikely that this cat, and some of the following examples, were accidentally trapped in buildings. A dried cat was discovered at St Cuthbert's Church, Clifton, near Penrith in Cumbria. It was discovered between slates and plaster in the roof of the church during restoration in the mid-1840s. The church dates from the twelfth century but it is likely that the cat was added to the fabric during roof repairs at a much later date according to staff at Keswick Museum. A dried cat was discovered in the Tower of London during alterations in 1950 (Rushen 1984: 34). Two cats were reported to have been found in a sixteenth-century cottage in Lynsted, near Sittingbourne, during renovations in 1968 – a child's shoe was also found in the same property. A dried cat was found wrapped in panels of woven reeds beneath the floorboards in the King's Dressing Room at Newton House in Llandeilo's Dinefwr Park (*Carmarthen Journal* 2000: 7). It is reported that Kettering Museum holds a dried cat which is said to have come from the roof of a house on the corner of Lower Street and Bakehouse Hill during demolition in 1966 – the cat's neck was hooked around a joist under the roof. In Wales a cat was found in the wall of the coach house stable of the King's Head Hotel, Usk.

At their house in Parracombe, North Devon, Jean and Phil Griffiths found a dried cat, a thick glass jam jar, a sardine tin and a horse-shoe, all discovered together in an iron bread oven which had been bricked up. They are likely to have been concealed at the end of the nineteenth century or early twentieth century. A cat was discovered in a seventeenth-century cottage at Black Moss reservoir in Pendle. It had been found in an internal room which had been sealed off in the nineteenth century. Its location led to much press speculation about it being a witch's cottage.

In an e-mail received in June 2002 the following cat was reported: 'Hi. Under the flags, immediately in front of the fireplace at [a house in] Stanley St, Ulverston, Cumbria a neighbour found a squashed kitten quite mummified! This was 5 years back. The house was built c1860'.

Two dried cats were discovered in the thatch of a farm at Wrington, North Somerset. The house dates from the seventeenth century and the discovery was made during re-roofing. A hand stitched paper bag was also discovered. The cats were found in different parts of the roof and are thought to date to different periods. The owner reported that the cats are now in a cardboard box in the loft of the property (reported by Ian Evans via e-mail in July and October 2002).

There are quite a few reports of cats where it seems that they were deliberately placed above the main entrance to the building. This was the case at Llancaiach Fawr Manor in South Wales (in the ceiling near the main entrance), at the Abbey Hotel in Bury St Edmunds (beneath the floorboards of the first floor above the entrance) and in Camberwell in London (above the main entrance to a building on the High Street).

In 2003 a dried cat was discovered in the thatch of a sixteenth-century cottage in Eckington, Worcestershire. It was found in a very old part of the thatch so may be a very early example. Two dried cats were found inside a Tudor cottage in Sittingbourne, Kent. Another was found in a house in Mexborough, South Yorkshire. A dried cat was discovered in 1915 in Woburn Abbey during demolition work – according to a TV report it was found 'in an airtight brick container' and retained its skin and whiskers but its fur was gone. The cat was on display at the

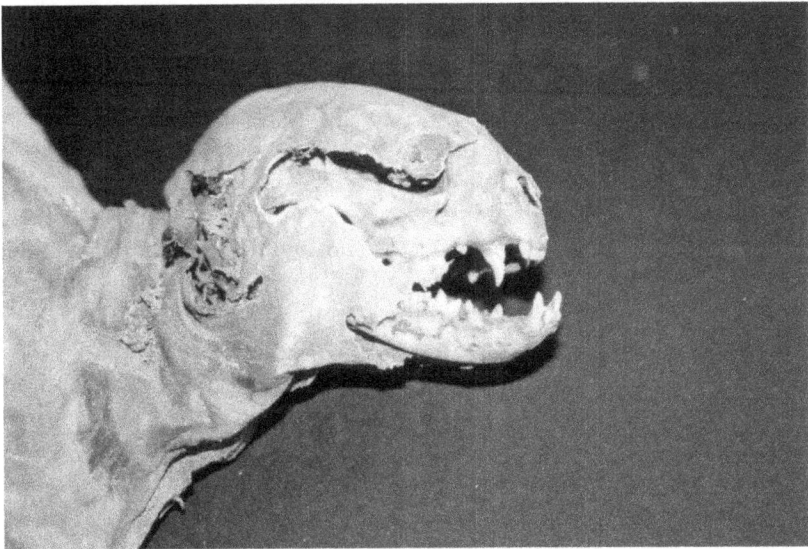

Figure 4.2 Dried cat from Eckington, Worcestershire. © Brian Hoggard.

Walter Rothschild Zoological Museum in Tring, Hertfordshire. Another cat was found at a windmill in Fulbourn near Cambridge. A lady who used to regularly visit the place as a child told me in May 2007 that the 'legend was, as I remember, that it used to belong to a past miller, and that if it were taken out, the mill would fall down'.

An example of a dried cat was found in a sealed wooden box beneath the floorboards of the Mill Hotel in Sudbury, Suffolk. The local builder reported that concealing cats was once 'a common practice … to protect the place from fire and evil spirits. It was a sort of sacrifice'. He went on to say that he had discovered about a dozen in the area and had always put them back. The story in this case continues that during the time he had the Sudbury cat inside his custody, three fires broke out in three different locations associated with the cat. Thankfully all this misfortune ceased when he returned the cat to its original resting place (Pleasant 1995).

An unusual example from Charmouth in Dorset was discovered in August 2007. A lead covered box was uncovered around 20cm below the surface around a metre outside an outbuilding belonging to a cottage there. Inside the box was the dried body of a cat which had been 'positioned in a life-like crouching pose, with its tail wrapped round one side'. The animal had been packed into the box with pieces of blanket and is thought to date from the 1920s or 1930s (Le Pard 2008: 181).

Two metropolitan cats were found in government buildings in central London. In one case the skull of a cat (no other bones) was discovered beneath the floor of a room dating to the 1850s in the Foreign and Commonwealth Office, Whitehall. In the same room a pair of boots was also found. A dried cat was also discovered in the Treasury building in SW1, London. According to those who know the history of the building, the cat must have got into the cavity in around 1912 or 1935.

In Scotland dried cats have been reported at Comlongan Castle. Elgin Museum has a cat in their collection which was found in 1896, together with with a rat and a starling, in a wall of the Old Greyfriars Abbey in Elgin. They also report that a similar cat was found beneath tiles at an old cottage in Spey Bay. Joyce Rushen reports that in 1703 an Elder of the parish church of Oyne in Aberdeenshire was 'charged with burying a cat under his hearth; the charge referred to as one of witchcraft and charming' (Rushen 1984: 34). Staff at Groam House Museum reported that a dried cat was found on top of the wall-head of a two-storey building in the village of Rosemarkie in Ross-shire. However, dried cats are not known to be commonplace north of the border. Many examples have been found in Ireland.

In France the remains of a cat buried behind a main beam by its owner in the sixteenth century and discovered by workers in the eighteenth century can still be seen today by visitors to Combourg Castle. A cat which had been buried inside a pillar was found at the church of Saint-Jacques de Saint-Quentin. In the region of Neuchâtel, Raoul Cop provides many examples of entombed cats in two separate locations on the Comtoise border, three at La Chaux-de-Fonds and one at Locle. These cats were found variously under the floor and in the ceiling and are thought to date to the nineteenth century when renovations were taking place. In Alsace a cat found in a cob wall was brought to the Écomusée d'Alsace and another was reported found in Rixheim (Vernot 2014: 379). The son of a property developer reported that they would often find cats and pine martens in the Dordogne region. A dried cat, which was clearly a deliberate deposit, was found between planks in the attic of the castle of Aspelt (Blaising 2016: 34).

A dried cat was found beneath the theatre in Hobart, Tasmania. Australian researcher Ian Evans reported in March 2004 that a dead cat had been found under the building during renovation work. The animal was found by builders working on the site and they were emphatic that it was located in an enclosed area under the front of the theatre. The building was constructed between September 1874 and June 1875.

Dried cats are also fairly widespread in Germany. Petra Schad has done considerable research in the area of Ludwigsburg in particular and noted at least 18 different discoveries of concealed cats in her 2005 paper. The buildings in which they were found ranged in date from the fifteenth to the twentieth centuries. For example, in a private house in Markgröningen cats were found under the floorboards in two different upper floors. In Besigheim a cat was discovered beneath the floorboards sitting on clay in the middle of the hall area (Schad 2005: 159).

Dried cats have also been discovered in Transylvania, Romania, where it is thought the tradition was imported by German settlers.

A dried cat was discovered during the remodelling of the Bishops Palace in Santiago, Chile. The Palace dates from 1852. Another dried cat was recovered from the roof of a property in Argentina, as reported by Daniela Àvido.

From the USA Geoff Rogers reported to me in May 2002 the discovery of a dried cat beneath the floorboards of his 1848 home in Shutesebury, Massachusetts while renovations were taking place. He learned that someone from the same town with a house of a similar age had also found a cat beneath the floorboards. Another deposit of a cat was found at the early eighteenth-century Holmdel Baptist Church, New Jersey. It was apparently shot in the head then immediately buried

(Scharfenberger 2009: 12–29). Bethany Myers reported to me that the previous owners of the house she had just moved to in Pennsylvania had discovered a dried cat under the foundation of their house at the back porch. There was some discussion about whether to keep it or not and it ended up being sprayed with a lacquer and now hangs in an out-house. Another dried cat was found in the attic of an 1840s house in Warren Center, Pennsylvania in 2004.

A very recent example reported to me in August 2017 by home-owner Bruce Warden was found beneath the porch of their 1924 bunga-low in Ann Arbor, Michigan. They decided to keep the cat so placed it in a glass display case from where it continues to protect the property.

From the other side of America, Alfred Eberle told me that while helping his friend jack up the foundations of his 90-year old house in Berkeley, California, they discovered a dried cat which had been placed inside a small hollow in the foundation. He described it as follows:

> We assumed that it had crept into the hollow and had died there, but what made me wonder about it was that the cat looked as though it had been *propped* there, in a standing position against the back of the niche, and even with a front paw stretched out as if to scratch someone, and with the teeth bared. I wondered about whether rigor mortis could actually do that.

Alfred went to explain that the house was constructed by immigrant Finnish farmers.

Simona Falanga told me about the discovery of a dried cat and rat in Newfoundland, Canada. They had been concealed in a plaster wall of a farm called the O'Brien Farm which was founded by Irish immigrants and dates from the 1790s. The farm is in the City of St Johns, between Mount Scio Road and Oxen Pond Road.

Many more examples of cats which have been concealed with obvi-ous intent could be provided here. Taking all the cases as a whole, there does not appear to be any obvious evidence that cats have been concealed alive; however, several individuals reported modern cases where cats have gone missing during building and were later discov-ered sealed into places where it would have been impossible not to have noticed the presence of a cat.

Howard relates an example from Gibraltar where a family cat dis-appeared during building works in 1879. This suggests both that the practice still occurs in some areas and that, on occasions at least, they are sealed in alive. Another correspondent informed me that a pet cat went missing during some building work on a property belonging to a relative in Dorset in the second half of the twentieth century. Upon investigation it turned out the cat was trapped in a very small cavity in the new build and the builders claimed that the animal had got there by accident. Those who saw the space were sure that the presence of a cat could not have been missed and that the animal had been trapped inside on purpose.

Much more recently, the *Daily Telegraph* of 29 August 2007 reported a short story titled 'Firemen find cat buried in floor'. In this story a 12-year old tabby had gone missing for three weeks and was eventually found trapped in a six inch pipe beneath a concrete floor in the garage of a new house. It had survived by licking condensation from the side of the pipe. The cat had been sealed in by workmen pouring concrete over the pipe. The owners of the house were alerted by the loud meowing; they dug up the floor to rescue the animal and then were able to reunite it with its family in the neighbouring street. It is not clear if this was indeed a case of a cat being interred alive but it does raise the possibility that the practice continues. In many of the cases from previous centuries, however, the evidence of cats being manipulated and attached to beams suggests that they were already dead.

At Morelinch Vineyard near Bridgewater a toy cat was found on a ledge up a chimney. The toy had pads on its feet, amongst other details, but unfortunately workmen burned it. At East Hendred a wooden figure of a cat was found in the thatch of an old house. Jo Seaman reported in September 2017 that a toy cat was found built into the wall around St Mary's Church, Willingdon in East Sussex. These all seem to be clear examples of toys being used as a substitute for cats.

Of all the objects found in buildings, dried cats are the most frequently disposed of, for obvious reasons. They are usually thrown away or burned and as a result very few well documented cases survive, compared to the very large amount of anecdotal references which exist for them. In the survey only 161 documented cases of dried cats have been reported for England and for those which have been dated according to their context within the building, there is a fairly even spread from the seventeenth century through to the early twentieth century. At present only around 20 per cent of all the dried cats contained within the author's database have been dated. This clearly illustrates how difficult it can be to arrive at a date for when these animals were placed in the buildings. The age of the building where they were found (if known) gives us a maximum age, but there is often evidence that the animal was interred within the building at a point of restoration, modification or simple repair which, without expert analysis, is not always easy to date and can sometime be a couple of centuries later than the original building.

From conversations with builders it has become apparent that a very large number of dried cats are discovered but never formally reported. In 1998 I spoke to a former builder from Pershore named Dave Parker who reported an interesting example which demonstrates what can happen when one is discovered during a project. He told me that he was working on converting an old stable block at Croome Court (Worcestershire) into apartments sometime in the late 1970s/early 1980s when they discovered a dried cat 3-4 feet off the ground lying down on a 'noggin' (beam) between two lath and plaster panels. The foreman on the site ordered someone to get rid of it by throwing it into the skip but no-one wanted to – they all felt deeply superstitious about it and did not want to touch it. He also reported that he felt it would be bad luck to move it. Ultimately Dave was ordered to move it which he did, reluctantly. After placing the cat in the skip he returned up the stairs into the stable block where a plaster panel from the ceiling fell down and struck him across the forehead, resulting in a nasty cut. Dave and his friends remained convinced that this happened because they moved the cat.

It is clear that this practice was widespread throughout the British Isles, mainland Europe and as far as Australia and the Americas. The concept of the witch having an animal helper with magical qualities was clearly one that those who feared witchcraft could harness to their own ends by effectively having one of their own attached (sometimes literally) to the home. So it can be argued that the dried cats were intended to act as wards against the witch's familiar and other bad energies that might enter the home. The concept of ritually killing something to make it function on a spiritual rather than physical level is one that is found in the practice of making witch-bottles (discussed elsewhere in this volume) and it seems that the same idea is being utilised here but with cats. The difference is that this spirit is active in death, on the prowl seeking out vermin.

Note

Some passages in this chapter were first published in Hoggard. 2016b. 'Concealed Animals', in R. Hutton (ed.), *Physical Evidence for Ritual Acts, Sorcery and Witchcraft in Christian Britain – A Feeling for Magic*. Basingstoke: Palgrave, pp. 106–17.

Chapter 5

HORSE SKULLS

Horse skulls have been recovered from under the floors and within the walls of buildings throughout the British Isles, Europe and the USA. There are not as many recorded examples of horse skulls as there are for the other objects discussed in this book but this could be because they are often beneath floor level and so are only discovered when a building is reduced to its foundations. The author's survey has collected a total of 54 examples of these in England, Eurwyn Wiliam cites 27 examples from Wales in his paper on the subject (Wiliam 2000: 136–49), Seán Ó Súilleabháin collected numerous testimonials of the practice being carried out in Ireland (Ó Súilleabháin 1945: 49–50), and there are reports from Scotland too. There are practices involving horse skulls repelling evil and pests in Romania, Finland and Russia, and in the USA there are examples from Illinois, Massachusetts and New Hampshire.

It is likely that many finds of bones and skulls in buildings meet a similar fate in rubbish tips as the dried cats which are discovered. It also seems to be the case that many of these objects are not reported when they are discovered. The fact that some of them are buried beneath the floor of buildings will account in part for this but a further complicating factor in the case of bones is their use as a building material in some houses and farm buildings. There are many examples of entire floors or walls which have been created out of animal bones or teeth (Armitage 1989a: 147–60). In the examples presented here only those which do not appear to have a structural function have been included.

In 1879 at a pub called the Portway in Staunton-on-Wye, Herefordshire, 24 horse skulls were discovered screwed to the underside of the floorboards. The reason given for the skulls being there was that the floor made 'a hollow sound when the dancers stamped their feet, as was the custom in some old country dances' (Gooley 1993). At High House in Peterchurch, also in Herefordshire, renovations revealed the presence of 27 horse skulls under the floorboards (*Hereford Times* 1987). Ralph Merrifield reported that many horse skulls were removed from beneath the parlour floor of Thrimby Hall where they had reputedly been placed 'for purposes of sound'.

During repair work to Bungay House, Earsham Street, Bungay in the 1930s, the contractors discovered horse skulls lying under the floorboards. On lifting two of the floorboards, 'beneath the joists were rows of horse skulls, laid with great regularity, the incisor teeth of each resting on a square of oak or stone ... The (floor) boards, which were of red pine, rested immediately upon the skulls'. The room contained up to forty horse skulls, each 'carefully prepared and boiled, and ... placed in position with great care and accuracy'. The adjoining house also revealed several horse skulls under the floor but these have been removed (Armitage 1989b: 201–23; Pennick 1986: 6). Ivan Bunn describes this one as 'A large number of horses skulls found beneath the floor-boards of two houses (formerly one house dating from the 1620s). The skulls had been carefully placed and firmly fixed, each having its incisor teeth resting on a square of stone or oak' (Mann 1934: 253–55).

In Manuden, Essex, a horse skull was discovered in 1979 in a seventeenth-century cottage. The owner uncovered a brick-built bread oven which had been sealed up at some point and inside it was a horse skull. Merrifield also reports a horse skull which was found concealed in a cavity between a chimney flue and two enclosing brick walls at Little Belhus, South Ockendon – thought to date from the sixteenth or seventeenth century (Merrifield 1987: 123). A complete and articulated horse skull and neck was found in a well at Grove Priory, Bedfordshire, dating to the first part of the fourteenth century. Two horse burials are noted at Blackden Hall in Cheshire. A horse skull is reputed to have been found at Hailes Abbey in Gloucestershire. A horse skull was discovered in a house known as Squeen Lodge at Ballaugh, Isle of Man: 'While the builders were removing the first floor joists they uncovered what appeared to be a skull and hip bone set into a joist hole ... [on investigation] ... it was in fact a horse's skull with twin boar tusks inserted into the tooth sockets of the upper jaw'. The find is thought to date from the eighteenth century (Hayhurst 1989: 105–107). In Wales a badly decayed horse skull was found beneath the farmhouse kitchen floor at Modrydd Farm, Libanus. At Yewdale Cottage, 8 Quickwell Hill, St David's, Pembrokeshire, former resident Robin Oakley reported that a horse skull is on display in a case which was reputedly discovered in foundations during renovations.

At Halton East, North Yorkshire, horse skulls were discovered beneath the flagstones of a cottage during restoration (Pennick 1986: 6). It was also reported to me that several field lime kilns excavated in 2007 in the Yorkshire dales have a horse skull set in the flues.

There is an example from Scotland on file where it is reported that horse skulls were found in the vicinity of the pulpit of Edinburgh Meeting House (Pennick 1986: 6). There is also a report that one was found within the Old North Bridge in Edinburgh.

Excavations at Hornby Castle in Wensleydale revealed a horse head buried within an early fourteenth-century wall. Correspondent Rubyna Matthews reported in November 2013:

> I am the Field Officer of the Architectural and Archaeological Society of Durham and Northumberland and since 2010 we have been undertaking a programme of fieldwork, mainly comprising excavation on a site within the grounds of Hornby Castle in Wensleydale North Yorkshire. The site comprises a 'pleasaunce' or detached structure for the entertainment of important guests of the owners in the 14th and 15th Centuries, a branch of the Nevilles and later the Conyers family. During Season 3 (2012) much to our surprise we uncovered a horse's head that had been deliberately buried within the core of a wall of early 14th Century date. The horse had been decapitated below the third vertebrae. We have found little comparative evidence for this other than from a handful of sites in Northern and Eastern Europe associated with the recruitment to the Order of Teutonic Knights. Interestingly, the builder of our structure Sir John Neville, one of King Edward III's inner household was a known participant in the Lithuanian Crusade. We also have other evidence of Medieval folk belief in the form of a series of fossils and reused Prehistoric worked flints.

In the USA four horse skulls were found in the Jarrot Mansion at the Cahokia Courthouse Historic State site, one in a cavity right beside the fireplace, the others under the floor. The building was constructed for French settlers by English Americans in the late eighteenth century. In Goffstown, New Hampshire a horse skull and some old shoes were found underneath the back of an old shop. The owner was convinced that the skull protected his store from several fires which affected the property over the years.

In South Deerfield, Massachusetts at the Bryant Homestead, built in 1776, a horse skull was discovered in a thick wall near the chimney. The finders, Rocky and Kathy Foley, reported that when they removed it from the wall they discovered a piece of paper in the eye socket reading, 'Colonel David M Bryant and Family took possession of this farm on April 29, 1848'; the note also listed the names of his wife and six children (Foley and Foley 1991: 49). This latter example clearly suggests a belief that the horse skull would protect those named in the letter.

In April 2011 it was reported that 'about 28 horse skulls' were found in a 1770 three-storey house placed in the floor joists between the first and second floors from a house in Kent County on the Upper Eastern Shore of Maryland. The home-owners were taking down the 1770 house to build a new home and planned to include some of the skulls in the new build to 'carry on the tradition'.

Sonja Hukantaival reports that in Finland horse skulls are often mentioned in folklore as being concealed within the hearth to ward off pests. She says:

> Even though horse skulls are often mentioned in the folklore, there are few documented finds of concealed horse skulls in Finland. Still, it has been pointed out that in some areas finding a horse skull in an old hearth when demolishing it is very common. Perhaps a bit too common, since people do not think that it is something they should report to the local museum. Only remarkable finds tend to get reported; this is evident in two cases where the complete skeleton of a horse was found in the hearth foundation. (Hukantaival 2016)

An example of a horse skull being used to ward off pests from bee-hives exists in the Museum of Ethnography in St Petersburg in Russia. It is said that a horse skull was often attached to a beam near a beehive because it was effective against bee diseases and intrusions by bears.

Adina Hulubaş from the Romanian Academy told me that in Romania horse skulls are placed in orchards to ward off evil.

Three main theories have been put forward by different authors to explain the presence of concealed horse skulls in buildings. There is the acoustic theory, the idea of foundation sacrifice and the general idea that it brings good luck.

Before discussing these theories, we should take a moment to appreciate that horse skulls are very impressive looking things and have a certain presence. This aspect of the skulls is bound to have been recognised and harnessed by magical practitioners. Their use in folklore attests to this with practices such as the Mari Llywd from South Wales where a creature with the skull of a horse attempts to gain entry into people's homes. There is also the tradition of soul caking in Cheshire where a figure performs a ritual dance, topped by a horse skull known as the Wild Horse of Antrobus. Both of these figures are rather spooky to look at and show that horse skulls in folklore have associations with threshold traditions and with the dead.

Many works on British folklore suggest that the horse was thought to be clairvoyant and vulnerable to the evil eye, hence work horses

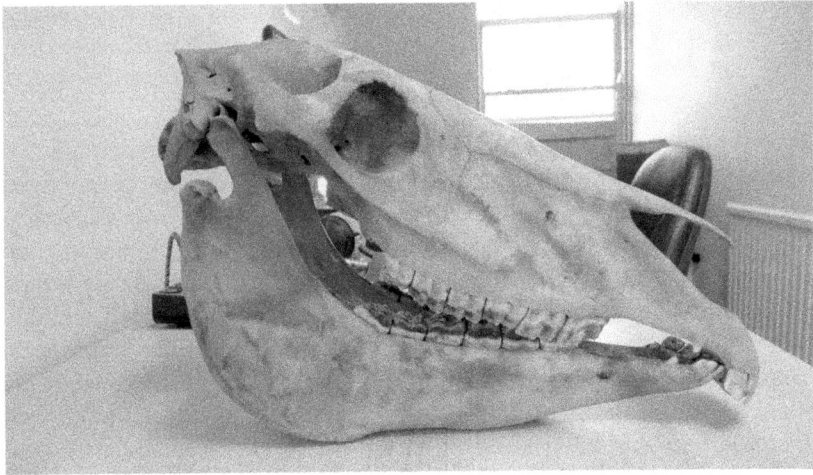

Figure 5.1 Horse skull from the author's collection. © Brian Hoggard.

were covered in horse brasses originally designed to protect the animals with images of the sun, moon and other symbols. It is possible that this vulnerability was sought by those who concealed the skulls to act as a lure for harmful forces coming into the home. There is also folklore suggesting that horses had the ability to see witches and evil spirits. There are many examples in prehistory of horse burials which there appears to be an association with the passage to the other world.

In 1945 Seán Ó Súilleabháin undertook a survey of concealed horse skulls in Ireland by asking members of the Royal Society of Antiquaries of Ireland to enquire about the practice in their local areas. In almost every area of Ireland it was reported that horse skulls were concealed in several houses, most usually under a stone before the hearth. The explanation given in many cases was that this improved the sound when dancing took place before the fire (Ó Súilleabháin 1945: 45–49). Similarly, in Herefordshire at the Portway Inn in Staunton-on-Wye at least twenty-four horse skulls were found screwed to the underside of the floor where they were reputed 'to make the fiddle go better' (Merrifield 1987: 123). Ó Súilleabháin was not convinced by the acoustic theory, believing that this was a modern interpretation which had evolved in order to explain the presence of horse skulls in buildings long after the original reason had been forgotten:

> It can hardly be doubted that the now popular explanation of the burial of horse-skulls under the floors of houses, churches, castles, or bridges (to produce an echo) is a secondary one. It may indeed be a practical

explanation but a little consideration of the problem must inevitably lead to the conclusion that this custom is but another link in the chain of evidence regarding foundation sacrifices. (Ó Súilleabháin 1945: 49–50)

Ó Súilleabháin's conclusions were disputed by Albert Sandklef of Sweden who undertook research into the custom across Scandinavia. He found that it was a common practice in southern Scandinavia to conceal horse skulls and pots beneath threshing barn floors and the reason provided was that it helped to produce a pleasant ringing tone while threshing. Sandklef's ultimate conclusion was that horse skulls were only concealed for acoustic purposes and that the foundation sacrifice theory was invalid (Sandklef 1949). Eurwyn Wiliam, in his study of horse skulls in Wales, concluded after consideration of both theories that the real answer to this practice is still elusive. He did, however, think that it is possible that 'it may be that we have here a custom, weakened by no longer serving its original function and with that function metamorphosed over time, rejuvenated and given a new imperative by fresh factors'. This essentially supports an ancient origin for the practice but in Wiliam's view this was changed in Wales from the eighteenth century onwards by an interest in the acoustic properties of the new chapels and the growing importance of the horse in the agricultural revolution of the nineteenth century (Wiliam 2000: 146).

Another contributor to the debate, Caoimhin Ó Danachair, provides some good evidence in support of the acoustic theory. He states that the horse skulls were placed under the hearthstone but were sometimes replaced by an iron pot. He describes how 'a hole was made in the clay [beneath the hearthstone] and in it a small flat-bottomed pot-oven was hung from two thin iron rods laid crossways over the hole. An irregularly-shaped piece of worn-out iron plate (possible part of a large griddle) was laid over the hold and the flagstone was set in place to cover the lot'. He states that this occurred particularly in Clare, Kerry, Limerick and Tipperary, and that the hearthstone is the spot where people would demonstrate their dancing (Ó Danachair 1970: 22). This account appears to demonstrate that iron pots did a much better job of enhancing the acoustics than a concealed horse skull.

In several cases where horse skulls have been discovered, the acoustic theory does not appear to be relevant and in some cases it does. For example, Northumberland National Park Authority state that a box containing three horse skulls was discovered in the bell turret in Elsdon Church during restoration work in 1837. These skulls may have been placed there to enhance the sound of the bells but this could also demonstrate an association with one of the original functions of church bells, to scare away evil spirits. An example which has no apparent acoustic function is cited by Merrifield where a horse skull was found concealed in a cavity between a chimney flue and two enclosing brick walls at Little Belhus, South Ockendon, Essex (Merrifield 1987: 123). Evidence from horse skulls found at Bay Farm Cottage, Carnlough, Co. Antrim also suggests that no acoustic function could be derived from the placing of at least ten horse skulls beneath a floor (Mallory and McCormick 1984: 50–53). There are also examples from Portmarnock, Co. Dublin which were clearly set into the clay (Colm 2015).

In Bryn Ellis' *Halkyn Mountain Communities in Times Past*, there are images of the 1726 house called Lygan Y Wern which include a picture of horse skulls. The text claims that the skulls, one black and one bleached white, were found in October 1965 during floor repairs in one of the front rooms. A local researcher named Garfield Bagshaw interpreted the two skulls as meaning that the unbleached one was set into the earth to 'propitiate the spirits of the soil, which had been disturbed to build the house', and the bleached one was there to prevent evil from entering. The skulls were apparently replaced afterwards (Ellis 1993: 40). This example appears to encapsulate two points of view regarding the purpose of concealing horse skulls, foundation sacrifice and warding off evil.

There is the evidence of ritual to consider too. In 1897 during the building of a chapel in East Anglia, England, a ritual using a horse's head on a stake was undertaken to 'drive away evil and witchcraft'. The head was 'annointed' with beer before being covered with bricks and mortar. A young boy was sent off to a knackers' yard to fetch one for the purpose (Merrifield 1987: 126). In several of the Welsh examples there was a clear belief that the skulls in the properties were to protect against evil and witchcraft, with some from church roofs thought to 'dispel the spirits' (Wiliam 2000: 138). Certainly, many of the skulls which have been discovered could not have had any kind of acoustic functions and in those cases apotropaic explanations fit rather well.

As in the case of dried cats, it may be that some of the perceived qualities of the horse also played a role in this practice. The horse serves humans in a direct way through transport and work and they are not generally regarded as food animals. They are also seen as particularly sensitive creatures, highly alert and are generally valued above other animals. It is also the case that they can sleep with their eyes open, lending weight to their watchful and sensitive qualities. Perhaps it was hoped that these qualities would be effective in protecting the house. One report suggested that the head of a favourite horse (upon its natural death) be used for this purpose; this seems to endorse the idea of bringing the good influence of an animal into the home (Buchanan 1956: 60).

Some of the finds of horse skulls have been explained by correspondents as bringing luck into the house, but how this association began is not clear. The placing of horse skulls within buildings can be said to have dubious acoustic worth in many instances. There are reports that they were placed there to ward off evil spirits at the foundation of buildings and also later on in other parts of the structure. The concealed nature of the items suggests that they were positioned in secret which may have contributed to the perceived importance of the act and also suggests their use as a ward against evil.

Without conducting tests on floors beneath which many skulls have been placed, it is difficult to know for certain whether the acoustic theory carries any genuine weight, but it does remain a popular explanation. Quite a few examples of skulls have been found located in the pulpit of churches or, as Sandklef reported, in large quantities beneath threshing barn floors in Scandinavia. These could provide evidence for this explanation but there are other ways of enhancing acoustics and it must be remembered that there are clear examples of horse skulls apparently being used for apotropaic purposes. If they were used for acoustic purposes, then it seems clear that there was already an association between the horse skull and averting evil and that perhaps this brought an additional benefit to the practice.

Horseshoes are commonly displayed as good luck charms throughout the British Isles, the USA, Europe and, it would seem, the rest of the world. In Britain and Ireland the preference is often to hang the horseshoes with points upwards, 'so that the luck doesn't run out'. In other parts of the world they usually point downwards. Aside from the close relationship between man and horse, it is also significant that horseshoes are made of iron, a known form of protection against witchcraft and the fairy folk.

The practice of concealing horse skulls in buildings must also be set against the widespread folk customs which also involve horses or horse skulls. The Hobby Horse, the Mari Lwyd and other folk customs were once very widespread, with traditions in Wales, Kent, Lincolnshire, Cheshire, the south-west and Ireland. Graffiti representing the Hobby Horse can be found in a number of churches in Hertfordshire.

Although it is difficult to pin down a date of origin for these folk traditions, it is safe to say there are records of hobby horses from as early as the fourteenth century. Hobby horses would often accompany folk dances and were sometimes also used in church collections. They could range from a pole with a skull on the end with fabric draped over it to something somewhat smaller with a model horse head on the end. The Mari Lwyd of south Wales, which is a human carrying a horse skull on a pole with a costume draped over it, first appears in records in the eighteenth century but may be considerably older; there was also a similar tradition in Pembrokeshire (Cawte 1978: 10–47).

These and other traditions attest to the impressive appearance of horse skulls and also a familiarity with them as being symbolic or powerful in some way. We know that people included horse skulls in new builds, particularly with nineteenth-century chapels, at a time when these folk traditions and practices were still current.

It is interesting to consider that prior to the advent and subsequent dominance of the motor vehicle as form of transport, it was the norm to encounter live and well horses in everyday life. The fact that the horse skull also had a widely experienced folk presence on certain occasions or even during church collections and that people were routinely concealing them beneath new buildings is a testament to the depth and richness of folk beliefs in the past. Accidental discoveries and archaeological investigation are slowly revealing the physical extent of these beliefs.

The evidence suggests that the use of horse skulls in buildings appears primarily to have been to ward off evil. If the acoustic theory were the genuine reason, it would be demonstrable, openly and widely known and encountered in every instance, which it is not. The averting evil explanation is found just as frequently and would account for the secrecy around the use of horse skulls in buildings. The evidence provided by Merrifield in the Norfolk example does suggest a ritual deposit or foundation sacrifice, presumably to appease the local spirit of place and protect the future occupants of the building. It is likely that the established church in any of the areas these are found viewed the practice as superstitious or heretical in some way, so the opportunity to explain the practice as having a legitimate acoustic function would have provided a welcome excuse for those caught red-handed. The location of some of the horse skulls next to the fireplace, and in particular the evidence of the note recovered from the eye socket of the Massachusetts example, seem to point clearly at a protective function.

Note

Some passages in this chapter were first published in Hoggard. 2016b. 'Concealed Animals', in R. Hutton (ed.), *Physical Evidence for Ritual Acts, Sorcery and Witchcraft in Christian Britain – A Feeling for Magic*. Basingstoke: Palgrave, pp. 106–17.

◦☀◦ Chapter 6

WRITTEN CHARMS

Written charms are the result of a person's need to have their property protected by a supernatural spell. They are often recovered from gaps in timbers where they have been folded many times and tucked away. It will come as no surprise that these are rarely found owing to the fragility of paper and its susceptibility to decay. The evidence shows that the person in need would generally contact the local cunning man or wise woman and ask them for a charm to protect the desired creatures or buildings. The charms themselves, through their combination of symbols and carefully laid-out text, are quite artistic in appearance. They frequently include astrological and occult symbols as well as invocations to God or Jesus to protect the required items.

It is not sufficient to look at the text alone when studying a written charm as clearly a great deal of effort and care goes into the appearance and nature of the symbols. Often the charms include symbols from astrology and grimoires such as the Key of Solomon, and the magical word triangle of 'abracadabra' is also often encountered. Written charms are as much artefacts as documents and the act of deliberately concealing them in buildings is equally as important as the text found on them.

The text and associated symbols are all usually squeezed onto a small piece of paper which is then folded and placed into a gap between timbers at the most convenient threshold or other location in the building concerned. One example was found folded inside a small sheet of lead and inserted above a door-frame and sometimes charms are found inside bottles.

Ralph Merrifield investigated a charm which was found buried in a cowshed in Sarn in Wales. When an old trough was dismantled, a cylindrical stoneware bottle was found underneath which had been

Figure 6.1 Written charm from Sarn in Wales. © Brian Hoggard.

broken during the work and a paper charm was discovered inside. The farmer's parents recognised it as a conjuror's charm and recalled that there had been a series of unexplained cattle deaths in the past and that the local conjuror (or cunning man) had been summoned to deal with it. Apparently, the conjuror would recite his spells around the boundaries of the farm over a period of seven days and on the final day bury one charm on the land and another within the farm buildings. The charm is hand-written and thought to date from the beginning of the twentieth century. The main body of text on it reads:

> In the name of the Fatha and of the Son and of the Holy Gost Amen xxxx
> and in the name of the Lord Jesus Christ his redeemer and saviour he will
> releve William _____ Pentrynant his cows calves milk butter catle of all
> ages mares suckers horses of all ages sheep yews lambes sheep of all ages
> piges sowes and prosper him in all his farm and from all witchcraft and
> all Evil deseases amen xxx Gasper fert myrham thus mechor balthasar
> auraum hec tria quregum salvatir a morbo a Christ pietate ea duco amen
> xxx ineducto unversanilam amathuram _____ positis sarah adverus
> artedovalis amen xxx Eructavit cor meaum verbun bonum dicam cuncta
> opera meregi domino labia mea aperies and os meum annutiabit vertatem
> cuntre brachna iniquet lingua malusqua subvertatur a Lord Jesus Christ
> homnoum he hereth the preserever of William Pentrynant his cows calve
> milk butter catle of all ages mares suckers horses of all ages yews lambes
> sheep of all ages piges sows and prosper him on this farm to live luckly

saved from all witchcraft and evil men or women or spirits or wizards or hardness of hart amen xxx and this I will trust in the Lord Jesus Christ my redeemer and saviour from witchcraft amen xxx and this I trust in Jesus Chris my redeemer and saviour he will releve William _____ Pentrynant his cows calves milk buter catle of all ages mares suckers horses of all ages yews lambes sheep of all ages piges sowers and everything (that) is his posesion to liv lucken and proster him on this farm and from all witchcraft by the same power as he did cause the blind to see the lame to walk and the dum to talk and thou findest with unclean spirits spirits as wilt Jehovah amen xxx the witch compased him about but the Lord will destroy them all pater pater pater noster noster noster ave ave ave maria creed car of acteum x on x adona x tetragra amen xxx and in the name of the holy trinity and of _____ preserve all above named from all evil diseases whatsoever amen x. (Merrifield 1955: 1612–13)

Beneath the text there are two rows of astrological symbols including those for Jupiter, the moon, possibly Venus and the sign for Pisces. Interspersed between them are four six-pointed line-drawn stars, echoing the six-pointed daisy wheels we see carved onto surfaces within buildings. Below these the words 'Jah Jah Jah' are written. In the bottom left-hand corner of the charm is the abracadabra magical word triangle, and in the bottom right-hand corner is an eight-spoked wheel symbol with different symbols adorning the end of each spoke. This latter symbol is taken from the key of Solomon.

The juxtaposition of astrological symbols, magical symbols, the magical word triangle and invocations to God and Jesus show that the intention is to take supernatural power from any source available, even if the Christian source would normally regard the others as heretical. The thrice repeated 'Lord Jesus Christ be the preserver' seems to be a part of the spell in itself. Merrifield suggests that the mention of Ave Maria and other Latin components mean that the writer of the charm is following a pre-Reformation tradition. His research in the area led to the discovery of other charms written in the same hand and others of identical structure but in a different hand. He later learned that this was because a father and son were both producing the same charm as part of their services (Merrifield 1955: 1612–13). An almost identical example made to protect Thomas Ellis was later discovered (Owen 1959: 253–54).

This example from Merrifield is the only one which provides evidence of rituals associated with the installation of the charm. It may be that similar practices were undertaken with all the charms cited here which would add a significant extra dimension to their meaning.

The Museum of Welsh Life at St Fagan's, Cardiff holds a written charm which was found in a bottle. Ceredigion Museum in Aberystwyth holds three of them, Brecknock Museum in Brecon has an example from the Honddu Valley, and there is one known to date from 1905 from Carno in Powys. At Cascob Church, Radnorshire, an abracadabra charm was found. The National Library of Wales at Aberystwyth has at least thirteen examples of written charms in its archives.

The abracadabra charm was not only written onto charms for installation into buildings but was one of a great many portable charms that people would carry. William Paynter from Cornwall reports the following example:

> Just a few miles to the north we meet a woman who used to draw circles on the road so that whoever crossed them was ill-wished. A man from the parish accidentally walked into one of these circles and suffered all manner of bad luck. 'I know it's true about the circles', he told me, 'because I have proved it.' This same man showed me an ABRACADABRA charm, which he assured me he always carried to keep him safe from witchcraft. (Paynter 2016: 44)

At Hill End Farm, Harden, West Yorkshire, a written charm was found which had been sealed in wax and placed into a gap in a two-foot thick wall. A demolition worker found the charm while working in November 1944 and a local curator dated the charm to around 1750. The charm reads:

> Good x Lord x Jesus x Thy powers is above all powers that is Evil. Good x Lord x grant that Thy powers may overcome all powers that is Evil. Good x Lord x Bless Thee Samuel Lund from all Evil Spirits, from witchcraft and fore-speaking and blasting and the cramps x all Diseases whatsoever in the name of the Father, and of the Son, and of the Holy Ghost Bless Thee Samuel Lund be Thou whole and guarded by the Angels of God x Fiat x Fiat x Fiat x. (*The Yorkshire Observer* 1944: 2)

This example appears to comprise purely of text although we can suspect that some ritual was associated with it prior to concealment, as in the example from Sarn. The sealing in wax and hiding in the wall is a deliberate and purposeful act to place secret power against evil within a wall. The repeated concern about evil spirits and witchcraft clearly demonstrates the ever-present fears that supernatural danger was all around. Another written charm was found behind a door panel in a West Yorkshire cottage in Netherend Road, Hilltop, Slaithwaite (*Colne Valley Chronicle* 1984).

A written charm from Chirk had been 'folded into a long thin spill and then folded again into a pentagon and pushed into a wide crack in the main beam in the kitchen living room'. This particular charm reads:

In The Name of God Let god Arise and scatter These mine Enemies let Them/be as The Dust before The Wind and The Angel of The Lord scattering Them [hieroglyphs] Put on the whole Armour of God That we may be Able to stand against The / wiles of the Devil [Hieroglyphs] Dei gratia Illum quod Sacrument Ingrato [Heiroglyphs] Appogageon. (Owen 1960: 1)

The hieroglyphs in this case were primarily astrological symbols, including the moon, Libra and Pisces.

An example from Church Street, Sturminster Newton in Dorset included phrases such as 'Let this be a safe guard to this house', and 'Remove the Evil from this house'. This particular example was found inside a six-sided bottle beneath the floorboards of a house in the village. Another charm in a bottle was found in Stalbridge and shown to curator Jeremy Harte who reported:

> piece of paper found in a bottle in a house in Stalbridge ... written, seemingly in a 19th century hand, two magic squares – one with columns adding up to 34 (symbol for Jupiter), and the other adding up to 111 (symbol for the sun), eight sigils, including two Solomon's Seals, and in two cases accompanied by words Adonai, and Agla and Omega; few astrological glyphs, and these words – 'The Lord the Faithfull King give commandment O God to thy strength conform o God thy strength in us. El. Elohim. Elohai. Zebraoll. Elion Exeerchie [letter 'h' placed above word] Adonai. Jah. Jehovah Tetragrammaton Jof Eheoi so good lord take [?] heare Remove the Evil from this house in the Name of Jesus Christ Amen Fiat Fiat Fiat Cito Cito Cito'.

One charm reads 'I charge all witches and ghosts to depart from this house, in the great names of Jehovah, Alpha and Omega'. It was written on folded paper and sealed with red wax, found in the crevice of one of the joints of a kitchen chimney in 1882 in Madeley, Shropshire (Dyas 1993: 50).

A most unusual example of a written charm recovered from behind the brass plate on an old tombstone in a Lancashire churchyard was reported in *The Reliquary* in 1870. In the top right-hand corner is a square of the sun, which takes the form of a square with six rows and columns, each of which add up to 111 whether read horizontally, vertically or diagonally, with the whole adding up to 666. The charm also has symbols for the sun and moon in addition to some other magical symbols (Dodds 1870: 129–31). Jennie Cobban looks at a virtually identical charm, which was discovered in 1825 in West Bradford, in her *The Lure of the Lancashire Witches* and states that similar charms have turned up in Pendle, Ribble Valley and Rochdale (Cobban 2011: 78–81). Another very similar one, thought to date from the late eighteenth century, was discovered under a leather square in a press bed at Dawber's Farm, Foulridge, near Colne, Lancashire in 1914. Press beds often had an 'all-seeing eye' carved on them to protect the occupants from evil spirits. This charm was reported via Cobban's Lancashire Folklore and History Facebook page during August 2015. All these charms are very similar and appear to be the work of the same cunning person.

Cobban has carried out extensive research into witchcraft and magic in Lancashire and beyond and has kindly shared examples of written charms via her Lancashire's Folklore and History group on Facebook. An example from Syke, near Rochdale, reads: 'Omnis Spiritus laudet Dominum Mosen habent et Prophetus Exurgat. Deus et Dissipentus Inimici Ejus. Let every spirit praise the Lord God. Almighty that comes unto this place abode abode Fiat Fiat Fiat' (Cobban, Lancashire Folklore and History Facebook group, 2 September 2015).

Another example from her archive is this one from Rochdale, found at Simonstone at the end of the nineteenth century. It reads:

> I abjure, and cunjure you spirits, Analu, Anla, Annala, Anner, Anag, ankur, or three Belphoru, in the name of God the Father, God the Son, God the Holy Ghost, to make either a witch, Witches, Wizard or Wizards, blasst, or blassts, evil eye or decietful [sic] tongue, Socerer or Cunjeror, to burn and consume to atoms every individual belonging to the diabolical art of Witchcraft that is made use of to work iniquity upon the body of ..., or any of his family. For the sake of Christ, Amen.

This charm is mentioned by Clifford Burne in his booklet on Newchurch-in-Pendle (Cobban, Lancashire Folklore and History Facebook group, 31 August 2015).

The chimney lintel of Camp Green Farm, Debenham, dated 1592, has an array of marks along it. There is also a double-sided hand-written text pasted onto the beam. This is thought be date from the early seventeenth century (Easton 1999: 22–29).

Some charms are more simple in their construction. Ian Miller kindly told me about the following example from 26 August 1626. Elizabeth Griffyn (wife of William Griffyn), accused of making a charm against Hughe Patye and his wife, was bailed to appear at the next Assizes. At the local court in Reading on 26 August 1626, in front of the mayor, various statements were made about this accusation. Here is one by Ellyn Beale about the charm or curse:

> Saith that upon Tuesdaye last in the evening, about 8 of the clocke, Hughe Patye came to her house discontented in mynd, in the company of his wief, Mistris Welbecke, Goodwife Glover, An Glover and Margery Coverye, and asked leave of this Examinate to come thoroughe her

house to goe into the next house, wherein William Griffyn did dwell, and requested them to goe with him to see the wickednes of Griffyn's wief, and the witchery she intended against his wief and her husband, and then requested Mathewe Beale to pull downe certen brickes in the chimney, and within 4 or 5 brickes they should see her villany, but at that tyme they could fynd nothinge; yett afterwardes this Examinate had further speches with the said Hughe Patye, whoe still was vexed, he using wordes of discontent; the said Examinate upon Thursdaye morning went agayne into the said house, and in the same place pulled downe a bricke more, and there she found a small paper with a rusty pyn in it, and upon the paper was written the word Elizabeth 4 tymes, and the word Paty once, and with all a peicc of browne paper waxed or pasted^ and almost consumed, whiche she presently delivered to Robert Harbert to deliver to the Constables. All whiche Hughe confesseth is true.

William Griffyn saith he can saye nothing of any practise he knoweth against him by Hughe Patye or Griffyn's wief, but upon Tuesdaye last and Wensdaye at night the said Hughe Patye was at this Examinate's house, where he nowe dwelleth, and did misuse him in wordes and did kicke him grevously; and at his goeing away said, at thy other house there lyeth under 4 or 5 brickes that whiche will consume the, and said further that this Examinate's wief this twelvemonth hath intended to poyson him.

Hughe Patye not denyeing theise thinges saith he was not himself. (Guilding 1892: 311–12)

It appears that Elizabeth Paty's name was written on a piece of paper by Elizabeth Griffyn, a pin was put through the paper and then the paper was hidden in the chimney of the Griffyns' house. The idea is that destroying the paper affects the person whose name is written on it.

This is similar to a charm investigated by Pat Winzar from Charing in Kent:

Early in 1993 a sealed chimney was opened up in no.32 High Street. From the architectural and documentary evidence the chimney had been built in the seventeenth century. A charm was found about five feet up on the right-hand side inside the chimney. It had been set in wet mortar and so presumably was placed there when the chimney was built. It consisted of a piece of paper sealed with animal glue. For further security the paper was tied on with a length of linen string with a tassel at each end. (Winzar 1995: 23–28).

Analysis of the charm revealed no text but there were some traces of red paint.

A similar charm was reported by Phil Rogers from a flat in Windsor Street, Dundee:

I lived for 5 years in an attic flat in Dundee. Having access to the roof space (which was small, due to it having a flat roof) I was surprised to find a length of red wool knotted around an iron nail. There is a Scots saying 'Red thread, Lammer bead, all put witches to their speed', or something like that - and this could be part of the significance of the item. The building was built in the 1850's and I felt that the item had been there for as long as the building.

At Gressenhall in Norfolk an iron nail, wrapped in hemp, was found hammered between bricks beneath the floor of an eighteenth-century fireplace at Rectory Cottage. There are probably a great deal more of these nail charms out there, some with, some without paper attached.

In the USA several examples of written charms have been found in Pennsylvania barns; they often carry what have become known as hex signs. These charms would be written by the local cunning folk who were generally known as Pow-wow doctors. An example from 1827, which had been folded and concealed in one of the cow stalls of a barn, reads:

F[ather]. x. S[on]. x. H[oly Ghost]. x. God help this person for his livestock from all harm and evil. x.x.x amen in the name of Jesus amen. May these cows be led, this undertaking is done, that nothing evil should be able to harm the flesh and blood of these cows. F. x. S. x. H.x. amen. In the name of the Father, this shall stand from 1827 until 1831 under the 7 planets and under the 12 heavenly signs.

One of the fascinating aspects of this particular charm is that it was written in German which was then crossed out. Here we have the words being ritually 'killed' to make them more potent on a spiritual plane (Donmoyer 2013: 86). The charm has an assortment of astrological symbols and roughly drawn six-pointed stars at the bottom.

Another example from Pennsylvania was found beneath the threshing room floorboards of a barn from around 1840 in Maxatawny Township. It is written in English and reads: 'help success come to this barn and stock, Horses and [illegible] ... hieroglyphs and symbols ... Success and good health come to all of our stock'. The symbols are in a line across the middle and are of the moon, the sun (with a face), Saturn, a six-pointed star, a triangle and a symbol like an 'M' turned on its side. Two more, which appear to have been written by the same pow-wow practitioner, were found in a barn in Bitner's Corner. They were hidden behind plaster in the stable walls (Donmoyer 2013: 87). The use of charms such as this continued into the early twentieth century (Donmoyer 2014: 193).

In this part of the USA it was fairly normal to have a Himmelsbrief hanging on the wall too: this was an ornate letter invoking divine protection or blessing upon the household and its inhabitants. These were often made by pow-wows, or folk practitioners, and a well-made one could be very expensive.

These written charms are all deposited in a manner similar to that of witch-bottles, shoes, horse skulls and cats, and secrecy was clearly an element in how these charms were handled. Unlike the other objects found in buildings, however, the meaning and reason for concealing a written charm in a building is usually clear from the wording of the text. The juxtaposition of astrological and occult symbolism in the same document is very informative regarding the nature of the beliefs of the people who had reason to use them.

It appears that the emphasis was on invoking power, whatever the source, and the methods of putting this down on paper varied according to the knowledge of the individual cunning person producing them. Many of the Lancashire charms have a strongly occult flavour compared to those from Wales in which that element of the charms is there but toned down in comparison. They all essentially use the same mixture of invocations of the power of God and Christ, magical symbols usually borrowed from popular magical texts, astrological symbols for signs and planets, and a description of what is to be protected.

As we have seen in the example from Sarn, there may have been a significant amount of ritual involved too. These charms and the associated rituals would have been commissioned for a fee so there must have been a need for protection or at least a fear of not being protected.

These charms for protecting property and people were just one of many types which people would request. They would also purchase charms for healing, love and hate. One example of a love charm involved a lovesick young woman wearing a folded paper charm inside her armpit, inside which was a tiny bag containing nail parings and hair. The text of the charm reads:

> Susan Lebway to draw the
> Affections of Theobald Young
> to Herself, So that he Shall
> Never have any Rest or peace
> until he Do Return unto her
> And Make her his Lawfull Wife
> Let the Spirits of the Planets Continualy
> Torment him untill he do fulfil this
> My Request, Cossiel Lachiel Samuel
> Michael Araiel Raphael Gabriel
> I continually stir up his mind thereto.
> Fiat Fiat Fiat Cito Cito Cito Amen

The charm contains the same square of the sun and solar and lunar symbols as found in the Lancashire examples although the bulk of the charm is written in English instead of in cipher (Jewitt 1870: 139). Exactly the same principle is at work here as in the house protection charms and it is clear that cunning folk could make money quite easily using the same formula but with slightly different wording.

Charms for all sorts of reasons could be worn as amulets, ingested as potions, stitched into garments, cast as sigils using movement, spoken or carved onto objects. In addition, religious symbols and actions could also be deployed. In the case of charms for magical house protection, it would seem that ritual and deliberate concealment of the charm was an important part of the process too.

⚙ Chapter 7

PROTECTION MARKS

Scratched onto all kinds of surfaces within all kinds of buildings and several caves can be found a range of marks which were deliberate attempts to add a further layer of protection to a location. Although technically regarded as graffiti, these marks reveal a whole world of symbolism which was employed by builders, home owners and, indeed, cave dwellers alike. There are compass-drawn 'daisy wheel' patterns (sometimes known as hexafoils), shoe outlines, large areas of criss-cross or 'mesh', circles and long passages of slashed lines which sometimes grace chimney and door lintels. In addition to this the letters W, V and M crop up regularly. Another type of mark actually looks just like a burn mark but these were also done deliberately. Ideas about the meaning of these marks have remained fairly tentative owing to the lack of any contemporary explanations but I believe that, when considered in the light of medieval and later magical beliefs, it is now possible to put forward some strong theories which may explain them.

These marks have become known as ritual marks largely through the work of Timothy Easton who pioneered this area of research. More recently, the English Medieval Graffiti Project has been set up by Matthew Champion. This project has a huge army of volunteers all surveying churches and other buildings around the country. They are building up a huge archive of all kinds of graffiti which includes ritual marks.

Daisy Wheels

One of the most common types of mark to be found in both secular and religious buildings is the compass-drawn pattern known variously as the daisy wheel, hexafoil or flower of life. It can be found in literally hundreds of churches, other buildings and objects through Britain, the USA, Australia and Europe. Within the field of magical house protection this symbol was first encountered as graffiti, scratched onto surfaces, in varying configurations and executed to varying degrees of accuracy. However, it later transpired that this symbol was in earlier times deliberately included into decorative designs in many parts of the world from at least as early as 1600 BC. It is only later, as we get further into the medieval period, that they begin to be found as graffiti. They should not be confused with consecration crosses with which there are some similarities. The general consensus on these symbols is that they are protective marks but there are other points of view.

For example, it has been suggested that the daisy wheel should be seen as purely a geometric device which was used by masons and builders in the design of their buildings. Laurie Smith has demonstrated the elegance of the daisy wheel as a geometric tool from which many kinds of shapes, angles and designs can be generated. Concluding his 1997 paper, he says: 'Because we no longer think or design in this way it is easy when observing daisy wheels or cut circles to perceive them in mystic terms, to attribute our own ignorance to them'. He goes on to say: 'Cut circles are evidence of carpenters at work', and 'The daisy wheel in full bloom symbolises this geometrical knowledge and marks the presence of a geometrical design system for the buildings upon which it is found' (Smith 1997: 5). Smith is clearly a huge admirer of the daisy wheel as a tool for construction and design and demonstrates this even more clearly in a later work where he explains much of the ornament and design of a sixteenth-century house using the daisy wheel as one of the principal design tools (Smith 2007: 35–47). He has published several other papers on geometrical building design.

It is clear that the daisy wheel would have been a useful part of the geometric tools available to carpenters, masons and builders but this does not explain the huge number of them which appear in some buildings, the distinctly variable quality of them, or the clustering of them along with other meaningful marks. This explanation also does not account for their appearance in objects from at least as early as 1600 BC on items as varied as gold discs, silver belt buckles, tombs and butter moulds. While the daisy wheel is a relatively simple design to create using a compass or any implement with two points (with some practice), the absence of other geometric designs useful in the building process in similar contexts is also notable.

Marko Manninen has been collecting early examples of the daisy symbol which he terms the flower of life. He has constructed a timeline of its appearance on objects and architecture from 1600 BC to 1600 AD. Examples can be found in India, Cyprus, Bulgaria, Russia, Ukraine, Israel, Iran, Turkey, Italy and Spain, variously carved on surfaces and objects made of stone, ivory, silver and as part of floor mosaics. Aside from the objects already mentioned, it can be found on candelabras, gateposts, grave slabs, waffle moulds, stelae and most notably there are some circular gold foils dating from 1600 BC from Mycenae in Greece which bear the symbol. Manninen has uncovered many fine examples which appear to establish that the earliest examples occur in the eastern Mediterranean, spreading outwards from there (Manninen 2015: 21–22). There is a nundinal calendar from Rome which depicts the market days for several cities where the information is written on the petals of a daisy wheel.

In Britain there is something akin to a six-petal circle on a building stone from the Roman 6th Legion from Hadrian's Wall or possibly Carlisle fort and in Saffron Walden Museum there is a small Roman panel made of jet which has a beautiful carved daisy wheel on it. Overlapping circles, related to daisy wheels, appear on fifth/sixth-century slates from Tintagel churchyard in Cornwall (Johnson 1994: 2). From that time we have a gap until the later medieval period when Timothy Easton writes: 'A relationship which continues through medieval times, as shown in an English manuscript of 1272, on astronomy, where John Hollywood uses a daisy wheel to represent the sun in diagrams showing an eclipse. The symbol's possible geometric importance in medieval building layout may have been derived from, and in turn, fed into its good luck associations' (Easton 1999: 26).

Leonardo da Vinci uses the symbol in his 'Principles for the Development of a Complete Mind'. It even pops up in China, decorating one of the balls beneath the foot of one of the guardian lions at the Forbidden City which was commissioned in the fifteenth century.

The daisy symbol was in wide usage in medieval Bosnia, Herzegovina and Croatia, Montenegro and Serbia on funerary monuments known as stecak between the twelfth and sixteenth centuries. There are around 60,000 of these monuments still standing and many of them display daisy wheels as one of their key symbols amongst others including the moon, hunting scenes and vine or leaf decorations. Some stecak are upright carved grave slabs while others take the form of box tombs, of which there is a fine example at Sarajevo Museum.

Manninen notes an Ottoman sarcophagus bearing large daisy wheels at Smyrna, Izmir, in Turkey, dating to around 1400 (Manninen 2015: 47). Another fascinating Turkish example is held at the Bodrun Underwater Archaeology Museum. It is a stone tablet comprising a body of text but there are two daisy wheels on either side and two other circular web patterns. My Turkish colleague Buket Akgün kindly arranged for it to be translated for me and it says, 'Milas was in dire need of water. God enabled him [meaning the person whose name is written on top, El-Hac Muhammed Aga bin Abdulaziz] to build this work [fountain] This work is unique. He who drinks from it shall find life'. The date is Hijri year 1166 which in the Gregorian calendar would be 1753.

Folklorist Adina Hulubaş informed me that the daisy wheel is also regarded as a solar symbol in Romania where it is often carved onto gates and furniture. We can think of it as a symbol which brings light and dispels darkness. There is tracery in the window of Cozia Monastery which has a daisy wheel pattern. There is an incredible wooden gate from Bacău, Moldova which bears the daisy symbol on both uprights either side of the main gate. Another fabulous example of these gates can be found at Berzunți. During a visit in 2018 I discovered a large pair of them either side of a door to a stairway in Golia Monastery in Iași, built during the sixteenth and seventeenth centuries.

Preston Barba also categorises the daisy wheel as a solar symbol in his impressive work on Pennsylvania German Tombstones (Barba 1954: 8–9).

In his foreword to Donmoyer's book on hex signs, Don Yoder states that daisy symbols have been found all over Germanic Central Europe with examples being found on the tombs of bishops in Rhineland Cathedrals and also on houses, barns, gates, portals and doors (Donmoyer 2013: 10).

In Britain the daisy wheel can also be found on furniture, usually much more neatly carved than when carved onto building surfaces. There are many examples of coffers and beds with the symbol on it and in my own collection there is a corner cupboard and old chest which both have the daisy carved onto them. Sometimes the daisy wheel is incorporated into the original design of the furniture item and at other times it has clearly been added in graffiti style at a later date. Some church coffers are incredibly elaborate; for example, Broxbourne Church in Hertfordshire dates from the fourteenth century and displays an impressive arcade of gothic arches along its nearly two metres length with two large daisy wheels at each end and six small ones between the arches. The frequency of daisy wheels on coffers, whether scratched or designed, suggests that it was seen as an additional layer of protection.

In the USA there are many bible boxes which are very richly decorated with daisy patterns in exactly the same way as you would find them on chests and elsewhere in the British Isles. In India and Pakistan it can be found as a common design on dowry chests with many examples being made well into the twentieth century. I have an example of this in my own collection, with both main forms of the daisy wheel pattern on the sliding door.

In Sherborne Museum in England there is a drinking horn decorated with daisy wheels. The symbol can also be integrated into artistic designs such as on a beautiful door from a farmhouse in Somerset. There are also excellent examples of daisy designs on the tympanum of Egleton Church, Rutland and on a corbel in the porch at Beckford Church in Worcestershire. A stone lintel over a passageway in Kirkby Stephen, Cumbria is dated 1636 and sports a fine carved daisy wheel. There are also examples of the design on fonts in England, notably at the church of Altarnun in Cornwall and also at St Peter's Church, Newenden in Kent (the opposite side of the country). There are also daisy wheel patterns built into some decorative stonework at Salcombe Regis Church in Devon. One can be found on the keystone above the door surround of the Lutheran Swamp Church in Montgomery County, Pennsylvania, dating from the 1760s (Huber 2017: 209). There is another to be found on the Great Conewago Presbytarian Church in Adams County, Pennsylvania, built in 1787 (Donmoyer 2013: 56–57). In France there is a daisy wheel very neatly carved on to a door jamb capital of a barn door in Haute-Sierck. Apparently, it is common in this area to have daisy wheels on the stone elements of barns (Blaising 2016: 33).

Figure 7.1 Daisy wheel symbol from a stone lintel in Kirkby Stephen. © Brian Hoggard.

This design is also one of the most commonly found patterns on lead tokens from the medieval and later periods. Lead tokens were a minor, unofficial form of currency in use from the mid-thirteenth century to the seventeenth century. They display many different designs, usually just on one side. A large number of them carry a daisy wheel design, some of them identical in form to the type encountered in buildings. I have many in my collection bearing daisy patterns and several with the VV mark. It would seem that these commonly encountered protective symbols were often carried as part of people's small change. These tokens were the popular answer to the shortage of low denomination coinage in England; people would simply make their own subdivisions of the smallest coins using lead. They could also be used as tallies, as a way of keeping track of specific quantities of material or crops. Moulds were carved into a large stone joined together by a channel forming a kind of tree pattern and molten lead was poured in and allowed to set. These tokens were not only used as low denomination coinage, but could also be purchased as part of pilgrimages and would allow access to various holy sites. The fact that so many of them carry the daisy design is probably a testament to their use as protective symbols for the pilgrim. These tokens usually carry simple geometric designs or initials. Wheel designs with dots are fairly common as are concentric circles and the daisy wheel.

The symbol crops up not only on buildings, furniture and low denomination coinage, but also on butter stamps and moulds. The

Figure 7.2 Lead token with daisy wheel design, from the author's collection. © Brian Hoggard.

design is fairly commonly found on butter stamps in the USA, UK and I am told that in rural areas of Romania people still stamp cheese and butter in this way. I have three examples dating from the eighteenth century in my own collection. There is quite often a focus of protection on food production and preparation areas so it is interesting to see this symbol finding its way onto the food itself. There is also a fine waffle mould in the Musée Lorrain à Nancy which has a daisy wheel as its central motif with two smaller circular patterns either side (Blaising 2016: 40). In the Cambridge Museum of Archaeology and Anthropology there is a horoscope which was made for 'Captain Lawrence and his son' at Mount Abu in the Sirohi District of Rajasthan, thought to date from 1912; the central design, on to which the planets are drawn, is constructed of interlacing circles forming a daisy wheel.

The examples cited so far are all designed into the objects or buildings. The symbol was specifically chosen at the time of the objects' creation. However, there are a huge number of examples of the daisy wheel which have been applied later, graffiti style; these vary between being incredibly clear and deliberate to being very subtle in form and difficult to see. Of the latter there is an example on a stone window surround at Lacock Abbey in Wiltshire. At the more extreme and clear end, one can find a whole host of daisies in various states of completion at the tithe barn in Bradford-on-Avon, also in Wiltshire. Some of the designs can be very elaborate, involving several interlocking daisy wheels such as those found on an internal window sill on the first floor of Fiddesford Manor, Dorset or on stonework within Orford Castle, Suffolk. There are also some fine sets of overlapping daisy wheels on walls in Acton Court, south Gloucestershire (Rodwell and Friel 2004: 272). There is a ceiling in Conwy which is literally covered in daisy wheels. Many complex versions of these interlocking daisy wheels can be found in ecclesiastical buildings too, such as one I discovered on one of the columns in the nave at Ripon Cathedral. Susan Mitchell reported to me in 2005 that Culross Palace in Fife, Scotland has many circles, concentric circles and daisy wheels. At Godolphin House, a large National Trust estate near Helston in Cornwall, a number of daisy wheels have been reported. Karen La Borde e-mailed on 16 April 2012 with the following: 'Just for your information and in case you do not know already. There are large and small daisy wheel marks scribed into the plaster at the rear of a 17th century fireplace. The largest wheel probably measures half a metre across. There are also about a dozen smaller circles over the wall at the rear of the chimney'.

An unusual example of a daisy wheel engraved onto the case of a fine clock was reported to me in September 2007 by Christopher

Figure 7.3 Butter stamp carved with daisy wheel design, from the author's collection. © Brian Hoggard.

Bryant. He had just taken ownership of a clock dating to 1800, made by famous London clockmaker Louis Recordon, which he had acquired from the estate of the Duke of Cumberland (King George III's fifth son) and noticed the mark very subtly engraved onto the case over some

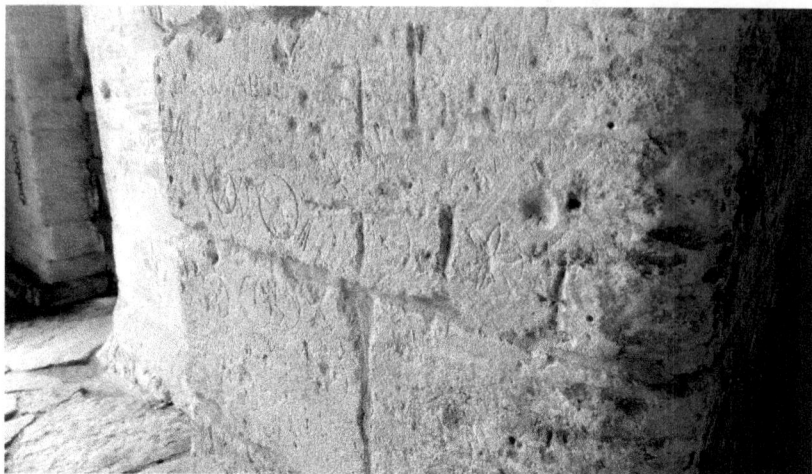

Figure 7.4 Multiple daisy wheels from Bradford-on-Avon Tithe Barn.
© Brian Hoggard.

yew veneer. There was a layer of shellac polish over the top of the mark indicating that it had been done during the making. The mark is incredibly fine and difficult to see but it has definitely been deliberately applied during the making process.

They are widespread in France too, particularly in the Dordogne. Linda Wilson discovered several daisy wheels in the Abbey Church at Souillac in the seventeenth-century choir stalls.

Daisy wheels can sometimes be found on tombs and gravestones as well. In the church of St Stephen in Kirkby Stephen, Cumbria, a tiny daisy wheel measuring just a few centimetres across can be found on the fifteenth-century tomb of Richard Musgrave – there is also a VV mark on the tomb. In York a gravestone was discovered beneath the lady chapel of All Saints Church which had a daisy wheel symbol carved onto it. That particular tomb contained the body of a pregnant woman along with the bones of her unborn child and a second chamber contained the bodies of three men. It is thought that the daisy wheel here was a direct response to the dark circumstances surrounding the death of these individuals.

The daisy wheel symbol appears to have been carved onto buildings from the medieval period and through the early modern period. In his work on early brick chimney stacks, mainly dating from the sixteenth century, D.F. Stenning noted that in Suffolk, 'there are an abundance of "daisies" on fireplaces, doors and ceiling which may represent charms to ward off evil spirits' (Stenning 1989: 101).

At Baltonsborough in Somerset Andy Letcher reports that there is a cottage with very clear daisy wheel carvings on the door frame at the bottom of the stairs. Mark Button reported that in Boreham, Essex, a daisy wheel is carved onto a brick house dating from 1837 along with lots of names. Christopher D. Robinson from the University of Lincoln reported in January 2002 the following example of daisy wheels:

> The Conservation Unit of the University is based in what was the old theological college and original county hospital dating from the late 1700s. I recently came across an overlapping double daisy wheel engraved on the (Victorian) brickwork of the old warden's wing. Below it two more daisy wheels have been adapted to represent a penny farthing bicycle!

These two examples clearly demonstrate the symbol's continued use well into the nineteenth century.

In the USA there are a number of excellent early examples which have been recorded by Allysa Conary. In the Curier Museum of Art, Manchester, New Hampshire there is a seventeenth-century chest with a daisy wheel inscribed as part of the central pattern. In the attic of Jackson House, Portsmouth, New Hampshire, which was built in 1664, there is an impressive set of overlapping daisy wheels. A single daisy wheel was recorded on a beam in the Clemence-Irons House, Johnson, Rhode Island which dates from 1691. There are also daisy wheels integral to the design of gravestones in Deerfield and one of 1752 in Lexington, Massachusetts. There are several examples illustrated in Barba's 1954 work on Pennsylvania German tombstones too. Here we have the prospect of daisy wheel symbols being used to afford protection to mortal remains.

Greg Lang reported to me in November 2000 the discovery of a daisy wheel which was found at the Dritt Mansion in York County, Pennsylvania. This mansion dates from the first half of the eighteenth century and was first lived in by a Yorkshireman. Another fine example of twenty interlocking circles can be seen in a Standard barn from Upper Milford Township in Lehigh County, Pennsylvania. This mark can be found scratched into the wooden wall of the barn (Huber 2017: 213).

At Nuestra Senora del Socorro near El Paso, Texas, daisy wheels form the principal part of the decoration of the roof supports, known as vigas. These are thought to date to the eighteenth century. The same correspondent, David Hill, told me in July 2000 that there are also 'similar hexafoils in Spanish missions in the San Antonio Texas area, also carved on the roof support timbers. In the case of the San Antonio missions and the Socorro hexafoils, like your English examples are scribed into the wood with a compass'.

Ian Evans has discovered numerous daisy wheel patterns and individual symbols in Australia and Tasmania. For example, several hexafoils were discovered in the mid-nineteenth-century house known as Wolston at Wacol in Brisbane's south-west outskirts (Evans 2016: 1). He also describes a daisy wheel found in a sandstone block next to a window in the stables at Shene, Bagdad, in Tasmania (Evans 2011: 20–21). Just like the examples found in the USA, he also reports the use of daisy wheels in graveyards in Norfolk Island and Black Heath, New South Wales, mainly dating to the nineteenth century (Evans 2015: 2). In the British Isles its appearance on tombs or gravestones is mostly restricted to graffiti but there are examples in Scotland at St Magnus' Cathedral in Kirkwall, Orkney where a highly ornate daisy pattern appears on the grave slab of a knight; there are also daisy wheels on graveslabs and gravestones on the island of Iona and also at Kilmartin.

In Pennsylvania, there are a number of barns known as Hex Barns due to the symbols which are boldly painted on the outside. There are a wide variety of styles of these hex symbols but the most popular type are the six- or eight-pointed stars. These can be found on the exterior of the barns painted in bright and bold colours, such as with these three examples in Berks County: at a barn near Lenhartsville there is a six-pointed star dated 1829; at Albany Township there is a barn with three six-pointed stars dated 1857; and at Pike Township there is a barn with what Greg Huber describes as a celestial motif with three concentric rings of points – this looks like many complex daisy patterns I have seen. There are a huge number of these hex symbols on barns in Pennsylvania. Inside the barns there Huber found that the most commonly found decorative marking was the six-pointed rosette (Huber 2017: 201–13). Patrick Donmoyer describes large numbers of these six-petal daisy designs in his book on hex signs. The book is profusely illustrated with designs from Brecknock Township, the Kistler Farm, Lynn Township, Upper Macungie Township and the Oley Valley. This rosette in England would be called a daisy wheel but in the Pennsylvanich dialect they are known as Blumme-Schtanne (flower stars) or Sechschtanne (six-pointed stars). They are also often referred to as barn stars and can have a varied number of points but are all essentially regarded as celestial symbols (Donmoyer 2013: 21–77). He writes of the walls in the barns: 'Scribe marks, consisting of circles and arcs are very common throughout the interiors of local barns, while painted designs are more rare, but not uncommon. These more developed, complex designs are almost always in close proximity to doors, passageways and stairwells'. He says this is due to them being thoroughfares and hence more prone to be covered in graffiti whereas this pattern in Britain would be regarded as protection of thresholds. He goes on to say that the place most covered in symbols and rosettes is the granary (Donmoyer 2013: 78). The similarities with European daisy wheel symbols and their use strongly suggests a protective role for this symbol in the USA.

Matthew Champion dedicates a chapter of his book *Medieval Graffiti* to compass-drawn designs in which he concludes that 'it becomes apparent that these compass-drawn designs, and particularly the hexfoil and all its many variations, were seen as offering a level of spiritual protection to both places and objects' (Champion 2015: 44). My view is that daisy wheels were, as suggested by Timothy Easton and confirmed by the practice in Romania, a potent solar related symbol which by the early modern period had taken on an additional role as a decoy or spirit trap. The geometrical elegance of the symbol, being a never-ending line, was believed to have an almost hypnotic effect on spirits or energies, acting as a trap or snare, preventing further progress.

In graffiti form they can be found almost anywhere in religious and secular buildings and on all types of surfaces: on plaster as at Tretower Court in South Wales, Baddesley Clinton in Warwickshire or Pear Tree Farm at Yoxall in Staffordshire (Meeson 2005: 42); on stone as at Chelvey Court in Somerset, King's College Chapel in Cambridge and in Great Malvern Priory in Worcestershire; on wood as in a cottage at Mansell Lacey in Herefordshire or the Oak House in West Bromwich; and on lead such as on the wall bracket for a drainage pipe at King's Nympton Park house in Somerset.

At St Mary and All Saints in Chesterfield, Darren Matthews reported via social media that there are a number of daisy wheels on a wooden screen which have been deliberately scorched or had bits of wood chipped away from them. It is possible that, as with pins in witch-bottles, they have been deliberately 'killed' to make them more potent on a spiritual plane. The notable thing about these daisy wheels is that, although not part of the original design of the screen, they are highly ornate and artistically rendered. They sit in between the deliberate design-in daisy form that we see in earlier times and the graffiti versions.

The elegance and simplicity of the design was very appealing to people and, once learned, could be perfected and developed into more elaborate patterns. The daisy wheel symbol appears to have been originally a solar symbol in the earliest times in the eastern Mediterranean and was incorporated into designs on objects, buildings and tombs. Later it began to be applied graffito style to furniture, buildings and tombs instead, perhaps because it came to be viewed as superstitious and belonging to an older time, so people avoided using it overtly and instead surreptitiously applied it to places deemed in need of extra protection. As a solar symbol, the daisy wheel shines light into dark places, making it more difficult for dark forces to lurk there.

Overlapping Circles

These belong in the same kind of category as daisy wheels although visually they sometimes look like a random collection of circles rather than a concerted attempt at a daisy wheel. Examples can be found at Harvington Hall in Worcestershire where they are somewhat disguised by a wall painting. The interesting thing at that site is that the marks occur on an upper floor on a door which leads to nowhere as the wing behind it was demolished. A good example which looks like an incredibly scruffy attempt at a daisy wheel can be found in King's College Chapel, Cambridge at the west end. In the USA a great example was reported to me from Marshfield, Massachusetts where some can be found on the main post to the right of the front door of a home there.

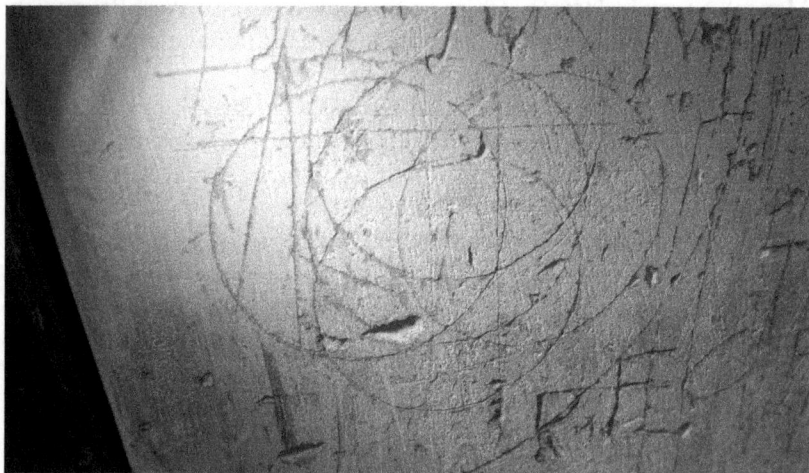

Figure 7.5 Overlapping graffito circles, King's College, Cambridge.
© Brian Hoggard.

The W, M and V Marks

These marks are also known as Marian marks because they are thought to refer to the Virgin Mary. Another very commonly encountered mark is the VV or W mark which upside down looks like the M for Maria. It was Timothy Easton, once again, who first wrote that this mark stands for Virgo Virginum, or, Virgin of Virgins, the latter being a fairly well-known saying amongst Catholics. Matthew Champion asserts that the phrase Virgo Virginum was little known in England and was not a phrase used outside of England, yet the VV symbol appears widely throughout Europe. For these reasons he believes that Easton's theory is now proven incorrect. However, there appears to be no reason why a symbol derived from a phrase (however little known) could not 'catch on' due to its simplicity and spread to the same places where English people went. There is of course no proof that this spread occurred.

In favour of the Marian interpretation of the VV is that it forms part of the Virgin Mary monogram which is widely found throughout Europe. Perhaps the most obvious point backing up the Marian theory regarding the VV and M marks is quite simply that they form the initials of the Virgin Mary when read upright or upside down. Many examples of the M letter found in isolation can be found to have extended initial and terminal lines which taper outwards and fade, a feature which can be seen clearly on the palm of a human hand. Although a collision of coincidences I think that people felt a little differently about M's and VV's, even when part of initials they are often executed with a flourish, almost as if people are proud to have a Marian association within their own name. There is certainly an abundance of VV and M marks to be found on all kinds of surfaces on buildings and furniture.

Timothy Easton has put forward an additional interpretation which is that the VV may in fact be intended as a double 'U' to form Omega, so where it occurs with an 'A' character it may mean Alpha and Omega, or Christ (Easton 2018: 26).

There are also instances of the letters A, M and R forming patterns and this is thought to stand for Ave Marie Regina. In his 'Ritual Marks on Historic Timber' article, Easton cites many Suffolk examples, including Ulveston Hall in Debenham, The Swan in Worlingworth, Bedfield Hall, Camp Green Farm in Debenham and Elm Tree Farm in Mendlesham. (Easton 1999: 24).

The 'VV' symbol is exceptionally common when looking at graffiti in medieval or later buildings where one will often find it mingled in with initials. In stone carvings the W letter is often carved as two overlapping V's but its occurrence in graffiti contexts is far too widespread for it to solely represent the initial W. If it were all just initials, the population would be full of William Wilberforces, Wally Winterbottoms and Willemena Wileys – but this is improbable. For example, the church of St Kenelm at Romsley has a large area of graffiti on the outside wall on the south side which is full of initials. One block in particular is covered solely in VV's. There are other solitary occurrences on the exterior of the building. Likewise, in the passage through Evesham Abbey tower there are several clearly visible VV's on one side and a consecration cross on the other.

Other examples from England which have been reported to me include marks inside a cupboard in a town house in Tewkesbury, on Pershore Abbey tower, on oak panelling in Llancaiach Fawr and on wooden shutters in a Georgian house in Shropshire. A tiny Marian mark was discovered in the side chapel of All Saints Church in Evesham and there is a fine example on Elmley Castle Church door. There are several large examples on stone in Prince Arthur's Chantry in Worcester Cathedral, a large number can be found in King's College Chapel, Cambridge and they have also been found at Kew Palace in London. A huge number of examples of this mark can be found on the English Medieval Graffiti sites on social media. In the USA, Alyssa Conary recorded a clear VV symbol on the mantel beam at Fairbanks House, Dedham, Massachusetts. The house dates from 1641 and is regarded

Figure 7.6 Marian marks and a butterfly mark from within Prince Arthur's Chantry, Worcester Cathedral. © Brian Hoggard.

as the oldest timber framed house in the USA; four concealed shoes were also discovered here. Greg Lang told me in October 2000 about a very clear VV mark at 'The Dritt House' which is on the west side of the Susquahanna River in an area of Pennsylvania thought to date to 1758. An unusual English example of the VV mark which appears on a gravestone can be found in the graveyard of All Hallows Church, Gedling, Nottingham. It appears on a slate gravestone with a mid-eighteenth-century date.

At a house called La Chenais des Bois in the parish of St Martin on the island of Jersey, a lot of 'M' 'V' 'W' and 'P' shapes are scratched into the three top stones of the arch along with crosses, triangles and other shapes. The fireplace at this house is quite unusual in being arched and also made of limestone instead of the more typical granite. The house was originally built in the sixteenth century, but has had many alterations and additions since.

Pilgrimages led to people acquiring all sorts of souvenirs from their travels, including pilgrim badges, ampullae and lead tokens. The portable antiquities scheme website (www.finds.org.uk) holds records of many ampullae which were used to hold small samples of holy water from the site of pilgrimage. Many of the examples include a VV, or M design on one side. The interpretation often given for this is that there is some connection with the shrine of Our Lady at Walsingham but archaeologists are also open to the idea that it represents Virgo Virginum or Maria (when upside down). Examples of ampullae with these marks have been found in Hampshire, Suffolk and Cheshire. Daisy patterns, or at least radial petals, are also often encountered on ampullae. A great example of this was found in Blackden in Cheshire where a lead ampulla was discovered with a very clear VV on one side and a daisy wheel pattern on the other. The VV symbol also appears quite often on lead tokens which were often used during pilgrimages. I have several examples in my collection. I even have had a report of the VV mark being found on a leather costrel.

Archaeologist James Wright speaks in his lectures of an image held in the British Museum (cat no 1880,0710.582) described as a 'broadside against witchcraft in the Bishopric of Trier and elsewhere', thought to date from around 1600. It was exhibited as part of the Witches & Wicked Bodies exhibition and contains a wide range of depictions of alleged witchcraft activity, notably amongst them a 'VV' on a chimney lintel which has been crossed out by the witches so they can safely come down the chimney.

As Jon Hughett from Milwaukee pointed out to me, another very interesting fact about the double V or M mark is that one only has to look at the palm of one's hand to see the symbol there too. Examples which looks exactly like this, even down to a tapering outwards of the long strokes of the 'M', can be found in Prince Arthur's Chantry in Worcester Cathedral and also in Wookey Hole amongst numerous other places. This raises the possibility that the hand outlines sometimes found carved onto buildings are also intended as Marian marks of a different kind. In 2014 Timothy Easton featured the south door of Ampney Crucis Church, Gloucestershire in one of his articles (Easton 2014a: 57). It is a fascinating door with seven hand outlines inscribed onto it, two of which have the Marian 'M' symbol drawn within them, exactly as is found on the palm of one's hand.

Christograms

Just as there are Marian marks, there are also marks for Christ. These are less common in graffiti contexts than the M, V and W marks but can often be seen in conjunction with them. The main type of character is similar to a capital I but with a small dash through the middle, a little like a hyphen, and it represents 'Jesu'. This is quite often found with the VV mark.

There is also the Chi-Rho symbol which is three lines crossing to form a six pointed wheel type figure where the top limb is turned into a letter P. This represents the first two characters of Christ's name in the Greek alphabet. Although visually not that similar, it does share the six points of a spoked wheel like a daisy wheel and it is sometimes depicted in a circle. This mark does not crop up in graffiti as it is part of the widely known symbolism of the Christian churches, but the P figure is quite often included in graffiti, particularly on chimney lintels in the south-east of England, and its presence may be derived from the Chi-Rho.

Sometimes the IHS monogram is derived from the letters of Christ's name in Greek. This can be sometimes found as graffiti and occasionally can be found in an elaborate interwoven pattern resembling a portcullis.

It is likely that many of the combinations of letters found in graffiti contexts are actually abbreviations for Catholic phrases and terminology. For instance, Alison Fearn pointed out to me that an example of 'I B' found at Donington-le-Heath Manor in Leicestershire may represent Jesus Benedictus.

Slashes and Mesh Patterns

One type of mark which predominantly occurs in the south-east of England is a series of angled slashes usually traced onto door or chimney lintels. Timothy Easton has identified numerous examples of this in domestic settings in Suffolk and elsewhere in East Anglia where this practice appears to be particularly concentrated. A very similar example was also reported from a Scottish house in Shore Street, Anstruther, Fife, so it does occur elsewhere too (Darwood and Sherriff 2003: 126–27). These marks quite often include the 'W', 'V' or 'M' letters too which are thought to be an invocation to the Virgin Mary (as mentioned above). Their location at points of access within a building, particularly the hearth, suggests a protective function. The slash marks however have long been something of a mystery although they are considered to be ritual marks due to context and a lack of any practical reason for their presence. It is my contention that these angled marks are the only visible remnant of the creation of spiritual pins or spikes. As we saw with witch-bottles where pins and nails are deliberately 'killed' in order to activate them on a spiritual plane, here tiny parts of the surface of the lintel are being killed in order to create a fearsome line of spikes on which any malevolent entity plunging down the chimney could become impaled.

When combined with invocations to the Virgin, perhaps a witch-bottle beneath the hearth and a shoe somewhere within the chimney stack, we can see a fairly formidable array of counter-witchcraft measures.

In the same way, the large panels of 'mesh' patterns provide literally a kind of magical grid which could trap negative energies coming into the home. An example of this is visible at an eighteenth-century house near Caer Caradoc in Shropshire where a wooden shutter was completely covered in one of these mesh patterns and also a large area of plaster in the wash-house. At Pentre in Bronygarth there is also a mesh area on a timber on the upper floor. At the Timothy Hyde house in Newton, Massachusetts (built in 1729), a whole wall in the attic is covered in a large mesh pattern. A fine example of a mesh mark which also has a burn mark in the centre of it can be found on a wooden screen in Exeter Cathedral. Another example from Knole (a National Trust property) in Kent was found beneath floorboards, demonstrating that these measures could be found in upper-class properties too.

Shoe Outlines

In Canterbury Cathedral there are literally hundreds of shoe outlines carved onto stone benches and other surfaces. These marks are very widespread, with examples being found in Bredon Church (Worcestershire), St Clement's Church Tower (Norwich), the church at Edmondthorpe (Leicestershire), Wath upon Dearne Church (South Yorkshire) amongst numerous other locations. Hand outlines also occur, for example at Pershore Abbey tower (Worcestershire) and Stathern Church (Leicestershire), but shoe outlines are far more commonplace.

The instinct on first learning of these types of marks is to assume a connection with the practice of concealing shoes which is discussed in Chapter 3. There are, however, some major differences. Firstly, these marks are not in any way subtle or visible only in specific lighting conditions; they are blatantly carved in plain view onto surfaces. Secondly, the locations of these marks usually have no specific relationship with entry or exit points in the building so no site-specific protective function within the building can be assigned to them.

June Swann has pointed out to me that in past times it was fairly common for visitors to an area to walk out on the roof because it afforded great views. While there it was not unusual for people to leave their mark. For example, in 1592, Fred, Duke of Württemberg had carved his

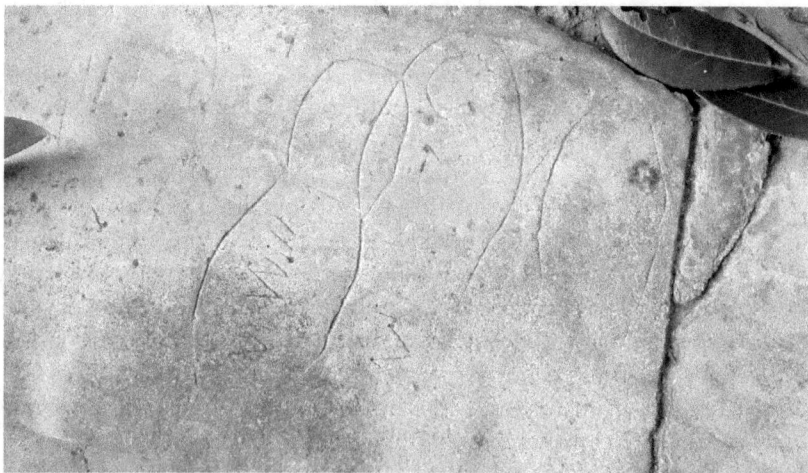

Figure 7.7 Shoes outlines from the porch at Bredon Church, Worcestershire. © Brian Hoggard.

name into the leads of Windsor. In 1599 Swiss physician Thomas Platter visited St Paul's cathedral in London where he said, 'I climbed 300 steps to the roof, which is broad, covered with lead so that one may walk there... every Sunday many men and women stroll together'. He also climbed to the lead roof of a very high tower at Windsor Castle 'on the top of which I wrote my name' (Henderson 1983: 8). More interestingly, in 1606 Christian IV (1577–1668) King of Denmark, visiting his sister Anne in London (the wife of King James I), after surveying the city, 'hee held his foote still whilest Edward Soper keeper of the Steeple, with his knife cutte the length and breadth thereof in the lead' (Rye 1865). In this last example we must assume there is a meaning behind carving the shoe outline as this visitor could surely have written his name. Yorkshire archaeologist J.R. Mortimer wrote in his memoirs *A Victorian Boyhood*, 'we occasionally climbed the church porch, and then ascended to the flat roof of the church, on which we cut the outlines of our feet in the lead and initialled them' (Billingsley 2014: 9).

Timothy Easton is of the opinion that most of the marks in lead on church roofs were made by plumbers or other craftsmen as they would have been more likely to have had access to certain parts of the roof. While this may have been the case in some large churches with complex roofing arrangements, it would seem from the evidence above that it was actually fairly common for all sorts of people to pay visits to church roofs where access was fairly convenient.

My own view is that we are dealing here with a form of sympathetic magic. As is evident with written charms, it is clear that people were not fussy about the source of supernatural power or protection they called upon, they just wanted the job done. So here we have people leaving a unique mark through the shape of their foot on a building which is the 'house of God' and therefore a source of supernatural power, the idea being that the positive and protective energies within the building would be sympathetically transmitted from the outline to the actual foot.

Many soldiers signed their names or initials within churches before heading off to fight in the two World Wars. In Ely Cathedral there are a large number of these on the tower. It strikes me that this is a similar practice, asking for protection while at the same time leaving your mark.

I can imagine that creating one of these marks might be particularly useful before setting off on any kind of journey, but I can just as easily see it happening as a general protective device – something people would do as part of their supernatural protective armoury.

Burn Marks

In many properties burn marks can be found on timbers, frequently on chimney lintels, but they can be found on any timbers within a building. It has become clear that these marks can also often be found on furniture (Morton and Maddison 2017: 22–25). These marks have the shape of a candle flame but are usually burned quite deeply into the timber. At first glance it is often assumed that these are the result of accidents relating to candles or rush lights but they are very commonplace and often occur in places where there appears to be no need for a light and there is no evidence of a hole where a rush light or taper could be attached. Sometimes they occur in such huge numbers that, had they been made accidentally, it would have been a miracle that the whole building had not burned down. For example, at Llancaiach Fawr Manor in Wales there is an attic space which was used as a servant's chamber – not generally part of tours of the building – which has over 100 of them on both sides of a beautiful curved beam. There are many other burn marks in the same manor. Similarly, at Stokesay Castle in Shropshire there are a huge number in the timber framed portion of the building. Anywhere there are timber framed buildings, one will find burn marks, for example in Lavenham Guildhall and Little Hall there are huge numbers on chimney lintels and elsewhere in the buildings. There are a large number of them in Donnington-le-Heath Manor in

Figure 7.8 Burn marks from beam at Llancaiach Fawr Manor in Wales. © Brian Hoggard.

Leicestershire and in my native Worcestershire they are also widely encountered.

Those of us who have an interest in protective marks have always noted these burn marks when exploring buildings, thinking of them as being unexplained and likely to fall into the 'apotropaic' category, but it was not until John Dean and Nick Hill published the results of their research into the marks that we could categorically state that these marks were deliberately made and not the result of accidental burnings (Dean and Hill 2014: 1–15). During their research they tested candles, tapers and rush lights on several different kinds of timber and they concluded that making the marks would take at least five minutes of burning with the flame at a forty-five degree angle to the surface. To make a more substantial mark took up to fifteen minutes by which time a layer of charcoal had formed preventing further burning, but in many cases this charcoal layer had clearly been scraped away to allow further, deeper burning. This was therefore a time-consuming, deliberate practice which also had a cost to it in the shape of wasted candles. Dean and Hill note that in terms of geographical spread these marks occur throughout northern Europe and also in the USA. Ian Evans has reported to me that he has found large numbers of burn marks in Australia and Tasmania, particularly in stables belonging to large estates.

Regarding the meaning of the marks, they state that 'Burn marks are occasionally found together with other incised ritual or "apotropaic" marks on building timbers, but the bulk of the evidence suggests that there is no close association between burn marks and other ritual marking' (Dean and Hill 2014: 10). The authors do not attempt to explain what the purpose of making these marks was, aiming only to demonstrate that they were made deliberately.

The idea that a deliberate burn mark is a kind of inoculation against fire has been suggested several times over the years, but I think if this was the reason then it could have been done discretely, in parts of the building not usually visible to the occupants, or it could even have been done by builders during construction. Burn marks are normally highly visible however and, although they can be found on any timbers in a building, are often found in highest numbers at hearths and thresholds. One of the themes linking all the practices described in this book is the concept of the ritual death of an object so that its shade, ghost or spirit form can take on a new role working to protect those who need it. In the case of burn marks, I strongly suspect that the creation of the burn mark is, in effect, creating some illumination on a more spiritual or astral plane, shining some light into the darkness. There was a belief that bad spirits and witches lurked in dark corners so making these burn marks set up a bright shining light in the unseen world which no dark force could tolerate. The number of marks might relate directly to the levels of fear which people felt, or it could be a sign that the occupant could afford the time and candles to ensure their security. Either way, the occupants of the Steward's Attic at Llancaiach Fawr must have spent considerable time and energy securing that room.

Alison Fearn has noted a German rhyme related to Christmas and Twelfth Night traditions recorded in 1553 which reads:

> And round about the house they go, with torch or taper clear,
> That neither bread nor meat do want, nor witch with dreadful charm,
> Have power to hurt their children or do the cattle harm. (Fearn 2017: 94)

Candlemarks

Timothy Easton has recorded seventeen examples of symbols and patterns being made on ceilings using sooty candle marks. They are predominantly focused in East Anglia, where he is based, with nine in Suffolk, two in Norfolk, three in Essex, one in Kent, one in Derbyshire and another from the USA. If it was not for the two in Derbyshire and the USA it would be tempting to think it was all the work of one local cunning person who had developed a new ritual practice in the area. However, it seems likely that there will be many more discoveries of this type as awareness spreads about it. There appears to be a mixture of letters, Christian symbols, the VV or M signs, ladders and many other characters which appear to be magical symbols. Easton suggests that some of the symbols share similarities with some found in the work of Cornelius Agrippa. There certainly appears to be some kind of ritual protection being carried out here, most likely in a highly ceremonial manner (Easton 2011: 56–60).

Concentric Circles

Orford Castle in Suffolk has an excellent example of concentric circles on otherwise very coarse stonework. In a very different context there is a good example on a tomb in Salisbury Cathedral in Wiltshire and in a private house near Bronygarth, Shropshire, a fine example can be found on the upper floor – coincidentally this house also has a pentagram near the same room. It would appear that these concentric

Figure 7.9 Concentric circle marks from Pentre, Bronygarth.
© Brian Hoggard.

circle marks are cosmological in nature and relate to hierarchies of existence as portrayed in widely distributed magical texts and pamphlets of the time, sometimes known as celestial spheres. Linda Hall cites three examples from Hampshire including one from the Manor House at Old Burghclere, another from Great Brook in Warsash and one from St Cross, Winchester which is quite complex in form, looking rather like one of the diagrams from these texts (Hall 2003: 99). Alternatively, circles were widely thought to be effective symbols against witchcraft because there were no corners for the witch to hide in. At the Fleece Inn, Bretforton in Worcestershire there are still three white circles in front of the fireplace to keep witches away. They are now painted in white emulsion but formerly were done in white-wash, as were all the gaps and cracks in the building – highlighting areas of vulnerability in the building, making it more difficult for dark forces to lurk. There is also the connection between circles and daisy-wheels, that they are a form of solar imagery, bringing light to vulnerable areas.

Pentagrams

With regard to pentagrams, there is a good example in Worcester Cathedral in the cloister near to the refectory, there are three on the Wharton tomb in the church at Kirkby Stephen in Cumbria, several in Whittlesford Church in Cambridgeshire, and a very unusual example on a stone on a garden wall at Llancaiach Fawr Manor in Wales. There is a pentagram amongst the graffiti in the Chateau at Domme in France.

David McNally reported in 2001 the existence of a carved pentagram on an inglenook fireplace in a farm cottage near Crewkerne in Somerset which is believed to be around 400 years old. In the 1970s workers found the pentagram carved into the wooden mantle on the inside; they decided to turn it around so that the sign now faces into the room.

In the current era we tend to think of pentagrams as occult symbols related to modern witchcraft or, if inverted, even with Satanism or black magic. They also have associations with freemasonry. However, in the past the pentagram had an important role within Christian symbolism as a representation of the five wounds of Christ and as such was seen as a protection symbol. It also features prominently in the medieval tale of Sir Gawain and the Green Knight as the symbol which he carried on his shield. Matthew Champion explains how the pentagram's connections with the Key of Solomon may have meant that the symbol was thought to be particularly effect at protecting against demons (Champion 2015: 47–52). In Troston Church, Suffolk, there is graffiti depicting a demon who has a pentagram clearly imprinted over its neck suggesting that its role is to protect against demons.

Butterfly Marks

These marks are of uncertain meaning. They appear to be the same as the rune known usually as Dagaz or Daeg which is broadly interpreted as meaning day or daylight. Runes were known in Britain via the Viking influence and there are around twenty examples of runic carvings found here but they are not widely found written or carved onto surfaces so most people tend to dismiss the idea that this mark is runic in origin. However, Scandinavian languages were still spoken in the Isle of Man as late as the twelfth century, in parts of England until the eleventh century and of course in key trading cities there would be regular Scandinavian visitors bringing their language and culture thereafter (Page 1971: 189). In some of the Scottish islands it was still spoken up until the modern era. Therefore, the question is really whether the meaning of this mark was known and transmitted into popular culture.

The daisy wheel is an ancient solar symbol which has worked its way through the best part of five thousand years with its original meaning largely forgotten in popular culture, and yet its use has persisted. It is possible, however unlikely it may seem, that the same thing has happened with the Dagaz rune. It may be that it retained some importance related to its daylight meaning but this remains just a possibility – there is no clear evidence for this.

This mark is quite commonly used as a mason's mark so it is important to verify that it is not simply a label identifying who has worked which stone. It appears in Worcester Cathedral, in Prince Arthur's Chantry, alongside two large M marks, clearly not a mason's mark in this case.

If the mark is runic in origin, then its meaning of daylight would be akin to the purpose of daisy wheels or burn marks, bringing light to an area to protect it from darkness.

One other possibility is that this mark can also be found as a significant part of the monogram of St Michael, which combines into one symbol the letters MIXAHA. Vandenbeusch and Antoine from the British Museum report the discovery in 2005 of the body of a Christian woman in Sudan who died between AD 655–775 (Vandenbeusch and Antoine 2015: 15–19). What is of interest here is that the woman had a tattoo on her inner right thigh of the monogram of St Michael so it seems that this symbol was widely applied and may have ended up being simplified or reduced over time into just the butterfly cross.

Alternatively, it is possible to view the mark as a saltire cross with the vertical lines joining it at the sides. In that case it bears similarities to the crosses found on top of 'witch-posts' and the huge quantity of these marks which can be found designed into latches and ironwork in the early modern contexts. These are clearly meant to be protection marks so it could be that these butterfly marks are simply the graffiti version of them. Walter Wheeler notes the use of the saltire cross on many buildings, fixtures and fittings in his paper on apotropaic practices in New Amsterdam, which later became New York (Wheeler 2017: 382–83).

Protection Marks and Other Graffiti on Tombs

Around Britain there are many box tombs with alabaster effigies on top which are literally covered with graffiti. Clearly the material is one of the principal reasons why this happens as alabaster is very easy to carve. There are two examples in Wells Cathedral which are at the extreme end of this practice.

The Harewell tomb has in the region of 500 marks and initials all over it including the face, feet and everything in between. Christopher

Binding analysed every single mark and determined that around 25 per cent of all of the marks were Marian or Christograms and so fall into the apotropaic category. The Harewell tomb has an effigy of the Bishop on it and also a sculpted hare, a clear reference to his name (Binding 2015: 5–11).

There are several other alabaster effigies which are heavily adorned with graffiti and which would benefit from similar analysis. There is certainly a lot of apotropaic graffiti on the other alabaster effigy in Wells Cathedral, belonging to Ralph de Salopia. At Salisbury Cathedral, which is not a huge distance away, there is a great deal of graffiti including apotropaic symbols on the effigy of John, Lord Cheney and also on the hard stone effigy of John Blyth.

My contention is that there were two different things going on with the personal initials and apotropaic marks on tombs and that these are both an amplification of the more normal discovery of marks and initials within ecclesiastical buildings. When people marked their initials on church buildings, it was not simply an idle 'making your mark' effort – many of them are nicely carved with gothic lettering. The idea seems to be similar to the shoe and hand outlines in that it represents an effort to channel some of the divine protection of the building through highly personal initials – a sympathetic link. On the tombs of influential people, particularly those of clergy, this is somewhat heightened by the importance and status in the eyes of the Lord of the individual concerned. In other words, there is likely to be a higher concentration of divine energies around the mortal remains of priest or a local dignitary for whom prayers are regularly sung – not unlike the way people regarded shrines containing saints' relics.

The use of apotropaic marks at these tombs is not unrelated to this. Invoking the protection of the Virgin Mary using Marian marks of different kinds at the tomb would serve to protect the mortal remains and, in doing so, make the use of one's own initials on the tomb more secure. Imagine if you had placed your initials on the tomb in the hope of hitching a ride on the divine forces flowing to the site only to find that the tomb had been corrupted by witchcraft or the activities of a demon – those same harmful forces could now flow in your direction. Much better to help ensure the site is protected by adding additional marks.

Most marks on tombs or gravestones are more restrained than these alabaster examples. By and large these are Marian marks but there are some tombs with daisy wheels, concentric circles and pentagrams on them too. When the marks occur on gravestones which are out in the graveyard, away from the protection of the church, then here we are looking at efforts to keep evil away from an individual's mortal remains.

Caves and Mines

Protection marks occur not only in buildings or on objects, they can also be found in caves. Christopher Binding and Linda Wilson have pioneered work in this area with papers about their discoveries in Somerset.

In 2004 they published their initial discoveries from Goatchurch Cavern, Burrington Combe in North Somerset, in which they described the discovery of three VV marks on the left wall of the cavern above an area known as the Giants' Steps (Binding and Wilson 2004: 119–23).

They subsequently made a huge number of discoveries in Wookey Hole and Long Hole in Somerset where they found a huge concentration of Marian marks in a part of the cave called the Witch's Chimney. The authors explain:

> It is worth noting that the area in Wookey Hole where the majority of the ritual protection marks are located is a closed aven, which results in a convection draught caused by the body heat of those standing below it displacing the cooler surrounding air which then descends noticeably. It seems reasonable to suggest that early observers experiencing the appearance of chill draught may have believed this to indicate the presence of some form of evil spirit. (Binding and Wilson 2010: 48)

I was given a tour of the cave by the authors in March 2017 and I can confirm the chill draught. The marks range from Marian M and VV symbols to Christograms and initials. There are also reports of Marian marks in a cave in Dovedale, Derbyshire. Andy Bentham reports the discovery of Marian marks in Peak Cavern and Pooles Cavern, both also in Derbyshire. In 2006 Peter Burgess reported to me that he had been discovering chalked VV and M marks in mines in Surrey. Having seen the VV marks described from Goatchurch Cavern, he said:

> I have become aware of very similar marks, in chalk, on the walls of ancient underground quarry workings in Surrey, and although research is in its early stage (we still need to record location and style of all the marks we have found) … The workings are very extensive, and we believe they were active from at least the 12th century until the early 18th century. From what little evidence we have, we believe the area where the ritual protection marks have been found dates from some time in the 16th century, or these workings at least existed at that time, but may of course have been older.

Witch-Posts

It would not be right to leave out the subject of witch-posts from this chapter. These beams, usually a significant upright beam associated with the hearth of the principal ground floor room, are normally topped with a saltire cross and other horizontal marks which have a scroll-like appearance and are sometimes called fillets. For a long time the pre-vailing belief was that these were created specifically as some kind of counter-witchcraft measure which was particularly unique to just two valleys in Yorkshire, those of Ryedale and Eskdale although there is one example in Rawtenstall, Lancashire. These posts first appear in the mid-seventeenth century, a time when many homes in Yorkshire were having chimney stacks inserted.

Mary Nattrass conducted some of the first serious research into them in 1962 where she mapped, surveyed, produced beautiful measured drawings, collected folklore and appealed for information in the local press. The posts were all reputedly made of Mountain Ash (Rowan) and then marked with the saltire cross. A local stonemason told her what she believed to be a traditional rhyme expressing the complaint of the witch:

> Oh Master, oh Master, we cant do no good
> She's got a witch cross made o' mountain ash wood. (Nattrass 1962:
> 255–56)

This stonemason was apparently a reader of verse in the Yorkshire dialect so was probably regarded as a reliable source for local folklore. Nattrass provides some tantalising glimpses of protective practices in her paper aside from the witch-posts themselves. Regarding a lost post from a demolished building known as 'The Nest' at Ainthorpe, Danby, she spoke to one Mr Jack Weatherill who reported that there was no writing on it, 'only some V-marks' – she was unable to trace the post to verify this herself (Nattrass 1962: 257).

In 1972 another serious piece of research appeared as a chapter in a book which identified a total of eighteen witch-posts including the one in Lancashire. Importantly, the authors point out that the first use of the term 'witch-post' in print appears to have occurred in 1936 when two of them were presented to Whitby Museum. The term is not used in any of the papers relating to one of them which now resides in the Pitt Rivers Museum in Oxford. They also assert that all the posts they had examined were made of oak, not Mountain Ash, as befits a structural beam in that area. They do state that the posts may have been used to prevent witches entering the house or to protect the hearth but that little of the superstition had survived and that it seems to have lost most of its significance by the latter part of the eighteenth century (Hayes and Rutter 1972: 87).

More recently Nicholas Rhea has argued that the marks actually relate to a travelling priest in the area known as Father Nicholas Postgate who was sixty when he was executed in 1679. The theory is that the priest would mark with an X houses which he would use for conducting Catholic ceremonies and rituals, this being an illegal activity at the time. He had a network of local houses and families which could be used for these purposes. He suggests in one of his papers that the varying number of scrolls or horizontal marking beneath the cross were one of the ways of numbering the houses so people could communicate which house was being used at any given time (Rhea 2011, 2014: 13–15).

There are various problems with Rhea's hypothesis, mostly based on the work involved in creating these posts. He suggests that the priest or possibly the occupants would carry out the work themselves yet many of the designs are highly decorative and quite beautiful. One would also think that these posts would be an extremely easy way for the authorities to identify Catholics, precisely the activity he suggests they were attempting to conceal.

So, the saltire cross at the top of the witch-posts and its close proximity to the hearth accords well with many of the evil averting practices discussed elsewhere in this book. The occupants of the house would surely have regarded the symbol as affording them some protection. It must also be pointed out that the saltire cross at the top of these posts is remarkably similar to the butterfly mark, or dagaz rune, which was widely used as a protection mark on wood, stone, plaster and iron fixtures and fittings. This similarity cannot have gone unnoticed and so it is likely that whatever the origins, these posts came to be regarded as having a protective function.

Conclusions

Many buildings will contain an assortment of these marks within them. For example, at a cottage in Mansell Lacey, Herefordshire, there are a lot of burn marks, VV symbols and daisy wheels. Many ecclesiastical buildings will have lots of daisy wheels and VV's, shoe outlines and other types of graffiti. The daisy wheel symbol stands on its own as having a very ancient origin as a solar symbol and has ended up travelling all around the world.

One of the principal ideas behind magical house protection is that objects are transformed through their death, for example, the deliberate bending of pins and nails in witch-bottles, the killing of a cat for it to act as spirit guardian, the re-use of a shoe which is no longer fit to wear. The idea seems to be that through death, a spirit form of the animal or objects becomes active and can then function in some way to trap evil influences entering the home or protect the inhabitants against these influences. In the case of ritual marks, it would seem that where the surface of the material has been scratched or burned away, whether it be wood, plaster, stone or lead, a ghostly form of the mark was believed to be created which would be highly visible to negative forces. This is particularly the case with mesh patterns and burn marks. The Marian marks were intended to invoke the protection of the Virgin Mary but I am confident that they were also thought of in a similar way. The daisy wheel pattern seems to have its origins deep in the ancient past as a solar symbol and migrated throughout all of Europe, Asia and into the USA and Australia where it came to be regarded as a general protective symbol, included in designs and also as graffiti. In a way its meaning is similar to that of the burn marks: shining light in dark places. The hand and foot outlines appear to have been to establish a sympathetic link with the holiness of a place but at times were also fun ways of making your mark, particularly when on pilgrimages.

⠿ Chapter 8

Other Concealed Objects

This chapter will discuss some of the many other types of objects that pop up fairly regularly in this subject area. Some of the items may seem a little odd but this all informs on the way people interacted with the supernatural world around them. If things ever get too scary in your home, you could always take the advice of my old friend and former builder Dave, who told me in 1998 that 'If you take the roof off a house the spirits are let out. It gets rid of all the spirits'.

Other Animals Remains

Many other examples of animal remains have been discovered in buildings. Examples of dogs, donkeys, horses, bulls, rabbits, chickens have all been found in deliberately concealed contexts. The broad reasons for burying and secreting these animals are essentially the same as for cats and horse skulls but they are worthy of note because they are exceptions to the norm and occasionally they represent something very different.

Cow skulls have been found in several locations in Ireland and elsewhere and appear to have been used more specifically for warding off illness in other cattle. Paul Sieveking relates a modern account of the use of a cow skull from the USA in an article in the *Sunday Telegraph* in 1999. He described how a farmer in Maine had a large herd of cattle but was losing animals periodically to an unidentified illness and had been reminded that his grandfather always kept a cow skull on the barn to ward off evil. He had always thought it was superstitious nonsense but after sufficient losses thought it worth a try and the illness rate of his cattle dropped significantly. It was reported that he extended the practice to having 16 cow skulls adorning his fence (Sieveking 1999).

Hearts stuck with pins are reported mainly from the south of England although they do turn up elsewhere. Many bulls' hearts stuck with pins have been recovered from chimneys in the south-west in particular. Folklore tells us that if a person stuck a freshly removed heart with pins, it could remove any witchcraft placed on the person doing it. Archaeology tells us that people then regarded these hearts as potent objects in the fight against evil because they were then placed within many chimneys. For example, a farmer called Mr Hart took over Devenish Pit Farm in East Devon in March 1899 and shortly afterwards discovered that a bullock's heart stuck all over with pins had been placed in a paper bag and nailed to the back of the chimney lintel in the kitchen. It is said that Mr Hart was a superstitious man so chose to leave the heart there undisturbed until he retired from farming in 1917 (Coxhead 1959: 111). The Pitt Rivers Museum in Oxford holds a sheep's heart stuck with pins and nails which was found in south Devon.

The skeleton of a pig was discovered in 1982 under the floor of a house in South Wootton, Norfolk. The animal was buried in front of the fireplace at a depth of about 1 foot 6 inches (Pennick 1995: 8).

William Paynter describes some accounts of hearts stuck with pins in his book which was published posthumously by Jason Semmens. He says, 'When a pig or other domestic animal met with a mysterious death it was formerly the custom to have its heart stuck full of pins and white thorns and put up the chimney in the belief that as the heart withered so would that of the black witch who had ill-wished the animal' (Paynter 2016: 12).

Several hearts stuck with pins have been discovered in Dorset, for example, at Frampton a builder discovered a bullock's heart stuffed with pins while fitting a new fire grate to the police station there. Another was discovered at Hawkchurch which had been stuck with pins, nails and some of the prickles of a white thorn. At Marshwood near Lyme Regis, 'A farmer complained his cattle had been "overlooked" and were all gradually dying off. He was told to take the heart out of the last animal which had died and push the heart, stuck all over with pins and nails, up the chimney so that the "overlooking" would pass back again where it had come from' (Lang 1969: 222–23).

There are just five examples of concealed dogs in my files. A Pekinese dog skull was found beneath the foundations of a house dating from 1750 in Douglas, Isle of Man (Garrad 1989: 110). A mummified whippet was discovered beneath the floorboards of the tack room of a pub called the Carlton in Leigh-on-Sea, Essex. The pub dates from 1898 (Collins

1985: 9–18). At the Crown Hotel, High Street, Alton, Hampshire, the skeleton of a dog was found behind a wall during alterations in 1967. This place was reputedly haunted by 'dog-like scratchings' which alarmed the owners' own pets prior to this discovery (Playfair 1985: 75). A dried puppy was found amongst forty sacks of straw and dust which existed beneath the floorboards of two rooms in the roof of Walnut Farm, in the region of Corfe Castle, Wareham. A child's cloth shoe was also discovered along with some coins, leading to the conclusion that these finds dated from the eighteenth century. Ullapool Museum reports that a dog skeleton was found after a severe gale undermined a wall at an archaeological site at Achnahaird Sands.

At Birkenhead Priory in 1896 the bones and skull of an adult sheep complete with horns was discovered in one of the buttresses. The author states that 'The stones were all properly faced inside, showing that the cavity had been intentionally built', and 'It seems clear that the sheep was deliberately immured in the recess prepared for it, and whether or not this constitutes a genuine example of a foundation sacrifice the facts are here recorded' (Irvine and McMillan 1969: 56–57).

During the demolition of the Pig and Whistle pub in Sedgeley, West Midlands, bones were discovered beneath the hearth. There was some concern that the bones were human but a doctor who was called confirmed that they were not. This seems to have been some kind of foundation sacrifice. The find was reported in the Birmingham Daily Post on 31 August 1860.

At a house in Corve Street, Ludlow, a horse vertebra was discovered in the roof of a house painted in the form of an angel. This is possibly of seventeenth-century date.

In 2002 Lucy Trench reported that beneath the floorboards of the non-conformist chapel at Newchurch in Powys, Wales, a large animal bone, perhaps a femur, had been discovered. This appears to have been a deliberate inclusion.

In a cottage in Gressenhall, Norfolk, said to be of the 1550s, two leg bones of a cow were found during restoration work beneath the hearth as a charm. In the same building Ivan Bunn reports that a charm comprising 'a lock of human hair and two nails' was found upstairs in a fireplace dated 1630 which had been covered by an 18th century one'.

A whole donkey was apparently buried in a barn in Caldecote, Hertfordshire. This was reputed to have been done to ward off a local beast which had been roaming around. The BBC News website reported that a headless horse was discovered during a new development for Stafford College on 19 November 2003. This was thought to be a medieval find and it was reported that experts were puzzled as to why a horse might be buried instead of just its hide and bones used, let alone that it has no head.

All types of apotropaic objects are just as likely to be found on church property as anywhere else and there are two excellent examples from a pair of England's finest cathedrals. Two bulls are reputed to have been buried beneath Canterbury Cathedral. In a similar ecclesiastical deposit, ox skulls and boar tusks were apparently found in the foundations of old St Paul's cathedral (Pennick 1986: 6). Both of these would be very early deposits compared to most of the other finds listed in this chapter.

In *Periods of Highland History* the authors describe the use of animals in foundation practices in Scotland:

> The burial of animals alive as a cure has been recorded so far apart as Kintyre and Moray. The bones of animals were also sometimes buried under the foundation of a building. One of the writers was told by the former owner, Mackintosh of Raigmore, that bones of cattle were found under the foundations of the farmhouse of Cradle Hall, and workmen told her that they had come across chicken bones in the foundations when restoring the farm of Dalraddy in Badenoch. Cradle Hall was built in the eighteenth century and Dalraddy is unlikely to have been as old. (Grant and Cheape 1987: 2)

Marianne Lines reported the discovery of horse bones used in the wall of a house in Braefoot, Collessie (*Dundee Courier* 1995).

At Rockview Cottage, in Bettyhill, Caithness, the remains of a lamb were found in one of the walls around the property. A mixture of glass and ceramics had been laid all around the body of the animal with a food tin and small bottle at its head and two jars containing small leather shoes at its hind quarters. This appears to have been intended as a lure, decoy and trap all at the same time. Within the cottage itself many other shoes were discovered.

The stretched hairless skin of a rabbit (or a young hare) on a stick was found embedded in the wall of a house near Hitchin, Hertfordshire. At Calke Abbey in Derbyshire, the skeleton of a hare or rabbit was found in a stone-lined grave in the foundations of the building, possibly of Tudor origin. In Falmouth a rabbit was discovered buried in a coffin at the top of a wall in a house (Pennick 1986).

Former builder Dave Parker reported to me in 1998 that during the early 1980s he was working on a brick cottage in Lower Moor, Worcestershire. He stripped the plaster off the ingle-nook fireplace and discovered a loose brick; behind this he discovered a chicken skull and leg bones. A chicken was found in the chimney of Potterne House, Devizes, Wiltshire in 1874. At the Bedern Foundry in York, a pit was discovered which contained the skeleton of a cat and several chickens – thought to be a foundation deposit. At the Broadgate East site in Lincoln, the skeletons of a cat and three hens were discovered in the infill of a stone-lined pit beneath a seventeenth-century occupation floor (Richard 1993: 182). At Porch House, Potterne, Devizes (built 1470), a dried chicken was found in the great chimney in 1874.

One of the most well-known examples of chickens being found is the assemblage which was found at Lauderdale House in Highgate, London. In a cavity next to the hearth on the first floor, a basket was found which contained two shoes, a broken glass goblet, a candlestick and four chickens. Two of the chickens had clearly been strangled and one of the others had laid an egg, suggesting that they had been concealed alive. The presence of the shoes and the location next to the hearth clearly imply a protective role for the deposit. The chickens could have been a kind of offering or foundation sacrifice, the candlestick perhaps to provide some symbolic light in this small void in the building. If the goblet was already broken when it was concealed, it is possible that it had been 'killed' in order to provide sharp spiritual shards to damage any negative forces which became trapped in this zone.

It is important to point out that sometimes animals remains were not used for any kind of magical purpose. There are many examples of bones or teeth being found in buildings – sometimes this is clearly a case of them being used as rather novel building materials and at other times it is not clear whether there was any element of folk magic being utilised. Philip Armitage has written that the peak of activity for using animal bones as building materials is from the seventeenth to the late eighteenth centuries. Features such as knuckle-bone floors and floors made of sheep bones crop up in various places and the floors of some follies and summerhouses were also made of knuckles and bones. Horse teeth were used to repair the floor of Hart's Horn Inn, Ash, Surrey and cattle horn cores were spread out on roads in London and covered in sand to form a 'firm and durable' surface. In these cases there was a readily available supply of animal remains from a nearby food production site and this must have seemed like a sensible use of what would otherwise have been a waste product.

It is clear that animal bones were regularly concealed in buildings in central Europe too. Iris Nielsen describes many examples of bones and parts of animals including cats being found in the fabric of domestic and religious buildings in Switzerland for example (Nielsen 2017: 325–36). Morten Søvsø has also recorded examples in Denmark (Søvsø 2017: 337–46).

Knife Blades

These crop up very frequently. They are often broken, or at least the handle has broken away and common places to find them are beneath window sills and in roof spaces. The idea that objects are 'killed' or at least 'dead' before use in magical actions is a recurring theme in this field and these are no exception. There seems to be two ideas at play here, the folkloric idea that witches fear iron, and of course the dangerous sharp edge of the now dead knife.

An excellent example was found in Manuden, Essex in the late 1970s. The knife dates from the eighteenth century and was embedded in a thick layer of wall plaster about 1.5m above floor level (Hooper 1988: 3). Ralph Merrifield reported that two sixteenth-century knives were found built into the wall at Cade House, West Malling (Merrifield 1969: 99–104).

Two knives were found in the thatch of a cottage at Dunham, Norfolk, during repair work in 1965, described as 'two small steel bladed knives and a leather sheath … possibly early 19th century, found with the blades crossed as a preventive against witchcraft, homemade and unused'.

At a farmhouse in Bishop's Castle, Shropshire, Philip Evans described the discovery of nails and a knife blade under a hearth slate:

> While restoring what was the parlour I took out the tiled 1940's fire place, the original hearth stone of slate had shattered, so I decided to replace it with new. Before replacement I dug out the remains, to find piled in what would have been the centre a pile of rusting nails (hand made) and the remains of a small knife blade directly beneath them.

The house dates from the mid-seventeenth century but was substantially altered in the 1740s. This example neatly combines the use of a knife with the use of iron.

David Rees reported in May 2002 a discovery at a cottage in Gasworks Lane, Llandovery in Carmarthenshire. Three bone handled penknives were found wrapped in cloth in two find-spots – both bedroom chimneys.

A knife was recovered from an inglenook fireplace in a cottage in Ibberton, Dorset during restoration work. The workman was turning around damaged bricks to show their best side and in doing so discovered the knife which Dorchester Museum dated to the eighteenth century.

A hand-made knife was found in the roof of a house in Footscray, near Melbourne, Australia. The house dates to the 1880s and the knife was found concealed in the roof. The owner subsequently buried it in the back garden so as to avoid any possible superstitious repercussions.

In the USA a knife was found concealed in the attic beneath a window at Marshfield, Plymouth County, Massachusetts, and Walter Wheeler describes the discovery of wooden carved dirks as concealed objects in his paper on early finds in the New York area (Wheeler 2017: 377).

In Garsington in Oxfordshire a resident reported to me in 2002 the discovery of lots of knives and other cutlery which was found hidden in the gaps between the stones in the dry stone wall which surrounded the garden of a cottage there. The cutlery was thought to be was around 100 years old and over forty pieces were found concealed in the wall. This struck me as being a late re-interpretation of the idea of concealing knife blades.

Use of Iron

Iron was thought to be effective in the fight not only against witchcraft but also the fairy folk. In West Sussex it was not unusual for people to create thresholds made of iron. It is said that iron thresholds protect against witches, fairies and other evil influences. Examples were recorded by the late Mr C.F. Tebbutt at the Priest House in West Hoathly, at Pepper Alley and Sedges in Danehill (Leppard 2002). Another example was in use at East Grinstead where the iron grave slab of Anne Barclay was used as the step to the scullery door in the vicarage that burnt down in 1908 (Golding-Bird 1933: 11).

A similar idea was employed at Llancaiach Fawr Manor in Wales. When the threshold timber between the servants' hall and kitchen was taken up from the floor, which is otherwise large flagstones, it was found to have a huge number of nails hammered into the underside. This is in addition to numerous burn marks in the door surrounds.

At the Lion Inn, Lamarsh in Essex, an iron fireback was found concealed behind another hearth. This was reported to me in November 2005 by Alastair Scot-Villiers who added that he had heard of 'a few examples of firebacks being found bricked up in fireplaces for ritual reasons. It seems that they are also sometimes found broken and the pieces hidden up chimneys!'

At a house in Foxholes Road, Horwich, Bolton, Lancashire, a number of pins and needles were found behind an old fireplace. Helen Scholar reported in January 2007: 'We have just prised away an old mantlepiece from a disused fireplace in our old stone house in Bolton ... A number of rusty needles and hatpins fell from behind the mantlepiece along with a brass weight marked a quarter of an ounce'. The farmhouse is nineteenth-century throughout but with possible earlier origins.

In Nova Scotia, Canada, four forged iron objects were found in the four corners of the parlour ceiling of an old property. The same house also contained two concealed shoes.

A knife, nail and piece of material were found enclosed in the wattle and daub wall of an old house in Brentwood High Street, Essex (Merrifield 1969: 99–104).

The use of iron as a deterrent is clear although it seems it was thought to work particularly well with sharp or large objects. The use of horseshoes for luck or protection, although not concealed objects, also falls into the use of iron category. This practice is world-wide and a cursory glance at any regional folklore study will reveal the local variant of this practice. This overlaps with horse folklore of course. Iron pins or nails are also a key ingredient of witch-bottles, as seen in Chapter 2.

Concealed Garments

When garments are found concealed within walls and elsewhere in buildings, it seems that the decoy principle of house protection is usually at work. An item of clothing, well used and usually bearing some marks of the life it had with its owner, acts as a lure for any dark energies that may be seeking out the occupants of a building.

Here are some examples. Four cotton dresses were found between the plank ceiling and the thatch of the bedroom at Causeway House, Northumberland. They were thought to be working clothes dating from the late nineteenth century and were heavily patched by the time of inclusion in the roof (Emery, Warner and Pearson 1990: 137). A corset dating from the 1870s was found in the wall of a house in Weymouth. A sailor's hat and glove dating from around 1875 were recovered from the wreckage of the George Inn, Portsmouth after it was bombed during the war (Keverne 1947: 136–54).

Siobhan Ratchford from Dumfries and Galloway Museums reported to me in 1999 that a man's brown skin waistcoat was found under the floorboards at Glenmidge, Auldgirth, Dumfriesshire. In Arundel House, Troqueer Road, Dumfries, a black hat with a velvet band and leather skip was found beneath the floorboards. Both of these finds are thought to date from the nineteenth century.

At the Talbot Hotel, Stourbridge, during work carried out on a small bridge building within the hotel, a number of objects were discovered. These included bone combs, a corset and a shoe, all apparently from the nineteenth century. At Barnoldswick, Lancashire, a single child's clog, a tiny slipper and a hand-made child's bodice were found in a bricked up oven.

Several other examples were investigated by the Textile Conservation Centre's Concealed Garments Project, including a seventeenth-century doublet from Reigate in Surrey found in a wall cavity. Another find mentioned by them is of five linen garments and a pouch from under the floorboards of Alpirsbach monastery in Southern Germany (Eastop 2001: 79–81).

A sad example from East Rutherford, New Jersey was reported in 2000 by Sandie McIlwaine. Apparently, some friends

> decided to renovate the attic so that they could rent out the rooms on the second floor. When they went into the attic they had found mass cards (small prayercards usually given out at funeral masses as remembrances of the deceased) hanging on strings from the ceiling. Weird but ... Anyway, they pulled up the flooring also and found a layer of old infant clothing under the floor boards.

In this case it would seem that the objects in the attic served as a memorial to a lost child although there is also the possibility that this was simultaneously intended to act as a decoy to other occupants in the building. Sandie reports that after the discovery there were strange noises in the night so they decided not to investigate further.

A similar example was reported by Tom Murison from Oakville, Ontario in Canada. He reported that:

> a child's dress, probably for an infant under the age of two ... was found laid out on a clean floor under a stair, but completely enclosed with walls so that no one had disturbed it since that portion of the house was constructed in 1859. The dress was face up, with the 'head' facing due south, even though the house did not align with the cardinal directions, and it was held down with a clay brick at both ends, (collar and hem) ... What struck me immediately was that this was a deliberate and very odd way to leave a child's dress concealed in the center of the house, on the main floor, and that it had been done very deliberately while the house was under construction ... What I saw in this case suggested that the dress was from a young child which may have died while the house was being constructed.

This could have been for a deceased child, or it could be another example of a decoy. An attempt was made to find a grave beneath the house but none was found. If the child had died and was buried elsewhere, then the concept of a combined memorial and decoy carries some weight.

Clothes appear to have been used in a similar way to concealed shoes although there seems to be more room for unusual practices too. Sometimes they were concealed as decoys, sometimes due to extreme loss and at other times they represent sentimental caches, although all three can often be at play.

Spiritual Middens and Hoards of Objects

This term was coined by Timothy Easton who in the course of his research in Suffolk and the surrounding area found many hoards of material in close proximity to the main chimney stack. He explains that the favoured locations for these hoards of material were, 'the spaces between brick chimney stacks and adjoining timber framed walls – these voids were accessible from the attic spaces' (Easton 1997: 568). In some cases people would add to the midden over generations of continued use.

Timothy Easton reports a large collection of objects from Barley House Farm, Winston, Suffolk. He describes that the objects came to light when there was 'a fall of bricks above the supporting ceiling joist which runs parallel to the chimney lintel'. Four shoes fell out but sixteen more were inside the cavity along with tally sticks, clothing and skeletal remains (Easton 1983: 29).

Cambridgeshire Sites and Monuments Record reported that a large collection of assorted objects was discovered behind the chimney breast of a house on the High Street, Brampton (Huntingdon district) during repairs in 1985. This hoard included post-medieval glazed sherds, a wine bottle, a sharpening stone, slag from a neighbouring forge, bones from horses, sheep, pigs, a duck skull, oyster shells, iron nails and window glass.

A very large hoard of objects was found during alterations to the chimney at 'The Barracks' in Nutley, East Sussex. This comprises more than sixty items of footwear, gaiters and undecorated brass and is one of the largest finds of footwear on record so far from England. The objects are all being held at the Weald and Downland Open Air Museum in West Sussex.

At the National Trust property at Chastleton near Moreton-in-Marsh, a hoard of seventeenth-century artefacts was found in a hole in the basement of the east stair tower. These included bellarmine stoneware bottles, pottery, clay pipes, and several onion-shaped glass bottles. The hole lies centrally within a room between four columns supporting the existing staircase (*Mosaic* 1994: 25). Although not associated with a chimney in the typical manner for a spiritual midden, this does appear to serve the same sort of function. Daisy wheel protection marks have also been found at Chastleton.

In an outbuilding behind Debdale Farm on Loughborough Road, Bradmore, near Nottingham, a hoard of objects was found inside a bricked up inglenook fireplace. The correspondent is of the opinion that the outbuilding was formerly the kitchen and that the objects are Victorian although the date of a book found amongst it all implies that the objects may be very late Victorian or Edwardian and almost certainly were not concealed prior to 1910. The objects were found behind the actual hearth and, it is thought, had been there long before the bricking up. They comprise two sliver thimbles, a silver broach with a bow and heart on it, a bone knitting needle, a round flat disc with a hole in it possibly made of bone, a pair of black elbow length cotton gloves with mother-of-pearl buttons, a narrow crochet tie, two bow ties and some wrapping with a picture of a jester on it and the words 'round corners' and 'pantaloons' written on it. There was also a little paper book from the International Bible Reading Association dated 1910. The building was originally built in the 1700s but was later divided into a labourer's cottage and a farmhouse, with the outbuilding behind the cottage.

In Howells Farm, Halls Green, Weston in Hertfordshire, a large hoard of objects was discovered behind an inside wall of a bedroom. The list is as follows: a red ceramic costrel with basketry cover; a hair comb; a cheek snaffle horse bit created from two different bits, with the cheek pieces cut with sharp knife; a sword scabbard, assembled incorrectly with hangars twisted; slipware sherd; a black leather shoe of adult male date between 1695 and 1720; two small pieces of white fabric block printed in red with floral design, dated 1675–1690; fragments of a woman's corset in white linen with wooden bones, 1650–1750; red ware sherds; other sherd; two stones; stoneware sherds; a deep green-black glass bottle with deep conical frog; a blue ceramic bead; a fragment of leather jacket, 1600–1700; and the blade of a metal knife. This material was all deposited through a hole in the attic. Other fine examples of middens in Hertfordshire have been found at Walsworth and North Mymms.

A fine example of a midden was discovered in Scotland at a property in Shore Street, Anstruther, Fife. Concealed within a lath and plaster wall near the foot of the stair was a collection of objects including a home-made doll made from a piece of fabric, a page from the bible showing psalm CXIX, a page of hymns, a George II half-penny, a bottle with a broken neck, a piece of stained glass, some wine corks, ears of corn, some dried peas, a bobbin and some chicken and pig bones. There were also some fine ritual marks discovered at this site (Darwood and Sherriff 2003: 127).

In 1999 Angela Walker reported that a hoard of objects was recovered from the left-hand side of the fireplace during renovations at a cottage in Nestor Square, Narberth in Wales. The finds included nine shoes, three of which were children's, a substantial quantity of broken crockery and a number of bottles.

During the demolition of the Plough at Sittingbourne, a huge number of shoes and other material was discovered from a large spiritual midden associated with the chimney. Sittingbourne Heritage Museum now holds this huge collection in cabinets specifically acquired to house them all. The Plough was original built in a couple of phases in the second half of the seventeenth century and many of the finds came from voids created by the boxing in of the chimney stack with lathe and plaster panels and from locations beneath the floor. There were eight different assemblages in total. The finds included footwear, garments, glass and hats ranging in date from the seventeenth to the twentieth centuries (Abbey 2010).

A report from Normandy in November 2012 by Frederick Allanic described the following find:

> we are currently restoring an old farmhouse in Normandy. Earlier this year we came across a cavity in the wall of the house where an old ceiling beam had been removed and the void filled with broken lamp globes, two medicine bottles, pieces of broken crockery and a small burner – the items are not very old and probably date to the early decades of the twentieth century.

Here we have the idea of filling voids with jagged, broken belongings. Voids in houses were seen as dangerous areas where evil could hide so here some 'dead' household items provide a lethal barrier to occupation.

Some shoes were discovered in Brisbane, Australia in what appears to be another spiritual midden. Ian Evans reported as follows:

> The story is that I've been contacted by someone in Brisbane who is fairly sure there are concealed shoes in the chimney of his 1880s house. He's been up into the roof cavity and can see down into the cavities on either side of the chimney flue. There appear to be shoes, or parts thereof, in each cavity, plus some other stuff.

These large collections of objects which occupy voids are intended to draw evil down into them where it would then be harmed by the dead and broken objects within. The idea is that lots of objects which had been part of the family's life and are now dead could act simultaneously as a lure and a trap.

Dolls and Figures

A number of dolls have been found deliberately hidden. Some of them form part of curses which are described in more detail in Chapter 9, 'Evidence of Darkness'. Some have been deliberately damaged, and others appear to have been concealed (along with other toys) as decoys to lure harmful energies towards them instead of the children to whom they belonged.

Janet Pennington reported that in Spinners, High Street, Upper Beeding in West Sussex, two shoes were discovered and a doll was found near the hearth which was blackened in parts. The shoes were dated to the first half of the eighteenth century. The doll remains near the hearth and the shoes were re-deposited in a special place made for them by the carpenter under the attic floorboards.

One example which appears to have been of the decoy type was reported to me from a seventeenth-century cottage in Mollington near Banbury in Oxfordshire. It was a small child's doll made from rag, together with a ball also made from rag, a turned stick possibly used to turn a spinning top, and a piece of stained glass all wrapped together. The objects were found together at first floor level next to a former window in a wattle and daub wall.

A doll is on display at the Museum of Witchcraft in Boscastle which was found near Padstow in 1998. It is reported to have been bricked up in a recess and uncovered during renovation work. Initially the doll was sold to an antique dealer before coming into the possession of the Museum (Semmens 2000: 25–30).

In 1999 the Museum of Kent Life had recently acquired an eighteenth-century weather-boarded farmhouse and during the dismantling of the building, they recovered a child's boot from beneath the floorboards of the main bedroom which was subsequently dated to 1850. They also recovered a doll from debris on the floor which they think had been concealed around the front door-frame or nearby window behind the plaster. Curator Octavia Kenny described it as

a small wooden doll, with a plaster and painted face, but no hair, holes for arms but no arms, and the trunk of the body crudely cut off at an angle to form an asymmetrical 'v' shape. The body was painted pink and wearing no clothes apart from a scrap of material knotted around its neck, with a design of red triangles.

Staff at Lewes Castle and Museum reported a wooden figure that was found lying in the roof of a sixteenth-century farmhouse. There were traces of colouring on the figure and there was apparently an unidentifiable object lying at its feet. Norfolk Rural Life Museum reports that they hold a witch-doll in their collection which is believed to have been discovered somewhere in King's Lynn. An individual at Liverpool Museum reported that during the restoration of a cottage, she found a doll within an inglenook chimney and marks beneath flag-stones. In Bullocks Café in the High Street, Droitwich, Worcestershire, a doll was discovered in the rafters in 1999 which workmen refused to touch. East Grinstead Museum in West Sussex notes the discovery of a nineteenth-century doll in their *Compass Magazine* in 2002. Staying in the same county, a doll was found under the floorboards at Glaysher's Shop in Horsham when the building was dismantled, and moved to Singleton Museum.

When a doll or figure is found which does not have any obvious sign of deliberate damage or cursing associated with it, my impression is that it is there to act as a decoy for any harmful forces entering the home. A certain amount of wear and tear type damage could be a reason to use it as a decoy, as it is felt that the doll has 'died' and in theory will now provide a useful target which negative forces will attack instead of the occupants.

Spoons

Hoarding silver or other valuable objects was not unusual in the past and people could be very creative about how they hid things to keep them safe. Some of the spoons which have been reported could have been simply a way of hiding a bit of valuable silver but some of them are not made of precious materials and have been found with other objects which were definitely concealed for protection reasons.

In 1962, the then rector of Abberley Church in Worcestershire, Richard Bevan, made safe the ruin of the church and closed off and restored the chancel. During this work, five fifteenth-century diamond point spoons were found which are now in the British Museum. This does appear to be an example of keeping safe some valuable silver.

Now for some examples which are less easy to explain. Two spoons were discovered in a wall in a very old hall house in Nibley, Yate, in the

Bristol area. Between the farm house and the barn there was a passage for the oxen and the spoons were found in this wall when a new passage was created. One was made of pewter with a broken stem and the other was a replica made of wood.

At Harome Hall in Yorkshire, a silver spoon was found in the rye thatch and was thought to date from the fifteenth to sixteenth century (Emery, Warner and Pearson 1990: 137).

A spoon was found buried horizontally at the base of infill to reduce the width of a doorway at Wellington House, Cheddar, Somerset. The spoon has been dated to 1660–1680.

A silver spoon was discovered in Combs Ford, Stowmarket in Suffolk, thought to date from the seventeenth century. It is described as having been deliberately hidden (Emery, Warner and Pearson 1990: 137).

A concealed shoe and silver spoon were discovered at a house in Wythall in the West Midlands. The house is thought to date from around 1800. Correspondent Eric Flavin reported the following in November 2012:

> just over 17 months ago we purchased an old cottage … we have just had some work done which involved having a small part of a chimney removed, as the builder was taking part of what looked like an old stove built into the chimney he found a small child's shoe and a silver spoon hidden in the wall of the stove, the shoe looks like a Victorian one black hard leather and very small, the spoon is solid silver and looks as though it has a letter H on it.

A number of items were discovered in the walls at two properties in Whitecross Street in Barton-on-Humber, Lincolnshire. This includes iron Saxon sceax, possibly dating from the seventh century (probably recovered from a nearby Saxon cemetery), an undatable triangular piece of iron, a wooden patten dating from the late eighteenth or early ninetheenth century, and a spoon of the late eighteenth or early nineteenth century found in the north wall of an entrance passage just below ceiling level (Williams 1998: 4–6).

A spoon and other items were discovered at a house in Narborough, Norfolk. The house is thought to date to between 1790 and 1920. There are several Marian marks in the building, some daisy wheels and a hand carved wooden spoon approximately 185mm long which was found concealed in between the main ceiling timbers of what is now the kitchen. The owners were told that the second floor of this house was added in the 1850s when the railways came to this part of Norfolk, so this spoon may have been put into what was the attic.

A spoon was found at Gomez Mill House, New York. This house is the oldest in Orange County, originating in 1714. During a restoration project, the bathroom and built up floor were removed to take them down to the 1772 floor. In replacing the floor boards, they found in the adjacent wall a child's shoe, a 'last', a purse and a spoon.

At various times in the past a spoon was seen as something of a status symbol. The materials it was made of would have a bearing on how you might be perceived by your fellows. You might take your own spoon if you went to eat somewhere and you would be unlikely to share it with someone. It was a highly personal object and has an intimate connection with your body that other objects would not have. For that reason I think it possible that spoons were intended to be used as decoy objects in a similar way to shoes and garments. Perhaps someone perceived themselves to be bewitched but did not have a spare shoe or garment, or could not afford the services of the local cunning person, and needed something they could place between themselves and the source of danger. The spoon could fit the bill for this.

Clay Pipes

Often found with concealed shoes or just on their own, clay pipes are also a fairly common find as a concealed object.

During the renovations of an old cellar at a house in Manchester, New Hampshire which was built in the 1860–1970s, an old clay pipe turned up in the earthen floor in the northern corner. A window in this area which had been used as a coal chute in the early twentieth century had a hollow area within the wall and here the workman found a woman's shoe, smallish and without laces.

At La Rigondaine, Jersey, the following is reported: 'When uncovered, a niche beside a fireplace in the earlier house contained a curious assortment of objects, suggestive of folklore. Amongst them was a clay pipe with a macabre and emaciated face and prominent cheek bones, probably about 1850 in date, but a type not otherwise recorded in the Island' (Stevens 1977: 183).

At the former Horse & Farrier at Oakshaw Ford, Bewcastle in Cumbria, a number of artefacts have been discovered. In July 2003 Heather Scott reported, 'I was currently gouging out some old lime mortar from the listed building my partner and I are renovating and two clay pipe bowls fell out. They appeared to be broken off at the very same point and one was large the other much smaller, possibly a woman's'. Horses' teeth and coins were also found.

At Fields Farm, Castleton, in Derbyshire, there are marks on a door lintel (Marian) and a clay pipe was also found in a bit of wall that was blocking up an old doorway. At Battersea Square, Wandsworth, a cat's skull, part of a bellarmine and a fragment of clay pipe were found together behind a wall during the excavation of a house. At Algakirk in Lincolnshire, a decorated clay pipe of the nineteenth century was found behind some panelling at the rectory. An earthenware jar was found concealed beneath the floor of a house in Salthouse Norfolk with four fragments of white salt-glazed pottery, one fragment of brown salt-glazed pottery and nine fragments of clay pipe stem, thought to belong to the eighteenth century. In a farmhouse at Sandford, Winscombe, in North Somerset, dating from the seventeenth to nineteenth century, a mid-nineteenth-century clay pipe was discovered beneath a window seat in a mortar mass. At the Old School House, Bucknell, Shropshire, a Victorian shoe and clay pipe were recovered from the fireplace.

At Lancing College in West Sussex, Janet Pennington reports that two clay pipes were found behind the panelling in the Great School which was built in 1882. The carpenters who found them replaced them with a tobacco tin and a coin when they made their own twentieth-century deposit in the 1990s.

Janet Pennington also reports the discovery of a large collection of objects at the Hall, The Green, Southwick in West Sussex. This included oyster shells, pottery and clay pipes. A fork with a split bone handle 'fell down the chimney' here and two coins dating from 1753/1755 and 1806 (pennies) were also found. A separate find was made here of a broken wine glass and part of a boar's upper mandibles with the front part of its skull and tusks tucked into the wine bottle. The front part of the boar's skull was found together with a newspaper dating from 1782, but the broken wine glass was dated to about forty to fifty years earlier. This was found behind panelling in the 'parlour', mortared into the top of a very thick flint rubble wall.

These pipes may have been concealed at the point where they may otherwise have been discarded to be used as a decoy item, the idea being that as they were regularly in contact with saliva and people would breathe smoke through them, they have an intimate connection with their owners. Clay pipes could often be important at wakes where people would sometimes partake of a communal tray of tobacco, break a pipe and cast it into the earth with the coffin of the deceased or alternatively keep the pipe as a memento. There are also folk tales which associate the pipe with the ability to defeat the Devil by challenging him to catch smoke rings, which he could not do.

Wooden Stakes or Rods

From Padside Hall, Ray Wilson reported in December 2001 the discovery of a

> wooden stake slung between two iron hoops under the boarded ceiling of what would have been the screens passage leading from the Hall door. The stake or pole is round, roughly fashioned, approximately 80mm in diameter and 1.25 metres in length and tapers at both ends. A local historian tells me that such stakes were positioned at the entrance to the house to protect and ward off unwanted guests. The stake is not carved. I have yet to discover whether it is fashioned from rowan.

Other objects were discovered at the building including a girl's shoe from the early nineteenth century which was found behind a blocked fireplace opening. A nineteenth-century flat iron was found within the fabric of a wall, concealed by plaster. A brown glass bottle containing liquid with a cork stopper was also found with a wall of the early nineteenth century.

A virtually identical wooden stake suspended on hoops is thought to have been found at Hill Top, the National Trust owned former home of Beatrix Potter. This is at Hawkshead in Cumbria.

In June 2016 Bill Fergie reported a slightly different example of lengths of wood being used with a possible protection function intended:

> With a colleague I have been studying timber framed buildings in Hampshire for many years. Some years ago we came across a hazel rod – about 25mm in diameter and 1500mm long – in the roof of a former medieval hall house dendro dated to 1365. The rod was tied with cords fastened to the thatching battens, and it ran just under the slope of the roof between two of the rafters. Some of the thatching battens and rafters were still smoke blackened but the roof had been repaired with various new timbers and the hazel rod was not blackened. It occurred to us that it might be some form of apotropaic protection but we thought no more about it until we found two more examples in fairly quick succession in late 16th century buildings. All three examples are in north Hampshire.

Timothy Easton notes the discovery of three rods which formed part of a spiritual midden at Cutchey's Farm in Suffolk (Easton 2014b: 20).

Walter Wheeler reports the discovery of a rod, thought to be cherry or apple wood, measuring 92.7cm and 2cm diameter from the roof of the Phoenix Hotel, Lansingberg, New York. The rod was found lodged between the roof boards and the truss and is thought to have been placed during renovations after a fire which occurred here in 1851 (Wheeler 2017: 387–88).

At present, apart from the testimony of the local historian who said they were to ward off unwanted guests, there is not a great deal of evidence to explain how these wooden stakes or hazel rods were understood by the people who installed them. These otherwise hidden objects clearly had a function, and concealed objects are usually for protection purposes. More examples will hopefully emerge and the meaning will become clearer.

Clear Builders' Foundation Deposits

Sometimes objects are found where there can be no doubt that they were deposited at the foundation of a building or by builders during some major work.

Lisa Graves reported in September 2017 a discovery beneath a chapel in Winterbourne which was undergoing restoration. The owner found a concealed bottle, reporting: 'I found it set in a solid block of stone, with carved chamber to hold the bottle. The bottle has the cork intact but not fully sealed. Within, a note with very faint writing, a silver coin and something else unidentifiable, possibly just sediment. The chapel date is 1868'. The bottle was an oval shape and turned out to be a mineral water bottle known as a Hamilton and was dated to the third quarter of the nineteenth century by Matthew Slocombe. The purpose-made cavity in the stone to receive the bottle must have been carefully planned by the builders. This strikes me as a cross between a votive offering and a witch-bottle. Coins are quite commonly included in new structures, additions and alterations. It is unfortunate that the note cannot yet be read, as it almost certainly holds the key.

Simon Walker sent me this extract from *The Bedfordshire Advertiser* relating to a foundation deposit discovered in August 1903:

> Alterations at old houses in Hitchin during the past week or two provided a good deal of interest for antiquaries … An interesting discovery was made by the workmen engaged in pulling down the shop lately occupied by Mr. Raban in Golden-square. They were pecking away part of the foundations and found, at a depth of about four feet, a small cinerary jar, containing what are supposed to be human ashes. The jar, which was unfortunately broken by a pick, was about six inches high, of globular form, and is glazed green. In front of the hole in which it was found was an old tile. The same men dug out a human leg bone. (*The Bedfordshire Advertiser* 1903)

Matthew Champion reported this example of a builders' deposit to me in April 2016. It involves a concealed rat and postcard which were found concealed in a purpose-built cavity in a hearth at Waterloo House, Litcham, in Norfolk. This is a substantial red brick building dating from 1815 but extensively remodelled in 1850–1851:

> During renovation works in 2005 the owner, Mrs Elizabeth Williams, detailed workmen to remove a fireplace from the dining room that had been inserted into an earlier chimney breast, to reveal the original larger fireplace beneath. When the later fireplace was dismantled a 'secret' compartment was found built into the shoulder of the brickwork (the shoulder on the opposite side was solid brick throughout). Inside the compartment were found the remains of a rat – curled up and mummified by the heat from the fire. Alongside the remains of the rat were found a postcard, complete with stamp, containing details of the builders who had constructed the fireplace, which was dated to 1851. Close examination revealed that the compartment had been formed to leave only a small hole at one end, which was subsequently sealed with a rough brick and mortar bung. The rat had been inserted through this hole whilst still alive. The rat had then partially chewed the postcard, before curling up in the wet mortar to fall asleep – and subsequently pass away.

The rat was buried nearby, with the postcard remaining in the possession of the householder. This find is clearly a foundation sacrifice, albeit a small one, as well as a kind of time capsule in the shape of the postcard.

Daniela Ávido reported another fine example of foundation deposits from the La Elvira site in Buenos Aires, Argentina. The building dates from the early to mid-nineteenth century and was originally built as a two-room house but was later split into four small separate dwellings. Several items were found deliberately concealed in purpose built voids within the walls. These include a glass bottle, a playing card, a bone and a pot. In addition to these items there were also some empty chambers within the walls which may have contained something perishable or perhaps the builders did not get around to putting objects in these cavities. There are no comparable examples yet recorded from South America so it is difficult to draw firm conclusions from this case but the existence of hidden objects in walls in other parts of the world is normally considered evidence of magical house protection (Ávido 2013: 6–13).

Jean-Marie Blaising relates another example from Rodemack in France, very close to the border with Luxembourg. During the archaeological investigation of a chapel, one of the stones forming part of a corner of the main wall was found to have a purpose-built hole in the centre of a carved heart, crosses and other signs clearly engraved onto its surface. It is suggested that the hole was intended to receive the consecrated host (Blaising 2017: 353).

Thunderstones

Throughout the British Isles many prehistoric artefacts have been included in buildings. Flints, in particular arrowheads, were known as thunderstones. There was a belief that they were created where lightning struck the ground and as lightning never strikes the same place twice, they could provide immunity from a lightning strike to one's building (*Folklore* 1938: 48–49). They could also be boiled so that people or animals could drink water imbued with their magic, or worn as amulets (Penney 1976: 70–75). This practice has been recorded widely in the British Isles and also Denmark (Søvsø 2017: 337–46).

Toads

Witches of the dark kind are often associated with toads in popular fiction. William Paynter from Cornwall described an old witch called Betsy who was much feared and would collect toads. It is said that she kept a slate over a hole in her kitchen floor, within which she kept her toads so they were always available for her nefarious magical activities (Paynter 2016: 43). That account dates from the early twentieth century. When toads turn up having been concealed in buildings, we must wonder what kind of magic was occurring. In a property on the High Street, Melbourn, in Cambridgeshire, a dried toad, apparently pierced, was found embedded in a wall (Pennick 1995: 10). and in a cottage at East Bilney in Norfolk dried toads were found nailed to the walls. It is reported that this latter example was possibly as a charm against illness.

Coins

Examples of coins being found in the structure of inglenook fireplaces, beneath door lintels, beneath posts and in gaps in door-frames are extremely numerous. People generally say that it is done 'for luck' but I think it may be a descendant of the foundation sacrifice concept, except a little less barbaric and adding a different kind of value. Foundation sacrifices can be seen as an offering to the spirit of place to make compensation for the modifications made to the site, as an offering of a life to the building so it won't take one later on by falling down. Offering a coin is not the same as offering the life of a creature, but it is certainly much easier and is a reflection of our changing ideas over time. The instinct and desire to make an offering is still there, if not the original method of doing so.

Marie Ellsworth from New York State recalls that in the 1960s her father made some improvements to the porch and 'We were called over to put some coins in a corner of the foundation to "keep it from cracking". I believe this was probably passed down in our family, or in my grandmother's family who were also masons'.

Simon Walker sent me this extract from *The Bedfordshire Advertiser* relating to a foundation deposit discovered in August 1903:

> During alterations to the business premises of Mr. J.R. Jackson, Market-place, three coins were found cemented in a wall, one being a Charles II. halfpenny, dated 1660, one a George III. penny, dated 1770, and the third a George III. penny, dated 1779. It is supposed to have been an old custom to insert coins in the walls of housed so as to denote the date of the building. These coins, despite their long imprisonment, are in remarkably good preservation.

Many coin discoveries are almost certainly not reported due to the desire to keep the coins when found.

There are a huge range of objects which have been used for a sacrificial, magical or time capsule purpose. The objects described in this chapter hopefully give a flavour of the material which has been reported to me over the years and demonstrate how easily objects can be transformed from one existence to another.

⚙ Chapter 9

Evidence of Darkness

The purpose of this book is to bring to light the objects and symbols which people used to protect themselves from supernatural harm. Along the way many examples of exactly the opposite have also come to light as proof that this counter-magic was indeed necessary.

Many objects are reported, including innocent things like time capsules and some not-so-innocent things like hidden swords and a crossbow recovered from walls and in one case a child's preserved arm. In addition to these, there are those finds which clearly point to forms of dark magic. Most humans are, as we know, capable of both good and bad and this is clearly evidenced in some of these cases. Here we will explore some of the curses, dolls and other objects which appear to suggest that some ill will was at work.

Before detailing some of the examples, it is important to consider the act of performing dark magic. When the magic is not instinctive, such as being ill-wished or given the evil eye, it is normally a pre-meditated act which may or may not involve magical tools or ingredients and a degree of ritual. Let us consider a scenario where an actual witch desires to harm the health of a person who has crossed them in some way. We can imagine the witch (if working alone) summoning energy in some way, possible utilising a human effigy, and at some critical point releasing that magical energy so that it can be sent on its way to find the target. This 'energy' will now have to negotiate its way past all the obstacles we have described elsewhere in this volume in order to reach its target.

Alternatively, an individual could pay someone to create a curse for them. For this they might seek out a magical practitioner such as a cunning person or, if they wanted more discretion, they might travel beyond their local area to find a practitioner who would not know the area they were from. Another way would be for them to create a doll or image and write their own curse (assuming literacy). Again, the magical energy created in these acts was believed to be a real force which could, if anticipated, be trapped, repelled or diverted from its target.

Many written curses have been discovered. Perhaps one of the most spectacular examples was one written in lead which was discovered in a cupboard in 1892 at Wilton Place, Dymock in Gloucestershire. It reads: 'make this person to Banish away from this place and country amen to my desier amen', with Sarah Ellis' name written backwards at the top (see Figure 9.1). There are a variety of sigils on the curse which all relate to the moon (Hartland 1897: 143). Just as with written charms, we have a magical object combining sources of supernatural power, in this case astrological and demonic magic symbols and the amen from prayer. The Dymock curse is held at Gloucester Folk Museum and their interpretation cards state that there is 'A local legend that Sarah Ellis was so affected by the curse that she took her own life and was buried at a crossroads with a stake through her heart. There is indeed an Ellis' Cross on the boundary of the parishes of Dymock and Oxenhall about two and a half miles from Wilton Place'. The curse dates from the second half of the seventeenth century.

The author of the paper about the Dymock curse believed this type of curse to be derived from Cornelius Agrippa's *Three Books of Occult Philosophy*. He cites an example of a similar curse found on Gatherley Moor, Yorkshire. That one was found on top of a pile of stones and read:

Figure 9.1 Curse on Sarah Ellis carved backwards onto lead from Dymock, Gloucestershire. © Brian Hoggard.

'I did m[a]ke this the James Phillip John Phillip and Aitkin Phillip and all The Issue of them shall Come to utter Beggery and nothine joy [or] prosp[er] w[ith] them [in] Richmondshire'. This curse is also engraved onto a lead plate; there is a small cross after the text and some large symbols which are of the Spirit of the Moon and of the Spirit of the Spirits of the Moon. On the reverse of this tablet is the complete table of the moon (Hartland 1897: 148–49). Another lead curse was found at St Mary's Abbey, West Dereham in Norfolk. And another possible curse, which comprised a silver coloured metal disc engraved with a number square and with non-standard English words, perhaps incorporating names of demons, angels or elementals, was found in a leather bag in a cottage in Oaksey, Wiltshire. It is thought to have been used by a witch.

In the Forest of Dean in Gloucestershire an unusual charm was discovered beneath the floorboards of an 1837 house. It consisted of a small bundle of strangely plaited hair, a tiny piece of what looks like a page from a book, and a bird skeleton. Part of the printed text on the paper says 'Saturday' and 'Stolen'. It is not clear what the purpose of this assemblage is but interpretations lean towards the dark side.

In 2008 an Atlantic storm blowing in from the sea dislodged a slate from a granite barn in the parish of Mabe, Cornwall. On close examination it transpired that some words had been etched onto the surface. It reads (the layout approximates the appearance of the words on the slate):

MAY HE WHO STEALS
MY ROUND STONES
MAKE EARLY DRY
   BONES.
REPENT
  RETURN AND
    LIVE
    FOREVER.

No-one is certain what is referred to by the round stones. The author of the paper, Steve Patterson, suggests it could relate to the work of a mason, to a magical Kenning stone or possibly to testicles (Patterson 2018: 1–3). The 'dry bones' is a clear reference to being nothing but a skeleton but the remainder of the passage appears to promise a reward of eternal life if the stones are returned. The slate is back on the farm from which it came.

Hereford City Museums have a good collection of charms and curses. One nineteenth-century curse was found in East Street, Hereford. It consists of a crudely made doll, with the body made of wood with arms

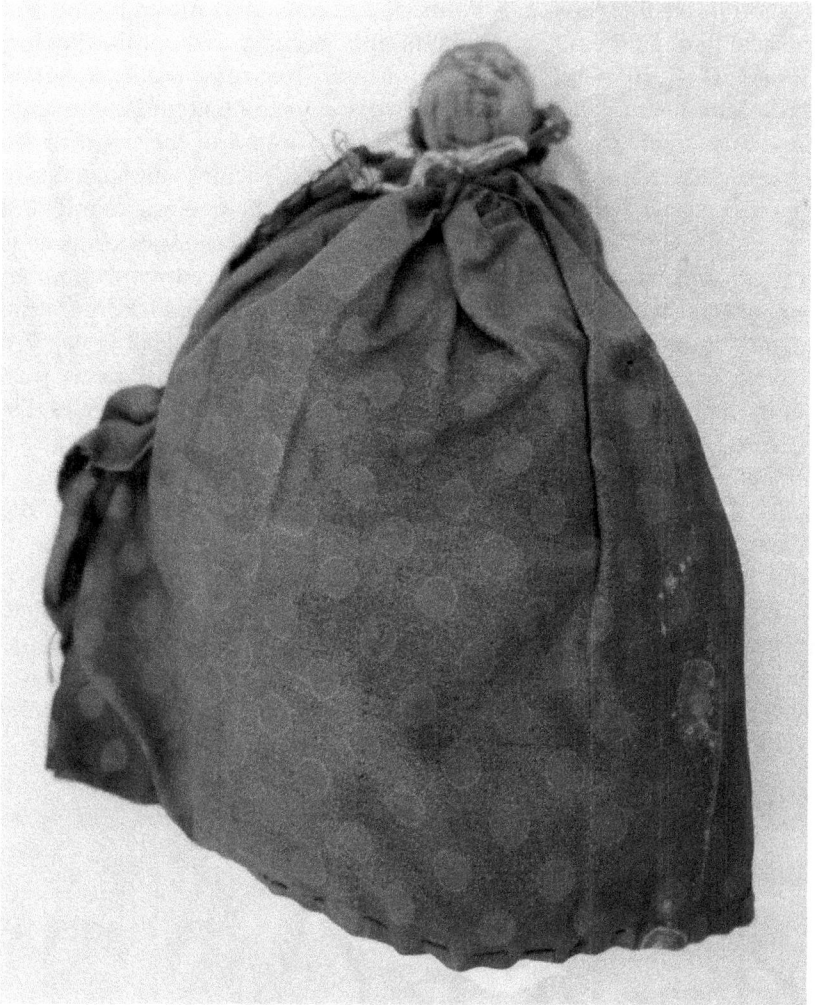

Figure 9.2 Curse doll from Hereford. © Brian Hoggard.

and legs of red checked cotton material. The doll is wearing a dress of red spotted dark blue cotton material and with the skirt area of the dress was found a curse written in black ink on paper. The curse reads: 'Mary Ann Ward, I act this spell upon you from my holl heart wishing you to never rest nor eat nor sleep the rester part of your life. I hope your flesh will waste away and I hope you will never spend another penny I ought to have. Wishing this from my whole heart' (Figure 9.2).

In Alfred Taylor House, 43-49 St Johns, Worcester, dating from 1500, some interesting objects were discovered. An extract from 'The

Medieval Hall House That Defies Destruction' by Gladys Keithley is available at the house which states

> But behind the early twentieth century fireplace, among the brick rubble in the damaged ancient stone fireplace was found an old wooden doll. This is probably early twentieth century. It may be a witch-doll. Its face, square, like the old wood Betsy dolls of Victoriana, is masked in plaster. Its foot is peg-like and etched with a pattern of claws. Its black chest is faintly marked with a drawing of a goat's head. On the back is a light patch where paper has covered it. On this patch, is faded ink where the words 'help me to –' but these words have faced from exposure.

The current whereabouts of this doll is unknown but it certainly sounds like it was involved in some nefarious activity.

The Moyses Hall Museum in Suffolk reported a witch-puppet, described as a cloth doll with a crone's head made of wax. The clothing includes an underskirt, dress, cloak and wide-brimmed black hat, the point bent forwards. In the left hand is a paper 'booklet' marked in ink with rows of squiggles, perhaps a written charm or curse.

Nigel Pennick reprints the headlines of an article about a collection of finds from Billericay in Essex: 'Horrified workmen have uncovered a black magic shrine at St Andrew's Hospital, Billericay. Their shock find in an attic close to the hospital chapel includes bones, voodoo-type dolls and a pin box. Now police may be called in ...'. Pennick states that what was found was actually two four-inch long effigies, part of a ruminant jawbone and thighbone, a piece of coal, and a notched wooden tine about three inches long (Pennick 1986: 7).

A wax effigy of a woman with marks where steel pins were placed through stomach, heart and head is held at Lewes Castle and Museum. Wax dolls have been in use for a very long time. John of Nottingham was said to have plotted to kill the Despensers using wax effigies back in 1324.

A written curse was discovered behind a skirting board by Lyle Armstrong in his home in Isleham, Cambridgeshire. He described it thus: 'Found a note behind skirting boards. Difficult to decode but reads something like this':

> I damn those that are employed and stoe this letter dwelling for none payment for carpentry work undertaken
> Joseph Datton
> May 5th 1892

Naomi Stevens reported the finding of a wooden doll from Tilford, Surrey in April 2001. She described it as follows:

> I was clearing out this old house for a friend of my and I found this doll it was laying face down under a floorboard that my dad happened to lift up I wondered if you could tell me what this is it's like a very old wooden doll it looked pretty strange.
>
> The doll had no hair when I found and it as it looked like the hair had been burned off because the head had like black marks all over it, it was in an old house under the floorboard in Tilford I didn't find anything else but the doll had very faded like knife marks all over it it does look like a very old wooden doll.

It very much sounds like this doll was deliberately burned and possibly deliberately cut with a knife.

Another fascinating find from Woolhope in Herefordshire is of a nineteenth-century coffin curse. This consists of a small human effigy lying in a coffin. The body is pinned to the back of the coffin with a nail. It was found concealed in a wall in 1987.

At the Bakers' Arms Pub at Thorpe Langton in Leicestershire, a dried kitten was discovered 'at the back of a mud wall'. The cat was found 'spread-eagled and its guts had broken out through its belly wall'. The wall is thought to date from the eighteenth century and clearly the animal had been handled in some way for it to have been found in this condition.

At the Church Inn, Church Lane, Prestwich, workmen discovered that there was a bricked up alcove in the cellar. When they removed the wall they discovered a small bag containing three carved wooden female figures which were naked. They also found a pile of vegetable matter and a dried cat. It would appear that some kind of ritual was being enacted, using roots or other plant matter, a sacrificial cat and these figures. The direct proximity to the churchyard suggests a possible connection with the dead. The figures were deemed to have been stylistically similar to sixteenth- to seventeenth-century country carvings but it was not possible to say with any certainty. The pub does date back to the first half of the seventeenth century. The fact that these objects were bricked up strongly suggests a secret activity was taking place along with a desire not to disturb the objects.

In effect, these examples are proof that activities related to black magic really happened and that people had just cause to attempt to counter this by implementing measures that could variously trap, repel or decoy these harmful intentions. Belief in magic as a real force for good or ill was visceral and normal which explains the huge amount of effort which went into handling the fear around black magic and goes some way to explaining the popularity of the cunning folk.

These examples represent just a small portion of the objects out there which appear to have been used to cause harm. Most people would have been fairly careful, for obvious reasons, about leaving evidence of their nefarious activities lying around so there is not as much of this material remaining as there is for material used for protection. Also, fear of witchcraft was probably far greater than the actual practice of dark witchcraft – perhaps analogous to crime and the fear of crime in the current era. Much of dark witchcraft was actually concerned with ill-wishing, or the evil eye, which in itself would leave no physical trace. William Paynter captured the essence of witchcraft in Cornwall in his writings, skilfully revived by Jason Semmens. In his descriptions of interactions between people and alleged witches, the power of a dark look, or an ill-timed crossing of paths comes across clearly. Paynter seems to have captured the very essence of what it was like to live with widespread witchcraft beliefs.

When a culture strongly believes in magic, there will be those who are regarded as witches (whether male or female), those who become experts in it such as cunning folk and wise women, and everyone else. The general population will largely feel at the mercy of more powerful players and will rely on folk magic for their security and well-being. Occasionally they will need to interact with experts for help which might mean paying a cunning person for their services.

Everyone in the society will have a view on magic and will probably believe that good or evil intent exists in that realm. The need to protect and the desire to harm using magic appear to have manifested in every age and every part of the world. It is remarkable how similar many of the beliefs and methods are, suggesting that magical thinking is integral to the human condition.

⚙ Conclusion

In the past there was a fairly clear understanding in popular culture that supernatural power could be used by people for good or ill; witchcraft was the main focus of this knowledge. The same ideas existed in elite culture too but tended to focus more on high magic with theories and cosmologies being more prevalent in the explanations for it. There was of course every level in between these two positions, often with cunning folk transmitting parts of elite ideas into their dealings with their customers. Print also brought many of these ideas into popular awareness through pictures and people sharing knowledge of the text. As time moved on and education improved, popular knowledge of science has led to increasing cynicism regarding magical beliefs of all kinds, leading to a gradual fading away, but not the complete disappearance of, magical building protection techniques.

The pervasiveness of beliefs in supernatural evil were very well known. In Rowland Parker's *The Common Stream*, the author writes:

> Even the most cynical of those yeomen, when building his house, would take care to incorporate in its structure a talisman to ensure that it and its occupants would enjoy some measure of protection from bad fortune, evil spirits, witchcraft and the like. This talisman usually took the form of animal bones, or a shoe, or a piece of iron, embedded in the chimney-stack, under the threshold, at the base of a wall, wherever the evil spirits were most likely to sneak in when the occupants were asleep or off guard. In the case of my own house the protective talismans were half a sheep's jawbone complete with teeth, and a little old shoe. (Parker 1976: 135)

It would appear that people have always had methods of repelling, trapping, diverting or confusing harmful supernatural forces which they perceive to be threatening their property, family or self. The marks and objects discussed in this book take us from the medieval period to well into the twentieth century and in some cases to the present. It is clear that methods of protection existed prior to this point too but that is for another book.

The practice of concealing horse skulls on their own appears to have been happening in the medieval period and ritual horse burials clearly took place from the earliest times, but the practice of concealing horse skulls under buildings is at least as old as our earliest known example which dates from the fourteenth century. Horses were reputed to be able to see evil spirits, perhaps because they sleep with their eyes open, and they also have a hugely beneficial relationship with humans. Their use appears to have been for foundation sacrifice, as an offering to the local spirit of place, but my feeling is that their heightened senses, their good relationship with humans and the distinctive appearance of a horse skull also play a strong part in their use.

It would also seem that concealing cats is for foundation sacrifice purposes but there is, I think, also the notion that the spirit of the cat might go about its vermin catching duties on a more spiritual plane. The examples where the cat has been positioned as if it were in the hunt reinforces this idea.

Concealing shoes for magical protection appears to be linked to the legend of the unofficial thirteenth-century saint John Schorn, around whom a hugely popular pilgrimage arose spreading his imagery of casting the devil into a boot far and wide. However, during the period of the witch trials, all methods of magical building protection saw an upturn in popularity. In addition to this, there are strong fertility connections with shoes and definitely a connection with infant mortality.

The many and varied protection marks described in this book range in date from the medieval through to at least as late as the nineteenth century. The daisy wheel appears to have its origins in prehistory as a solar symbol and was used widely as a deliberate design feature. Later it found its way into the canon of available marks which could be discretely scratched onto surfaces to bring light and protection to those around it. Marian marks were widespread for a long period, invoking the Virgin Mary's maternal protection and love to ward off evil influences. Christograms also appear but less often, perhaps because Christ's presence was the main focus in churches and many buildings would already have crucifixes as part of their décor. Mesh marks acted as a symbolic net which could either trap or bamboozle energies that encountered them, the idea being that the scratched marks literally leave a ghost-line highly visible to those existing on an ethereal plane. The same concept applies to burn marks which are the physical vestige of an ethereal flame forever shining a light in a vulnerable spot in a building.

Bottles and other vessels have always been used for mixing concoctions of any kind, whether culinary or magical. The emergence of witch-bottles around the third quarter of the seventeenth century was a direct response to the period of the witch trials. Although the literature which mentions witch-bottles focuses on boiling the bottle and its contents specifically to undo bewitchment, the physical evidence appears to suggest that bottles were routinely concealed in the area of the hearth specifically as a lure and trap for harmful energies entering a property via the chimney.

Written charms are more self-explanatory than the other find types. They declare their intention and focus of protection in the text but are supplemented by Christian invocations, astrological symbols, magical words and occult symbols. The act of concealing these charms and the rituals which precede it are also highly significant. The actual charm is the end product of a serious amount of effort.

Other cases like Pentre at Bronygarth demonstrate that there were a range of foundation practices which may pre-date or have run alongside many of these find types. Stones with crosses crudely cut onto them, piles of bones beneath wall foundations and probably some element of ritual appears to have been used here. I strongly suspect that foundation sacrifices were not uncommon and still occur in some places, for example in Albania where a colleague recently showed me a video of a goat being sacrificed in modern concrete foundation. In Romania there is a ritual of sacrificing one's own shadow to a new building plot, as Adina Hulubaş related in her lecture in Salisbury in April 2018. In her paper she says:

> Deposits with ritual characteristics managed to preserve up to the end of the last century a magic practice mentioned in 1894 by G.W. Speth and two years later by Clay Trumbull: the shadow of a person is measured with a piece of a thread or a stick, and then the instrument used is walled up. This represents the second phase of the human sacrifice. (Hulubaş 2018)

Merrifield relates the ritual where a horse skull is placed on a stake and has beer poured over it prior to commencing the building of a chapel in Norfolk in the late nineteenth century (Merrifield 1987: 126). Clearly there is a whole area of ritual and practice relating to setting out the plot and laying the foundation which we know less about, for obvious reasons, than those parts of the building which remain above ground. These rites and rituals seem more about sacrificing to the spirit of place than a reaction to witchcraft, but were intended to bring more security, prosperity and protection to a building.

All this material is very important for developing a true understanding of what witchcraft actually meant to real people. For a long time historians have been producing vast quantities of literature looking at the documents relating to witchcraft and this inevitably focuses on the literature around the witch trials and pamphlets which were often spin-offs from these. The elite view of witchcraft, represented through the judiciary and clergy, was one which tended to concentrate on the heresy of witchcraft and attempted to interpret all the testimony through that lens. One should also bear in mind the fact that the vast majority of individuals who ended up being tried for witchcraft often had nothing at all to do with it. There were many reasons why an individual could end up in court for witchcraft, usually to do with mis-interpretation of actions, being in the wrong place at the wrong time, or being ill-regarded by their neighbours. The occasional use of torture or extended periods of imprisonment could also take their toll on the truth. The result is that we have often ended up with fascinating books about witch trials, opinions about witchcraft, miscarriages of justice and interesting social histories. What we rarely get from the documents is any real sense of how people perceived magic and the evidence for their interactions with it. The objects and symbols discussed in this book were made by real people as a direct result of their beliefs in witchcraft and they tell us a good deal about the way in which magic was perceived and witchcraft was experienced.

The physical evidence explored in this book is just a tiny portion of what was actually concealed in buildings or scratched onto their surfaces. We must remind ourselves that only a fortunate few buildings have survived intact for many hundreds of years affording us the opportunity to explore their nooks and crannies for artefacts of magic. It is also important to remember that it is normally only through alteration, demolition or accident that these objects are discovered, and then only if someone has the initiative and desire to report it to someone.

When people sought to protect themselves from supernatural harm, they would tackle it in a multitude of ways which could include hiding a charm about their person, saying a charm, consuming a potion, using a religious blessing, performing an action or a combination of all of these. Concealing objects in their walls, up their chimneys, beneath their floors, in their roof spaces or through charms or markings was a choice that demanded much effort but was thought to be highly effective.

PART II

EVIDENCE AND EXAMPLES

:●: Case Studies

Some buildings seem to have a bit of everything going on inside them, such as Church Farmhouse in Wormleighton, Warwickshire, which is reputed to have hosted pentagrams, daisy wheels and witch-bottles. Here are a few examples where we can look at a building as a whole instead of just at individual find types. Doing this helps to build an appreciation of the way in which people approached the subject of house protection.

Forncett, Norfolk
At a house in Bentley Road, Forncett End, Forncett, many deposits were found. The house dates from the early seventeenth century at the latest. Edwin Rose provides the following information: 'In the back of the fireplace several fragments of scythe blades and pieces of iron, and four small bones with holes drilled in them were found. Apparent inscriptions on first floor with possible ritual significance. The ground floor ceiling of the main room has been removed and three painted circles with crosses within them have been found on a joist. Two other crosses occur in a similar position. The main fireplace bressumer, now stripped of laths, has a complex of Sussex marigolds (or "hexes"). Above the ceiling were found nine pieces of flint, and a lanyard with a piece of turned wood.'

La Vignassa, Italy
In the village of Torre Pellice in Northern Italy there is a B&B run by Ian Stimpson. In November 2007 he reported discoveries including daisy wheels, shoes and two bottles from within the house. The house lies in a Protestant valley which is historically the heartland of the Waldensian region. The building dates from multiple periods, having been begun

in the 1500s, added to progressively up to the 1700s, with a few smaller changes in the early 1800s. Daisy wheels have been found on two plaster walls, on a door lintel and on a door. They also found two glass bottle ends cemented into the rear wall, although Ian thought this could just be '18th century builders having a bit of fun'. Also found were '3 coins from the 1700s one placed above each door lintel in the mid-part of the house and in the oldest room which we think dates from the early 1500s'. A small dish was found bricked up in the chimney and, although not concealed, several single shoes dating from the 1800s were found in the loft spaces. This is a fascinating range of finds which are probably fairly common in that area.

Llancaiach Fawr

Not far from Merthyr Tydfil and Caerphilly in Wales is the sixteenth-century Llancaiach Fawr Manor. The building is largely in the same condition as it was when the grand staircase was added in the mid-seventeenth century. Many objects and marks have been found within the walls and fireplaces of the building and more recently staff member, Alicia Jessup, has discovered a large number of protection marks.

Near the front entrance the first discovery to mention is that of a dried cat which was uncovered in the ceiling.

When the threshold timber between the servants' hall and kitchen was taken up from the floor, which is otherwise large flagstones, it was found to have a huge number of nails hammered into the underside. It is well known that iron is thought to repel witches so this could be a

Figure 11.1 Llancaiach Fawr Manor, Wales. © Brian Hoggard.

deliberate counter-witchcraft measure. The door frame here has more than twenty burn marks on it. At Llancaiach Fawr almost every original door frame and chimney lintel that remains is protected by at least one, though many have several.

The servants' hall fireplace is the site of a number of discoveries. The chimney lintel has an array of deep burn marks and a number of deeply carved angular symbols – possibly Marian marks. Fireplaces are almost always the principal focus of protection because they are always open to the sky and therefore particularly vulnerable to evil forces. In this one a niche was found inside on the right-hand side which contained two different colours of human hair, a knife blade, a hare's foot, a small bag, a twist of paper, linen, cloth and a piece of scarlet cloth with lamb's wool attached. The knife blade and hair are particularly diagnostic of this being a counter-witchcraft deposit. Hair is used in witch-bottles as part of the lure to fool evil energy into attacking it instead of you. Knife blades are made of iron and hence useful against witchcraft. The hare's foot was considered a lucky charm. The fabrics were likely to have been taken from garments belonging to the occupants, again to act as a lure or decoy away from the real person. The linen bag contains herbs; these bags were often carried to repel 'miasmas' or bad air that was thought to carry disease. The twist of paper has been very carefully formed, and although it now appears blank, it seems likely that it once contained some manner of charm. Beneath the fireplace itself a number of deliberately placed pins were found along with an 1806 halfpenny.

The grand staircase was added in 1628 and a number of shoes, leather-work, textiles, ceramics and bones were discovered in voids beneath it. The bones included articulated bones with flesh still attached, vertebrae and a jawbone, all belonging to a medium sized animal. The headboard from a child's crib, a child's whistle and a dried bat were also found. The child's whistle and crib headboard are here as a decoy, drawing any evil looking to prey on a child into this area instead of wherever the actual child lay.

Images of the shoes were sent to footwear expert June Swann who dated them largely to the seventeenth century. Interestingly, one of the shoes is of a much later date than the others, suggesting that in the nineteenth century the cache of shoes was discovered and, rather than being removed, was added to.

Other items found beneath the stairs included fine linen, scarlet fabric, a piece of silk, unbleached servants' linen, brown servants' linen, part of knitted hose, bits of broken pot and bone, a bit of kid skin, pieces of glass, a large boring device and a board bearing the Pritchard seal (the family who built the manor). So here we have more fragments of personal attire which could act as a decoy, luring evil away from its intended target. The fragments of glass and pottery no doubt formed part of the trap.

Upstairs, above the entrance porch, is a small attic space once used as a servants' chamber. It has a huge number of burn marks on the main beam and door frame. Alicia has counted over one hundred marks in this small space alone. The marks not only cover the roof beams and door: there is a small draw bar which would have been used to lock the space from the inside, and even the inside of the socket for this is scorched.

Other marks in the building include numerous Marian marks on oak panelling, beams and elsewhere on stone and incised into plaster. These run through all levels of the house, but are most prevalent in the parlour, the highest status room.

There are also several small and large carved crosses occurring in wood and stone in the building; they are particularly concentrated around staircases, doors and windows. As the house is semi-fortified there are many places where oak beams can be drawn across to barricade doors. Only one of these original beams remains and carved into it is a small cross, which has also been scorched. Alicia has also discovered some interlocking circles and in the main attic spaces two meshes carved into the beams. There are also numerous undeciphered marks and symbols, one of which is the outline of a coffin with a cross carved into its centre.

The final discovery from Llancaiach Fawr is that of a pentagram carved onto a stone which was found in the outer wall. The stone was facing inwards to the wall so the carving was not visible at all. This is not a crudely scratched pentagram but a well carved one and clearly of considerable age, perhaps contemporary with the building, 1550 (Hoggard and Jessup 2017: 51–55).

Pentre, Bronygarth, Shropshire

This house has layers of protection going back to the medieval period. I am not sure if any building has been so meticulously investigated as this one thanks to the enthusiasm and curiosity of its current owner and custodian, James Lloyd, whose family have lived at the same house for well over a hundred years.

In this house there are numerous burn marks on a chimney lintel and other timbers, there are several examples of concentric circles carved onto timbers, a pentagram, mesh marks, a spiritual midden, foundation sacrifices, a re-used ecclesiastical stone, an ancient stone head, large pebbles placed at the corners of a room with crosses and other marks on them, use of iron blades, glass, pottery, and that list is not exhaustive.

A large cavity was found above the front door which had some paper in it which had been shredded by a mouse. To have paper concealed in a cavity suggests the presence of a written charm but in the absence of a whole piece of paper we can only speculate.

When excavating the old front door threshold, a very old black-smith-made cut-throat razor was found, as well as cat vertebrae and two stones with scratched crosses on them, identical to the one under the main hearth. One of these was found under the step and the other in a strange alcove build into the wall at chest height. This alcove was originally thought to be the door beam slot but no other reciprocal slot existed when the plaster was removed on the other side of the door entrance wall.

Also found under the door threshold was one bright white bone (probably belonging to a goose) with two deliberate 'stab' marks through it. Also found under the step was a stone bearing a cross, carved concentric circles and the letters 'SyP'. The character of the marks on this slab appears medieval, in the style of high-quality graffiti.

All this material was covered in charcoal where someone had clearly had a small fire in the middle of the threshold. In addition, some broken, buried, worn stone fragments and some shards of pots were found.

From beneath the hearth a stone was found with a large incised cross going through it, similar to a St Andrews cross, and beneath that a copper alloy (bronze?) ring with circle and dot decoration, awaiting cataloguing but understood to be Celtic or Romano British with 'evil eye' decoration.

During an excavation to recess a radiator, bones were found which had been placed beneath large foundation stones under the external walls in the dining room. They had clearly been placed there and not discarded following feasting. They were identified as cat, lamb or possibly dog bones. Further and possibly later incised voids along the whole length of the external walls were found to contain bones (likely to be cat and goose) and broken glass (port bottle) pushed between the foundation blocks. One also contained a partially broken medieval pilgrim's badge and folded lead object.

One of the foundation stones in the corner of the room was found to have numerous criss-crossing marks on it, resembling mesh marks and a cross. These have been deemed to be glacial striations but in my experience it is quite rare to find a site with glacial striations which is also a quarry for foundation stone. It has been surmised that these stones

Figure 11.2 Foundation deposit of bones from Pentre, Bronygarth.
Reproduced with permission of James Lloyd.

were chosen specifically because they bear these marks which added to the spiritual armoury of the building. I think there is a fair chance that these marks were applied to the stones; it is a much simpler approach than finding a site with striations and ordering someone to quarry out that surface material for use as building material.

A stone loom weight (iron age to early medieval) was found built in to the wall beneath an exterior window. Five years earlier the owner found a similar stone in the same position under the adjacent kitchen window of the property. These are fairly crude in appearance and I take their deliberate concealment beneath the window to mean that they were seen as holed stones in this context. Hag-stones (stones with naturally occurring holes) were often hung outside buildings to ward off witchcraft.

The lintel over the main fireplace has burn marks, overlapping circles and also some short but deeply carved characters carved into the edge. These characters take the form of short, thick lines angled to form M, V and W marks, so they may be Marian marks, but in a very different style to those we normally see elsewhere. Also present is a large symbol '6' on the underside of the lintel.

There are burn marks on several other timbers in the building including in the stairwell and on timbers on the upper floor, mainly around doorways.

There is also a circled pentagram clearly carved onto a timber above one of the bedroom doors. This was discovered after the removal of later Georgian lath and plaster covering the beam.

In the attic there are several examples of concentric circle marks (as seen on the cover of this book), more burn marks and also a range of marks that are somewhere between Marian marks and a kind of mesh pattern. There are also numerous carpenters' marks throughout the building which are identical to marks on timbers at nearby Chirk Castle.

A cache of objects was found beneath the floor at the left-hand side of the main fireplace. It contained bones, fragments of glass, pottery and a quantity of some rusted metal objects (iron), a padlock, an iron loom weight and iron spikes, as well as numerous children's 'marbles', some made of pottery with painted dot decoration.

Immediately above this 'midden' of objects was a concealed compartment in the ceiling containing hundreds of carefully placed walnuts and a child's spinning top. Witches had an association with walnut trees from ancient times and so this may have been an offering to persuade a witch to leave a child alone.

The ceiling in the adjacent room sealed in between the rafters contained the soles of children's shoes, spinning tops, glass, broken pots, clothing, a leather belt and some carved objects. Also present are hand prints in the original wattle and daub panelling.

There is a natural spring in the garden on the site and it appears to have been venerated. Numerous coins and objects have been found in the vicinity and approximately forty years ago an ancient stone head (50 to 200 BC/early medieval attribution) was dug up by a farm hand. It has now been included in a wall around the property. The head is considered to be in the same tradition as, and likely related to, two stone heads previously discovered a few hundred yards away at Well cottage in Bronygarth, now in the care of the British Museum. The heads, one of which is janiform, are believed to represent Celtic gods Amon and Mabon.

Also present are numerous large white quartz stone blocks that are thought to have once surrounded the spring. Similar quartz blocks have been found around burial cairns and holy springs throughout Wales.

The house, dated 1591, is built on top of the foundations of at least one much earlier building; the timbers of the earlier building were reused, clearly evidenced in the arched truss and plank and muntin screen elements seen throughout.

This building really does have a bit of everything.

Looking at buildings as a whole like this, particularly in the case of one like Pentre, shows how protection was considered at so many different points in the evolution of the structure, from foundation deposits to items hidden in the walls, from marks added to timbers to more objects inserted during renovations and rebuilding.

⚫ Finds Gazetteer

These lists comprise finds which were reported to me personally or which have worked their way into the database over the years. Many researchers have compiled their own lists in areas where they live and I do not intend to duplicate those here or copy every find reported in every paper. Over the years many finds have been reported anecdotally and I have not sought to include all ofthose reports in this book – it would take up far too much space. What you see in this list is a selection which convey something of the character of the reports I have received. The spelling and use of language in the reports has been preserved to maintain authenticity, any inconsistencies are the product of that decision.

The precise addresses and names of many of those involved in these discoveries have been removed in the interests of data protection but bona fide researchers can make a request for information to the author via www.apotropaios.co.uk.

England – by County/Area

Bedfordshire

A dried rat was found in the wall of the now demolished White Horse Inn, **Bedford**. From Pennick 1995.

VV marks and others exist at **Biddenham** Church.

A dried cat in hunting position was found in **Bletsoe**, Bedford. The house is a thatched eighteenth-century extension to a medieval house and the discovery was made in the 1970s. The builders who found it disposed of it.

At a cottage in Town Lot Lane, **Felmersham**, Bedfordshire, a bellarmine witch-bottle was discovered beneath the site of the old hearth by builders in late 2001. The house is estimated to be around 300 years old. The tiles were taken up because the floors were damp and beneath the dirt, cobbles were found. One area of the floor did not have cobbles and it was while digging in this area that the bottle was discovered inverted and with a clear blockage in its neck (excepting a small hole). The bottle was discovered at around the same level as the cobbles. The builders washed the bottle and almost certainly destroyed the liquid evidence it contained. I collected the bottle on 22 November 2001 and within a week took it to Dr Alan Massey in Loughborough for analysis of its contents. A large lock of dark hair was discovered in addition to a congealed mass of nails and pins. When consulted, Dr David Gaimster, the foremost expert on stoneware, reported 'The bottle appears to be a good example of a Frechen stoneware *Bartmann* bottle, typical of the cargo of so many Dutch East India Company wrecks, particularly the VOC *Vergulde Draeck*, lost off Western Australia in 1656. So lets say mid to third quarter 17th century'. The finders eventually sold the item on ebay despite our arranging for a local museum to purchase it from them.

A complete and articulated horse skull and neck was found in a well at **Grove Priory**, Bedfordshire, dating to the first part of the fourteenth century.

The **Harlington** Heritage Trust journal reported, in early 2006, 'A pair of boots, date circa 1760, were found in an alcove at "Asphodel Cottage", the former village butchers'.

At Church Farm in **Little Woolstone**, a small glass phial was found when the first-floor ceiling of this seventeenth-century building partially collapsed.

In the grave of a young adult at All Saints Church, **Loughton**, a late seventeenth/eighteenth- century glass steeple bottle was discovered lying between the left humerus and upper chest. The bottle contained several copper pins and a number of pins were also stuck into the cork. The bottle contained liquid which may be urine, although no analysis has yet been attempted on this substance. The author of the report into the bottle, David Bonner, notes that witch-bottles are unusual in this context. Source: Bonner 1994.

A dried cat was discovered in 1915 in **Woburn Abbey** during demolition work. According to the TV report, it was found 'in an airtight brick container'. It retained its skin and whiskers but its fur was gone. The cat was on display at the Walter Rothschild Zoological Museum in Tring, Hertfordshire. According to the expert interviewed, the cat was 300 years old.

Berkshire

At **Boxford**, two women's leather shoes dated to the late seventeenth century were found in the chimney of a cottage.

A devil figure (photo on file) in unfired clay was discovered by a thatcher while replacing old thatch in a cottage at **Chieveley**; the owner returned it to its original location after recording.

A group of objects were found concealed in the fireplace of a cottage at **Eastbury**. They comprised an iron heel 'protector', a large iron horse shoe, a knotted and twisted stem (photo on file) and iron nails.

At **East Hendred**, a wooden figure of a cat was found in the thatch of an old house. From *Country Life*, 1955, p. 1682.

A dried cat was discovered in a cottage at **Lambourn**. After being recorded, it was returned to its 'resting place'.

During demolition, a single leather man's shoe dated to the seventeenth century was found between the wall of the Plaza (formerly the King's Arms Inn) and the adjacent building in Market Place, **Newbury**.

A single leather woman's shoe dated to 1680/90 was discovered under floorboards on the first floor of a property in Cheap Street, **Newbury**.

Concealed shoes from **Sonning** were reported in Perkins and Edmonds 1999: 74: 'Some years ago, a small fabric shoe was discovered in a chimney in Old Cottage, Pearson Road. The blue, green, soft rust and pink scroll and flower pattern of the brocade can still be followed... shoe is dyed 1720-30 when wealthy girls had their footwear covered to match their dresses, and this one had been recovered twice if not three times'.

An 8 inch lock of hair was discovered in a chimney breast in a house in **Speen.** The house dates to 1890. Reported in May 2004.

A concealed shoe was found in a loft in **Windsor**. The find was reported by Janet Pennington.

In a house at **Wolverton Common** near Basingstoke, a single leather man's shoe dated to the late seventeenth/early eighteenth century was found built into the fireplace.

Buckinghamshire

At an early seventeenth-century Manor House in Buckinghamshire, there are various marks on the lintel of the kitchen fireplace including spectacle marks, and other marks on the staircase.

A bellarmine witch-bottle was recovered from a fireplace in **Winslow**, Buckinghamshire. Reported in Farley 1978.

A report of a concealed shoe was e-mailed on 27 October 2015. 'Some years ago I was restoring a late C16th cottage in **Wooburn Green**, Buckinghamshire, and on removing a small zinc plate fixed to the floor boards in a bedroom I found beneath a beautiful little fabric shoe with leather sole and toe cap and blue stone buttons, which although small (approximately for a 4 year old today) was well worn on the sole and toe cap. It intrigued me sufficiently to take it to the V&A where a conservator directed me to the children's museum in Bethnel Green ... She was able to date the shoe at around 1867, amazingly precise but apparently styles of the day can be quite accurately dated'. See Figure 3.3.

Cambridgeshire and Peterborough

A large collection of assorted objects was discovered behind the chimney breast of a building in the High Street, **Brampton** (Huntingdon district) during repairs in 1985. This hoard included post-medieval glazed sherds, a wine bottle, a sharpening stone, slag (there was a forge next door), animal bone (horse, sheep, pig, duck skull, oyster shells), iron nails and window glass. This appears to be a spiritual midden.

A dried cat is preserved at Eaden Lilley's Department Store in Market Street, **Cambridge**. The cat was discovered in a basement wall in 1811 with a dried rat in its mouth. From Pennick 1995. There is a photo of this cat and rat in Pennick 1986: 7. Ivan Bunn describes it as follows: 'According to tradition a mummified cat with a rat in its mouth was discovered in the cellar wall in 1811. The cat and rat are still preserved at the store; the former is painted shiny black with the date 1811 AD painted on it. For many years after its discovery it hung in the cellar from a piece of string. Today the cat and rat have been moved from the cellar and removed to a first floor office suite where they still remain, wired to a green baize board. They are not on view to the general public but are brought out at talks on company history and similar occasions!' Ivan quotes his source as the *Cambridge Weekly News*, 23 April 1981, in addition to personal communications with W. Eaden Lilley.

A dried cat was found in 1988 during building work in a cavity over a second-floor door in a house in King's Parade, **Cambridge**. From Pennick 1995. A report of the same cat was made by Cambridgeshire SMR Office in September 2001.

A leg bone of a horse, dating to the sixteenth century, was discovered in the stables of the former White Horse Inn, **Cambridge** (now Cambridge Folk Museum). From Pennick 1986: 6. Ivan Bunn adds that the horse bone was found in a cavity beneath the foundations. Ivan's source was Porter 1969: 181.

A ruminant leg bone was discovered concealed in the chimney of a room at Magdalene College, **Cambridge**. From Pennick 1986: 7. Ivan Bunn describes this as follows: 'During the restoration of a 17th century room a dog's leg bone was found carefully inserted in the bricks of the chimney breast. Now in Cambridge Folk Museum'. Ivan's source was Porter 1969: 181.

Ivan Bunn reports that at the Three Tuns Inn on Market Hill, **Cambridge**, 'ancient shoes (now in Cambridge Folk Museum) were discovered when this 17th century inn was demolished'. He quotes his source as Porter 1969: 181.

A dried cat was discovered during the renovation of King's Parade, Cambridge. It was reported by and is now retained by the builder who found it. My correspondent Tim Reynolds reports, 'The cat was found at the back of a chimney/fireplace on the ground floor of a late medieval building'. It is thought that the cat must have been deposited in late medieval / Tudor times based on the builder's description of recovering it.

In 2004 I received the following e-mail concerning the discovery of a miniature shoe in a Victorian house in **Cambridge**: 'I thought I would mail you re: a find made in my parents' Cambridge Victorian home in 1986. The house itself was built in the 1880s and in 1986 my parents were having the first floor bathroom renovated. This involved pulling out and replacing one of the original windows. In the space between the wall and the frame the builders found a tiny but perfectly formed leather shoe. It is about 2 inches long with a 2cm heel, and the leather is sewn together with exquisite stitching. There was just the one shoe found but the other original sash window was left in place so we don't know whether it was part of a pair or a one off. We assumed it was a doll's shoe – is that likely? The builders who found it told us they often find shoes and other objects in old houses, and asked us for something of ours to put in the new wallspace for later generations to find. I believe we gave them a pair of swimming flippers!'

A concealed snake skin was found at a house in **Cottenham**, Cambridge. This was reported by Joff Duck who 'had discovered a few items concealed within two spine beams, in her parlour and her hall. These included a button with a note wrapped around it, dated 1617, a coin from the 1630s, a playing card from the 1680s, a few pages of an C18th bible and several rat skeletons in the daub in the external walls ... she discovered a snake skin wrapped up and stuffed into a small "compartment" as she called it, in the underside of the beam'.

At Ely Porta, **Ely**, two Elizabethan boys' shoes were found in a bricked-up cavity.

In Broad Street, **Ely**, a dried cat was found in a fifteenth-century cottage.

A dried cat was discovered in a house in 'the old part' of **Ely**. The house is close to the river Ouse and is between the river and the cathedral (no further details provided). The house is thought to date to 1350, has a brick ground floor and timber framed first floor. The cat was found during restoration work and had been concealed in a fireplace. A short article was published in the *Cambridge Evening News* of 19 May 1984 with the following title: 'Cat is clue to ancient past. Feline clue to one of the country's oldest houses'. In the article it is said that the cat is thought to be 600 years old. The cat is currently kept in a box in the attic.

Medieval (this term is used extremely loosely in this context) shoes were apparently discovered in a builders' spoil heap in High Street, **Ely** and taken away by an expert from the Antiques Roadshow television series. It is quite likely that they were formerly concealed.

A dried cat is reputed to be kept in the windmill at **Fulbourn**. From Pennick 1995. Deborah Oliver reported the same cat in 2007 via e-mail saying: 'I don't have any particular information about dried cats in general, but know of one (I'm not sure if it's already been recorded) in the windmill in Fulbourn, near Cambridge. It belonged to the family of a schoolfriend and as you walked up the stairs there was a small alcove in an internal wall (lit up so you could see it) with a mummified cat in it. The legend was, as I remember, that it used to belong to a past miller, and that if it were taken out, the mill would fall down. As far as I know, it's still there – it certainly was in 1989 when I saw it'.

A slightly faint and maybe incomplete daisy wheel can be found at the church at **Guilden Morden**, Cambridgeshire.

Half a horse jawbone was discovered, dating from the seventeenth century, between two courses of brick in the chimney in a house in **Histon**. A horse leg bone was found in another house in the village, also adjacent to the chimney. From Pennick 1986: 6. Ivan Bunn describes this one as 'a number of horse bones, found between two courses of brickwork during restoration. The largest of these is preserved in the Cambridge Folk Museum'. He quotes his source as Porter 1969: 180–81.

Ivan Bunn reports the discovery of a pot in an unidentified cottage in **Histon**. He says, 'during alterations to an old hearth in the cottage a 17th century salt-glazed pot was discovered behind the original fireback'. He quotes his source as Porter 1969: 181.

A written curse was discovered behind a skirting board at a home in **Isleham**. Reporting the find in an e-mail in July 2012, the correspondent said: 'Found a note behind skirting boards. Difficult to decode but reads something like this:

> *I damn those that are employed and stoe this letter dwelling for none payment for*
> *carpentry work undertaken*
> *Joseph Datton*
> *May 5th 1892'*

At **Linton** a dried cat was found in the Anchor public house (now an antiques shop). From Pennick 1995. Ivan Bunn says this about a Linton find which must surely be the same one Pennick refers to: 'skull of a cat discovered in the brickwork of a chimney in the [unidentified] house'. Ivan quotes his source as the Cambridge Folk Museum.

Two dirty shoes dating to the early seventeenth century were discovered at the Green Hill public house in **Linton**. Reported in the *Cambridge Evening News*, 25 May 1979, p26.

In the *Cambridge Evening News*, 25 May 1979, p26, 'Witchcraft in Pub', it was reported that a greybeard jug, knives, a riding crop and a reaping hook had all been discovered in **Linton.**

In **Little Downham** a witch-bottle was discovered beneath an entrance stone. The bottle was retained by the finder.

At a house in the High Street, **Melbourn**, a dried toad, apparently pierced, was found embedded in a wall. From Pennick 1995.

A dried cat was discovered in a wall of the Angel Hotel, Narrow Street, **Peterborough** and donated to Peterborough Museum in 1900 – now lost. From Pennick 1995.

A photograph of a witch-bottle reputedly found at **Sawston** appears in Porter 1969.

A daisy wheel can be found in a house in the High Street, **Swavesey** – the house was built in the 1600s.

A bellarmine jug (Bartmann ware) was discovered beneath the hearth of Pond Cottage in **Wennington** in January 1914. The jug had been used as a witch-bottle and when discovered had pins protruding from the neck which crumbled to pieces soon after discovery. Yeatherd 1920; there is also an article on the donor of the bottle in *Cambs & Hunts Life*, August 1988.

A dried cat was found in a wall during the renovation of a property in the High Street, **Willingham**. The animal was replaced at the request of the workmen. From Pennick 1995.

A shoe and 'mummified animal' were recovered from the chimney stack in the attic of a farm at **Witcham**, near Ely.

At **Yaxley** a bellarmine bottle was found in the rubble of old buildings.

Channel Islands

The following was reported on the BBC News website, 23 September 2005: 'A hidden collection of personal items has been found in the roof of the Priaulx Library in **Guernsey**. The objects were unearthed during work on the building by the foreman in charge of the repairs, Ken Laine. He discovered a child's boot in the roof space below a window. Other items including a purse, a coin, a pipe and a newspaper from 1889 were also found. They could have been put there as part of a tradition of hiding tokens in buildings to ward off evil spirits. The Priaulx has a piece of timber signed by workmen who carried out alterations to the roof in the late 1880s and it is thought they may have been the ones who concealed the objects. The find has been fully recorded and will be registered with the Concealed Garments Project at the University of Southampton'.

At a house in St Peter Port, **Guernsey**, Linda Hall notes a daisy wheel on panelling or wooden partition wall. Reported in February 2009.

John Billingsley reported in May 2016 that he had found some 'spectacle marks' on a door in Cliff Street, St Peter Port, **Guernsey**.

Six large animal bones were in an outbuilding by the house of L'Anciennete on **Jersey**. They are described as 'placed at regular intervals parallel with the slope of the gable. It was a curious building, impossible to date, with an irregular façade and few windows. In Guernsey one has heard of witches' steps made of bone inside a chimney, and one can only conclude that these projections, for which no practical purpose can be imagined, were for the use of witches' – from Stevens 1977.

At a house called Douet de Rue on **Jersey**, the following was reported: 'A door in the south wall of the oldest building on the property, the house in question, has been blocked at an unknown period and in the infill two small pottery jars were found, 5in. maximum circumference, and slightly under 3in. high. They are of Normandy ware, impossible to date accurately, put there to propitiate or repel witches incensed at finding a familiar door no longer open' – from Stevens 1977: 119.

At La Ferme, **Jersey**, the following was reported: 'This is a house where a square bottle, probably a Dutch gin bottle, was found embedded in a wall, with some stones, two at least of which were artefacts; there were also fragments of pots, and some seaweed. These objects must indicate "insurance" against witchcraft and lightning. There is a recess in the east bedroom wall which if investigated could prove to be a "paute"; it extends the full length of one's arm into the thickness of the wall, quite straight' – from Stevens 1977: 122.

In a house called Fontis on **Jersey**, dated 1714, the following was discovered: 'A garden wall running north-south must have been part of an earlier house as it contains a pair of fireplace corbels, on either side of which a square gin bottle was found buried, one being broken and the other whole. These were no doubt placed there as protection against the ubiquitous witch' – from Stevens 1977: 124.

At Highland Farm on **Jersey**, the following was reported: 'The fireplaces are simple, with wooden lintels, and in a recess in one of them were found a glass bottle, part of a cowhorn, and a stocking which must have been knitted locally; although rather tattered, it showed very fine stitching and well-made clocks in cinnamon brown wool. These objects were almost certainly concerned with witchcraft' – from Stevens 1977: 138.

At Le Mourin, **Jersey**, the following was reported: 'Perhaps the most interesting thing here is the square bottle found buried in the north wall, when a beam had to be replaced, and it is fortunate that it was recovered unbroken. In that position it was certainly intended as a specific against witches. Although popularly supposed to be gin bottles, such a design could be used for any sort of beverage. It is of a 17th century date' – from Stevens 1977: 162.

At La Rigondaine, **Jersey**, the following was reported: 'When uncovered, a niche beside a fireplace in the earlier house contained a curious assortment of objects, suggestive of folklore. Amongst them was a clay pipe with a macabre and emaciated face and prominent cheek bones, probably about 1850 in date, but a type not otherwise recorded in the Island. This motley collection of objects was probably intentional as a charm to avert evil spirits, or as a specific for curing an illness, such as rheumatism. The inclusion of an egg in the collection is a reminder that eggs were regarded as charms against whooping cough' – from Stevens 1977: 183.

At St Clement's Rectory, **Jersey**, two pale green glass witch-bottles were found in a space three feet from the summit of the outer wall while the building was being demolished in 1948. These bottles are held by Jersey Museums Service and this information was shared with me by Dr Alan Massey.

At a house in St Martin, **Jersey**, a home owner reported in June 2001 extensive 'graffiti' on her stone fireplace. The house dates from the sixteenth century, though with many alterations up to the nineteenth century – the fireplace is in the oldest part of the house in an upstairs bedroom. Drawings of the marks are on file.

In March 1999 a find of witch-bottles was reported to Dr Alan Massey: 'My husband and I bought a farm in St Ouen, **Jersey** where we retired in 1965. During the alterations we found buried in the walls two queer gin bottles which must have been witch-bottles. The chimney has a ledge on it for the witch to land on! They only contained shells – no gold coins to our sorrow. I now ... have the bottles on the top of a cupboard, with an antique taper holder, as a reminder of happy days before my husband's death'.

Mary Gibb reported in 2001: 'You may be interested to know that here in **Jersey**, when investigating a house in the parish of St. Martin called

La Chenais des Bois, a lot of ritual "graffiti" was found on an upstairs fireplace stone. The fireplace is in the form of an arch (most unusual in Jersey) and is of a limestone (probably Caen Stone). This is also most unusual in Jersey as most fireplaces are made of granite. The house was originally built in the16th century, but has had many alterations and additions since, notably in the 19th century. There are a lot of "M" "V" "W" and "P" shapes scratched into the three top stones of the arch, also crosses and triangles joined to these and other shapes'. Drawing of marks are on file.

Daisy wheel reported from **Jersey** by Stuart Fell (architect working on the island) in March 2008. He says it is on a beam above an entrance to a courtyard in a seventeenth-century building.

Cheshire

At **Blackden Hall**, Holmes Chapel, I was informed of the following finds:

– The owner, author Alan Garner, told me that a holed stone was hanging in the chimney of the building known as Toad Hall as it just fell down while he was working there.
– Also, in an attic space in Toad Hall there was a void by an inserted mid-seventeenth-century chimney. Alan spotted the void because a big lump of daub covered in gorse covered it. When he broke into it he discovered six shoes, two adult and four children's. The shoes have been dated to the 1680s.
– In a gable behind a tie beam he discovered the saddle stirrup.
– In the cross passage of Toad Hall on top of a rail in the framing, a glass phial was discovered which still contained some liquid/residue.
– A portion of a bellarmine bottle was discovered in a garden boundary (possible significance).
– Also in Toad Hall Alan discovered under a purlin a large smooth black stone which everyone present described as 'highly tactile!'. Clearly the stone was placed there on purpose.
– Many pieces of jet from Whitby have been found at the back of Toad Hall. Alan quoted an interesting passage from Bede on the properties of jet and amber.
– Under the doorstep of a former farm building an entire skeleton of a cart-horse was discovered in a foetal position.
– Another nearby former building also has an unexcavated horse burial beneath it.

– A dried cat has also been discovered in Blackden Hall. The hall was turned into a farm in 1880 and the fireplace was inserted at this time. Beneath the hearthstone was a constructed chamber into which the live cat was placed.
– Also discovered on adjacent land was a lead ampulla with a daisy wheel on one side and 'VV' on the other.

In a cottage in **Bollington**, near Prestbury, a creature of some kind was found beneath the small landing of an inserted staircase. 'The cottage was probably once a single open hall and then a chamber was inserted above. Then a staircase and small landing were inserted to access this bedroom. During maintenance work about ten years ago an object was found under the floorboards of the small landing. It has been described to me by the owner who saw it at the time it was discovered as looking like a "prehistoric animal with a long snout, curled up into a nest". Unfortunately the owner gave it to a relative who has since died. All the owner knows is that the relative put the object in a glass case'. Reported in January 2015.

In Astle Hall, **Chelford**, Cheshire, a dried rat was apparently walled in alive. The hall was built in 1645.

At **Little Moreton Hall** in 1992 eighteen assorted boots and shoes were discovered – all from the nineteenth century. From Brooks 2000.

There is a daisy wheel marked on a screen in St Oswald's, **Lower Peover**. Reported by Andy Bentham, February 2015.

At a farm in Weston Lane, **Shavington** near Crewe, a report of a concealed shoe recovered from chimney breast '20 years ago' was received in June 2007.

Cornwall and Isles of Scilly

An unusual report is of a stable boy's jawbone which was discovered beneath the floorboards of the stable-block at an eighteenth-century cottage in Castle Street, **Bodmin**. This information was included in the advertisement in the *Sunday Times* Home (section 10) for the house being sold which has five bedrooms, stables and a walled garden. Reported 3 February 2003.

The Museum of Witchcraft, **Boscastle** have their own modern witch-bottle created by the former curator Cecil Williamson. It seems that while living there he concealed his own in the soil at the back of the museum. According to the Museum who reported this to me, they found several of Cecil's witch-bottles there. There is an image on file of one of them which appears to be a large glass jar filled with urine.

Jason Semmens (2000) cites the discovery of some apparent witch-bottles from beneath **Bossiney Cross**. It was H. Mitchell Whitley who in 1881 while sketching the cross was told the story by a local farmer. The farmer told him that he had recently re-erected the cross, which had been overturned at some time, and that during the course of doing this he had 'found several bottles full of water, and with many pins in them, buried around its foot'. Jason continues in his article, 'These bottles were evidently fairly recent and it was not until Mitchell Whitley reached Boscastle that he discovered the meaning of them, for he was informed that: "If you are ill wished you must take a bottle, fill it with water, and put some pins in it, cork it tight, and then bury it at the foot of a holy cross; and the ill-wish will fall on the person who ill-wished you."' The original report of this appeared in *Devon and Cornwall Notes and Queries* 1921.

In the village of **Callington** it is reported that a witch-bottle was discovered. Jason Semmens kindly informed me of the relevant passage which is from Paynter 1929, viz: 'During a recent visit to a village not far from Callington, I was informed by a mason that while repairing an old fireplace he discovered a bottle of pins and needles, which had been placed there by a previous occupant as a talisman to preserve him and his family from the effects of the Evil Eye'.

In **Falmouth** a rabbit was discovered buried in a coffin at the top of a wall in a house. From Pennick 1995.

In **Gerrans** a witch-bottle was found buried inside a hedge at the entrance to a pre-Elizabethan manor house. Photo on file. An expert on bottles put this type of onion bottle at around 1700 or certainly in the early years of the eighteenth century.

In **Gerrans** a child's patten was discovered walled up in the chimney.

At **Godolphin House** (a large National Trust estate fairly near to Helston) a number of daisy wheels have been reported. Karen La Borde reported the following in April 2012: 'There are large and small daisy wheel marks scribed into the plaster at the rear of a 17th century fireplace in Godolphin House, Cornwall. The largest wheel probably measures half a metre across. There are also about a dozen smaller circles over the wall at the rear of the chimney'.

Jason Semmens (2000) reports a discovery near **Helston**. He states that one bottle containing earth and ash has been discovered built into the wall of a cob-built house near Helston.

A doll is on display at the Museum of Witchcraft in Boscastle which was found near **Padstow** in 1998. It is reported to have been bricked up in a recess and uncovered during renovation work. Initially the doll was sold to an antique dealer before coming into the possession of the Museum. Reported in Semmens 2000. The information card in the museum cites slightly different information, saying that the doll was donated to the museum in 1997.

In **Padstow** during repairs to an old cottage, a small cupboard was found hidden behind several layers of old wallpaper. Inside it was a nineteenthth-century corked and sealed wine bottle. The bottle was filled with liquid and contained a mounted group of carefully carved wooden 'instruments of passion' in miniature comprising a cross, two spades, two axes, a pair of pincers, two stakes and a ladder. Merrifield states that this bottle is unique; however, one was also found in Worcestershire. From Merrifield 1955. This bottle is referred to in Merrifield 1987. Jason Semmens (2000) reports that the name of the area where this bottle was found is Trevone.

In **Padstow** during alterations to the back kitchen of a shop, a witch-bottle was discovered in a chimney. It was a cod liver oil bottle that had been labelled by a firm in Exeter. Eight slightly bent pins and a needle were stuck in the outside of the cork. There were no pins inside the bottle, which otherwise contained a malodorous brown, slightly turbid liquid. It was found to be decayed urine. The bottle is now held in the Horniman Museum, London. From Merrifield 1987: 180–81 (excellent photograph on p. 181). Jason Semmens also mentions this in his article (2000) and adds that the discovery was made in the 1930s.

The Museum of Witchcraft at Boscastle has on display a small witch-bottle said to have been found during bomb damage clearance in the Barbican area of **Plymouth**. When the bottle was drained, the sludge within it was found to contain hair and small pins and little bits of painted bone splinters. I am grateful to the Museum for this information.

It was reported in the *Western Morning News* on 25 April 1970 that a witch-bottle had been found in the walls of a cottage on **St Mary's**, Isles of Scilly. The cottage was apparently due for demolition. The bottle is thought to date from the eighteenth century and its current whereabouts are unknown. Thanks to Jason Semmens for reporting this to me in December 2001.

Jason Semmens (2000) reports a discovery at a cottage near **Sennen**. Apparently, a bottle containing earth and ash was discovered within a recess in a chimney place there. The precise address is not known.

A glass witch-bottle from **Stratton** is on display in the Museum of Witchcraft, Boscastle. It contains hair, pins and what looks like chicken bones. I am grateful to the Museum for this information.

A witch-bottle and dried cat from a cottage in **Stratton** were reported in October 2006 by Graham King from the Museum of Witchcraft: 'The find consists of a cat, witch bottle and some "sticks with something wound round them". These objects were all found together in a wall. They were found by the owner of the cottage. I notice that the bottle is not very old – perhaps around 1850. The bottle has brown staining inside and no contents. It has not been opened since the find. Around the edge of the stopper are what looks like the remains of feathers. The owner has lost the "sticks with something tied around them" but thinks that they might turn up! I attach some photographs of the cat and bottle'.

'Two finely scribed daisies, placed on the top rail, on an early c17th Court Cupboard in **Cotehele House** (Tamar Valley, Cornwall, NT). The conservators seem well aware of them and of their significance'. Reported by Malcolm Dyer in April 2016.

A witch-bottle was discovered during work on one of the Railway Cottages at **Tresmeer** in 1928. Quoting from Jason Semmens (2000): 'The workmen were surprised when a bottle fell from the chimney and smashed upon the hearthstone. Upon inspection the bottle was found to contain pins and a lock of human hair, and it was removed to the window-sill where the curious came to see it. There was apparently "an unwillingness on the part of some of the inhabitants … to touch the broken bottle, lest some evil come upon them."' This extract came from the *Cornish and Devon Post* of 6 October 1928 and was quoted in Jason Semmens (2000).

Objects have been discovered at a house in Churchtown, **St Veap**, Lostwithial, reported in September 2001. In July the owner decided to remove the fireplace in the front room as it was not to her liking; in her words: 'To my complete surprise I found a very large fireplace with two ovens in it. One of the ovens is complete with door, hinges and catch. The other no longer has its door but it was in this one we found some interesting artefacts! There was the base of a wooden "shoe" which may have been a patten or overshoe! There was a piece of fabric and a wooden ball on a stick which is the size of a cricket ball. When we took up the floorboards we found pieces of broken glass one of which is the neck of a bottle. Further investigation ie in the roof leads us to believe the house may have been built in the C16th-17th'.

A pair of miner's boys boots are on display in the Wayside Folk Museum at **Zennor**. They are labelled as having come from the cottage chimney at old Boswednack Farm and the discovery was made in 1988.

Cumbria

At a former pub in Oakshaw Ford, **Bewcastle**, a number of artefacts have been discovered. In July 2003 it was reported as follows: 'I was currently gouging out some old lime mortar from the listed building my partner and I are renovating and two clay pipe bowls fell out. They appeared to be broken off at the very same point and one was large the other much smaller, possibly a woman's. We have also found horses teeth, bits of leather and a 1799 penny with unusual stamps marks on it and 5 holes punched in it (but not a pentacle formation as such)'. In a subsequent message she added, 'The pipe bowls were found in the upper part of the gable end wall (eastern end) – perhaps only 12' from the wall head. The horses teeth were also found in this wall. The penny was found in the middle rubble of the wall under one of the windows (south-facing). The bits of leather were found in one of the outhouses I think (north-facing)'. She adds that as there was a smithy next door, there would have been a ready supply of leather and horse teeth.

At Scarrow Hill, **Brampton**, Cumbria there are daisy wheels, dating from the seventeenth century.

Keswick Museum and Art Gallery reports a find of a dried cat at St Cuthbert's Church, **Clifton**, near Penrith. It was discovered between slates and plaster in the roof of the church during restoration in the mid-1840s. The church dates from the twelfth century but it is likely that the cat was added to the fabric during roof repairs at some later date.

A looped and socketed spearhead of the Late Bronze Age was discovered built into the walls of the fourteenth-century castle at **Dalton**. From Penney 1976.

At **Kirkby Stephen** there is a decorated stone lintel above an alley way leading off from the Market Place – it has a designed daisy wheel and the date 1636. In the church there are pentagrams on one tomb and a daisy wheel on another.

A looped and socketed spearhead of the Late Bronze Age was discovered built into the walls of the fourteenth-century castle at **Piel**. From Penney 1976.

At **Sedburgh** it was reported that 'The House Detectives' were enquiring locally to discover more information regarding some shoes which were found in a house there.

At **Thrimby Hall**, Westmorland (Cumbria) in 1860 a quantity of horse skulls was discovered under the parlour floor where they are alleged to have been placed for acoustic reason. From Armitage 1989b.

In June 2002 the following report of a cat was received from Ian Lewis: 'Hi. Under the flags, immediately in front of the fireplace [of a property in] Stanley St, **Ulverston**, Cumbria a neighbour found a squashed kitten quite mummified! This was 5 years back. The house was built c1860'.

In another e-mail Ian Lewis also reported: '20 years ago I had a house [in] Soutergate, **Ulverston**. Deeds went back to 1750-ish when it was a "cotton factory" split into 2 c1830 & into 4 c1870. I had one quarter! In the upstairs bedroom, of three floors, there were three successive fireplaces. The earliest was c1830 (Georgian). As I removed it a small glass bottle with dark liquid fell down the chimney. Gave it a chemist at Glaxo to analyse he never came back to me!'

Derbyshire

An early nineteenth-century short boot of black leather was discovered behind a chimney stack on the ceiling joists of a property in Church Street, **Ashbourne**. The building dates from the mid-eighteenth century. Reported 20 August 2001.

All Saints Church, **Bakewell** has daisy wheels, concentric circles and other marks. Reported by Andy Bentham, November 2014.

At Haddon Hall, near **Bakewell**, there are concealed shoes on display in the mini museum there. Reported via Andy Bentham, September 2017.

At a cottage in Waterswallows Road, Fairfield, **Buxton**, there is a daisy wheel on the cottage door. The house was built about 1600. The daisy is about 9 inches in diameter according to the cottage owner who reported the find by e-mail in February 2002.

A dried cat was discovered at the old post office in The Quadrant, **Buxton**. Apparently, it dropped from a ceiling during restoration in early January 2017. Reported via the Buxton Museum and Art Gallery blog. The cat is now preserved at the museum. Reported by Andy Bentham on 28 February 2018.

At **Calke Abbey** the skeleton of a hare or rabbit was found in a stone-lined grave in the foundations of the building, possibly of Tudor origin.

At a property in Main Street, **Calver**, Hope Valley, a child's shoe was discovered beneath oak floorboards in an upstairs room. June Swann examined the shoe and reported the following: 'The photographs enlarged well on the screen, but not all the detail I need (to be certain) is visible. Sadly, there is nothing to suggest a 17th century date. But it is not at all unusual that the date of the shoe is quite different from that of the building, and you may find some re-flooring or other alterations tally with the shoe date. What I can see is the oval toe, which suggests 1820s (or 1792 at the earliest), and 1820s would fit well with the 3 (or 4?) pairs of holes and the crossed front lacing. The practice of placing one pair below the side seam, and the rest above also fits with 1820-40s date, but square toes became pretty general in 1830; so I do not think it is after 1830. I cannot see if there is a little wedge of leather above the sole at the back, which would be called a spring heel, but that is what I would expect with this style – or just a single lift below the sole. I know on children's shoes, this often gets worn away if worn too long, or passed on to too many younger brothers. This style was usually boy's. It is a common style found in concealments, but usually with 3 pairs of holes – I have presumed the number to be significant, though 4 have also been found. The sole at this date could made either straights, or shaped right/left (note they often get moulded to one foot, even if made straight)'.

At a farm in **Castleton** there are marks on a door lintel (Marian) and also a clay pipe was found in a bit of wall that was blocking up an old doorway. Reported by Andy Bentham, November 2014.

In **Chesterfield** it is recorded that a witch-bottle was found during restoration on a building of around 1500 which is believed to have been a merchant's house. It is suspected that this bottle went into a private collection and no further details are available.

At a property in St Chad's Road, **Derby**, an eighteenth-century child's shoe with leather soles and uppers was discovered under floorboards.

At Pountain's Premises (a wine merchant) on Market Place, **Derby**, parchment, pencil and three pieces of chalk were found in a bottle in the corner stone of the stables.

An e-mail report of Marian marks in a cave at **Dovedale** was received in October 2013.

Eyam Church has a 'plague cupboard' which has complex overlapping daisy wheels on it. Reported by Andy Bentham in November 2014.

Millstones from **Froggatt** and **Gardoms Edges** in Derbyshire can sometimes be found with VV marks on them. Photos on file. Reported by Steve Wood in March 2018.

A bottle was discovered during the rebuilding of a dry stone wall on the **Gritstone Heights** to the north-east of Matlock in Derbyshire. 'The precise location was not given to me but I believe the vial together with an almost identical one was found placed in a gap between two of the base or foundation stones when the old wall was stripped back to ground level in order to rebuild it. The other vial was empty except for the dried up cork. Slender cylindrical bodied vial. Circa 1750 ish. Height 4 inches. English manufacture in a pale smokey green glass. The vial contains the remains of some grass or straw and other vegetable matter and what is left of the cork'. Reported by David W. Barker in June 2004.

A concealed shoe was found in a cottage in **Stoney Middleton**. Andy Bentham reported in February 2015: 'Met a chap recently who found this shoe about 50 years ago! It was in an old cottage in Stoney Middleton, Derbyshire. It was found underneath a window board (sill) of a downstairs front window, within the rubble wall. So nice context'.

June Swann's analysis, received in February 2015, is as follows: 'It would be 1 of the most common children's shoes ever designed: style starts with pointed toe c1790 in definitely female colours, and my impression is it was usually a girl's shoe, worn as soon as they got out of baby bootees, ie when they start walking. Of course toe shape changes, and the rivetted construction (the corroding brass nail-heads you can see on the sole) doesn't become volume production until after 1853. This one is very sturdy, with leather top edge binding, holding lining and upper together and reinforcing the weak points, though it looks as though the centre throat of the upper has been cut to enlarge, the usual place – of course, children grow, and this is one solution – for a week or 2. It is probably patent leather, and of a type I can't date. But with the one-lift heel, may be 1860-70s. Still around 20th c. until ?quite recently.

1930s were often patent leather, but not as tough as this. I'm pretty certain it's likely to be pre 1900, and prob. nearer to 1853 than 1899'.

At the Crown Pub, High Street, **Tibshelf**, a human skull and crossbones were found during the expansion of a skittles alley. The pub dates back to 1895.

A dried cat is preserved with a mouse in a pub called the Three Stags' Heads between **Wardlow** and **Tideswell**. It is kept in a glass case in the bar. From Pennick 1995.

Shoe and cigarettes were found behind panelling. Reported by Andy Bentham in November 2014. 'This group of objects was found during some building work at the Three Stags Heads, **Wardlow Mires**, Derbyshire. (incidentally one of the finest pubs in the country!) Found behind some paneling under the stairs. Unfortunately I didn't ask the date when it was found but it was some time ago (I can get some idea another time). The cigarette packets are all full, I'm told the De Reszke was a posh smoke'.

At the Old Shoulder Of Mutton, West Bank, **Winster**, Derbyshire, some clay pipes and an old coin were discovered. Reported by Andy Bentham in October 2017. He said: 'Went photographing graffiti up the church tower in Winster this weekend. The chap who took me up winds the clock and lives in a very interesting old property. Whilst renovating the place in 2008 he found four clay pipes within an altered 17th C fireplace – pipes circa 1800. Also interestingly, the house has some 18th C baluster staircase remaining. The handrail is made up of several bits of wood sandwiched together to form the decorative profile. Whilst making some repairs to the handrail, a hollowed out cavity was found, containing a 1700's coin. He put the coin back and added another to it!'

Devon

At a house in **Appledore** 'potion bottles and shoes' are reported to have been discovered by the owner, Colin Graves, during renovations in 2001. Reported in an article entitled 'Renovations Reveal Link to Witchcraft', *Western Morning News*, 12 October 2003. In a personal communication between myself and the property owner, the objects were described as 'an Elizabethan shoe, sealed bottles and animal bones together with a pocket history of the area in the form of pottery shards'. I endeavoured to get more information about the objects and possibly some photographs but the owner was not interested and instead attempted to persuade me to purchase the items.

A dried cat was discovered in the roof space of a house in Holy City, **Axminster**. The house dates from 1634. The cat's paws were pulled aside. From Pennick 1995. Ivan Bunn reports the find as follows: 'Mummified cat in a good state of preservation discovered in the roof space. The cat had its paws pulled apart on either side of its body. There is a local tradition that cats were 'crucified' like this and placed in the roof as a charm against witchcraft. The house was built in 1634'. Bunn cites his source as one of Theo Browne's reports on folklore in the *Report and Transactions of the Devonshire Association for the Advancement of Science, Literature and Art*. Another cat was said to have been found in the workshop next door to this property. From Pennick 1995.

In the **Bradworthy** churchyard of St John the Baptist, a corked jar was discovered while digging up the path. The jar contained several spikes broken from a thorn bush and some pins. A local legend added to this discovery is that, in order to destroy the power of a witch, it was necessary to bury such a bottle in three different churchyards.

Two shoes were discovered at a house in **Brampford Speke** near Exeter. The house was built in 1884–1885. The shoes were recovered from beneath the cupboard under the stairs. The builders were sure that the shoes were put in during the initial build.

During recent building work at a Manor near **Buckfastleigh**, 'a worn leather boot or farm patten was found under almost every threshold'. This find was reported to Dr Alan Massey by a local from Harbertonford.

At a house in New Street, **Chagford**, a dark coloured bottle was discovered neck downwards while digging up the ashlar floor. When the bottle was pulled out the cork flew off with a 'great explosion' and a black foul-smelling liquid spurted out. Seventeen large thorns and seven old pins were in the bottle. The house dated from 1446.

At **Chambercombe Manor** in North Devon, a tiny double 'V' mark can be found on one of the external panels of the seventeenth-century oak front door. Reported by Malcolm Dyer in April 2016.

Chard and District Museum refer to two dried cats discovered in **Chardstoke**, just across the border in Devon, thought to date from the sixteenth and seventeenth century respectively.

At a farm in **Countisbury**, near Lynton, a rusty horse shoe and half a pair of scissors are nailed to the wall by the main entrance. This appears to be some sort of protective measure. Reported by Simon Walker in October 2005.

A dried cat was discovered in a house in **Crediton**, Devon. This was reported in September 2006 as follows: 'We found a dried/mummified cat in the roof, thatched, of a very old cob dwelling when it was pulled down. The cat was in a defensive position and it looks as though it were alive when incarcerated. I have been trying to find out why this was done. We have hidden the cat in a leafy place in the garden – the kind of place our live cat likes to hide in. It seemed unkind to bury it; we wanted to release the spirit'. She later added: 'The house we live in is dated as 1790. The cob dwelling was attached to our house and had been used as a barn for a long time. No idea how old the thatch was. We suspect that our house is a later more comfortable building than the "barn"'.

In a village near **Crediton**, a dried cat and a few old coins were found. This was reported in February 2001 as follows: 'This is just to inform you that about 17 years ago my great Aunt and her husband discovered a dried cat and a few old coins concealed in a wall close to the fireplace in a thatched cottage they lived in. The cottage (which was about 300 years old) was situated in a small village outside of Crediton, North Devon. I can't remember the name of this village, but I remember it has an unusual name as it is in Latin'.

A pitcher type bellarmine jar with a bearded man's face is on display in the Museum of Witchcraft, Boscastle, Cornwall. The information card on display with it reads: 'When found the jar was fitted with a wooden stopper and sealed with wax. When opened it contained some stinking black liquid and a quantity of sludge. This mess was originally human hair and urine. Found concealed in a table tomb close to **Exeter Cathedral**, 1950'.

Fleur Fox reported in March 2016 that when volunteering with the stonemasons at **Exeter Cathedral**, she saw a large hexafoil design in the leads.

In 1951 the skeleton of a cat was discovered buried under the ashlar-lime floor of Church Gate House, **George Nympton**. From Pennick 1995. Ivan Bunn adds the reference for this as *Report and Transactions of the Devonshire Association for the Advancement of Science, Literature and Art* 103, 1971, 266.

A hoard of shoes, probably dating from the nineteenth century, was discovered in a house near **Hemyock** in East Devon.

A cat was found in the wall beside a bake-oven next to the hearth in a house in **Higher Brimley**. From Pennick 1995. This cat is reported in the

Report and Transactions of the Devonshire Association for the Advancement of Science, Literature and Art 110, 1978, 214.

Ritual marks including numerous daisy wheels, overlapping circles and vertical lines have been recorded on a lead wall bracket and drainpipe at **King's Nympton** Park House. The house dates from 1740 and the drainpipe can be found on the north elevation.

Near the church door at **Monkleigh**, a green glass bottle with a cork stuck with pins was discovered and reburied by the Sexton when digging a grave. See also Merrifield 1987: 180.

In 1973 the skeleton of a cat was found behind the hearth of Tucking Mill, **North Lew**, during the construction of a flue. The cat was replaced after the work was completed. From Pennick 1995 and repeated by Ivan Bunn.

A written charm is recorded from near **Okehampton**, dating to around 1890.

In a house at **Parracombe** in North Devon, a dried cat, a thick glass jam jar, a sardine tin and a horseshoe were all discovered together in an iron bread oven which had been bricked up. They are likely to have been concealed at the end of the nineteenth century or early twentieth century.

Jason Semmens was told by a former resident of **Princetown** of the discovery of a possible witch-bottle there sometime in the 1970s. His report read: 'she was helping to clear a rubbish tip that had built up against the side of a barn, and dislodged a bottle from its hiding place on the window lintel of the barn. It was sealed at the time but she couldn't describe any particulars and doesn't now know what became of it. Very vague I know but she was convinced that it was a witch-bottle'.

A dried cat was reported here: 'Item 35 in the Mill House Working Cider Museum at Owermoigne is a "cast iron fluted roller cider mill from Lower Mincombe Farm, Roncombe, **Sidbury**, near Sidmouth, Devon... The date is about 1750. The top half of the mill was at cider loft level". And they helpfully add "It was in this cider loft that the mummified cat was found". The cat is on display on top of a barrel, to your left as you go through the passage from the museum shop to the displays'. Thanks for Jeremy Harte for reporting this in August 2002.

Ritual marks have been identified in the screen passage of a house at Hayne Barton, **Shillingford**, Bampton, Devon. These marks include numerous daisy wheels and other marks.

A dried cat was discovered in the roof space of the church verger's cottage in a row of houses adjoining The Church House Inn, **Stoke Gabriel**. The cat was lying at the base of the original roof, which was thatched and covered with straw. The roof was enclosed by an outer roof in 1817. The cat appears to have been disembowelled and stitched up, a seemingly very deliberate mummification process. From Pennick 1995.

A concealed shoe is reported from the railway station at **Tavistock**. This was reported in November 2007 as follows: 'this is not a question really it is some more information for your research. We are restoring Tavistock Railway Station in Devon and the builders have found a boot behind the plaster in the old Porters Office. The building was finished in 1890. The boot is a man's and we presume it is from one of the builders probably Irish'.

A dried cat was discovered in **Ugborough**. Reported in April 2009.

The skeleton of a cat was discovered in the roof of a cottage being re-thatched in **Woodbury** prior to 1965. From Pennick 1995. Ivan Bunn adds that 'It is believed from its position and attitude that it was a sacrifice' and cites the source as *Report and Transactions of the Devonshire Association for the Advancement of Science, Literature and Art* 110, 1978, 214.

Dorset

A dried cat was found in a house in **Abbotsbury**. From Pennick 1995.

Peter Thomas reported shoe fragments from his chimney at a cottage in **Blackney**, Bridport. He sent images to Northampton for identification and they said they dated from the 1770–1790s.

At **Briantspuddle** Dr Andy Russell, archaeologist at Southampton University, reported: 'Another dried cat to add to your list. My parents lived at Briantspuddle, Dorset, thatched cottage next to the village school as then was. When they extended the roof in the 1980s a dried cat was found. It had been damaged by the builders but appeared to me to have been dried in a sitting position. It was put in the skip but I replaced it in the roof so it's still hopefully doing its work'. Reported in August 2014.

An unusual example from **Charmouth** in Dorset was discovered in August 2007. A lead covered box was uncovered around 20cm below the surface around a metre outside of an outbuilding belonging to a cottage there. Inside the box was the dried body of a cat which had been 'positioned in a life-like crouching pose, with its tail wrapped round one side'. The animal had been packed into the box with pieces of blanket and it's thought that the example dates from the 1920s or 1930s.

At the Corfe Inn, **Corfe Mullen**, a dried cat is said to exist.

At **Fiddesford Manor** a complex of daisy wheels can be found on a first-floor interior windowsill. They comprise a central circle around which six daisy wheels are formed, each with six petals.

A scribed circle was found opposite an inglenook fireplace in a 1686 cottage in North Street, **Fontmell Magna**.

An ox leg was discovered concealed in a wall at **Hazelbury Bryan**. Reported by Jeremy Harte in June 2001.

A knife dated to the early eighteenth century by Dorchester Museum was found within the structure of an inglenook fireplace at a cottage in **Ibberton**, Blandford Forum. The fireplace had been filled with rubble and plastered over and was restored when the correspondent took over the property. During this restoration the builder discovered the old knife while turning some bricks and pointing. The knife was discovered at the right-hand side of the fireplace.

A bottle was discovered by workmen rebuilding a boundary wall which was the parish boundary of **Langton Matravers** and Worth Matravers. The glass bottle is a deep blue colour and contains a substance which becomes more fluid as it is held and moved. Matthew Slocombe has provisionally dated this bottle to the mid-eighteenth century. Research by Dr Alan Massey at the University of Loughborough suggests that the main ingredients of this substance could be beef tallow and spring water.

Some marks have been discovered in a working mill at **Mangerton**, near Bridport. This was reported in April 2002 as follows: 'Whilst we were having some refreshment in the tea room which adjoins the mill. I noticed highlighted by the sunlight some distinct scratch marks engraved on the left wooden bracket supporting the mantel shelf. I have regularly visited the Mill and tea rooms on more than several occasions and have never noticed them before probably due to the fact that the light can be dull in the tea room when the sky is overcast and also for the wood to be very dark in colour'. There is also a dried cat on the premises.

A dried cat was discovered at Michels Square, **Marnhull**. The animal was found under a roof of pantiles in a small row of eighteenth/nineteenth-century cottages. Reported in *Proceedings of the Dorset Natural History and Archaeological Society* 74, 1952, 110.

A number of objects from a cottage in **Marshwood** had been brought into Dorset County Museum for identification. They are: 'a glass bottle, a stoneware bottle, a lump of yellow material, and a salt cellar. There was also a lady's white glove, now lost. The glass bottle was five inches high, and had contained some brown stuff, the cork having fallen in; the bottle was of the sort which is blown, not cast in a mould, and the surplus glass at the top had not been nipped off. The white glazed stoneware bottle was five inches high and three inches in diameter. The lump was of some material much like resin, evidently cast in a bottle which had been six inches high and two-and-a-half inches in diameter; it had been broken to let out the lump, which bore an interior cast of it. The salt cellar had a rough knob on top and three machined rings halfway up, and the words Chrome Plated were stamped on the base, though it had lost its chrome. Judging from the salt cellar, the whole assemblage cannot have been placed in the wall any earlier than the late nineteenth century'. Thanks to Jeremy Harte for reporting this in July 2004.

A hoard of objects has been discovered in **Piddletrenthide** – reported in the *Dorset Evening Echo*, 30 April 1987. The article reads: 'The other interesting find was made by Mr Binoy Roy in Saddlers Cottage. He found a big old fireplace hidden behind a smaller modern one. In the fireplace he found a pair of child's boots from the 1870s, a woman's boot of the 1890s and a shoe from the 1930s. There were also the remains of old leather gaiters, the broken tine of a pitchfork, a trivet, a pen-knife and a small card-board box. The box bore the name of Cooke & Kelvey, Diamond Merchant, Jewellers, Watch, Clock and Chronometer Makers, Scindia House, Queensway, New Delhi. Mr Roy discovered the reason for the old shoes. A superstition dating back to the Middle Ages says it is lucky to conceal worn footwear in new or altered houses'. Clipping sent by Jeremy Harte.

A dried black cat was discovered 'installed' in a building at the Verne, **Portland**, now in Weymouth Museum. From Pennick 1995.

A black cat with the skeleton of a mouse in its mouth was discovered in the nineteenth century in a house in **Portland**. The cat is now in Avice's Cottage. From Pennick 1995.

At **Puddletown** Church, Linda Hall noted a daisy wheel on a 1635 box pew. Reported in February 2009.

It is thought that a witch-bottle was found in the **Shillingstone** area.

At **Stalbridge** a witch-bottle was found. The find was reported in the *Proceedings of the Dorset Natural History and Archaeological Society* 117, 1995, 142, including illustration. The bottle was found at 1 Grove Lane, Stalbridge and is described as follows: 'During the removal of 19th century blocking from an inglenook fireplace at 1 Grove Lane, Stalbridge, a corked glass bottle filled with urine and containing a small number of steel pins was discovered by the householders, Mr and Mrs Finch. This was presented for identification at the Dorset County Museum. The cylindrical bottle, either a medicine or a sauce bottle of mid-19th century date, was mould-blown in pale blue glass, 145mm high and 41mm in diameter. It was not possible to ascertain whether the bottle had been placed in the chimney at the time of blocking or had been there for some time'.

In Church Street, **Sturminster Newton**, a bottle was found containing an apparent charm. A photocopy is held in Dorset County Museum. It is described by Jeremy Harte as follows: 'Photocopy of piece of paper found in a bottle in a house in Stalbridge ... written, seemingly in a 19th century hand, two magic squares – one with columns adding up to 34 (symbol for Jupiter), and the other adding up to 111 (symbol for the Sun), eight sigils, including two Solomon's Seals, and in two cases accompanied by words Adonai, and Agla and Omega; few astrological glyphs, and these words – 'The Lord the Faithfull King give commandment O God to thy strength conform o God thy strength in us. El. Elohim. Elohai. Zebraoll. Elion Exeerchie [letter 'h' placed above word] Adonai. Jah. Jehovah Tetragrammaton Jof Eheoi so good lord take [?] heare Remove the Evil from this house in the Name of Jesus Christ Amen Fiat Fiat Fiat Cito Cito Cito'. From Waring 1977: 85. The photocopy of the charm (L1973.2) was presented to the Dorset County Museum by Mrs E.M. Rose of Stalbridge.

Two pots were discovered in the thatch of a cottage in **Upwey** near Weymouth. One of the pots is earthenware (5in high and 4in diameter) and the other is of metal (1.5in tall) with a screw fitting for a lid that is missing. The pots were found in dead space adjacent to the chimney. Reported in November 2000.

In the village of **Verwood** it is reported that 'several potters cottages ... had a clay bowl cast into the wall, usually near the outside door, but on the internal face. The bowls vary between about 200 to 400mm diameter and are cast in at different heights. There is one in each cottage. Being very shallow, it is not possible to store anything in them. They are plain and are not likely to be considered a form of decoration. ... the only suggestion submitted has been that they were to ward off evil spirits'. Reported on 30 August 2001.

At Middlebere Farm, in the region of Corfe Castle, **Wareham**, an eighteenth-century dried cat was found in a roof collapse at the side of the fireplace in the bake-house.

At Boar Mill, in the region of Corfe Castle, **Wareham**, another eighteenth-century dried cat was discovered under the floorboards of the main bedroom together with a George III coin.

A dried puppy (identification of which is not certain) was found amongst forty sacks of straw and dust which existed beneath the floorboards of two rooms in the roof of Walnut Farm, in the region of Corfe Castle, **Wareham**. A child's cloth shoe was also discovered, along with some coins, leading to the conclusion that these finds dated from the eighteenth century.

A dried cat or kitten was discovered in the roof of a cottage in Elwell Street, Upwey, **Weymouth** in 1987. The building dates from 1821 and the cat was replaced after the work was completed. From Pennick 1995.

A dried cat is said to exist at the 'Country Arms' near **Wimbourne**.

At **Winterbourne Kingston** a witch-bottle was discovered. A local chimney sweep remarked that he had 'met with hundreds similar'. The find is described as follow: 'In a farm-house in the neighbourhood a bottle was found hanging by a wire up in the old chimney, and, when it was cut down, was found to contain liquid. It was tightly corked and the cork stuck all over with pins. After the bottle was broken and the liquid spilled the family had nothing but bad luck and finally left the place'.

At **Worth Matravers** it is thought that a pot, apparently medieval, was discovered walled up in a house.

Shoes from around 1730 were found concealed in the wall of Robert Boyle's School, **Yetminster**, near Sherborne. Reported via Sherbourne Museum's twitter feed in September 2017.

Durham, Tyne & Wear and Other Regions

Three shoes were found around a window frame at **Eastgate**, near Stanhope, Co. Durham. Reported in July 2008.

At **Crawley Peel Tower**, Newcastle-Upon-Tyne, three shoes were discovered in the walls. Two of these belonged to adults and the third was a child's shoe.

A dried cat was discovered at Alderman Fenwick's House, 98 Pilgrim Street, **Newcastle-Upon-Tyne** beneath the fireplace slab. It was thrown away by the building contractors and was not included in the report in *Archaeologia Aeliana,* 1997. It seems that a concealed shoe was also found at this house at the same time.

The Wallsend News Guardian reported that a dried cat had been found in a cavity at Wallsend Police Station, **Newcastle-Upon-Tyne**.

In 1985 a dried cat was found under the floor of a Victorian house in **North Shields** which was being renovated. The animal was discovered by a homeless person who tried to exchange it for beer at the Dolphin Inn. It is now in the Hancock Museum. From Pennick 1995.

A dried cat was found at **Throckley**, Tyne and Wear – it is now in the Hancock Museum. From Pennick 1995.

East Riding of Yorkshire and Hull

Staff at **Goole** Museum and Art Gallery report that they hold a left shoe which was discovered in a fireplace and therefore must date after 1850.

East Sussex

Daisy wheels which look like consecration crosses were found at the Pilgrim's Rest pub in **Battle**, just beneath a window. Reported by Sinead Spearing in September 2017.

A child's shoe was discovered in the roof of Hayes Farm, **Beckley**, thought to date from the eighteenth century.

A phial/witch-bottle was discovered in ashes by the side of a duck pond at Pound Farm, **Blackham**. The house and barn were for sale and the finder saw the phial and other objects at that time. The bottle was corked and contained brownish residue. The bottle went to Dr Alan Massey for analysis of its contents. Reported in September 2003.

A dried cat was discovered beneath the floorboards above the shop in Sydney Street, **Brighton**. The correspondent and her colleagues have reported serious bad luck since the discovery. Workmen decided to varnish the cat.

Many daisy wheels and other marks were found on the beams and doors in a seventeenth-century house in **Etchingham**. The building was previously The Bluebeard Inn. Reported in January 2002.

Two dried cats were discovered in the Stag Inn, All Saints Street, **Hastings** and are now on display in a case on the wall of the bar.

A man's shoe was discovered in the roof of Malling House, **Lewes**, thought to date from the eighteenth century.

At 17 South Street, **Lewes**, a woman's leather buckle shoe, a buckle shoe (1760–1770s), a slipper (late eighteenth–early nineteenth), a cricket ball and two smaller balls were found behind the plaster of an upper room. From the files of Janet Pennington.

At the Royal Oak in **Mayfield** (now a private house), three shoes were found near the hearth. One was a child's shoe, another 'style' shoe with an almost curly toe – thought to date from around 1650. From the files of Janet Pennington.

Some ritual marks have been identified in a **Mayfield house**. Double V's, butterfly marks and Rx have been found on a bressummer there. From the files of Janet Pennington.

At a cottage in **Nutley**, fragments of salt-glazed pottery were discovered beneath a doorstep suggestive of the placing of a witch-bottle.

A very large hoard of objects was found during alterations to the chimney at 'The Barracks' in **Nutley**. This comprises mostly footwear, gaiters and undecorated brass. The objects are all being stored at the Weald and Downland Open Air Museum and will be displayed there. A report by June Swann details 56 shoes dating largely to the late nineteenth and early twentieth centuries.

An e-mail report from November 2005 reads as follows: 'Thought I might mention (as you are collecting data) that a shoe sole was recently found in our house under plaster over the fireplace in our house. It looks like it dates from the late 17th century, but not completely sure. Also the beam over the main fireplace (dated 1693) has a number of interesting "witch" marks. They were noticed by someone a few years ago who is quite knowledgeable about them. Our house dates from about 1520 and is in **Rushlake Green**, East Sussex'.

A collection of objects was found under the floorboards of one of the gatehouses at the Old Sanitarium, **South Chailey**, near Lewes. They consist of several bottles (one still corked though empty), a couple of tobacco pipes and a small doll's head. This was an anonymous report from someone on the site who was a carpenter.

In 1990/1 a concealed boot was discovered at **Vines Cross** in a labourer's cottage dating to the first decade of the twentieth century. The boot was found beneath the floorboards of the rear ground floor room and the sole had been torn away from the upper.

At **Westham** in the Old Vicarage, a very old green shoe was found. From the files of Janet Pennington.

At **Wivelsfield** a wooden patten was discovered on top of a domed bread oven belonging to a house of the seventeenth or early eighteenth century.

Essex

Ashdon Church has several four-petal daisy wheels inside it. Reported by Simon Walker in September 2002.

A collection of bottles and what look like pattens have been found beneath the floor of a building at **Abridge**, Essex. Reported in an e-mail from Matthew Slocombe in January 2009.

Pennick reprints the headlines of an article about a collection of finds from **Billericay**: 'Horrified workmen have uncovered a black magic shrine at St Andrew's Hospital, Billericay. Their shock find in an attic close to the hospital chapel includes bones, voodoo-type dolls and a pin box. Now police may be called in …'. Pennick states that what was found was actually two four-inch long effigies, part of a ruminant jawbone and thighbone, a piece of coal, and a notched wooden tine about three inches long. From Pennick 1986. Ivan Bunn repeats this information but cites his source as the *Southend Evening Echo*, 18 December 1981.

At Shottesbrook, Church Road, **Boreham**, Chelmsford, a report of a daisy wheel described as 'on the brickwork of the above address where there are many names and initials scratched into the bricks next to the pavement. This part of the house was probably built shortly before 1837, when it is mentioned in a will'.

A knife, nail and piece of material were found enclosed in the wattle and daub wall of an old house in **Brentwood** High Street. From Merrifield 1969.

A bellarmine witch-bottle, made in Frechen in 1620–1675, 22cm in height, with a stylised face mask and a flower design medallion, was found at **Chappel** near Colchester, Essex. It was found 'standing up' buried near the front door. The bellarmine was washed out at the time of discovery. Whilst travelling in the post, the iron mass inside broke up and was found to be mainly iron nails. Thanks to Alex Wright who supplied this information based on the bottle in his collection. Reported in March 2016 and published in Wright 2009.

A dried rat was found beneath the floorboards of a house in Springfield, a suburb of **Chelmsford**. From Pennick 1995.

At **Clavering** Church there are numerous four- and six-petalled daisy wheels. Reported by Simon Walker in September 2002.

A dried cat was recovered from the roof of a house in **Coggeshall**. From Pennick 1995. This find must be the same as the one 'from an unidentified house in Coggeshall' reported by Ivan Bunn: 'A mummified cat was discovered and removed from the roof space of this house which is reputed to be 600 years old. According to the owners the removal of the remains was followed by "a plague of accidents"'. This was reported in the *News of the World*, 14 April 1985.

Staff at Chelmsford and Essex Museum report that they hold a brown leather shoe which was found in the chimney of an old farmhouse near **Colchester** when it was demolished. The shoe dates from the late seventeenth century or early eighteenth century. It is possible that the cuts in the shoe were deliberately made.

On the Great Stairs of **Colchester** Castle there is a seventeenth-century daisy wheel symbol which has been engraved into stone.

Three witch-bottles have been discovered within a large house near **Coopersale**, Epping in Essex. The first two were discovered side-by-side set into plaster/cement within the structure of a hearth and adjacent to a former rear entry into the house. The bottles were broken on discovery by accident. The bottles are thought to date from the late eighteenth century (thanks to Matthew Slocombe for the date) and contained some residues of liquid and some hairs. Later work revealed a further bottle, apparently intact, further up the structure of the hearth and evidently sealed into the hearth in the same way. This third bottle will remain sealed, in-situ. Lorna Ellis' researches into the house revealed that the lady of the house died around the time of the concealment of the glass bottles – apparently the owner of the house was grief stricken and sealed the house with all furnishings intact. The house was only reopened in the early nineteenth century and was quite an attraction at the time, due to the the tragic story behind it. It may be that the bottles were placed in the house as the owner believed that his wife was bewitched. Numerous photos on file. This house, its bottles and myself and Dr Alan Massey featured in a documentary on Channel 4 in late 2001. Some bones were discovered in the floor by the hearth in an adjacent room but they turned out, after analysis by Philip Armitage, to be food waste and were from sheep.

At **Cricksea**, a dried cat and kittens are said to have been found plastered into a wall of a house. From Pennick 1995.

There is a painted 'daisy' on the display panel above the fireplace at Little Badcocks Farm, **Easthorpe**.

A wooden rattle was discovered in a thatch in **Essex** – the precise location is not known. It is currently owned by a retired antique dealer; photo on file. The owner thinks the item dates from the late seventeenth or early eighteenth century judging by the type and quality of the woodwork. It is entirely made of wood and, judging from the sound it makes, apparently contains seeds. The cross made on the handle is similar to the 'St Andrews Cross' found on witch-posts.

A bellarmine was found buried upright under the hearth of the Red Lion Inn, **Great Wratting**, with a twist of something in its neck. Its contents were discarded by workmen and tests revealed no traces of urine – possibly a witch-bottle. From Bunn 1982.

In **Harwich** Guild Hall it is reported that a daisy is inscribed, amongst other images, on the boarding of the prison there.

At the Lion Inn, **Lamarsh**, a fireback was found concealed behind another hearth. It was later acquired by Alastair Scot-Villiers who reported it in November 2005. He later added: 'After emailing you I did a Google search and found a few examples of firebacks being found bricked up in fireplaces for "ritual" reasons. It seems that they are also sometimes found broken and the pieces hidden up chimneys!'

A dried whippet dog was discovered in the stables of the Carlton public house at Leigh Broadway, **Leigh-on-Sea**. The dog was found buried directly before the hearth of the tackroom, the only part of the stables with floorboards. The animal was reburied after examination. The building was erected in 1898 and the animal was rediscovered during rebuilding work in 1984. From Pennick 1995. There is a photo of this dog in Pennick 1986.

A side wall of boarding at the barn or granary of **Little Leighs** Priory is reported to have many 'daisys' covering it.

The house called Winter's Armoury in **Magdalen Laver** has two dried cats inside it. A feature was made of the animals during the sale of the house which was reported in the *Daily Mail* in October 2002. The cats are preserved in a glass case. The house is reputed to have been used by Oliver Cromwell during the Civil War.

At Hill House, **Manuden**, a knife was found plastered into the chimney breast. The knife was identified as dating from the eighteenth century 'due to its distinctive 17cm long scimitar blade fashioned in iron'. This was first published in Hooper 1988 and subsequently cited in Collins 2003.

A horse skull was discovered in a seventeenth-century cottage in **Manuden**. The precise location of the cottage is not known but the skull was discovered in a bread oven which had been plastered over sometime during the eighteenth or nineteenth centuries. First published in Hooper 1989 and subsequently cited in Collins 2003.

In **Manuden** an ancient stone head was found buried in the walling above the arch of the west window of the parish church. The head was described as a medieval grotesque but seems to be fairly featureless. It is not certain whether this was magical or not but it is possible. It was first mentioned by Verry 1978 and subsequently cited in Collins 2003.

A possible witch-bottle has been discovered in a property of 1894 at **Mersea Island**. It is described as follows: 'The house was originally a 2-up, 2-down semi with a staircase between the rooms. One wall of this staircase is wood panelling fixed to timber framing, with a door giving access to an under-stair cupboard. We decided to remove this wall and in the process, came across a glass phial resting on top one of the timbers in the framing. It contained a dark brown liquid and there was a cover on the top tied with a cord. There was a large printed label with a picture of a sword and the word Harlemennis'. Reported in May 2001.

A witch-bottle was apparently found at Old Brook Farm, **Navestock**. It was reported in November 2008 as follows: 'while doing some damp proofing work to the chimney at [a farm] in Navestock an octagonal bottle was found containing some residue and fragments of bone, unfortunately the bottle was broken but has now been glued back together, the contents of the bottle replaced. the cement the bottle was found in is part of restoration works carried out in approx 1976, however a lump of clay with a similar octagonal indentation in was found and this is thought to be the original support for the bottle, the bottle itself has roman numerals down one side. A fragment of the now solid residue can be sent to you for analysis. photographic details of all items found has been attached to this e mail for you. The fragments of bone, cloth and other items along with the clay boulder have been placed in a white china urn and re concealed behind the chimney on 31st october 2008'.

A dried cat was found in a barn at **Newport** in 1986. The cat is now in the ownership of Nigel Pennick. From Pennick 1995.

At **Pebmarsh** some shoes and other objects were discovered in a previously blocked up oven. The owner of the building describes it as follows: 'We moved into a hybrid 16th century/Victorian house last July. The bread-oven (part of the inglenook) was exposed two or three years back by the previous owners – and contains a pair of child's shoes as well as a wooden spinning top and a fork of the kind used when carving meat (possibly 19th century)'. Reported in February 2001.

Merrifield refers to a witch-bottle being discovered at **Saffron Walden**. From Merrifield 1987: 174.

A horse skull was found concealed in a cavity between a chimney flue and two enclosing brick walls at Little Belhus, **South Ockendon** – thought to date from the sixteenth or seventeenth century. From Merrifield 1987: 124.

The Central Museum and Planetarium at **Southend-on-Sea** reported that they hold at least one dried cat and some witch-bottles.

A dried cat fell out of a chimney during building work at the Ship Inn, **Thurrock**. This was reported in the *Daily Star*, 13 October 1992. From Pennick 1995.

In the Abbey church of **Waltham Abbey** a dried cat was found.

It is also reported that a daisy wheel ritual mark occurs in the stone surface of one of the Norman pillars in the nave at **Waltham Abbey**. It is about 5ft from the floor and is a completed floret like that on the Corinthian Arch at Stowe (Bucks). From *Mosaic*, the archaeology newsletter for the National Trust, Summer 1994,.4.

At the Coach and Horses public house in **Wicken Bonhunt**, a collection of nineteenth-century shoes are on display in a glass cabinet. They were found in a blocked-off hole behind a wall during works. From the *Herts and Essex Observer*, 11 November 1999, 24.

Gloucestershire

At a house in **Blakeney** various 'burn marks and incised marks on 1st floor in bathroom and stair turret, and in attic'. Reported by Linda Hall in August 2013.

Ritual marks were found at a cottage, formerly an inn, in **Brockweir** in the Forest of Dean. Reported in December 2012.

A thatcher in the **Chipping Campden** area reported the following items discovered while working on a house in the area: a patten with a wooden sole and leather straps, a bottle, and the remnants of a corn dolly. The house dates from the 1680s.

At **Dymock** a small tablet dating from the second half of the seventeenth century with an inscribed curse on 'Sarah Ellis' was discovered. This curse is fully discussed in Hartland 1897. A document created by Gloucester Folk Museum for display about this item reads: 'This inscribed lead tablet was found in a small wall cupboard in Wilton Place, Dymock, in 1892. The curse is laid on Sarah Ellis whose name is written backwards at the top of the tablet. Symbols representing the good and evil spirits of the moon are followed by the figures 369 – the mystical number of the moon adding to the charm's influence. Then the demons Hasmodat, Acteus, Magalesius, Ormenus, Lieus, Nicon, Mimon and Zeper are called upon to "make this person to Banish away from this place and countery Amen to my desier Amen". Sarah Ellis has never been identified, but there is a local legend that the curse so affected her that she committed suicide and was buried at a cross roads with stake in her heart. There is indeed an Ellis's Cross on the boundary of the parishes of Dymock and Oxenhall, about two and a half miles from Wilton Place. The curse belongs to the second half of the seventeenth century and was probably based on Henry Cornelius Agrippa's "Three Books of Occult Philosophy", published in 1532 and translated into English in 1651. Apart from the identity of Sarah Ellis, the effectiveness of the curse, on whose behalf it was made, and whether the place of its discovery was that where it was originally laid, these are all questions that have never been answered'.

At a barn at **Elberton Manor**, Linda Hall notes daisy wheels in plaster on a long wall. Reported in February 2009.

At **Fiddington** a shoe was found in an attic. Reported in March 2016.

At Eastgate House in **Gloucester** (built in the 1790s), a dead cat with its skull missing was discovered buried in masonry when demolition work was being carried out.

A horse skull is reputed to have been found at **Hailes Abbey**.

Two shoes have been found in the attic of a farm house at **Haw Bridge**, Tirley. One shoe is adult size and the other is for a small child. These shoes were brought to a lecture I delivered in Cheltenham in August 2009. June Swann's analysis placed them around the first quarter of the nineteenth century.

At a house near **Joyford** in the Forest of Dean a dried cat was discovered in the roof while repairs were being undertaken.

At Clutterbuck House in **Leonard Stanley**, there is a daisy wheel etched into the stone window in the kitchen. It is a classic, neat six-petalled daisy pictured in the *Vernacular Architecture Group Newsletter* 67, July 2014, 15.

Linda Hall notes daisy wheels on the walls near doorways at the Barn at Villars Farm, **Meysey Hampton**. Reported in February 2009.

A daisy wheel was found at Mill End, **Mitcheldean**. Reported in March 2008.

At Weir Farm, **Oakridge**, intersecting zigzags were found along the hall fireplace lintel. Reported by Linda Hall in February 2009.

At Solomon's Court, **Oakridge**, multiple daisy wheels were found on stonework of the parlour chamber fireplace. Reported by Linda Hall in February 2009.

At Japonica Cottage, **Oakridge**, various multi marks were found on the hall fireplace lintel, including a series of curved parallel lines rather like part of a rainbow, with a small circle with a dot in the centre between two of the lines; a multi mark and a large group of intersecting circles were also found on the stone mullion of the hall window. Reported by Linda Hall in February 2009.

A variety of objects including shoes were found in a Victorian cottage in **Randwick**, near Stroud. They were reported as follows in December 2012: 'I dont know if you are collecting individual information, but

I thought I'd let you know about some finds in our early Victorian cottage which we are renovating in Randwick on the edge of Stroud. They were all located in the bricked up bread oven at the side of the fireplace, but I suspect they had all been moved to here from other places when a small extension was built in the 70s/80s and the fireplace was bricked up. There are 2 slip on leather shoes of a small adult size, but I dont think they are a pair. They have metal studded soles, and are quite pointy. They are in terrible condition due to the damp conditions they have been in and one of them is in pieces. There is also a small stoneware pot about 4cm in diameter and light grey in colour. This was upturned when I found it but is filled with what looks like mud, with a strange purple bloom on top. 2 clay pipes are also in there. These are in perfect condition. Finally there are 2 metal items in very poor condition. One appears to be a wick holder, the other seems to be an old door hinge. As the items have probably been moved from elsewhere I suspect the latter items may have no connection to folk magic, but I'd be interested if you know better'.

A dried cat was discovered in the wall cavity of the barn at **Southam Manor**, although it is unclear whether this was intentional or not.

A concealed shoe is on display in The Crown Inn, Gumstool Hill, **Tetbury**. Reported in January 2002.

Concealed shoes were discovered in a sixteenth/seventeenth-century town house in **Tetbury**. There were also three dried cat's paws (presumably the remains of a dried cat) and animal bones found in a compartment in a partition wall, as well as a seventeenth-century religious book of some sort. All this was reported in March 2008 as follows: 'It is a large property that started its life as a coaching inn, luckily for us no real renovation work has been carried out since 1880 so many bits and pieces have survived. Under the attic floor I found a single Ladies very worn working shoe pressed into the plaster 1790–1820 I think. A corn sheaf also deliberately placed and by that a tied cloth bag containing animal bones. There has been masses of other material finds, coins, lots of clay pipe fragments, bottles etc'. He later added: 'Give us a couple of days and I will photograph the finds and send them to you, by the way I forgot to mention we also found three mummified cats paws (cat found and removed at some point I guess) and animal jaw bones found in compartment in an old partition wall, plus a 17th century religious book of some sort in poor condition found in the shop at the front of the house'.

It is reported that a dried cat with a mouse in its mouth was discovered in an old house in **Tewkesbury**. From Pennick 1995. This find is also reported in Howard 1951.

In **Tewkesbury** High Street there is a town house with marks and objects. This was reported in December 2015 as follows: 'The house under its listing says C17 or earlier and we suspect parts may be C16/C15 or earlier. The house appears to have only undergone 2 main periods of "improvement" Circa 1870's and 1960's. The Georgian changes seem to have been moving a staircase and cutting off the timber front and putting up a brick one. The 60's saw only fireplaces replaced downstairs.
Attics:
Under the one or two elm boards we have lifted for electrical access, we have found many amazing bits and bobs – in amongst the half a ton of dust everything from musket balls to playing cards (dated to 1790), lobster claws, pins, beads, broken jewelry and bones which appear to be chicken bones (fingers crossed). We also found several white quartz pebbles which someone has suggested may be something to do with some kind of a Christian ceremony? These stones are not found in the soil in the garden as far as I am aware.
First floor:
In each of the three bedrooms (under the floorboards [in the SW corners]) we have found pieces of a pot (this has clearly had lime wash and paint in it at some time) each with some small bones near by: we also found a twisted willow? loop thing with other bits of wood (oak?) in it. There are also bits of leather but these just look like off cuts lost when making something???
Ground floor:
Several small bones with holes in either end of them… which suggests to me they were linked and worn… I really hope they are chicken!:\ some quite big iron blobs :) and more pot.
The house also appears to have some apotropaic marks on the stone shelves in the cupboard near the fire. Crossed V's (some very faint) and some strange marks that might be a stone mason mark?'

In the **Forest of Dean** an unusual charm of some kind was discovered beneath the floorboards of an 1837 house (address not supplied). It consisted of a small bundle of strangely plaited hair, a tiny piece of what looks like a page from a book and a bird skeleton. Part of the printed text on the paper says 'Saturday' and 'Stolen'.

Two eighteenth-century phials, alleged to have been used as witch-bottles, are illustrated in a pamphlet published by **Gloucester** Folk Museum.

A dried cat is said to exist in the museum at **Stroud**. From Pennick 1995.

City of London and Greater London

Merrifield refers to a bellarmine discovered on the site of the city ditch in Duke's Place, **Aldgate**. He refers to this containing a mass of corroded brass pins and having probably been put there no earlier than the third quarter of the seventeenth century. From Merrifield 1987: 164.

A dried cat is preserved in a wooden case without glass above the bar in the cellar of Dirty Dick's public house, **Bishopsgate**. From Pennick 1995.

A dried cat was found in a house in **Bloomsbury**, demolished in 1915. From Pennick 1995. This find is also reported in Howard 1951.

At White's Cottages, Hayes, **Bromley**, a child's shoe dating to around 1790 was found under floorboards [#059].

A dried cat was discovered in the ceiling above the front door of a property in Church Street, **Camberwell**. Reported in October 2017.

A dried cat was discovered in Lord Yarborough's old house in **Chelsea**, demolished for the construction of Chelsea Hospital. From Pennick 1995. This find is also reported in Howard 1951.

A possible bellarmine witch-bottle was discovered at **Chelsea Reach**, which contained a bent iron nail, cinders from a fire and some unidentifiable fibrous fragments. It is thought that this bottle was thrown into the water. From Merrifield 1969.

Merrifield refers to a broken bellarmine discovered at **Chiswick Eyot**. It contained a bent iron nail, small pieces of partly burned coal and fibrous fragments. This was found in the Thames. From Merrifield 1987: 163.

In **Clerkenwell** a boot was found under the floorboards in a house dating from 1835, reported in November 2011.

At Queen Elizabeth's Hunting Lodge, **Epping Forest**, there is a daisy wheel carved into wood next to the fireplace according to correspondent. Reported in November 2009.

An intact bellarmine complete with contents was discovered beneath a house in **Greenwich**. It was placed in the care of the Old Royal Naval

College and sent to Dr Alan Massey for analysis. Dr Massey has since published widely on it.

A carpenter reported having found several mummified cats beneath the floorboards of Victorian houses in **Hackney**. This was an anonymous report.

At Lauderdale House, **Highgate Hill**, a collection of items was discovered in a bricked-up recess near a first-floor fireplace. These comprised four dessicated chickens, two of which had apparently been strangled and two buried alive. There were the remains of an egg, a yellow glazed earthenware candlestick, a glass goblet, two odd shoes and a thong of plaited rushes – all from the late sixteenth or early seventeenth century. From Merrifield 1969.

A Bellarmine witch-bottle was discovered during excavations at **Holywell Priory**, Holywell Lane. It was a plain bottle with no face and contained bent pins. An image and a little further detail is given in the original article, Lewis 2010: 254.

Under the foundations of some 1719 almshouses in High Road, **Ilford**, a ritual deposit was discovered. It consisted of a seventeenth-century witch-bottle contained within a sixteenth-century chamber pot, both covered by a floor tile.

On 4 October 2005 Alison Lister reported to me via e-mail that **Islington** Museum had just taken possession of a dried cat from a nearby street. It was buried with a newspaper dating to 1894.

Some 'M' and 'W' marks have been found at **Kew Palace**. The find was reported in the *Guardian* on 29 April 2004 as follows: 'The closure has given historians a unique opportunity to study the skeleton of the building – which is where curator Lee Prosser found the witchmarks. They had been spotted before but dismissed as carpenter's marks, but these are quite different; sun symbols, eye shapes, M- shapes to invoke the protection of the Virgin Mary, classic witchmarks – and from exactly the period, and in the positions near the potential points of danger, the door and window entry points, where you would expect to find them'. The transcription was kindly provided by John Billingsley, July 2004. Many photos on file provided by Stella Eglinton.

A bellarmine described as Holmes Type VIII was discovered in Broad Street, **Lambeth**. The bottle contained a coagulated mass of rusty nails and is thought to have been buried either beneath a riverside house, or in open country on the fringe of the town, perhaps deposited in a ditch. From Merrifield 1954.

Apparently ox skulls and boars' tusks were discovered in the foundations of old St Paul's Cathedral, **London**. From Pennick 1986: 6.

Merrifield refers to a bellarmine discovered on the site of the Plaisterers Hall, Noble Street, **London**. The bottle contained nine brass pins, each carefully bent twice. An excellent photo is reproduced in his book. From Merrifield 1987: 165–66.

A dried cat was formerly preserved at the Marquis of Granby public house, New Cross Gate, **London**. It was destroyed before 1951. From Pennick 1995. This find is also reported in Howard 1951.

A rat was discovered walled up in the **Tower of London**.

A bellarmine bottle, described as 'Late form, with crude mask of Holmes Type IX', was found nine feet from steps by the River Thames at Paul's Pier Wharf, **London** in 1926. The contents of the bottle comprised a felt heart pierced with pins and iron nails. It is thought that the bottle was deposited in the river. From Merrifield 1954. The article includes a photograph. There is a small article about this bottle called 'Witchcraft in Stuart Times', which appeared in *The Times*, 14 February 1954, 8.

A dried cat is said to have been discovered in 1960 in a house in the **Tower of London**, rebuilt by Wren after the great fire. The dried cat was found against a joist beside the fireplace under the floor of an upper room. From Pennick 1995. This find is also reported in Howard 1951.

A dried cat was discovered under pews in the Church of St Clement Danes, Strand, **London** in 1899. From Pennick 1995. This find is also reported in Howard 1951.

A dried cat, described as 'starved', was found in the stables of Beaufort House, **London**. This find is reported in Howard 1951.

'The dried body of a cat' nailed up near the fireplace of 1, Dane's Inn, The Strand, **London** was discovered. It was found in 1890 when it was the studio of Thomas Robinson. From Lewis 1973. From Pennick 1995.

A dried cat was discovered in a sealed passage under the roof of the Church of St Michael Paternoster Royal, College Hill, **London** during repairs following the blitz. The church was rebuilt in 1687–1691. From Pennick 1995. This find is also reported in Howard 1951.

Merrifield notes the discovery of a witch-bottle on the site of the Alhambra on the eastern side of Leicester Square, **London**. From Merrifield 1969.

A dried cat in the hunting pose was found in **London**, A correspondent reported in March 2010: 'I have presently been working on renovating a property in London SE5 and discovered a well preserved remains of a cat under the ground floor floor boards. I initially thought that it may have been trapped and died there but on mentioning this to a family friend, she suggested it may have been put there to ward off evil spirits. On researching this I discovered your web site and read your suggestions. I still have the cats remains – it is in a hunting pose with its mouth wide open. Hope this info is useful to you' No further details were provided.

Staff at the Guildhall Museum, Newport, Isle of Wight recalled that five bellarmines were discovered in a culvert in **London** when an underground car park was being constructed opposite the Victoria Tower. The culvert was well silted and stone-lined and each of the bottles had its bellarmine mask defaced and contained bone, pins and urine residues. It is believed that this was some kind of curse.

A pair of old boots was found beneath the Foreign and Commonwealth Office, Whitehall, **London**. Photo and description. Reported in February 2006. The building dates from the 1850s and while clearing out under the floor area, builders also found a cat's skull, no other bones. The skull was found in the same room as the boots. The cat skull and boots were re-interred with a time capsule and an account of their discovery a couple of months later.

A dried cat has been discovered in the Treasury building in SW1, **London**. According to those who know the history of the building, the cat must have got into the cavity around 1912 or 1935. Reported in October 2003 by e-mail.

A cat with a rat in its mouth was found between a wall and wainscotting in a house at **Lothbury** in 1803. This was demolished to make way for New Building, Bank of England. From Pennick 1995. This find is also reported in Howard 1951.

A bellarmine, described as Holmes Type VIII containing half a dozen brass pins and a handful of corroded iron nails, was discovered at Rathbone Place, **Marylebone**. It is thought that this bottle was buried in open country on the fringe of the town before it was built over. From Merrifield 1954.

Merrifield notes that a witch-bottle was discovered at **Roehampton**, thought to have been deposited in a ditch or buried in a field. From Merrifield 1969.

A cat and two rats were discovered beneath sixteenth-century wood-work in a house in Borough High Street, **Southwark**. One rat was in the cat's jaws, and the other beneath it. This was reported in the *Illustrated London News* of 8 December 1948. From Pennick 1995. This find is also reported in Howard 1951.

Merrifield notes a witch-bottle found possibly in a garden in Pennington Street, **Stepney**. This bottle contained iron nails, brass pins, human hair, nail parings and a piece of cloth. From Merrifield 1969. A small piece on this bottle appeared in *The Times*, 19 March 1954, 3, with a photograph.

A dried cat and underpants were found in an 1890/1900 house in **Stoke Newington**, London. This was reported in March 2016 as follows: 'In the late 1990's I bought and renovated a house in Stoke Newington, London. The estimated date of building was somewhere between 1890 and 1900. During the works we came across a cat's skeleton, found under the wooden "door" of a deep sill under a dormer window (The house had a mansard roof). Some time later, lifting up the floorboards on the ground floor living room (therefore near the house's entrance) we found quite a large quantity of men's underwear. There were old-style y-fronts and vests, the first we found had obviously been used, but as work proceeded we found loads more still in cellophane wrappings. All vests and pants, all looking to be the same size and colour and style, perhaps dating from the 50s or 60s, I don't know when cellophane started to be used. There was nothing written on the packets, as far as I can remember'.

At Battersea Square, **Wandsworth**, a cat's skull, part of a bellarmine and a fragment of clay pipe were found together during the excavation of a house. They were found either under a floor or behind a wall.

In a house at South Kenton near **Wembley** a pair of old men's shoes were found nailed to the beams in-between the plasterboards. The objects are thought to date to 1934. Excellent photo on file.

At St Augustine's Church, **Wembley Park**, a bottle containing a liquid, possibly just water, and a small pottery figurine were discovered. The figurine resembled the modern stereotype of the witch and it is possible that this 1906 deposit under a concrete floor was a modern re-interpretation of the witch-bottle. From Merrifield 1987: 182.

A bellarmine is reported from **Westminster**. On the bottom was a note to say that it was 'found towards the end of the 19th century when the Gas Light and Coke Co. was being rebuilt in Horseferry Road, Westminster'. This bottle was reported by Pat Winzar who continues, 'I was visiting someone and on commenting on the pot used for flowers, was told that if it might have a connection with witches would I please take it away. It had been the property of her Grandfather. I took it because there was no way of finding its original home and it could have been one of the many "empties" that were thrown into the Thames'. Pers. comm. 20 February 2001.

A bellarmine witch-bottle, described as 'Late form with crude mask of Holmes Type XI', was found at the corner of Great College Street and Tufton Street, **Westminster**. The bottle was discovered 10-11 feet below street level in 1904 and contained a cloth heart pierced with pins, human hair and nail parings. It is thought that this bottle was deposited onto the bed of an old mill stream, or buried on its bank. From Merrifield 1954. Photograph in article. A good photograph of this is included in Merrifield 1987. This witch-bottle is displayed in the 'Sympathetic Magic Case', Pitt Rivers Museum, Oxford. Kindly reported by Jason Semmens, pers. comm. 7 November 2002.

A witch-bottle, apparently a bellarmine, was discovered in **Westminster** around 1904–1905 which contained pins and rusty nails. From Merrifield 1954.

A dried cat is said to have been discovered in a wall of **Westminster** Abbey. From Pennick 1995.

A dried cat, known as Dr Liddle's cat from a collar with a tag which it allegedly wore, existed at Ashburnham House, **Westminster School**. The cat is now lost. From Pennick 1995. This find is also reported in Howard 1951.

Greater Manchester

At **Gorton** a rosary was discovered concealed beneath the floorboards of Gorton Monastery: 'A ROSARY buried under the floorboards in Gorton Monastery for more than 140 years has been found during restoration work. The set of Roman Catholic prayer beads was discovered in the organ loft by members of the Monastery of St Francis and Gorton Trust, working on the £6m restoration of the historic building. Measuring just eight inches long, the rosary was probably designed to be used by a child or a nun as they recited their "Hail Mary" prayers.

Tony Hurley, of the trust, said: "We've checked the floorboards and they're quite tightly fitted together so it doesn't appear that the rosary could have got there accidentally. We believe it was placed there but we don't know why"'. From *Manchester Evening News*, 29 August 2007.

An old boot was discovered behind a back wall (built half underground) of a house in George Street West, **Macclesfield**. The house dates to the 1850s but older brickwork exists in part of it. Reported in October 2002.

A dried cat was discovered by a builder during the renovation of a butchers' shop in central **Macclesfield**. The cat was found in thatch adjacent to an old rats' nest containing bones from the butchers' shop, dried rats and the cat. The building is timber-framed, possibly six-teenth-century, but the area where the cat was discovered may relate to a late nineteenth-century alteration. Reported in October 2002 by the finder and also reported in the *Macclesfield Observer*.

In a house in Worthington Street, **Old Trafford**, a bottle labelled 'Poison' was discovered behind an iron fireplace in 1986/7. The house is thought to date to 1900 and the bottle is thought to be of the same date. There were no contents in the bottle which was of clear glass, 4 inches high, 1 inch diameter, with a neck of ¾ inch. From a discussion with the finder, it is clear that the bottle was definitely sealed in behind the fireplace and access to it would not have been possible, indicating that the bottle was concealed intentionally at the time of the addition of the fireplace. It seems likely that this bottle was used as a charm to protect the hearth.

An impressive group of finds emerged from a cellar in the immediate environs of the Church Inn and the Parish Church of **Prestwich**, Greater Manchester. The group was found in a bricked-up alcove within the cellar, which is of seventeenth-century date or earlier. The group com-prised a dried cat, a mass of vegetable matter and three wooden figures enclosed in a cloth bag.

At Ordsall Hall in **Salford** a child's shoe was found under the floor-boards during restoration work. The shoe dates from the seventeenth century.

In Langshaw Street, **Salford**, a shoe was found upstairs in a chimney breast behind firebricks. The shoe dates to c.1911.

In a house in **Stockport** bones were found by a hearth during altera-tions. They comprised the bones from at least four rabbits, assorted bones of a large mammal (perhaps sheep), mainly rib bones, a bird's wing bone and the vertebra of a hare. Egg shell, hairpins and parts of a doll were also discovered here. The find was not thoroughly recorded but the house appears to date from the nineteenth century.

The curator of Saddleworth Museum refers to a number of shoes which have been found at a cottage in Tunstead, near Greenfield, **Saddleworth**. The items comprised one child's shoe, one adult's shoe, the sole of a child's shoe, unidentified pieces of leather with stitching holes, five shuttle pins of turned wood bored down the centre, a rounded stick with pointed end and a bead, and some unidentified pieces of wood with a metal strip in-between, bound with string. All these items were found in a wall of the house which is thought to date from 1700 or earlier. The curator also drew my attention to the custom of leaving late eighteenth-century cartwheel 2d coins in rafters when the roof is repaired; labourers' felt hats found among rafters were also regarded as charms.

Hampshire

Four bellarmine stoneware 'witch-bottles' were discovered in Duck Street, **Abbotts Ann**. Two were found inverted and two upright. All were found in close proximity to each other and one clearly had been situated before a hearth. From Allen 1991.

A single bellarmine witch-bottle was discovered in **Abbots Ann** in 1976, embedded in a chalk floor in front of the central hearth and stack. From Allen 1991. In a report entitled 'Under the Floor They Found a Witch's Pot', *Southern Echo*, 3 June 1977, 4, the bottle is said to have been dated to 1700 and was discovered when the floor was being lowered.

At the Crown Hotel, High Street, **Alton**, the skeleton of a dog was found behind a wall during alterations in 1967. This place was reputedly haunted by 'dog-like scratchings' which alarmed the owners' own pets prior to this discovery. Guy Lyon Playfair, from whose book (1985) this extract comes from, describes the haunting as a Black Dog but does not elaborate. Presumably the book has categories of ghosts and he put this dog noise and skeleton into the Black Dog section for a convenient reason. My thanks go to Jeremy Harte for passing on this reference.

In **Burley Street** in the New Forest it has been recorded that a number of bottles were discovered secreted in a roof space.

A dried cat was discovered in a cottage at **Harley Wespall** between ceiling joists.

The skull of what appears to have been a monkey was discovered beneath the floorboards of a house in **Hinton Ampner** when the old manor was demolished. From Pennick 1986: 6.

At **Hurstbourne Tarrant** church there are daisy wheels and other marks. Reported in October 2010.

In 1997 Trevor Butler of St Helens, **Isle of Wight** found a mummified cat in his chimney. Reported in Sieveking 1999.

At **Lymington** it is reported that a dried cat was discovered.

At Abbey Farm Cottage, **Mottisfont**, there is a daisy wheel on the lintel of the parlour chamber fireplace. Reported by Linda Hall in February 2009.

At the Old Sun Inn, Holyrood Street, **Newport**, Isle of Wight, it was reported that 'hidden in a void behind the chimney he came upon a dusty bundle of rags and a bag of ancient leather shoes. Inside the bundle was very old white cotton nightgown decorated with broderie anglais … and heavily bloodstained'. From Baldwin 1992.

A deposit of a vessel of some kind is recorded as having occurred beneath an early seventeenth-century almshouse at **Odiham**. From Magilton 1992. Merrifield refers to this pot as having been found under the threshold of a bricked-up doorway during renovations in 1968 – from Merrifield 1987: 120.

A drying shed from **Petersfield**, now in the Museum of Buildings at Singleton Park, West Sussex, has many protection marks on it. See the illustration in Easton 1999.

A sailor's hat and glove were found in the wreckage of the roof of the George pub, **Portsmouth**. The items are thought to date from about 1875 and were discovered after the place was bombed during the war. This find is reported in Keverne 1947: 153–54. I am grateful to Janet Pennington for passing this on to me.

In the Tudor House in **Southampton** it is reported that a concealed shoe was discovered in the 1970s during restoration work.

Staff at **Southampton** City Heritage Services report that concealed items were discovered in the medieval merchant's house in French Street in the City.

In Spring Road, **Southampton** a Johnnie Walker bottle with liquid inside was discovered beneath the floorboards. The house dates to

1904–1909 and the bottle was found when taking up floorboards. The cork in the bottle perished and the liquid evaporated, leaving a reddish brown residue.

A bellarmine witch-bottle may have been discovered in **Southampton**. The evidence is not conclusive, so I will cite the words of the reporter who reported this by e-mail in March 2003: 'I have recently found what is believed to be a Bellarmine bottle, this was during the excavations for a new building in Southampton. The find was confirmed by the Resident Archaeologist and as far as I am aware my bottle is the genuine article. The archaeologist could not confirm what the purpose was and I found your site most helpful understanding this', and later also, 'The bottle alongside an amount of clay also contained a few iron fillings and was buried at a depth of approximately 2 metres below the level of the current street. The bottle was found buried just of the vertical facing upwards and was found outside the foundations of an older building that had been destroyed some time ago, as far as I am aware this was the front entrance of the building. The position and orientation to the foundations suggested burial this is further supported by the fact that no other items of rubbish/pottery etc where found in the vicinity'.

A shoe discovery from **Southsea**, Hampshire was reported in February 2007: 'I am a property developer and am used to renovating old houses but have found, for the first time, an old shoe underneath the floorboards. The building was built in the 1850s here in Southsea, Hampshire. My father told me that there used to be an old custom of concealing shoes which got me digging on the internet for information. I will describe the black shoe: It is 100% a woman's shoe, with four holes either side for laces. Instead of laces though there is a black ribbon. It is made of leather but is heavily worn but does not seem to have been repaired apart from a mini horseshoe on the heel. I would love to know whether this was placed under the floor when the property was built therefore dating the shoe'.

Bellarmine fragments were recovered from beneath the floor of a nineteenth-century cottage in **Titchfield**. It is thought this could be evidence of a witch-bottle that was buried beneath the previous dwelling on the site. Reported in December 2001.

It is reported that a shoe was discovered nailed to the wall in loft space at **The Vyne**.

At St Cross church, **Winchester**, Linda Hall noted a daisy wheel on one of the columns, reported in February 2009.

In **Winchester Cathedral** Linda Hall noted that an ancient massive bench has a daisy wheel as a decorative motif at either end of the back. Reported in February 2009.

In June 2016 the following was reported: 'With a colleague I have been studying timber framed buildings in Hampshire for many years. Some years ago we came across a hazel rod – about 25mm in diameter and 1500mm long – in the roof of a former medieval hall house dendro dated to 1365. The rod was tied with cords fastened to the thatching battens, and it ran just under the slope of the roof between two of the rafters. Some of the thatching battens and rafters were still smoke blackened but the roof had been repaired with various new timbers and the hazel rod was not blackened. It occurred to us that it might be some form of apotropaic protection but we thought no more about it until we found two more examples in fairly quick succession in late 16th century buildings'. All three examples are in north **Hampshire**.

Joanne Thornton reported in May 2007 the presence of a twist of hair attached to some roof timber in a seventeenth/eighteenth-century farm-house on the **Isle of Wight**. She thinks the hair is human.

Herefordshire

In Rainbow Cottage, **Almely**, a witch-bottle was discovered in the inglenook fireplace.

In the **Aymestrey**/Leintwardine area, a written charm of around 1800 was found. The charm invokes spirits to compel a thief to return missing sheep. The charm has an eight-spoked circle to the left with symbols and astrological symbols figure in the text.

Two phials were found in a wall in a house just a few miles outside **Bromyard** at a farm dated to 1577, but owners have also been told it may date from 1485. This was reported in November 2008 as follows: 'I have just (today) found two bottles similar to the bottles on your website found at Pershore. They are in a wall next to a window, which may have had a chimney to the outside. One is empty and the other has some white substance which has oozed out of the cork. There is evidence of there having been a label. I live 3 miles outside Bromyard, Herefordshire. I have put the bottles back, but my builder friend couldn't remember which way they were facing. We think they fit better with the open end facing inwards but would this be so? My house has 15th century origins, but the bottles are much later obviously'.

Burn marks and shoes were found in a farmhouse near **Bromyard**. The owner thinks the burn marks are grouped in threes, to represent the Trinity. Reported in December 2016 and beyond.

A concealed shoe buckle and leather strap were found at a cottage in **Cradley**, reported in April 2008 as follows: 'I have just found a hidden shoe buckle and leather strap in our 17th century, grade2 listed cottage that I am renovating. The 3' buckle was hidden in the gap between a beam and the chimney above the fireplace in the upstairs room. From websites it would appear that the type of buckle is post medieval'. June Swann analysed the items as follows: 'The style of buckle, and it is for shoes, is most likely from the 1770s, with the curves and piercing, and H-type shape'.

There is a VV mark in the attic of **Croft Castle** on one of the rafters in the servants' quarters. Reported in April 2016 by Ben Moule who works for Hereford Museums.

In **Garway Church** a concealed arrowhead was discovered while trying to hook some wire around a column for decorations. Reported by Frances Phillips in November 2017 via e-mail as follows: 'Hereford Museum suggested that I contact you about a recent find in the church, which has a long history of Knights Templars and Hospitallers. One of our parishioners was doing flower arrangements for a wedding (mine!), and wanted to poke a piece of florist's wire around a pillar which is immediately beneath our Green Man carving on the chancel arch. She worked some of the dust of ages out with her scissors to make room for the wire, and an arrow head popped out. The Museum in Hereford has had a look at it and confirms that it is a hunting/multi-purpose arrowhead, dates 1200-1300. There is absolutely no way this could have got there by accident--it was hidden on purpose. Whether it had a shaft all those years ago, or whether it was just the head that was hidden, we cannot tell'.

A dried cat was discovered in a barn at **Heightington**. Reported by Ben Moule in April 2016.

Nigel Pennick reports that a wooden doll with attached curse was discovered in the area and is held at Hereford City Museum. It is thought that this doll was discovered during rebuilding of an old house in **Hereford**. From Pennick 1986: 7. Further investigation reveals that the doll was discovered in a crevice in the brickwork below the basement stairs in 21 East Street. The curse was found folded within the dolls skirt and reads, 'Mary Ann Ward, I act this spell upon you from my holl heart wishing you to never rest nor eat nor sleep the rester part of your life. I hope your flesh will waste away and I hope you will never spend another penny I ought to have. Wishing this from my whole heart'. The doll body is made of wood, with arms and legs of red checked material. The head bears traces of paint, and string and a silk pigtail is attached. Thanks to Ben Moule from Hereford Museums for allowing me access in April 2016. The doll is currently in Museum Stores, Friar Street, Hereford, and is thought to date to the nineteenth century.

It has been reported to me that a concealed shoe is now on display in the Heritage Centre in **Ledbury** – the shoe was found in the building.

In **Leintwardine** a dried cat and shoe were found in the walls of a house.

A dried cat was reported from **Little Birch** in January 2002. The report reads: 'I am writing to tell you the story a lady in Little Birch, Herefordshire, told me – about her experience of a mummified cat. Just after the 2WW had ended, she and her husband bought their first house in the upper reaches of Little Birch. It was an old farmhouse, built around 1800. It was a very well built house, and the wattle and daub had survived for at least 150 years. This lady tells of a very strange experience in their main bedroom when they first moved in (she believes it to be true as her husband who "wouldn't see a ghost if it was under his nose" also experienced it). During the night, they would feel a cat jump up onto the bed, pad around, then settle down. They owned no cats at the time and whenever the light was switched on, there would be no sign of a cat, but a warm indentation in the duvet as if one had been there.

This continued each night until, deciding to have an extension, the West wall of the bedroom was demolished. Inside the wattle and daub frame of the wall, was found a perfectly preserved tabby cat. It appeared to have a little leather bag strung around its neck, filled with what looked to be teeth – whether human or animal I don't know. They gave the cat a proper burial in the garden and a tombstone, and were plagued no longer by a cat on the bed'.

Many marks can be found at a house in **Mansell Lacey**, Herefordshire, as reported in August 2011. These include burn marks and daisy wheels.

Twenty-seven horse skulls were discovered beneath the floorboards of High House, **Peterchurch** during renovations. 'We came across one skull and then found other lying between the joists'. From *The Hereford Times*, 26 February 1987.

At the Market House, **Ross-on-Wye**, Linda Hall reports the following: 'Ross on Wye Market House, supposedly built between 1660 and 1674, burn marks and incised marks on the wooden pillars on the first floor. Or are the incised marks merchants' marks?'

At an old inn called the Portway at **Staunton-on-Wye** twenty-four horse skulls were found screwed through the eye-holes to the underside of the floorboards in three rows. The skulls were allegedly placed there to make the fiddle go better. From Armitage 1989b. Discovery reported (including photo) in *The Hereford Times*, 8 July 1993 and also in *The Hereford Times*, 15 July 1993.

At a house in **Westhope** a variety of marks have been found including circles and a daisy wheel. A jawbone was also found at the base of a timber. The owners wrote in March 2018.

At **Woolhope** a nineteenth-century 'Witches Coffin Curse' was found. It is a human effigy lying in a coffin, both made of wood. The body is pinned to the back of the coffin with a nail. It was found concealed in a wall at Woolhope in 1987. Thanks to Ben Moule from Hereford Museums for allowing me access in April 2016. The item is currently in Museum Stores, Friar Street, Hereford.

Hertfordshire

A hand-blown green glass bottle was discovered in the tower of **Anstey Church**.

A dried brown rat was found behind plaster in 28 Hodwell, **Ashwell**. From Pennick 1995.

In June 2002 Simon Walker reported the existence of a daisy wheel variation from **Ashwell Church**.

A dried cat is said to have been discovered in the roof space of 83 High Street, **Baldock**. From Pennick 1995.

A dried brown rat was discovered between roof rafters at 11 High Street, **Baldock** on 23 June 1982. From Pennick 1995.

At a cottage in Berden, near **Bishops Stortford**, Herts, a series of objects have been discovered. The owner describes the finds as follows: 'I live in a 17th C. thatch cottage which up to 1963 belonged to the Priory, then it went into private ownership. We have lived here since 1984 and during our time here we have carried out extensive renovations. We found a single shoe lodged under the staircase when this was exposed (the outside wall was partially removed). But more interesting was the plough share which had been concealed over the lintel of the main door. The door had to be replaced by a window, so we decided to put it back over the lintel of the new doorway, somehow we felt it had to go there and be thoroughly concealed as it was before. My feeling was that it brought enough food into the house and ensured we would not go hungry. We also found a skull of a squirrel inside a wall near the inglenook (no other bones, just a perfect skull). Also found a wild boar tusk in the garden'. Reported in October 2003.

In **Caldecote** a complete donkey was buried in a barn. It is thought that this was to ward off a beast which roamed locally according to local folk belief.

At **Great Hormead** it is reported that shoes were found dating to 1700.

A dried rat was found in a house in Tilehouse Street, **Hitchin** in 1982. From Pennick 1995.

Simon Walker sent me this extract relating to a foundation deposit on 7 January 2017:
'*THE BEDFORDSHIRE ADVERTISER*, FRIDAY, AUGUST 21, 1903
Alterations at old houses in **Hitchin** during the past week or two provided a good deal of interest for antiquaries. The house occupied by Messrs. Passingham, which was at one time a religious house, is full of evidences of its great age. The well-known figures which ornamented either end of the roof have been brought down and found to be excellent specimens of tile work, which some consider to date from Pagan times. An interesting discovery was made by the workmen engaged in pulling down the shop lately occupied by Mr. Raban in Golden-square. They were pecking away part of the foundations and found, at a depth of about four feet, a small cinerary jar, containing what are supposed to be human ashes. The jar, which was unfortunately broken by a pick, was about six inches high, of globular form, and is glazed green. In front of the hole in which it was found was an old tile. The same men dug out a human leg bone. During alterations to the business premises of Mr. J.R. Jackson, Market-place, three coins were found cemented in a wall, one being a Charles II. halfpenny, dated 1660, one a George III. penny, dated 1770, and the third a George III. penny, dated 1779. It is supposed to have been an old custom to insert coins in the walls of housed so as to denote the date of the building. These coins, despite their long imprisonment, are in remarkably good preservation'.

The stretched hairless skin of a rabbit (or a young hare) on a stick was found embedded in the wall of a house near **Hitchin.** From Pennick 1995.

At Ransoms Barn in **Hitchin** some 'dagaz' or butterfly marks have been discovered by Simon Walker. Reported in October 2004.

Above the church porch at **Meesdon** there is a moulded brick 'daisy'.

At a cottage in Warrengate Road, Waterend, **North Mymms**, Herts, an apparent 'spiritual midden' has been discovered. The house is a mid-eighteenth-century farm cottage but the owner estimates that the arte-facts all date from the late nineteenth century. The finds are described as 'shoes, hat, scissors, bottles, lids, newspapers, bones, shells, platted bundle, large exotic sea shells found in rubble infill in fireplace, remain-der found in wall by door. Glass bottles late 19C newspapers dated 1894/5. Shoes leather laced 7 eye holed? childs size 3-4 shoe + felt shoe larger, bones – bird skulls, 2 x metal pot lids small metal lid. Wooden clothes peg, Under floor? ox tooth and pottery/bone'. Reported in August 2001.

A local legend says that a dried cat once existed in a house in the High Street, **Royston**. It is reported that a haunting ceased once the cat was removed. From Pennick 1995.

At **Shillington Church** shoe outlines have been carved into the stone bench in the porch. There is also a daisy wheel. Reported by Simon Walker in December 2003.

At a house just outside **St Albans** a child's shoe and two bottles were found in what is thought to be an animal shelter at the side of the house. The house dates back to around 1700. The items were found in the ground after removing a concrete slab. Reported in January 2012. Nearby there were also some bones, although I have found a good many bones in various places, and these may not have been deliberately concealed.

A shoe was discovered at a hall in **Tewin** dating to 1700.

A hoard, or spiritual midden, was found in a house in **Walsworth**, Hitchin. The following information was supplied by Simon Walker in January 2002: 'The house is of unknown age, though the present owners say that the people they bought it from claimed to have traced its his-tory to the 17th century, when they gave up, because earlier documents were in Latin. It looks 17th century to me – not much older, but I'm not an expert. It is timber frame, and when the current owners moved in several of the walls were covered with hardboard and wallpaper.

Behind the studwork supporting the hardboard was lathe and plaster, brick, and in one case wattle and daub. The house has two stories. Ground Floor Room 1: finds were from above a lathe, plaster and horse-hair ceiling, beneath two layers of floor boards, laid at 90º to each other; Julie thinks that the newer plaster boards were simply laid over the old ones when they wore out. The objects fell out when the old ceiling was removed. The hoard consisted of: one damaged shoe, three stone or clay marbles, a pair of scissors, a small horseshoe, perhaps 2.5' across, two iron items (hinge brackets?) though no hinge attached, brass buttons with four cotton holes, marked "Beales Cambridge", a button with brass loop fitting, depicting a figure holding a Greek cross to the left and a lion to the right. Behind the lion is a naval anchor. A very worn bronze coin, about the diameter of an old penny, or a little smaller, but thicker than a penny. No detail is visible. A second coin or perhaps a token. Roughly struck, reminiscent of the sort of quality of a lot of Roman coins. It feels like it's made of lead. It is not possible to make out the detail, though it is quite prominent. There may be a cross to the left on one side. Ground Floor Room 2: finds behind plaster above centre of fireplace: a dried and hairless cat, a dried and hairless rat. Both animals were pretty flat, though the skulls were intact. The cat was eaten by a family dog, and what remained was thrown away, along with the rat'. Information copyright of Simon Walker, January 2002.

In a farm in Halls Green, **Weston**, a large hoard of objects was discovered behind an inside wall of a bedroom. The list is as follows: a red ceramic costrel with basketry cover; a hair comb; a cheek snaffle horse bit created from two different bits, where the cheek pieces had been cut with a sharp knife; a sword scabbard, mis-assembled with hangers twisted; slipware sherd; a black leather shoe for an adult male dating between 1695 and 1720; two small pieces of white fabric block printed in red with floral design, dated 1675–1690; fragments of a woman's corset in white linen with wooden bones, 1650–1750; red ware sherds; other sherds; two stones; stoneware sherds; a deep green-black glass bottle with deep conical frog; a blue ceramic bead; a fragment of leather jacket, 1600–1700; the blade of a metal knife. This material is probably a spiritual midden as apparently the objects were accumulated over time having been deposited through a hole in the attic.

Isle of Man

A horse skull was discovered in a house known as Squeen Lodge at **Ballaugh**. 'While the builders were removing the first floor joists they uncovered what appeared to be a skull and hip bone set into a joist hole ... [on investigation] ... it was in fact a horse's skull with twin boar tusks inserted into the tooth sockets of the upper jaw'. The find is thought to date from the eighteenth century. From Hayhurst 1989.

A dried cat was discovered beneath the floor of a public house in **Douglas**, probably nineteenth-century. From Garrad 1989.

Two stone axe heads (thunderstones) were discovered in different structures at **Old Laxey**, Lonan. From Garrad 1989.

A stone axe head (thunderstone) was discovered beneath the earthen floor of a cowshed at Ballavell, **Malew**. From Garrad 1989.

A stone axe head (thunderstone) was discovered built into a wall at a farm at Ballastowell, **Maughold**. From Garrad 1989.

A stone axe head (thunderstone) was discovered in an old loomshed at Cregneash, **Rushen**. From Garrad 1989.

Kent

In a house in **Belvedere** which was built in 1803 some objects were discovered concealed behind a lock in the front door. They were wrapped in a cloth and included a worn farthing, a button and a bean seed.

Nine witch-bottles were discovered under the hearth of an old timber-framed building at Minnis Bay, **Birchington**, Margate.

At Whitefriars Abbey excavations, **Canterbury**, numerous daisy wheels on stonework were reported by archaeologist Tracey Smith in an e-mail of September 2008: 'The second example was from the Whitefriars Abbey excavations in Canterbury, Kent, where a number of crudely carved stone blocks were recovered from one of the rooms that had been backfilled with stone rubble after the dissolution of the abbey. These were covered in carvings, which included the daisy wheel symbol as well as a crude rendering of what looked like an eagle or bird of prey of some type and a person's name. This was thought to have been the work of an apprentice stone mason'.

Several eighteenth-century apothecary bottles were discovered within the walls of Latchmere House, Watling Street, **Canterbury**. They contained, variously, lizards, a snake and insects.

At 41 St Peter's Street, **Canterbury**, shoes and other finds from a chimney stack were discovered; they are thought to date from 1701–1750.

It is reported that two complete bull skeletons were discovered under the footings of the north-west tower of **Canterbury Cathedral**. From Pennick 1986: 6.

At a house in **Chartwell** a shoe from the 1930s was discovered. From Brooks 2000.

In Winzar (1995: 26), the following reference to a witch-bottle in **Charing** is found: 'Until 1993, only one instance of a witch jar had been found in Charing. In the 1960s the owner of The Old House in Station Road, asked for the help of Mr P Oldham and the Charing and District Local History Society to excavate the floor of the main room before it was laid with concrete. In the back right-hand corner of the seventeenth-century chimney hearth a "Bellarmine" jar was found. No contents were recorded and the jar was retained by the owner'.

In Winzar (1995: 26–28, with illustrations), the following charm from **Charing** is reported: 'Early in 1993 a sealed chimney was opened up in no.32 High Street. From the architectural and documentary evidence the chimney had been built in the seventeenth century. A charm was found about five feet up on the right-hand side inside the chimney. It had been set in wet mortar and so presumably was placed there when the chimney was built. It consisted of a piece of paper sealed with animal glue. For further security the paper was tied on with a length of linen string with a tassel at each end. The charm was sent for analysis and conservation to a specialist paper conservator, Miss C. Lewis, whose report states that: 'The paper was in a brittle and friable condition. Some areas of the paper were badly charred. Examination of the paper under ultra-violet and infra-red light was carried out. This revealed patches of animal glue but no writing. A microscopic examination of the paper revealed spots of red paint. (Red is a colour associated with witches). Fibre analysis was also carried out to determine the composition of the paper. This revealed that the paper is mainly made of linen with some hemp. The piece of string is made from linen. The iron nail is handmade and typical of those made up to c. 1750'. Contact with the current owner of the property confirms the details above and the fact that a special box has been created to museum conservation standard to house the charm.

Two bottles were found beneath the hearth of 27–29 High Street, **Charing** (once one dwelling). Reported in Winzar 1995, with photos and good description (photos on file). She writes: 'In the summer of 1993, nos 27 and 29 High Street, Charing (originally one building), were undergoing renovation during which another seventeenth-century sealed chimney was opened up. Under the bricks of the central hearth two small jars were found and removed by the builder. Jar A was all but complete but Jar B was broken into two pieces with about 50 per cent of the jar missing. It would seem that the jars were once identical in size and design with a hard light brown glaze speckled with blue. They were about 5in in height, depending on the original size of the neck which was broken on both jars.

The contents were examined using an Olympus VE3 x 40 microscope and found to contain in Jar A – the more complete pot:

17 round-headed pins of copper alloy, pointed ends, bent double. One of the pins has a lump of corroded matter attached. There seems to be iron, a hair and a spread of yellow gunge which I am told is sulpher.

2 small pieces of wood pierced with holes.

Burnt charcoal flakes.

Quartz – round grains.

Bone flakes and tiny fragments – possibly some powdered bone.

3 threads from a greeny colour textile.

Calcite dust with quartz grains.

Odd moulded pieces of calcium carbonate and quartz grains, the consistency of lime mortar.

3 small pieces of iron stained bone.

2 small pieces of iron.

Strand of hair, only visible under microscope.

Jar B, had lost most of its contents but contained:

1 pin as described for Jar A.

2 small flaked pieces of iron stained bone.

1 strand of thick hair (yellowish colour).

2 strands of textile fibre.

Debris containing iron granules with calcite and quartz'.

A Victorian child's shoe was discovered in the chimney of the Red Lion Inn at **Charing Heath**. Reported by Pat Winzar in February 2001.

At a cottage in Cooling Street, **Cliffe**, Rochester, a dried cat was found in the roof space in 1970. The house dates from the 1750s. Reported in January 2002.

In a house in **Cranbrook** a girl's shoe was found above the first floor – it is thought to date from 1725.

At a farmhouse in **Cranbrook**, two concealed shoes were recovered from an obvious 'spiritual midden'. It is reported that from the attic on the third floor it was possible to see down to the kitchen fireplace owing to the presence of a gap between the chimney and the outside wall. More shoes remain at the bottom of this gap. Of the two that were recovered, one was an ankle boot and the other was a shoe – both thought to date from the 1860s. During restoration to another ingle-nook fireplace in the house, a dried rat was discovered.

At another farm in **Cranbrook**, two shoes were discovered during the restoration of the chimney in the 1960s. One was a small boy's ankle boot and the other also appeared to be a child's boot. Both are thought to date from the 1840s–1850s.

A large assortment of finds was discovered beneath **Cuxton Chapel** including bottles, frying pan and a child's boot. The finder describes the finds as follows in January 2003: 'Just found out that the oval bottle is a urinary bottle, so quite excited about that as that fits with the anti witchcraft protection. I have listed the bottles in my inventory as such:

1 x oval urinary bottle flat based with "Tribe & Lamb Chatham – Chemists" embossed on upper surface
4 x small square ridged bottles
1 x small round bottle in orange glass
1 x large square sided corked bottle with chamfered shoulders ('2711' on base)
1 x tall bottle with high neck & possible remains of red label
1 x small bottle with high neck & remains of red & green label (cork inside)
1 x small square sided bottle with cork stopper embossed "Eiffel Tower Lemonade" on one side & "Foster Clarke &Co Maidstone" on the other.
1 x tall thin corked bottle with short neck
The frying pan as I may have mentioned before is badly corroded iron and has a deliberate hole in the end of the handle (possibly for hanging from?)

The Child's boot has been identified by Northampton Museum as late 19th Century having as it does a pointed toe. It has a machine sewn upper and riveted sole construction and has had a half sole repair. It has a "reasonably low heel" and could be either a girl's or boy's boot'.

During the demolition of Bugden Hall, Lowfield Street, **Dartford**, a child's hand-made leather bootee with square toe was found inside a wall.

During the demolition of Longfield Monastery, near **Dartford**, a hand-made left shoe with a square toe-cap was discovered. It is thought to date from the late eighteenth century.

It is reported that a dried kitten was discovered in **Dover Castle**, thought to date from the medieval period.

A hand-made shoe was found in the roof space of a Tudor dwelling at Riverside, **Eynsford**. The shoe has been dated to 1800–1810.

In June 2007 a bellarmine bottle and dried cat discovery was reported from a farmhouse on Bedgebury Road, **Goudhurst**. 'Alan Massey has suggested I contact you about a bottle found last week when we had the old worn brick floor of our cellar removed. The house dates back to about 1470, but I don't know when the cellar floor was put in. The builders who found it say there were no contents, but it has been suggested this could have been a witch bottle. Unfortunately the builders rinsed it out with tap water, so it seems we will never be sure now as to whether it was a witch bottle or not. They have confirmed that nothing was rattling inside, and did not see any spilled contents on the soil. It may also be of interest for you to know that we have been told there is a petrified cat and rat buried in the far wall of our house. There had apparently been a chimney there which fell down. Some builders were called in to block it off and found the cat and rat. Story is that they drove around with it in the boot of their car until they were told it was bad luck, and so came back and reburied in the wall. We cannot verify this unless someone in the village remembers'.

At a substantial house in **Goudhurst**, it was reported in November 2010 that 'We have many really clear examples of the "daisywheel" on two beams near our fireplace, the house was built in 1470. I will now get a torch and have a good look for any further sigils'. She added later on: 'following my previous mail, I got my torch and have indeed found further marks! We have one arrangement of the daisy wheel where five wheels are overlapped into a larger five petalled design. Also, there are smaller circles with the letters "IH" in them. We have also had a dried cat and a stone carved talisman which was buried at the north of the house outside'.

It is reported that a witch-bottle was discovered at **Gravesend**. From Streeten 1976. It is likely that this is the bottle that exists at Gravesham Museum, Gravesend. An article from 1965 describes the find in detail. The bottle was discovered on the north side of West-street, Gravesend. It contained over a pound of assorted metal objects, of which three quarters were iron nails and pins. The bottle was found embedded in undisturbed river mud at a depth of about five feet. The mask on the bottle is a very degenerate Holmes Type IX and the bottle is generally very distorted and misshapen. The jug was stoppered with a solid lead plug, which unfortunately was drilled out and the vessel emptied before a chance for analysis was allowed. 420 grams of the metal were iron nails, a further 30 grams were of iron wire and other fragments, hundreds of brass pins were also in the bottle, amounting to 32.5 grams and 35 grams of window leading were also present. Stones, pieces of bone, coal, coke, wood, grass and dirt comprised the remainder. A lock of hair, a glass bead and a small diamond shaped gilt ornament were also found. From Tilley 1965.

Merrifield refers to a witch-bottle being discovered inverted beneath the hearth at **Hoath** near Herne Bay. From Merrifield 1987: 174.

At **Ightham Mote** eleven boots and shoes have been discovered during ten years of conservation work. From Brooks 2000. There are also a number of marks on a first-floor hearth lintel.

The Cobtree Museum of **Kent** Life reported that a farmhouse they recently acquired contained some artefacts which were discovered during dismantling. A child's boot was found concealed under the floorboards of the main bedroom, roughly in the middle of the room. It has been dated to around 1850. A small wooden doll with the trunk of its body crudely cut off was also discovered and is thought to have come from the door frame or lintel, or possibly a nearby window frame from inside the plasterwork. The doll wore no clothes, had no hair, no arms and a plaster and painted face. The body was painted pink and it had a scrap of material knotted around its neck with a design of red triangles.

Pat Winzar (1986) refers to an article which details finds in a **Kent** house. It apparently concerns the discovery of some unusual clay pots. The pots were 'stuffed from a hole in an upper room in a 15th century house into the ceiling space at a much later time when the hall was floored at first floor level. ... It was in the same house that a collection of odd shoes were found behind plaster on the first floor. The said plaster had been put on the outside of the inserted brick chimney on the landing, sealing in the shoes. June Swann has seen the photographs, but the intriguing thing about them is the spread of dating. There were a number of shoes surviving from before the Civil War in the 1640s, a lot more from the 1660s period with very few from 1640–50. The collection also had a few tools connected with shoemaking or repairing. Most interesting to me was the portion of a knitted heel of a sock or stocking, turned in the traditional way'. Pers. comm. 20 February 2001.

A bellarmine bottle was discovered during alterations to the fireplace at The Elephant's Head, Hook Green, **Lamberhurst**. It is thought to date from the late seventeenth century and, although traces of a cork were found, there were no contents. Its location suggests its use as a witch-bottle. From Streeten 1976.

In the kitchen at **Leeds Priory** the lower part of a pottery vessel was discovered when part of the clay hearth was removed: 'one is reminded of the custom of burying Bellarmine jugs and other vessels in hearths, containing charms against witches, though whether this is the explanation in this instance is far from certain'. From Tester 1978.

The skeleton of a cat was discovered in the 1940s at Little Woodlands, **Lyminge**. The skeleton was attached to a chain consisting of brass emblems positioned high up the chimney breast. From Pennick 1995.

At the sixteenth century Tudor Cottage, Cellar Hill, **Lynsted**, Sittingbourne, two dried cats and a child's shoe were discovered during restoration in 1968. The shoe was of leather and is believed to date from the late seventeenth to the early eighteenth century.

At Salmestone Grange, **Margate**, three witch-bottles were discovered under a demolished out-building. The building is described as dating back 'several centuries'.

At **Minster** a pair of shoes were discovered in the chimney in a large space. The shoes were described as belonging to a male, having metal buckles and 'old maps on funny sort of paper, with old fashioned ships on them'. The shoes were discovered after a serious fire in the 1930s but have since been destroyed and the cottage has been demolished.

Dr Peter Rumley reported in September 2003 that 'During the conservation Newenden Oast, **Newenden**, Kent, a concealed shoe was discovered within the timber framework of the north first floor elevation of the structure. Just below the small window on the landing at the top of the staircase which was inserted in 1999'. The building dates from 1857. Dr Rumley is consultant archaeologist for the National Trust in the area.

At Queen's Court, Queen's Street, **Ramsgate**, a dried cat was discovered during excavation.

During alterations to a sixteenth-century building in **Rochester** High Street (a restaurant named Elizabeth's of Eastgate at the time of publication), a child's shoe and the lock from a flintlock gun, both circa 1800–1820, were found concealed in a chimney. From Moad 1976.

At a farm near **Sheperdswell**, an old child's shoe was found on a ledge up the chimney. This was reported as follows in August 2011: 'We are about to move into an old family house and when looking around tonight I found an old child's shoe on a ledge in the chimney, I'd like to make it a special feature perhaps putting it in a frame to protect it and house it on the ledge, but is the tradition that I hide it and never speak of it, to leave it be to protect the house and family, I'd so love to think it would bring fertility ... any suggestions and what's the traditional thing to do'. She later added in January 2012: 'I will take a photo and send it to you, the shoe was found about 50 years ago by the father of a friend of my other half, they had the house and grew up in it as children, oddly the friend dropped by just before Christmas and when we showed him around he went to the fireplace and pulled out the shoe he knew it would still be there, I hadn't mentioned it!!! He said his dad found it when they uncovered the fireplace years ago and placed a note by it ... that note is still there asking that the shoe was not removed as it protects the family from evil spirits. I think I will leave the shoe alone, although I'd like to preserve it'.

A report from the *Daily Telegraph* of 29 August 2001 mentions the rescue of a cat in **Sittingbourne**, Kent. The article reads: 'A cat has been rescued by firemen after being trapped for three weeks in a 6in pipe beneath a concrete floor in the garage of a new house. The 12-year old tabby, which survived by licking condensation on the pipe sides, was sealed in when workmen poured the concrete. A week after moving into the new house near Sittingbourne, Kent, Susan Mersh and her family heard the cat's cries and called the fire brigade. Firemen dug up part of the floor to reach the cat which was later reunited with its owner in a neighbouring street'. Thanks to Janet Pennington for sending me this extract.

A concealed shoe has been discovered under the floorboards of a first-floor room at The Plough, in East Street, **Sittingbourne**, Kent. This was reported in December 2002. The building dates from the seventeenth century but was radically altered in the mid-eighteenth century. Photos of the shoe were sent to June Swann for analysis and her considered opinion was as follows: 'Woman's tie shoe, with side seams fairly close to central and blunt toe, should put it c1760s'. There were further finds in The Plough, when a huge quantity of material was recovered from this building prior to its demolition. Photos and papers are on file. Thanks to Alan Abbey for organising access to the material. The visit to Sittingbourne Heritage Museum took place in August 2009. For full details, see Abbey 2010.

At the Red Lion public house in **Snargate** (sixteenth century), an old shoe was found up the chimney.

An eighteenth- or early nineteenth-century stoneware bottle containing nails and pieces of wood was discovered beneath the hearth of Clapper Farm, **Staplehurst**. From Tilley 1965.

A steeple bottle was discovered under the floor of Ely Court at **Staplehurst**. From Merrifield 1987: 123.

In **Tenterden** a concealed shoe was discovered in a house.

At The Old Vicarage, **Upchurch**, six concealed shoes were discovered during the demolition of the central chimney stack. These comprise three ladies' walking slippers and three shoes probably for male children of varying ages. All the shoes are of leather and are provisionally dated to 1740/1820. From Moad 1976.

At Cade House, **West Malling**, two sixteenth-century knives were found built into the wall. Merrifield believed they may have been put there as a charm. From Merrifield 1969.

Lancashire

At **Barnoldswick** a single child's clog, a tiny slipper and a hand-made child's bodice were found in a bricked-up oven.

A concealed shoe was found in **Blackburn**, Lancashire, as reported in October 2011: 'Hi there I read the article on hidden shoes on the apotropaios website with great interest having just recently found one in my house. It was a ladies strappy sandal high heel appearing like it came from the seventies and had the look of a prop from the film the omen which creeped me out a bit. It was nailed to the underside of the main roofing joist in the attic and I had seen it before but paid it no mind thinking of it as a builders prank. Only when it struck me as particularly odd did I ever inspect it closely. Just the other week I removed it but kept it in the garage just in case. No significant change has occurred but I think I will return it anyway. There are also a pair of lucky horseshoes nailed to the back fence so I can only presume a former occupant must have been superstitious. The house is a suburban semi in Blackburn Lancashire and was built in 1965 I believe. So this would be one of the later examples of this habit. Thank you for posting such an interesting if mysterious article on your website'.

A dried cat was discovered in a sealed room in a cottage at **Black Moss Reservoir**, Pendle. This was reported widely in the press as being a 'witches cottage' but was really nothing of the sort, although it does date to the seventeenth century. This was in a lot of press and Jennie Cobban also reported it to me in December 2014.

In the Museum of Lancashire in Preston there are four charms which were all found in a seventeenth-century farmhouse at **Charnock Richard**. One is what looks like a worn brick with a 'Y' shape in it, a cow's gall stone with a hole almost right through it, a piece of stone which is almost hollowed out and a spatula with rune-like letters on it.

A small metal skull (bass relief) was discovered in 1945 behind the fireplace of Warehouse Farm at **Glasson Dock** near Lancaster. The ornament is unusually detailed and has a frog on the front and a pine cone, flower and snail on the back.

At a property in Foxholes Road, **Horwich**, Bolton, Lancs, a number of pins and needles were found behind an old fireplace. This was reported in January 2007: 'We have just prised away an old mantlepiece from a disused fireplace in our old stone house in Bolton. There has been much modernisation work over the years and the chimney has not been used for many years. A number of rusty needles and hatpins fell from behind the mantlepiece along with a brass weight marked a quarter of an ounce. I vaguely remembered something about things being hidden in old houses from a radio programme and found your site, to discover the practice of sticking bullocks' hearts with pins. Although our needles and pins were not found up the chimney itself (and perhaps had simply slipped down behind the mantle shelf at some time) it made me wonder, and I thought you might be interested to hear about it'. The farmhouse dates from the nineteenth century but may have earlier origins.

The following was reported in November 2013: 'There is reference to 18th century shoes found in a void on the stairs in the Witches Tower **Lancaster Castle**'.

A written charm is recorded from **Pendle** dating to 1900.

In **Rawtenstall** two witch-posts have been discovered in houses.

In a house in Back Lane, **Trawden**, a stoneware bottle was discovered under floorboards in 1955. 'It was intact and contained nails, a ball of hair and an "unidentified liquid" which was no doubt urine. Trawden was an apt place to find a witch bottle as it was on her way to Trawden that Lancashire witch Alizon Device met the pedlar John Law with disastrous consequences'. This was shared by Jennie Cobban in May 2017.

About thirty years ago a shoe was found concealed in a hole in a beam in an eighteenth-century stone cottage in **Wheelton**, near Chorley. The find was made in an upstairs room forming part of the attic. Reported in March 2002.

At **Whittington** a perforated stone axe hammer which was ploughed up in a field was for some time hung as a 'lucky stone'. From Penney 1976.

A witch doll is reputed to have been found in a chimney in **Worston**. Reported by Jennie Cobban in November 2002.

Leicestershire

At New House Grange, Orton Lane, Sheepy Magna, **Atherstone**, there are many protection marks in the impressive barn which formerly belonged to Merevale Abbey. I am reliably informed that the barn falls just within Leicestershire even though it has a Warwickshire postcode. The barn has been dendro-dated to 1506 and one end of it was on many floors containing rooms where presumably the administration for the barn's contents took place. A large quantity of tally marks exists around the main door on the first floor of the barn in addition to numerous other marks. There are drawings of keys around the door done by a variety of hands, several 'P' characters, some patterns made with small holes, and some curvilinear designs. In the barn itself almost all of the major uprights (massive oak timbers) have either dagaz/butterfly marks on them, several have daisy wheels, and others have criss-cross patterns similar to many other ritual mark examples.

At the Lamb Inn, **Ashby-de-la-Zouch** (upper floors), it is reported that protection marks exist there.

In **Ashwell** it is reported that protection marks are to be found at a farmhouse.

Staff at Stranraer Museum in Scotland report the finding of a number of leather shoes and fragments of leather clothing in a late medieval bell pit in **Coleorton**, Leics. The finds are reported to be held by the County Museum and the correspondent states that this may be a particularly early example of the practice of leaving shoe offerings in metal mines in the eighteenth/nineteenth centuries.

Alan Massey reports that the witch-bottle found in Rutland is of 'bellarmine' type and came complete with contents. It is thought to date from the seventeenth century and was found below the hearth at 1 Malting's Yard in **Exton**, Rutland; the find is held at Oakham Museum. A short report by G.C. Morgan on the bottle summarises the contents as follows: 'In conclusion, we can say that the bottle contains a liquid of pH 7.4 (neutral) with probably plant extracts, animal and human hair and traces of grass, rootlets and bark, and an altered fat such as tallow'.

A large quantity of protection marks on plaster are recorded for a house in **Frisby-on-the-Wreake**. This was reported in November 2007 as follows: 'I am an archaeologist based in Leicester, also studying part time for an MA. I have recently been working on a 15th century timber-framed building, located in Frisby-on-the-Wreake, Leicestershire, where a number of plaster-filled panels within a closed truss have been covered in graffiti. I am still in the process of uncovering the plaster-work and so have yet to record much of what is there – but there are inscribed names, anthropomorphic figures, bells, creatures, scissors, large daisy wheels, Ms, Vs, all kinds of stuff – undated, but certainly pre-19th century. As a result of this work, I have decided to try and come up with a dissertation looking at evidence for ritual markings on the historic buildings of Leicestershire'.

Mr Stuart Warburton of Leicester Museums reports the discovery of numerous shoes in the medieval coal mines in north-west **Leicestershire**. Each boot was apparently recorded and accessioned into the museum collection and analysis has shown that all the boots were from different periods and all were in poor condition. In his words: 'I still believe that the boots were left in the mines as a form of "good luck superstition" for future pits dug. Some of the boots were found close to or at the bottom of shafts making me think that they were deposited as the shaft was back filled or left as the last miners climbed back to the surface'.

At a property in George Street, **Lutterworth**, a nineteenth-century pair of women's leather boots with elastic sided gussets were found hidden in a cupboard behind wall plaster.

At **Lyddington**, protection marks are said to have been found in the Prebendal Barn.

Rutland County Museum reported that a number of shoes have been discovered in **Rutland** (no further details) and that there was a report of a skeleton of a cat discovered in a lead coffin locally.

At the Bakers' Arms Pub at **Thorpe Langton**, a dried kitten was discovered 'at the back of a mud wall'. The cat was found 'spread-eagled and its guts had broken out through its belly wall'. The wall is thought to date from the eighteenth century and the animal had clearly been handled in some way for it to have been found in this condition.

Lincolnshire

At **Algakirk** in Lincolnshire, a decorated nineteenth-century clay pipe was found behind some panelling at the rectory.

Michael Field reported the following in May 2002: 'I run a small Rural Life Museum at Waltham, near Grimsby. A couple of years ago builders were demolishing Manor Farm at **Barnoldby Le Beck**, Lincolnshire, and when they got the walls down to about waist high they found in the gap between the two layers of wall a pair of children's shoes. These shoes are now on display in the museum, together with the Telegraph article, so visitors can get an idea of what used to be hidden in walls – we estimate the period when these shoes were placed in the walls to be around the early 1800s'.

At 17 and 19 Whitecross Street in **Barton-on-Humber**, three deposits were discovered which have a direct bearing on the presence of a Saxon cemetery which exists behind the property. David Williams, author of a paper concerning these objects, explains that these two houses 'are part of the terrace which forms the south-western side of Whitecross Street, to the rear of which lies the Castledyke cemetery. Number 17 dates to the 18th century, but has been substantially altered. Number 19 dates to the late 17th or early 18th century, but with 19th century alterations, and is part of a row of three contemporary cottages'. At number 19, an iron Saxon sceax, possibly dating from the seventh century, was discovered. It was concealed in a recess in the western side of the fireplace at ground-floor level, between 90cm and 1.2m above the floor. The recess was a gap in the mortar which separated two courses of bricks. An undatable triangular piece of iron was found on the east (street) wall of the property just above the footings and below the window, also on the ground floor. A spoon dating to the late eighteenth or early nineteenth century was found in the thickness of the north wall of the entrance passage just below ceiling level. At number 17, a wooden patten of late eighteenth- or early nineteenth-century date was discovered – details of its discovery are not provided. In the small article describing these finds, the author David Williams concludes with the following: 'The date of the deposition of the items is not known, though the spoon must have been inserted into the fabric after construction. If all three items at 19 Whitecross Street were inserted at the same time, the most likely explanation is that a grave was discovered to the rear of the property, during the late 18th or early 19th century, and that the finder took appropriate action to protect his house and family from any supernatural retribution. Whether the contemporary patten in number 17 was deposited for the same purpose cannot be known'. From Williams 1998. The information above was supplied by Kevin Leahy from the North Lincolnshire Museum.

Ivan Bunn reports that horse bones and the jawbones of sheep were found beneath the floor of St Botolphs Church, **Boston**. He cites his source as *Notes and Queries*, 1st series (v), p. 274.

At **Creeton** a leather shoe was found in a roof.

At **Crowland** a metal tipped arrow was found in the thatch when demolishing a cottage.

A witch-bottle was found buried beneath the hearth stone of a public house in **Crowland**. From Merrifield 1954.

In **Eaton**, near Grantham, a bezoar stone, a red glass disc with hole in the middle (diameter 12mm), and a dried cat were all found together under the floorboards next to the hearth, above the cellar. This was originally reported in May 2016 as follows: 'The items were found when our sitting room floor was replaced. It was more Victorian aged pine so not as old as wooden flooring elsewhere in the house. It was below the floorboards to the right of the fireplace in a room above the cellar. That's the oldest part of the house which was subsequently extended up in 1774. The finds were the bezoar stone, which I shared a photo of on Twitter, an old red glass disc with central hole (total c 12mm in diameter) and the mummified cat. I'm afraid I don't have photos of the cat as we were away when the floor was replaced (c 14 years ago) as the room is a bit of a through way. The carpenter said he just left the cat where it was although he did have to remove a good few sacks of dust/detritus!! If it's of any relevance the house was owned by someone called Thomas Wright (who was the one who extended the house in 1774). He was allegedly the owner of *Old Moores Almanac* and was referred to as "a gentleman of the starry science". He sounds like he was a bit of a character as he left the house to his daughter on the condition that his son in law never entered it!'

In **Flixborough** High Street, North Lincolnshire, a ritual deposit was discovered in an apparently Georgian cottage. It was found plastered between the brick work of the chimney and the oak beam which supported the inglenook fireplace. The deposit consisted of a piece of lead melt, pins and a cone made from material cut from a painting. In the absence of other evidence, it can be assumed that the find dated from the eighteenth century.

Protection marks were reported in September 2003 at a property in Castlegate, **Grantham.** The find was described as follows: '16th or early 17th century stone fireplace in ground floor room (believed to have been imported into the building from a house in St Peter's Hill, Grantham, c.1925) – a daisy wheel deeply cut into the left hand jamb of the fireplace and faint short diagonal scores'.

A child's shoe was found in the ceiling of a house in **Ingoldsby.**

At the School of Art & Design (formerly St Michael's Church) on Christ's Hospital Terrace, **Lincoln,** a pair of leather slippers was found under the floorboards. The church dates to 1865. June Swann examined photographs of the slippers and said: 'They look like a pair of men's patent leather Albert slippers, machine sewn upper, which would put them c1860+; oval toe-shape is also 1860s. The wear through the toe suggests they are made straights (no right/left). As they appear to be close to a man's size I don't think they would have been made much after early 1860s. Obviously well worn, 5+ years wear. Thus concealed just pre 1870, perhaps some re-flooring then?' Reported in January 2002.

The same correspondent also reported in January 2002 the following incidence of daisy wheels: 'The Conservation Unit of the University is based in what was the old theological college and original county hospital dating from the late 1700s. I recently came across an overlapping double daisy wheel engraved on the (Victorian) brickwork of the old warden's wing. Below it two more daisy wheels have been adapted to represent a penny farthing bicycle!' The address of this find is University of **Lincoln,** School of Art and Design, Conservation Unit, Chad Varah House, Wordsworth St., Lincoln, LN1 3BP.

At the Broadgate East site in **Lincoln,** the skeletons of a cat and three hens were discovered in the infill of a stone-lined pit beneath a seventeenth-century occupation floor.

All Saints Bracebridge Church in **Lincoln** has protection marks, reported in November 2008 as follows: 'The window, at All Saints Bracebridge, Lincoln, is reputed to have been a lepers' squint, allowing visual access to the altar without entering the church. I had assumed that the stone-work had been reused from elsewhere, but perhaps the marks were deliberately made to protect the congregation from the lepers outside! There are "M" and "W" markings as described, and also a symbol which looks like a capital "E" with an extra line on the right hand side. Further down and much more deeply etched are an "s" and what I presume is a capital "I" although it actually looks more like a "T"'.

At **Rippingdale Church** in Lincolnshire there is footprint graffiti. Simon Walker reported three examples in May 2013.

A witch-bottle has been discovered from a parish just north of **Scunthorpe.** This was reported in August 2008 as follows: 'I came across your website whilst researching a find I think that will be of interest to you. I'm an archaeologist who has been digging in a parish just north of Scunthorpe, North Lincolnshire for some years now. This summer a lady from one of the old houses (probably late 16th century in origin), next to my site brought me some artefacts she had recently found whilst removing the blocking of an old window. I've long been aware of Ralph Merrifield's work on witch bottles etc, but this assemblage is something quite different from the normal deposit I've read about before. Within the blocked window was a small corked late 17th-century phial with a string around the neck. It had been left lying on its side and a green (copper?) stain formed below it where the original liquid had leaked out and dried. Unfortunately the phial had recently been broken, but this allowed me to see the contents which included strands of a grass like plant fibre and a silty residue that appears to contain small pieces of a clear crystalline substance as well as a single light blue crystal, very similar to the copper sulphate ones I used to grow as a child! The whole residue has a very distinctive "spicy" aroma. Placed next to the phial were a small piece of 17th-century window lead that had been bent into a loop with its ends twisted together and a fine iron buckle – I think maybe from a shoe. The final artefact is the strangest; it is a portion of twisted branch or root that has roughly cut across the top and has a notch cut into its upper side. This shaping and the natural features of the wood make it look uncannily like a bird, and I don't think that this is entirely coincidental. But have a look at the attached pictures and let me know what you think. Have you come across anything similar? The absence of pins etc make it different from the "classic" witch bottle, and doesn't explain the presence of the other items'.

Near the Water Leisure Park (Butlins) in **Skegness**, a metal detector-ist reported finding the following finds all within one square yard: two bellarmines which were broken, brass nails (possibly from bel-larmines), and a horse skull with associated hooves, shoes and nails. A whole horse skeleton was recovered nearby. According to a 1819 map, this was on the site of a former gatehouse.

A bowl of grain and a clay pipe were discovered in a roof in **Sleaford**.

A dried cat was formerly preserved at Burghley House, **Stamford** – it has now been buried because of decay. From Pennick 1995.

A concealed shoe was reported in August 2007 from **Winteringham**, as follows: 'I read with great interest your web site about old shoes up chimneys. I thought that you might be interested in one found recently up a chimney of Walnut Farm cottage in Winteringham, North Lincolnshire which is in the process of being renovated at the moment'. June Swann dated the shoe: 'Front lace, probably originally stitched right across at the throat (called "closed tab"), which means it started life as Sunday best. Couldn't decide if it had had eyelets in the 7 holes, but if so, obviously long worn after they pulled out. Couldn't see either if it's machine-stitched. It appears to have no back seam, so a blucher boot, with what looks like double (waterproof) tongue. All this, plus toe-shape with quite high toe-spring suggests date fairly close to 1850s – perhaps towards the end or a bit later. The leather on the outside joint is of course a repair patch, quite neatly done, and in that position inevitably hand-sewn'.

Merseyside

At **Birkenhead Priory** animal bones were found in a carefully prepared cavity at the foot of one of the buttresses. The bones were found in 1898 and were described at the time as follows: 'In the course of this work of restoration, in one of the buttresses was discovered a cavity wherein were the bones of a kid with a skulls and horns complete. The stones were all properly faced inside, showing that the cavity had been intentionally built'. Later examination demonstrated that the bones were actually those of an adult sheep and the bones were the skull and both mandibles, pelvic girdle, sacrum, right femur, right tibia, right humerus, a scapula and numerous ribs. The paper written about this concludes: 'It seems clear that the sheep was deliberately immured in the recess prepared for it, and whether or not this constitutes a genuine example of a foundation sacrifice the facts are here recorded'. From Irvine and McMillan 1969.

An individual at **Liverpool** Museum reported that during the restoration of a cottage, she found a doll within an inglenook chimney and marks beneath flagstones.

In an article of 8 March 1954 in *The Times*, p. 5, mention is made of a stoneware jug which was found to contain a mass of handmade nails and pins. This witch-bottle was held in **Liverpool** Museum.

Norfolk

In Hargham Road, **Attleborough** (formerly a Public House), a lady's boot was discovered beneath the floorboards of an upstairs room. The boot is described as 'lady's black cloth boot with black leather winged cap with broad semi-square toes and black leather counter, slightly stacked leather heel, side lacing with eleven pairs of lace holes on the inside of foot and black cord lace'.

A sickle was found up the chimney of Church House Farm, **Aylmerton**, dating to c. 1700.

Ritual marks were reported at a farmhouse in Spa Lane, **Aylsham**, Norfolk. The finds were described thus: 'Recently uncovered timber chimney lintel in former kitchen (house dated c.1600) – a series of deep diagonal notches, and faint v, w and wavy line markings, interpreted by Edwin Rose of Norfolk Landscape Archaeology as ritual marks. I am currently awaiting his report on the building and will let you have any further information that comes to light'. Reported in September 2003.

At **Castle Acre** Castle a post-medieval witchcraft deposit was found.

In **Costessey** a complete mouse skeleton was found walled up with no possibility that it could have got there itself.

Alex Wright reported in January 2008 some witch-bottles including a bellarmine found near **Diss,** Norfolk prior to 1985 (the contents now in the possession of Norfolk Museum Services).

A charm was found in **Diss**, reported in February 2016 as follows: 'Some 20 years ago a friend restoring a timber frame property near Diss found a coarsely woven little bag stuffed into a knot hole in the jamb of a doorway that had once been external from the oldest part of the house which is probably late c15. Inside were little pieces of amber and beside the back was a twist of paper with dried herb leaves. I imagine that together they were some form of protection for the house and its occupants rather than directed against a specific evil person but I would be interested to hear what you think'.

Two knives were found in the thatch of a cottage at **Dunham** during repair work in 1965. They were described as 'two small steel bladed knives and a leather sheath ... possibly early 19th century, found with the blades crossed as a preventive against witchcraft, home made and unused'.

Another two knives were found in a thatch in **Dunham** in 1935. They were found crossed; a photograph exists in the Rural Life Museum.

At **Earsham**, in a seventeenth-century house west of Camphill, a bellar-mine witch-bottle was found in one of the two back-to-back fireplaces in an off centre stack. The bottle contained iron nails and bronze pins and was below the hearth in the western fireplace.

In a cottage at **East Bilney** dried toads were found nailed to the walls – possibly as a charm against illness.

At a farm cottage in **East Tuddenham** Amanda Staerck reported that several tiny horseshoes had been found in her chimney. Staff at the Rural Life Museum in Gressenhall said these were placed there to prevent witches from coming down the chimney. Reported in May 2002.

A shoe was discovered in a house in **Fakenham**, described as follows: 'leather shoe, c1840, leather uppers and sole, cotton lining, sole and heel very worn, lining has been poorly repaired, seam at heel has come apart, and leather has split along heel, found in cavity of exterior wall'.

At a property in Bentley Road, Forncett End, **Forncett**, many deposits were found. The house dates from the early seventeenth century at the latest. Edwin Rose provides the following information: 'In the back of the fireplace several fragments of scythe blades and pieces of iron, and four small bones with holes drilled in them were found. Apparent inscriptions on first floor with possible ritual significance. The ground floor ceiling of the main room has been removed and three painted circles with crosses within them have been found on a joist. Two other crosses occur in a similar position. The main fireplace bressumer, now stripped of laths, has a complex of Sussex marigolds (or "hexes"). Above the ceiling were found nine pieces of flint, and a lanyard with a piece of turned wood'.

At a property in Southwood Road, **Freethorpe** (c.1840), two children's boots were found behind the oven in the kitchen range. One boot is described as an 'ankle boot, laced, originally with six eyelets, hand-sewn leather, square toe, rounded off, low heel missing, half sole repair, later addition of toe cap, white stone inside'. The other is described as a 'child's ankle boot, laced, with eight pairs of brass eyelets, black patent vamp golosh and facing, red leather lining, fawn coloured twill lef, heel missing, half sole repair, worn on left foot, originally straight, worn out at toe, 1860s'.

A stirrup attached to an iron bar (possibly a sword) was discovered up the chimney of a farmhouse in Church Street, **Great Ellingham**. The house dates from 1746. Reported in March 2003.

The discovery of a witch-bottle was reported as follows: 'In 1948 I lived with my parents at the Manor House, **Great Walsingham**, Norfolk. My mother who was an avid gardener dug up a bellarmine jug in the garden and it contained nails, cloth and debris as mentioned'. He went on to say that the bottle was identified by staff at Norwich Museum and that he has no idea what happened to the bottle. Reported in March 2003.

In a cottage in **Gressenhall**, said to be of the 1550s, during restoration, two leg bones of a cow were found beneath the hearth as a charm. Ivan Bunn adds that 'a lock of human hair and two nails were found upstairs in a fireplace dated 1630 which had been covered by an 18th century one'.

At **Gressenhall** an iron nail, wrapped in hemp, was found hammered between bricks beneath the floor of an eighteenth-century fireplace at Rectory Cottage.

At a farmhouse in **Haddiscoe** a mummified rat was found sealed into a vent and an earthenware bottle was found beneath a wall thought to date from the early eighteenth century. Reported in January 2016.

At a house in the Waveney Valley, not far from **Harleston**, the following was reported in March 2003: 'when we took out a 1950's tiled fireplace and opened up the central chimney's original hearth, and removed Victorian plaster from the bressumer beam, we found extensive carved and scratched graffiti on the old oak beam. There are numerous circles and "B" shapes, "Y" shapes, and the scratched letters "RV" – might these be witchcraft deterrent symbols?'

At a cottage in Lynch Green, **Hethersett**, a witch-bottle was found. The house dates to around 1600. The bottle was a 'bellarmine' and was found standing upright in the hearth. There is a lime residue over the face and medallion area but not inside, suggesting it was corked. The handle was broken and an iron-bronze lump accumulated in the neck suggests that the bottle had stood upside down at one time. X-rays show at least two iron nails and lots of bent bronze pins. The bottle is 226mm high. The bottle is unlikely to be from before the mid-seventeenth century. Ivan Bunn states, 'House dates from c1600 but partly re-built in 1729'.

At **Hellington** a witch-bottle was found 45cm beneath the hearth of a cottage. It is a bellarmine bottle, Holmes type VIII with arms of Amsterdam, made 1680–1700. A short report on the bottle and its contents was written by John Walker, of the Department of Archaeology, University of Manchester.

Hall Barn at **Hemsby** in Norfolk has a 'daisy' inscribed on the plaster on the outside of the aisle wall.

At **Hevingham** a seventeenth-century complete bellarmine was dug up in the garden containing two iron nails.

At **Heydon** in lodges at the eastern end of village street, one witch-bottle was found under a doorstep and another under a hearth. Both bellarmines contained pins and vole and rat bones. Ivan Bunn adds, 'Lodge appears to be early 19th century, but may stand on the site of an older building'.

In **Hilborough** two shoes were found in the roof of a cottage which dates from the seventeenth century.

At a house in The Street, **Hindolveston**, a pair of concealed shoes were found. This was reported in December 2008 as follows: 'Hi, attached is a photo of a pair of shoes found while renovating my house. The shoes were amongst rubble in an inglenook style fireplace which had been bricked up to make it smaller. Norfolk Museum services has seen the picture of the shoes and believe they date to around 1800. The house itself dates back to the 16th century, possibly even earlier. The shoes appear to be a pair of children's possibly ladies, and don't seem to have used. I wonder if they were placed there when the fireplace was made smaller?'

A 'bellarmine' bottle without mask was found in foundation at a farmhouse in **Ingworth**; another bottle was said to have been found with it but there are no firm details. The contents were intact, and described as 'heavy mass'. The bottle was found under old foundations, with the handle broken off. Rust flakes were extracted but it was not possible to remove the rest.

At **Kenninghall Palace** the following was discovered in 1982: 'Inside the central stack was found a pottery handled footless bowl of large size, with orange glaze, found complete but broken by workmen. Also, a stick with hair attached, old shoes and clothes with lead buttons'.

South-west of St Peters Church, **Kimberley**, a post-medieval bent lead token incised with an X on one face was discovered. The report questions whether it was bent deliberately as a ritual object.

A Holmes type IX bottle was found under the threshold of a house in **King's Lynn** – possibly the Plough Inn, King Street. The contents were described as a 'heart shaped piece of cloth with eight bronze pins piercing it'. The building dates from 1715 and became an inn in 1739. This find was originally reported in Merrifield 1954. This find also appears in Ivan Bunn's list as 'Site of Plough Inn, 14 King's Street, King's Lynn, Norfolk. – c. 1905. A witch bottle (bellarmine of Homes type IX) found under threshold when demolition took place c. 1905. Contained a cloth hearth pierced with a pin. Now in Norwich Castle Museum (19.032). Inn was built as a customs house in 1715'. Ivan's sources were Clarke and Carter 1977 and Dutt 1905.

At Thoresby College, **King's Lynn** a bellarmine witch-bottle was found under the college. This case is reported in Clarke and Carter 1977, and was also mentioned in the *Eastern Daily Press* of 27 February 1963.

In **King's Lynn** a dried cat was found in the attic of a property in St Margaret's Place in the late 1970s; the cat is now thought to be lost. From Pennick 1995.

At 28 King Street, **King's Lynn** a dried cat was found by a surveyor from Cruso and Wilkin. The cat was found in the rafters between the first and second floors. From Pennick 1995.

In a letter to *The Times* of 29 March 1999, responding to a letter concerning witch-bottles by Dr Alan Massey, one G.L. Bolt of **King's Lynn** wrote: 'Sir, I was intrigued by Dr A G Massey's letter (March 24th) on witch bottles, having made a similar discovery a few years ago when repairing damaged brickwork here. My house, built originally in the 14th century, was refaced in the early 18th century when the medieval jetty was filled in. The bottle contained a number of non-ferrous pins with heads as Dr Massey describes, varying from just under an inch to an inch and a half long, together with a flat fish made of horn or bone about 1¾ inches long, which I took to be a gambling token. I was not aware of the bottle's function until I read Dr Massey's letter, but since we replaced the bottle, along with most of the pins, perhaps it will still appease any latter-day roving witches'.

Norfolk Rural Life Museum reports that they hold a witch-doll in their collection which is believed to have been discovered somewhere in **King's Lynn**. Reported in January 2001.

'About that time [1980s] I was asked by a couple to visit a cottage they were restoring in **Kings Lynn** to give my opinion. As you know the floors of almost all old cottages consisted of large tiles, or pammets, laid on a sand base. Now unfortunately by the time I got there everything had been "tidied up" and no photographic record made. But apparently when the tiles were lifted in the main room the couple found what at one time was half a pig, split from nose to tail, laid in the sand. Have you come across this before?' Reported in May 2002.

At **Langham** a child's black leather shoe was discovered – described as 'nailed at sole and heel, toe cap, two single eyelet holes for lace, split at heel, found built into the fireplace of a cottage opposite Langham School'.

In Waterloo House, **Litcham**, Norfolk, a rat and a postcard were discovered in 2005. Waterloo House is a substantial red brick dwelling in the main street, originally constructed in 1815 and extensively remodelled in 1850–1851. During renovation works, the owner, Mrs Elizabeth Williams, detailed workmen to remove a fireplace from the dining room that had been inserted into an earlier chimney breast, to reveal the original larger fireplace beneath. When the later fireplace was dismantled, a 'secret' compartment was found built into the shoulder of the brickwork (the shoulder on the opposite side was solid brick throughout). Inside the compartment were found the remains of a rat, curled up and mummified by the heat from the fire. Alongside the remains of the rat, there was also a postcard, complete with stamp, containing details of the builders who had constructed the fireplace, which was dated to 1851. Close examination revealed that the compartment had been formed to leave only a small hole at one end, which was subsequently sealed with a rough brick and mortar bung. The rat had been inserted through this hole whilst still alive. The rat had then partially chewed the postcard, before curling up in the wet mortar to fall asleep – and subsequently pass away. The rat was buried nearby, with the postcard remaining in the possession of the householder. Thanks to Matthew Champion who reported this to me in April 2016.

At **Morley** a complete stoneware witch-bottle was found broken, containing iron nails and tufts of short hair. In Ivan Bunn's list this appears as 'Complete stoneware witch bottle found under tiled floor in north room by the hearth of a 17th century, Grade II, house. Bottle contained iron nails and tufts of hair'.

Near Hollies Farm, at an old brickworks, **Morningthorpe**, a scythe blade was found in the stack.

The following was reported in March 2003: 'I was most interested to read your article in the EDP [*Eastern Daily Press*] on Sunday, especially concerning ritual marking found on timber in houses. My wife and I live in **Narborough**, Norfolk and bought our house in 1999. We have spent two and a half years renovating the property which used to be the village forge and have ended up with a beautiful home. I have however noticed a number of strange markings on internal wood work which we put down to "scratchings" made by children. I have attached a number of photos of these and would appreciate your comments as to what they might be and perhaps how old they are. My investigations into the age of the house have not been conclusive but our guess is somewhere between 1790 to 1820. The principal markings are in two places: 1. The oak beam over the inglenook fireplace, where amongst other 'markings' there are two daisy wheels and the letters "V" and "TT". One of the daisy wheels has 6 petals contained within a circle of diameter 70mm. The second is three interlocking circles each of approx 70mm diameter. 2. Two daisy wheels on a door which I had always suspected as being an external door due to its thickness. This door is now an internal door. One daisy wheel comprises of a number of interlocking circles each of 20mm in diameter and the second a 6 petal arrangement in a circle of 25mm diameter. As always when one "discovers" such things in an old house they seem to pop up all over the place. My attention was also drawn to the fact that people used to hide artefacts away in crevices in houses. This made me think about something we found concealed in between the main ceiling timbers of the now kitchen. The item is a hand carved wooden spoon approx 185mm long. We are led to believe that the house was originally single storey and thatched. The second floor was added in the 1850s when the railways came to this part of Norfolk (so I have been told) so this spoon may have been put into what was the attic?'

Staff at **Norfolk** Landscape Archaeology state the following: 'Horse skulls are not so commonly found with us, although apparently it used to be a practice in the Fens to place a horse skull beneath any nonconformist chapel that was being erected ... We have had two cases of complete pig skeletons found beneath houses ... There are a number of cases of the widespread practice of Neolithic axes being thought to be thunderbolts and thus built into towers and chimneys to guard against lightning. Various iron artefacts have been found in chimneys, the idea apparently being to keep the night mare out'.

In **North Wootton** near King's Lynn, a dried cat hangs over one of the bars of the Red Cat Hotel. The cat was found in 1946 on the table of a sealed off room in a house in King's Lynn and given to a customer of the Red Cat Hotel who then gave it to the hostelry. Peter Irwin, whose family have owned the Red Cat for generations, gave me full details of the animal including photos and an x-ray during many e-mails in the second half of 2001.

A dried cat was found during shop rebuilding in London Street, **Norwich**. This find was reported in September 2000.

At 11 Bank Plain, **Norwich**, a dried cat was discovered under floorboards during demolition; it is now held at the Castle Museum.

A dried cat was discovered under the floorboards of a house in **Norwich**, and is now held at the Rural Life Museum.

A bottle was found inverted under the remains of Chingleford House at the junction of Horn's Lane and King Street in **Norwich**. Donated to the Museum of London in May 1950. The contents were described as 'about eight iron nails and hair etc'. Merrifield describes this bottle as a bellarmine Holmes Type IX. From Merrifield 1954.

A bottle was found at Eastern Counties Newspapers site, Rosen Road, **Norwich**, near Woolpack Pit. The contents, now held in Castle Museum, comprise sixty nails, thirty-eight bronze pins and hair. This find appears in Ivan Bunn's list as 'Witch bottle found containing approx., 68 iron nails, 38 bronze pins and human hair. ... Human skeletal remains also found on site'.

At 67–73 Stephens Street, **Norwich**, a seventeenth/eighteenth-century witch-bottle was discovered under what in 1977 was the Key Markets frontage – found by mechanical excavator. Ivan Bunn states that the bottle was found during street widening in 1960.

In King Street, **Norwich** a bellarmine was discovered with iron nails, bronze pins and hair at a depth of 12ft in brick rubble and soil.

At the junction of King Street/Music House Lane, **Norwich**, a seventeenth-century bellarmine jar was found inverted with iron nails and human hair in the neck under the remains of a building at the corner of these two streets.

In Lower King Street, **Norwich**, two shoes were found under floorboards, thought to date to 1870.

In Pottergate, **Norwich**, a woman's clog or mule from the late seventeenth or early eighteenth century was found above a brick fireplace opening behind lath and plaster studwork. A pair of straps was also found and a child's shoe from the second half of the seventeenth century was found in a roof void.

In Duke Street (Hoppers Yard), **Norwich**, a bellarmine containing iron nails and pins was discovered when Duke's Palace Ironworks was pulled down. Merrifield describes this bottle as Holmes Type VIII and adds that it also contained bits of old iron. He states that the bottle was found in the courtyard or garden of the Duke of Norfolk's Palace or actually beneath part of the Palace, which was rebuilt in 1672. From Merrifield 1954. Ivan Bunn states that this bottle is now in the Pitt Rivers Museum, Oxford.

In Bethel Street/Little Bethel Street, **Norwich**, a witch-bottle (still corked) with a hole in it was found under the hearth. X-rays and tests for urine were carried out.

A child's lace up shoe from the mid-nineteenth century, a girls' shoe and a woman's shoe were all found in infilling at a property in St Andrews Hill, **Norwich**.

Shoes and other items were found behind the oven of a seventeenth-century house with nineteenth-century additions in **Oulton**.

Dead cats were found at a farmhouse dating from around 1600 in **Oxborough**.

In **Postwick** a witch-bottle was found in an eighteenth-century property. The bellarmine was found inverted in a courtyard. The bottle is 23cm high with a rampant lion motif. Ivan Bunn states, 'The building is 18th century incorporating earlier (16th century) work'.

At a cottage in **Roughton** a witch-bottle was found in the fireplace of a seventeenth-century cottage. The bottle was found still sealed with a cork but containing nothing except a dark stain. Ivan Bunn states,

'16th century cottage altered in 17th century. Witch-bottle found in 16th century fireplace'.

An earthenware jar was found concealed beneath the floor of a house in **Salthouse** with four fragments of white salt-glazed pottery, one fragment of brown salt-glazed pottery and nine fragments of clay pipe stem. The jar was lead glazed with a green patch in the centre of the body, thought to have been buried for superstitious reasons and thought to date to the eighteenth century.

A bellarmine with a stylized face mask, used as a witch-bottle, was found near **Scole**, Norfolk. The mouth is of hour-glass shape with teeth and tongue. The medallion is of a flower with long petals. It contained an iron mass which when x-rayed was found to be pins and iron, probably remains of nails. Thanks to Alex Wright who supplied this information based on bottles in his collection. Reported in March 2016 and published in Wright 2009.

At a house in **Seething**, near Brooke, a witch-bottle was discovered. This was reported in May 2002 as follows: 'We lived in an old farmhouse in Seething, Norfolk 1979–1983. During some renovation work around the old back door (wattle and daub) we found a small green glass bottle in a cavity above the door. We have kept it with us (being slightly superstitious !!) It is 10.5cm high, 4cm diameter with a 2cm indented bottom, a flared top with cork above a 1cm high/1.5cm diam neck. It is quite thin dark green glass and appears to contain a feather and a small amount of gunge'. Regarding the age of the property, he went on to say, 'The front of the house had been rebuilt with a Georgian brick facade, but I'm sure the remainder was 16th or 17th century'.

Daisy wheels have been found at a farmhouse in **Shelton Green**, Norwich. Interestingly, a flint with a hole in the middle was found 'on top' of a daisy in their barn. Reported during November and December 2002.

At a house in Market Street, **Shipdham** (seventeenth/eighteenth century), a boot and nails were found in the thatch.

In **Shotesham** in a post-1780 building, a scythe blade was discovered in the central stack.

The skeleton of a pig was discovered in 1982 under the floor of a property at The Green, **South Wootton**. The animal was buried in front of the fireplace at a depth of about 1 foot 6 inches. From Pennick 1995.

At a cottage in St Nicholas, **South Elmham**, Harleston, a witch-bottle was discovered. Rene Greville was the discoverer and home-owner. This was featured on 'History Detectives' where I made an appearance too. First reported in November 2006.

At **Stubb's Green** a stoneware witch-bottle without mask was found on the site of an old cottage. Other bottles were found which contained nine bronze pins and a nail which were all bent – fragments of other nails were also found. The tops of these bottles were sealed with clay.

A bottle was from in the area of **Swaffham** or Necton containing iron nails and bronze pins.

A bellarmine with a stylised face mask and a medallion with a double headed eagle, used as a witch-bottle and with its contents intact, was found at **Swardeston,** Norfolk. Alex Wright supplied this information based on bottles in his collection. Reported March 2016. Published in Wright 2016.

The remains of a cat were unearthed from beneath the doorstep of an eighteenth-century house at 3 Castle Street, **Thetford**. This was reported in the *Eastern Daily Press*, 27 July 1983. From Pennick 1995. Ivan Bunn repeats this information.

In the village of **Three Holes** a dried cat was discovered beneath downstairs floorboards. The owner thinks the cottage was built in 1902 so this is quite a recent concealment. The owner hopes to replace the cat once work is completed with an account of its discovery. Reported in May 2003. Owner told me in this new letter that the animal's paws have been amputated and there is no trace of them.

A shoe was found in the roof of the seventeenth-century Marsh Farm, **Thurlton**.

Concealed footwear was discovered at The Grange, **Tottenhill**, Norfolk, in 1977. The Grange is a fifteenth-century, two-cell dwelling, greatly extended in the sixteenth, seventeenth and nineteenth centuries to form a substantial farmhouse. Substantial renovation work in the late 1970s involved the opening up of the original fireplace. At the time a very large chimney breast (approx. 14ft across) was fronted by a small 1930s tiled fire-surround and grate. The first fireplace was removed to reveal another fireplace beneath it. This was then removed also. In total there were seven separate fireplaces, each built inside the previous one. Concealed in the cavity between the sixth and seventh fireplace was a carved wooden patten with neatly worked leather attachment straps. The straps were made of two layers of leather, finely stitched together, and secured to the timber of the patten with small iron nails. The timber was identified as willow or aspen. The patten was initially thought to date from the seventeenth century. However, identical pattens have since been recovered from sixteenth-century contexts. The whole fireplace was topped by a very large timber bressumer, approximately 18 inches by 18 inches, which contained numerous protection marks (conjoined V's, compass drawn), several coins concealed in cracks in the timber (all sadly Victorian or later) and numerous burn marks. Several of the taper burn marks had been repeatedly burnt and then had the charcoal scrapped away, before being re-burnt to create a deep hollow in the timber. The concealed item was reported to, and recorded by, Kings Lynn Museum before being returned to the house owner. Thanks to Matthew Champion who reported this to me in April 2016.

At a farm in **Weeting with Broomhill** a dead cat was found in the attic.

At a farmhouse in **Welney**, a complete bellarmine containing small bones and dust was discovered under the floor of the dining room – the house is thought to date from the seventeenth century. This was also reported by Alex Wright as, '48. Bellarmine Witch Bottle, 1650–1700, H 24.5 cm. Bellarmine with stylized face and sun spiral medallion. This Bellarmine was used as a Witch Bottle. It contained nails etc and was found buried and standing upright in the hearth'. Alex Wright supplied this information based on bottles in his collection. Reported via e-mail in March 2016 and published in Wright 2009.

At St Mary's Abbey, **West Dereham**, a lead curse was discovered.

A bellarmine with a stylised face mask and a medallion of a stylised ship, was found with another one in **Whissonsett**, Norfolk. It was used as a witch-bottle and contained iron nails, etc. Thanks to Alex Wright who supplied this information based on bottles in his collection. Reported via e-mail in March 2016 and published in Wright 2009.

Marks cut into lead can be found in the roof of the Old Rectory at **Weston Longville**. This was reported in February 2009 as follows: 'Another one has come to light, the outline of an adult's shoe cut into the lead covering of a dormer giving access to an internal roof slope at the Old Rectory, Weston Longville near Norwich (built about 1840) – photos attached. The leadwork of the dormer is covered with other grafitti including a nice dated one of 1843 and what looks like a nine men's morris'.

At a farm in The Street, **Weybread**, Diss, the following was reported in November 2006: 'The house is a Grade II listed, formerly Medieval Hall House dated as being built around 1590. There are currently builders in adding an extension and at the same time restoration work going on. Finds to date are:
1. Daisy Wheels on the ingle-nook lintels.
2. Carpenters marks in the roof (Queen Truss).
3. Initials stamped on various beams.
4. A Rat's skull, bottle and iron nail under the staircase.
5. What the restorer says are two ritual marks impressed in the wattle and daub, looking to have been made with a goat's or sheep's cloven hoof'.

Wiggenhall Church has a large daisy wheel on the main door, reported in April 2008.

At a farm in **Winfarthing**, a phial was discovered. This was described as follows: 'In the flint plinth beneath the sill-beams at the junction of the east wall and the original north wall a small phial or "lachryma-tory" bottle was found of early type and containing brown stains. It is possible this may be some sort of anti-witchcraft device, or possibly a charm against rats'.

Witchcraft material was discovered at the Old Vicarage, **Woodbastwick Green.** This includes the bones of at least three and a half rats, the lower left jaw of old cow, a small wooden box with lid containing paste, and a mid-eighteenth-century shoe. Ivan Bunn adds that some of these objects are set behind glass in a restored fireplace.

A seventeenth/eighteenth-century belt buckle was found in the chimney of a cottage, **Wood Dalling**, which dates from the seventeenth century.

A bottle was found near the Tumble Down Dick public house, **Woodton**, with an 'iron mass' (probably nails) still inside it.

A witch-bottle was discovered at **Woodton**. It is described as '18th century, earthenware, filled with iron nails, human hair, nail clippings and urine'. The contents have corroded and split the bottle.

A child's shoe dating to the seventeenth century was found in the stack at a property in Market Place/Honing Row, **Worstead**.

A candle holder was found in the chimney of the Abbey Hotel at **Wymondham** along with a child's shoe. Both date to the nineteenth century.

A child's shoe was discovered at **Wymondham**, described as 'leather sole, leather upper with four metal rivets for laces, stitching marks visible around edge, found in chimney ... poor condition, upper leather extensively decayed and only right portion remaining, 19th century'.

At a property in Damgate Street, **Wymondham**, several daisy wheels can be seen in wattle and daub. Reported in August 2002.

North Somerset, Bath and North-East Somerset, Bristol and South Gloucestershire

At Ellbroad Street, **Bristol**, a bellarmine flask was found which contained a few iron nails and several bronze pins.

The fireplace surround in the lower floor of a property on Redcliffe Parade West, **Bristol**, has numerous graffiti and daisy wheels all over it. The house dates to 1768. The site visit occurred in September 2001.

At a property in St Lukes Crescent, Totterdown, **Bristol**, two dried cats, one ginger and one black, were discovered laying side by side. The property dates from 1893. The cats were apparently concealed within the ceiling as they fell down on a builder working on the ground floor. Reported in June 2008.

In Goatchurch Cavern, **Burrington Combe**, North Somerset, some ritual protection marks have been found and examined. C.J. Binding and L.J. Wilson have co-written a paper on the topic – see Binding and Wilson 2004.

Shoe outlines in the lead were discovered at **Cameley** in North Somerset. Reported in June 2012.

A tricuspid head spoon was found buried horizontally at the base of infill to reduce the width of a doorway at a substantial property in **Cheddar**. The spoon has been dated to 1660–1680.

At Chelvey Court, **Chelvey**, near Nailsea, there are protection marks in the form of a daisy wheel and a scratched 'M' mark. Concealed shoes have also been discovered there. Reported in 2001.

Two spoons were found concealed in a wall between a barn and a hall house dating to between 1450 and 1500 in **Nibley**, near Yate. The barn was an addition. The first-floor ceiling dates to around 1650.

Protection marks exist on timber in a house in Blackrock Lane, Publow, **Pensford**, Bristol.

At **Thornbury**, north of Bristol, a hoard of shoes was found, possibly from the late 1800s, in a timber-framed building possibly dating to the sixteenth century. The building is on the High Street, Thornbury.

A bellarmine flask was brought in for identification from the **Wickwar** area near Bristol, which contained metal and also animal bone fragments.

In a seventeenth-nineteenth-century farmhouse at Sandford, **Winscombe**, a mid-nineteenth-century clay pipe was discovered beneath a window seat in a mortar mass.

An apparent witch-bottle or foundation deposit has turned up from beneath a Victorian Chapel. A curator at Bristol Museum reported in September 2017 as follows: 'working on restoring a chapel in **Winterbourne** near Bristol has just found this witch bottle ... I found it set in a solid block of stone, with carved chamber to hold the bottle. The bottle has the cork intact but not fully sealed. Within, a note with very faint writing, a silver coin and something else unidentifiable, possibly just sediment. The chapel date is 1868'.

In **Wootton-under-Edge** a lady's shoe was found in the roof by the attic. The shoe was found where a gap between a fourteenth- and eighteenth-century property was bridged.

Two horseshoes and a 'round' of wood (like a cheese) with a wedge cut out and nailed were discovered within a cavity inside the hearth of an upstairs room of the Ancient Ram Inn, **Wootton-Under-Edge**. The piece of wood has been heavily attacked by woodworm but the horseshoes, two different types, are in excellent condition. The owner says he discovered them quite by chance when he found a loose stone inside the hearth, which is of drystone wall construction. The building dates back to at least the thirteenth century.

Two dried cats were discovered in the thatch of a farm on Wrington Road, **Wrington**, North Somerset. The house dates to the seventeenth century and the discovery was made during re-roofing. A hand stitched paper bag was also discovered. The cats were found in different parts of the roof and are thought to date to different periods. The owner reported that the cats are now in a cardboard box in the loft of the property. Reported by Ian Evans in July and October 2002.

North Yorkshire, City of York

Two suspected witch-bottles have been discovered beneath the pathway to a cottage in **Addingham Moorside** near Ilkley. Reported in November 2000.

A pair of black leather open tab shoes was found in a house in **Bishopthorpe**, near York. The shoes date from the mid-nineteenth century, and are hand stitched, with a leather sole and lining, and a square toe. The heels have not survived. A fragment of the laces survives, and is made of textile (cotton or linen). They have a wide tongue and fasten by means of two eyelets punched into the leather; the eyelets are not reinforced. Reported in April 2018. Find reference in York Museum: YORCM: 2017.127.

A child's shoe was found in a wall at the Old Hill Inn, **Chapel-le-Dale**.

At Stangend house in Danby there is a witch-post. 'This cruck-framed long-house has been reconstructed at the Ryedale Folk Museum, **Hutton-le-Hole**, and the witch-post replaced in its original position. It bears a plain St Andrew's cross with two horizontal raised bands below'. There is an illustration on file. From Hayes and Rutter 1972.

At the Shoemakers Shop in **Danby** there is a witch-post. 'Canon J C Atkinson, Vicar of Danby, sent a witch-post with a drawing showing its original position in the shoemaker's shop in Danby to the Pitt-Rivers Museum, Oxford in 1893. The precise site of this shop is unknown. The post possesses the "St Andrew's cross" with no less than twelve narrow horizontal bands below'. There is an illustration on file. From Hayes and Rutter 1972.

At a house called Toad Hole (later The Nest) in **Danby** there was a witch-post. 'This house, demolished in 1939, is said to have contained a witch-post which had no carving on it but "only some V-marks" ... It is not clear why this should be classed as a witch-post. Unfortunately its present whereabouts is unknown'. From Hayes and Rutter 1972.

At **Danby Castle** there is a form of witch-post. 'Mrs Nattrass records ... that a window lintel in Danby Castle is marked with two crosses one above the other and some horizontal cuts and bands. It is not now visible, but in view of the witch-posts re-used as lintels at Church View, Gillamoor and Postgate Farm, Glaisdale, the Danby Castle lintel may well be the remains of another witch-post'. From Hayes and Rutter 1972.

At a property near the village of **Darlton**, the remains of a dried cat which had been fastened to the floor joint by wire was discovered. The house dates from the seventeenth century.

A dried cat was discovered in **Easingwold**. It was mentioned in Gutch 1901: 88. Thanks to Jeremy Harte for the reference.

In East End Cottage, **Egton**, there was a witch-post: 'The witch-post from this rebuilt cruck-house was presented to Whitby Museum by the late Mr R L Foster of Egton Manor in 1936. It has a "St Andrew's cross on the outer face." From Hayes and Rutter 1972.

At Bugle Cottage, **Egton**, there is a witch-post: 'A cruck cottage with a modern replica of the witch-post which was in the same position before the house was rebuilt in 1927 ... It bears a simple "St Andrew's cross". The replica is said to have been made from rowan wood'. From Hayes and Rutter 1972.

At Delves Cottage, **Egton**, there is a witch-post: 'The probable witch-post of this cruck-house is boarded in, but five horizontal raised bands are just visible'. From Hayes and Rutter 1972.

A cottage in **Egton Bridge** once contained a witch-post: 'Mrs Nattrass ... was informed that a cruck-cottage near the saw-mill contained a good example of a witch-post before it was pulled down. No description available'. From Hayes and Rutter 1972.

At a house called Murk Side there is a witch-post: 'Although situated below Jenny Bank Wood near Beckhole this house is in **Egton** parish. Mrs Nattrass ... figures a speer-post which was erected by the hearth after the house was rebuilt on a new site in 1915. It has one horizontal fillet across the upper part, but the portion with the cross may have been cut off'. From Hayes and Rutter 1972.

At **Farndale East**, in a house called Oak Crag, there is a witch-post: 'The witch-post in this interesting cruck-framed house is still in situ. It has a worn or polished appearance and the "St Andrew's cross" is faint. Below the cross are two bold horizontal bands followed by four faint horizontal lines and two lines of indistinct notches. There is a stout post behind the witch-post, with a slot for the ingle-nook seat'. There is an illustration on file. From Hayes and Rutter 1972.

At a house called Church View in **Gillamoor**, there is a witch-post: 'This witch-post was discovered in 1971. An ancient piece of oak used as a lintel over the doorway of a former byre was removed ... and about to be sawn up for firewood when the carved face of the post was noticed.

It bears the usual "St Andrew's cross" with a single raised horizontal band below and is similar to the example from Low Bell End, Rosedale East. Apart from cracks, nails and the portion cut off from the base, this witch-post is in fairly good condition. The most interesting feature is that the post is make from part of a ridge-tree. Peg-holes at intervals, on a slant, indicate the position of rafters. The notch at the base of the post may be where the ridge-tree was joined and two holes in the tongue at the top show where is was tenoned to the hearth-beam. [The occupants] … intend to preserve the witch-post at Church View. The byre, a former cruck-house, was probably rebuilt in the 18th century and the post was then placed in the position where it was found. The witch-post at Postgate Farm, Glaisdale has a similar history'. From Hayes and Rutter 1972.

At Quarry Farm, **Glaisdale**, there is a witch-post: 'This farmhouse, a much altered long-house, contains a fine witch-post standing on a base-stone at the end of a panelled speer. It has a deeply cut "St Andrews cross", above a series of five bands of vertical lines, a type of decoration not found on other local witch-posts'. From Hayes and Rutter 1972.

At Postgate Farm, **Glaisdale**, there is a witch-post: 'The elaborate witch-post at Postgate Farm was found used as a lintel in an earth-closet by the late Mr George Harland of Glaisdale. It possesses two "St Andrews crosses" with a central floral motif and below are four narrow horizontal raised bands, the date 1664 and initials EPIB (Eliz. Pruddon and John Brackon). On top of the post is a stout tenon with a peg-hole where it was formerly attached to the hearth-beam. Lower down are holes for attaching the ingle-nook seat. The witch-post was probably removed from its original position when the present farmhouse was built in 1784. It is of especial interest as it is the only example in the area which bears a date'. From Hayes and Rutter 1972.

At Lanes Farm, **Glaisdale** there is a witch-post: 'Lanes Farm, to the north-west of Glaisdale village, had its original witch-post removed during alterations in the 1939–45 war and replaced by a new post. The new post bears a simple incised "St Andrews cross"'. From Hayes and Rutter 1972.

At **Halton East**, horse skulls were discovered beneath the flagstones of a cottage during restoration. From Pennick 1986: 6.

At **Halton East**, a nineteenth-century cylindrical stoneware bottle was found near the edge of a field remote from the village. The bottle was buried in an inverted position and contained lumps of wet clayey soil, each stuck through with pins and nails. There were 22 nails, 35 pins and 16 needles. From Merrifield 1987: 180.

At **Harome Hall** a silver spoon was found in the rye thatch, thought to date from the fifteenth–sixteenth century. From Emery, Warner and Pearson 1990: 137.

Excavations at **Hornby Castle** in Wensleydale revealed a horse head buried within an early fourteenth-century wall. This was reported in November 2013 as follows: 'During Season 3 (2012) much to our surprise we uncovered a horse's head that had been deliberately buried within the core of a wall of early 14th Century date. The horse had been decapitated below the third vertebrae. We have found little comparative evidence for this other than from a handful of sites in Northern and Eastern Europe associated with the recruitment to the Order of Teutonic Knights. Interestingly, the builder of our structure Sir John Neville, one of King Edward III's inner household was a known participant in the Lithuanian Crusade. We also have other evidence of Medieval folk belief in the form of a series of fossils and reused Prehistoric worked flints'.

In East Road, **Northallerton**, an apparent witch-bottle was discovered during excavations. It was a stoneware jar which had been plugged with clay, although the seal was not intact when discovered. Inside was soil and a nail; any fluids may have leaked away owing to the broken seal. The bottle is thought to date to the nineteenth century.

From **Padside Hall** Ray Wilson reports the discovery of a 'wooden stake slung between two iron hoops under the boarded ceiling of what would have been the screens passage leading from the Hall door. The stake or pole is round, roughly fashioned, approximately 80mm in diameter and 1.25 metres in length and tapers at both ends. A local historian tells me that such stakes were positioned at the entrance to the house to protect and ward off unwanted guests. The stake is not carved. I have yet to discover whether it is fashioned from rowan'. Ray also reported that other items were found at the Hall. He went on to say: 'The other finds were concealed within the fabric of the walls prior to alterations, probably over a period of 80 years from the early 1800's; a young girls shoe, refined design early 19th cent. behind a blocked fireplace opening; a flat iron early 19th cent. within the fabric of the wall concealed by later plaster work; a brown glass bottle containing liquid still with cork stopper concealed within the fabric of the wall early 19th cent'. Reported in December 2001.

At a small Elizabethan house near **Ripon**, the principal rafter over the open hall has a number of compass circles with hexes. The timbers have been dendro-dated to 1580. From Armstrong 1998.

At a house called Low Bell End in **Rosedale East** there is a witch-post: 'The witch-post from Low Bell End is now preserved at the Ryedale Folk Museum at Hutton-le-Hole. It has the usual "St Andrews cross" with a single horizontal raised band below. Underneath the raised band is a second small and very faint cross. Mr Jackson of Low Bell End states that his father told him that the second cross was incised by the "Wise Man of Stokesley", a 19th century witch-doctor of repute. The witch-post was in its original position by the hearth until 1960. The top-most portion had been mutilated but has now been carefully restored at the museum'. From Hayes and Rutter 1972.

At an unknown location in **Scarborough** there was a witch-post: 'The exact provenance of the Scarborough witch-post is unfortunately unknown, but it is said to have been part of the hearth seat of an old house. It was obtained by the Pitt-Rivers Museum, Oxford, in 1870 and, therefore, many years before the acquisition of the Danby example. It is elaborately carved with two pin-pricked hearts and other symbols within a "St Andrews cross". Below the latter are five horizontal raised bands followed by a row of eight incised notches'. From Hayes and Rutter 1972.

At The Folly, **Settle**, North Yorkshire, two concealed shoes have been discovered (not a pair), as reported in January 2003: 'the Folly is a Grade 1 Listed building, built 1679 but with older bits at the rear. Besides the shoes, we have found two glass beads, some bones and a silver thimble, with a spool of thread therein. The plan is to display the shoe parts in the Folly Museum along with modern recreations of the shoes. They would then remain at The Folly and continue to ward off whatever evil spirits they were meant for'.

From **Sherburn-in-Elmet** comes this report of bottle tradition from October 2002: 'Reading about witch bottles on your site reminded me of two houses in the village I grew up, which had milk bottles cemented into the eaves. My friend lived in one of these and told me that if the bottles were ever damaged in any way, something bad would happen to the house. What's interesting about this is that these two houses were built as recently as the 1950's. Not archaeology, I know. But indicative of ongoing tradition'.

At Pond Cottage in **Silpho** a witch-post was discovered: 'A post 5ft 6in high stands on a base of stone at the end of an oak speer. On the outer face of the post are two horizontal raised bands and four lines of square notches. On the narrow space above these decorations is a modern coat hook. An elegant ingle-nook seat is attached to the hearth side of the post. It is possible that this is a mutilated witch-post, the topmost portion with the cross having been cut away'. From Hayes and Rutter 1972.

A dried cat was discovered in a cottage in Henrietta Street, **Whitby**, reported as a '400 year old cat' which must allude to the age of the cottage because no other evidence is given. Reported in the *Whitby Gazette*, '400 Year Old Cat is Found in the Walls of a Whitby Cottage', 24 April 2009.

During the redevelopment of a cottage in Church Street, **Whixley**, York, three odd shoes were discovered. According to the correspondent, 'They were black leather lace up traditional "clogs", and were still in reasonable condition'. One was a child's shoe, one was an adult's shoe and one was thought to be a teenager's shoe. The shoes were spotted by a neighbour who was observing the work taking place. The current whereabouts of the shoes is not known. The neighbour went on to say that during some work on her own fireplace a nearby cottage in the same street she ensured that a pair of her son's shoes were secreted into the fabric of the building there.

Daisy wheels were found on thirteenth-century grave markers re-used in a tomb in **York**, reported as follows: 'During recent excavations in All Saints North Street (York) we uncovered what appear to be early 13th century grave markers, re-used in a tomb. One of these had what you call a "Daisy-wheel" on it, while another was covered in circular markings, holes and "Daisy-wheels". The stones were only slightly worn, and un-weathered, and add weight to an early 13th century date for the Lady Chapel (where they were found). The "setting out lines" are still clearly visible on the stones. Is it possible that these are the same symbols which you refer to in your internet site? Is there evidence for their use as symbols to ward off evil as early as this?' This e-mail from Dr Robert Richards was received in October 2013. He later added: 'As far as we can tell, the marks on the grave slabs appear roughly contemporary with their original use. They were found, with other fragments, built into the sides of a large two chamber burial chamber (date pending, but probably 15/16th century). Most of the walls were rendered, but these were left largely exposed – hence we spotted them. Presumably, if the builders had recognised the symbols and there significance, they may well have deliberately left them "on view" to the dead. The chamber has a vast cover stone (some 2 1/2 tons) and rebated ends, so we imagine it was designed for coffin burials, with the coffins slid in through the west end openings rather than trying to lift the cover stone – thus it was designed not to be back-filled with soil. North chamber (no symbols observed) one heavily pregnant mature woman. South chamber, three males – the bones of the earliest were "shoved" up to the far (East) end, presumably to allow for the next coffin to be slid in. Central wall 9' late medieval brick, rendered to look like stone. The stones with the symbols on were on the south wall, facing north'.

At the Bedern Foundry site in **York**, J.D. Richards noted the following: 'Just inside the doorway a substantial pit, containing a cat skeleton and the remains of several hens, was set in the construction trench … At the time of excavation the pit containing the cat and hens was interpreted as a post-pit. More recently Dr T P O'Connor has suggested that it may represent a foundation offering. Although cat and hen bones were not uncommon in other deposits, whole skeletons of these animals were rare even in pit fills, so the small assemblage is distinctive and unusual for the site, as is its location. Dead hens and a cat seem unlikely post-hole packing material. As the deposit defies functional interpretation, a "non-rational" (sensu Merrifield 1969, 103) interpretation may be more appropriate. Foundation deposits of dead animals, or parts thereof, were probably more common in the medieval and post-medieval periods than has generally been allowed (Armitage 1989, 147-51). This need not imply any continuity of serious belief, merely the accommodation of superstitious habit. Two hen skeletons recovered from the backfill of the L-shaped gully cutting the northeast wall of Bays GHI may be seen as a second foundation deposit. There may be a parallel in currently unpublished material from the Broadgate East site in Lincoln. Seventeenth century fills of a stone-lined pit, apparently beneath an occupation floor, yielded skeletons of a cat and three hens, a type of assemblage not otherwise seen at that site'. From Richard 1993: 182.

At Mansion House, **York**, a shoe has been found in the eaves of the house and was found in the builders rubble; it appears to have been nailed to the wall and have part of it missing. On the ground floor, by a threshold, a cavity was found at floor level containing glass fragments and bones. Reported in April 2016. A further report in April 2017 mentioned a dried cat: 'The cat was buried in a floor/ceiling between levels and was seemingly "laid to rest" in a peaceful pose on a bed of hazelnut shells'.

A dried cat is said to have been found walled up behind studs, lath and plaster in the roof space of 73 Walmgate, **York**, dated 1650–1680. From Pennick 1995.

In March 2008 it was reported via e-mail that 'Several field lime kilns excavated last year in **Yorkshire** dales have a horse skull set in the flues'.

Northamptonshire

Marian marks were reported at a cottage in **Aston-le-Walls**.

In **Clay Coton**, the letter W is scratched on a beam above the threshing floor of a timber framed barn which probably dates from the early seventeenth century.

Some objects were discovered inside a wall at The Old Post Office, Whilton, **Daventry**, Northants. This was reported in January 2002 as follows: 'Book of Psalms, published Cantrell of Cambridge, date given 1623 (in Arabic numerals not Roman, does this mean it is later rather than earlier?) Candle holder in oolitic limestone. Both items found in a cob wall above a lintel of an old entrance in cottage thought to be Georgian. Whole thing was once two cottages, left hand one is prob. Georgian and the right hand one is prob. Victorian. Left hand cottage used to have an entry through what is now a side wall, into a porch. Items were concealed between beams above the lintel of this former entrance into the left hand cottage'.

A deposit was found in a property in Main Road, **Duston** within an inglenook fireplace. There were some bones (unidentified), the remains of a bag and part of a sign showing tollgate charges. This assemblage is thought to date from the first half of the nineteenth century.

At **Geddington**, a shoe was found in the thatch of an eighteenth-century building.

It is reported that **Kettering** Museum holds a dried cat. The cat is said to have come from the roof of a house on the corner of Lower Street and Bakehouse Hill during demolition in 1966. The cat's neck was hooked around a joist under the roof; it appears to have been hammered or stamped into place when supple, so that the imprint of the joist is still apparent. From Pennick 1995.

At the National Trust property of **Lyveden** there are many Marian marks amongst other graffiti.

Talbot Hotel, **Oundle**, Northants, constructed 1626 – marks were found on a stair newel and finial, as reported by Linda Hall.

A dried cat and rat were discovered in thatch at **Pilton** when the house was demolished in 1890. The cat is said to have been pegged down with wooden pegs. From Pennick 1995. This find is also reported in Howard 1951.

In the crypt of Holy Trinity Church, **Rothwell**, many animal bones and the neck of an old bottle were discovered.

In a priest hole at **Rushton Hall**, many small animal bones and a bottle neck were discovered. Whether these had any ritual function is not clear.

Merrifield mentions the discovery of a cylindrical glass phial, probably dating from the eighteenth century, which was discovered containing only 'the alkali salt of an organic acid' under the floor of **Thornhaugh Rectory**. From Merrifield 1987: 174.

At Church Farm **Wadenhoe**, the following find is described: 'a beam in the end parlour has raised lettering within the chamfer on both sides. On one side was the date 159(7)? And on the other side was short religious inscription. The inscription was carved upside down so it would be seen "skyward"'.

In **Wollaston** two very worn eighteenth-century shoes were found when an old house was being refurbished.

Northumberland

A Victorian worn shoe and jar were found alongside the string rim neck of an eighteenth-century bottle inside a stone wall during restoration around 2005 in the village of **Acombe**. The shoe is now lost but the vessels are still held by the reporter. The wall was near to an eighteenth-century barn. This was reported in January 2015 as follows: 'Around ten years ago while demolishing/rebuilding for some neighbours in my village (Acombe, Northumberland), a dry stone boundary wall that enclosed a small field behind an eighteenth century barn, I found in the centre of the wall what I believe was a Victorian boot, a small old pottery jar (possibly Victorian) and part of the string rim neck of an eighteenth century onion shape bottle. These seem to have been placed near each other. I suppose it is possible that the bottle neck and jar could have been pushed into the wall at a later date but the boot could have only been placed in the centre of it. It was placed between the two rows of stones in the middle of the wall and packed round with the hearting (filling) stone. The wall was higher than a normal dry stone wall and the boot etc was found half way up the wall 2½ -3 feet from the ground and in a section near to the barn. it was a farm workers/labourer's boot, left foot. The upper was in fairly good condition with a large part of the sole missing. Unfortunately, and to my regret, I did not photograph the boot at the time but showed it to the landowners who were interested and wanted to show it to their friends and to the builders restoring the barn. To my horror it was lost sometime during the barn restoration and was perhaps thrown out by the builders, I wish I had kept quiet about it. I managed to save the bottle neck and jar and I attach a photograph of these'.

In **Elsdon Church** a box containing three horse skulls was discovered during restoration work in 1837. Merrifield also refers to this: Merrifield 1987: 124.

At Causeway House, in the Northumberland National Park, near the **Vindolanda** Roman Fort, many artefacts were discovered in the heather thatch roof. They comprised: a child's right clog sole, a damaged, late eighteenth-century key, a pewter table spoon, an iron hook with a pointed tang and four cotton dresses, said to be working-class clothes from around 1890–1900, found between the plank ceiling and the thatch in the bedroom. All of this is detailed in Emery, Warner and Pearson 1990.

Nottinghamshire

In an outbuilding behind a Farm on Loughborough Road, **Bradmore**, near Nottingham, a hoard of objects was found inside a bricked-up inglenook fireplace. The correspondent is of the opinion that the outbuilding was formerly the kitchen and that the objects are Victorian although the date of the book (see below) implies that the objects may be very late Victorian or Edwardian and almost certainly were not concealed prior to 1910. It is known that the inglenook was bricked up only forty years ago and that the objects were not concealed at this time. The objects were found behind the actual hearth and, it is thought, had been there long before the bricking up. They comprise two silver thimbles, a silver broach with a bow and heart on it, a knitting needle (bone?), a round flat disc with a hole in it (bone again?), a pair of black elbow-length cotton gloves with mother of pearl buttons, a narrow crochet tie, two bow ties and some wrapping with a picture of a jester on it and the words 'round corners' and 'pantaloons' written on it. There was also a little paper book from the International Bible Reading Association dated 1910. The building was originally built in the 1700s but was later divided into a labourers' cottage and farmhouse, with the outbuilding behind the cottage.

At a cottage in Low Street, **Collingham**, a patten was found during restoration.

At **Newark** a whole lot of protection marks are reported to exist at a house in Little Carlton. Reported in April 2008.

A dried cat was found under floorboards in the 1876 Unitarian Chapel, High Pavement, **Nottingham** by a joiner in 1988. From Pennick 1995.

In Manor House, Main Street, **Wysall**, Nottingham, there is a daisy wheel inscribed onto a wall in the kitchen. Reported in November 2002.

Oxfordshire

At a house in East Helen Street in **Abingdon**, a child's wool doublet or jacket dating to the early seventeenth century was found under floorboards. It had been found during restoration work in the early 1990s in the attic (now a bedroom).

At another property in East Helen Street, **Abingdon**, an eighteenth-century lady's pocket was discovered containing an eighteenth-century baby bonnet, a variety of coins and some letters, possibly business letter dating from the late 1670s. The pocket was found in a wall amongst hops filling the cavity between the outer and inner walls in a manner similar to cavity wall insulation.

Also in **Abingdon** but with no precise address, a fragmented smock and man's shirt, probably from the nineteenth century, were found in a wall by a fireplace. These were found in 1997 and all details were given via correspondence with the finder.

Two dried cats are said to have been discovered under the floor of a landing in a house dating from 1640 at **Bampton**, near Burford. Some Queen Anne period playing cards were also found. From Pennick 1995. This find is also reported in Howard 1951.

At an unspecified house in **Banbury**, the following marks have been reported in an e-mail from August 2002: 'We live in a 17th century farmhouse and some of the beams and door furniture are marked with patterns and shapes. The beam above me now has two daisy circles of varying size each with 6 petals. There are also letters/initials stamped into the beam – may be carpenters marks (IG ?) or just residents graffiti. The latch on the kitchen/parlour door has an "x" cross inside a square with four circles punched in the four quadrants. The well has a stone engraved with what looks like a W sitting on the top of a capital A in a circle. The legs of the A stick out of the bottom of the circle'.

At a Farm in **Chalkhouse Green**, Kidmore End near Reading (actually South Oxfordshire despite the address), a pair of workman's boots were discovered in a barn. This was reported in April 2002 as follows: 'The barn is possibly early 1700's, tiled roof, weatherboard sides. The boots were placed in a timber within the side of the barn. Barn wall facing west and boots pointing north, both the same way. Boots-working, hob-nailed, eight eyelets and well chewed by rats! About a size 8/9. We have left the boots in situ'. June Swann (footwear expert) looked at photographs of the boots and thought they were from the 1880s or later.

At the National Trust property at **Chastleton** near Moreton-in-Marsh, a hoard of seventeenth-century artefacts was found in a hole in the basement of the east stair tower. These included bellarmine stoneware bottles, pottery, clay pipes, and several onion shaped glass bottles. It is not clear why they were put there. The hole lies centrally within a room between four columns supporting the existing staircase. Images of three daisy wheel ritual marks also found at Chastleton are on file. From *Mosaic* 1994.

At a Cottage in The Green, **Garsington**, a very unusual find has been made. The owner describes it in an e-mail from May 2002: 'I live in a 1690 cottage in Garsington, Oxfordshire. It has a tiny garden surrounded by a dry stone wall. When part of the wall had to be repaired we found it had a number of knives and forks poked into the gaps between the stones. On looking further this cutlery support system went right around the garden. I have found about 40 so far. I would guess they are no more than 100 years old'. In response to this I speculated that this may have been a way of warding off witchcraft, that is , using 'dead' blades made of iron as a ward. She replied, 'I will have a look for some more knives and forks and send you a picture. If they were to keep out evil they were most effective – since they were removed we have been overrun with rats. There were also some cow bones under the floor of a barn in the garden which was a bit odd. The barn is marked as a dairy in the village archives'.

An interesting collection of objects were reported to me via e-mail from January 2002. The objects were found at a property in **Mollington,** Banbury, described as follows: 'This house was built mid 17thC during renovation work concealed in a dividing wall of wattle and daub we found a small childs doll made from rag, together with a ball also made from rag, a turned stick as possibly used to turn a spinning top and a piece of stained glass all wrapped together'. He went on to say, 'Built about 1640 from local stone under a thatch roof, believed to have been home of a farmer or a small manor house, now part of a row of 7 cottages of which we own 4. Each gets progressively smaller. Finds were made in wattle and daub first floor wall between cottages. Finds not in any proximity to a door but were found next to what was possibly an external window. Objects were put back where found but are accessible, one theory is that a child died in that room and that these were his/her toys'.

The quotation here was copied for me by Janet Pennington: '(5) The Star Inn (Clarendon Hotel), **Oxford**. ... The Star Inn was rebuilt on a larger scale, probably about 1550; during the recent demolition, one of the chimney stacks was found to contain the mutilated head of a monumental effigy (a knight of c. 1300), perhaps taken from one of the suppressed religious houses such as Oseney – which may help to date the rebuilding'. From Pantin 1961: 175.

A dried cat was found under the floor of an old house in Paradise Street, **Oxford** in 1986 during renovation work. The cat was replaced on completion of work. From Pennick 1995.

'A dry'd cat found in Hart Hall Buttery' refers to a dried cat found in **Oxford** – in the *Old Anatomy School collection* (item 269), Gunther p. 267. From Pennick 1995.

Concealed shoes were discovered in a property on Howard Street, **Oxford** in November 2016, described as follows: 'It's a two-storey terraced house that we believe was built in around 1890. I think the shoes were in a corner of the front room, near the entrance, though I would need to confirm this with the builders. They did not mention finding anything along with the shoes or any kind of wrapping, except that nearby was a dead dried-out cat. We aren't sure if it was put there or just crawled under the house and died. Sadly by the time the builders told us about this they had thrown the cat in their skip so we don't have it. If it would be helpful I could ask them for more information about the position of the two objects. The builders said there was a lot of rubble under the floor in the same place that they thought had come from the demolition of the fireplace in the front room, so it's possible the shoes were originally under the fireplace and then got moved along with the rubble. The shoes are brown leather boots, with no laces, to fit a child of (as a guess) perhaps 6 years, by today's standards of child size. I attach a photo'. There is a photograph on file. These shoes are now in the collection of the author.

At the Bear Hotel in **Wantage**, a single leather shoe dated to the seventeenth century was discovered in the chimney stack.

At a cottage in **Woodstock** bones and coins were found. This was reported in August 2006 as follows: 'Underneath a slab of old and very rotten wood which divided the stone floor in the sitting room from the stone floor in the passageway we found a George II coin which seems to have been carefully placed. Alongside this were 3 bones, one rib bone, one other similar bone and a smaller, thin "cylindrical" bone. Underneath a nearby stone we have also found a thimble which seems to be made of brass and which has been flattened, probably by the weight of the large stone covering it. During other work on the cottage, we unearthed another coin in another entranceway although it is not possible to tell what that coin is. Our cottage was originally part of a larger establishment, a shop, which has now been converted into 3 other cottages to which we are attached. The chimney to the adjoining property is inscribed with 1742, although a building was standing on the site before this time and was damaged by fire before being rebuilt. We have no way of knowing whether our part of the property has been standing since 1742 or prior to that'.

Shropshire

At The Pentre, **Bronygarth**, Oswestry, Shropshire, numerous burn marks, carpenters marks and some protection marks have been found along with some shoes, crockery and glass. The protection marks are of three interlocking circles, some concentric circles, a series of angular marks on the chimney lintel, some solitary circles and a circled pentagram. This is all focused on the east wing of the building; the west wing is largely reconstructed. There is also an apotropaic stone head which was found by a spring in the garden to the rear, now mounted in a wall at the front of the building. See the case studies in Part II.

Shoes and other items have been found at a house in **Bucknell**, Shropshire. The owner described it thus: 'I recently became the custodian of an old half-timbered house in Bucknell in Shropshire. I have a shoe which was found in a chimney, together with the remains of a clay pipe. I am in the process of finding out from a previous owner the exact location of the shoe and any other details. I believe the shoe I have is a child's shoe of Victorian vintage, although the house dates back much earlier (possibly mid 16th century). The shoe is 6.5' long and 6' high, and would appear to be a well-worn child's shoe (Victorian?). It was discovered when a bricked-up chimney was broken into in 1968, and was located within a "secret" cavity, along with blocks of salt. This cavity could be accessed by climbing up the chimney and then dropping down into it, or possibly by a closed-off hatchway which entered through the side of the chimney. Also found in roof voids nearby were a variety of items, including a small wooden pipe, George 2nd pennies, an English coin dating from 1730's, and a match striker. Interestingly, this is not the only shoe to have been found in the chimney. Together with the one I have attached, was also a ladies shoe from the 1920s(?), the present whereabouts of which I am unclear. I have spoken with the previous owner who found the shoe, and she tells me that much older boot(s) and clay pipes were found in the same chimney by an earlier owner, probably in the 1930s – the boots allegedly dated from Cromwellian times and may have been given to Shrewsbury museum'.

In Abcott Manor, **Clungunford**, Craven Arms, Shropshire, two beams have daisy wheel marks and a shoe was discovered behind plaster in the sixteenth-century attic. The shoe is currently being dated. One of the daisies is above the kitchen fireplace. Reported in December 2001.

At a property in Corve Street, **Ludlow**, a horse vertebra was discovered in the roof of a house painted in the form of an angel. This may date from the seventeenth century.

A charm was found in the crevice of one of the joints of a kitchen chimney at **Madeley** in 1882. It reads: 'I charge all witches and ghosts to depart from this house, in the great names of Jehovah, Alpha and Omega'. The charm was of folded paper and sealed with red wax. From Dyas 1993.

A man's shoe dating from the mid-eighteenth century was discovered during restoration work at the Bear Steps Cottages, **Shrewsbury**. From Dyas 1993.

At Wilstone House, **Wilstone**, near Cardington, there are several ritual marks. In an outwardly eighteenth-century house which appears to be built on earlier foundations, there are marks and grafitti on the wooden internal shutters on the ground floor. In an outbuilding which is joined to the house there are highly complex grids and arcs along with Marian marks and daisy wheels. This covers a large area of a plastered wall which must be four to five metres wide and three and four tall at the apex of the roof.

Somerset

At a house in **Ashbuttle** in 1892, a heart stuck with pins and thorns was found in a recess up a chimney wrapped in a flannel bag. This item is on display in the 'Sympathetic Magic Case' in the Pitt Rivers Museum, Oxford.

At **Baltonsborough** there is a cottage with some daisy wheel carvings, as reported via twitter in July 2015. The carvings are on the door frame at the bottom of the stairs.

At a barn at a farm at **Blacklands**, numerous daisy wheels were reported in September 2008: 'During an excavation on a farm at Blacklands, Somerset a couple of years ago I examined the stonework of an old barn where we had set up our work room. There were a number of daisy wheel designs carved into the stonework around the main door posts and on the underside of the door lintel as well as around one of the visible windows. When I pointed these out to the farmer he was surprised as he had never noticed them before and since there were also marks from the later tallying of crops he had never paid the carvings much heed'.

At **Bridgewater** a dried cat was found in the roof of a fourteenth/fifteenth-century house south of the parish church in Little St Mary Street. Apparently, it was kept at the museum for a while but was eventually destroyed. From Pennick 1995. Margaret Howard mentions that the cat's mouth was open in a 'snarling' way – see Howard 1951.

In a house in High Street, **Bruton**, a dried cat, witch-bottle and ritual marks have all been found. In an e-mail from July 2009 it was reported: 'We live in a timber framed building on the High Street in Bruton, Somerset. The roof is dendro dated to 1450, but the main cellar beam is dated 1290. The house was probably a clothier's house in its early life but then was a shop and business for most of the rest of its history.
1. When we took up floorboards in our living room we found skeletal remains beneath a wall, on closer inspection we decided it was a cat. They were completely dried and appeared broken and fragile. We had them put back in the same place.

2. The previous owner found a small corked bottle, resembling the Pershore phials on your site, in the roof space tucked up into the eaves, he told us it was an ink bottle but our researches make us wonder if that is correct! It has been opened but is not broken. We have this in a frame now.

3. On several beams around the house we have marks which were looked at in 2005 or 6 by a visitor who was at a local vernacular buildings conference. We had not noticed them but he shone a torch and said he thought they were protection marks, AVM for Ave Virgine Maria. There are more in the roofspace which he found with a torch. I have tried photographing these but they don't show up very well. I have shown them to our local Conservation Officer but there is no mechanism to have them recorded as part of the listing!'

Protection marks exist in **Chelvey Court** in the form of a large daisy wheel on the chimney lintel and a scratched 'M' mark. The owner describes them as follows: 'Ours is on the lintol of a late 16thC stone fireplace surround. The scratch marks have survived largely because the fireplace was replaced in the mid 17thC with a smaller surround inside the larger – with successive, smaller fireplaces at later dates. We uncovered this "nest" of fireplaces in removing a 20thC cupboard which pulled off old plaster, revealing the past 400 years of history. The same stone surround also has an "M" scratch – very difficult to see to anyone untutored in such things (including me) but we have been assured by an elderly and learned visitor that the M refers to Mary, placed there to guard the entrance to the house via the chimney. We also have oxshoes on two thresholds – for similar reasons one gathers'.

At Shutes Hill Farm, **Chipstable**, Somerset, a bullock's heart pierced with large nails and thorns was found in a chimney in 1892. This item is on display in the 'Sympathetic Magic Case' in the Pitt Rivers Museum, Oxford.

At **Cleeve Abbey**, Washford, Watchet, there are some daisy wheel ritual marks in the passage between the Warming Room and the Corrodians' Lodgings. These are in plaster and incomplete. From *Mosaic* 1994.

A carved pentagram on an inglenook fireplace was reported in a farm cottage near **Crewkerne**. The owner believes it to be around 400 years old. Thirty years workers found a pentagram or five-pointed star sign carved into a wooden mantle on the inside; they decided to turn it around so that the sign now faces into the room. Reported in February 2001.

A series of ritual marks on an oak screen was reported at a house near **Dulverton**. Reported in May 2001.

Protection marks have been discovered on the chimney lintel of a cottage in **East Lambrook**, South Petherton.

A daisy wheel is reported on a window spandrel in the south wall of **Glastonbury Abbey**. Reported by Rebecca Ireland from the Churches Conservation Trust in June 2012.

At a farm in **Hillfarrance**, Taunton, Somerset, there is the most incredible daisy door. This appears to be a seventeenth-century wooden door with a beautiful and intricate design of two large daisy wheels. This is an example of the protective symbol being used overtly as a key part of a decorative scheme instead of being subtly traced onto a surface.

At Upton, **Long Sutton**, during a house restoration a seventeenth-century glue pot was found with the jawbone of a sheep and a pamphlet dated 1783 about Phoebe Hann's (?) being burned at the stake for counterfeiting. The items were placed carefully in a mitre over a doorway.

Protection marks have been found at **Meare Manor**. Reported in June 2001.

At **Morelinch Vineyard** near Bridgewater, a doll cat was found on a ledge up a chimney. The toy had pads on its feet amongst other details; unfortunately however, workmen burned it.

On the north end of the communion rail at **Otterhampton**, Somerset, daisy wheels can be found. Reported by Rebecca Ireland from the Churches Conservation Trust in June 2012.

Ritual marks have been found in a property in **Shapwick**. Reported in June 2001.

Scribed circles in plaster were reported in the pigeon loft/cheese storage room of a farm at **Southstoke**.

A heart stuck with pins forming the initials 'MD' was found nailed up on a beam in a fireplace at **Staplegrove**, Taunton in 1890. This item is on display in the Pitt Rivers Museum, Oxford.

It was reported that a dried cat was discovered in the vicinity of **West Quantoxhead**. It is said to have been found in the farm, parts of which are thought to be Elizabethan. Reported in February 2001.

A tiny wooden shoe/clog was discovered under the rafters next to the chimney stack at a cottage in **Wrington**, North Somerset. It is a remarkable little thing with a kind of hash-tag symbol on it and the word 'ANVERS' carved onto it. Reported in December 2011. ANVERS is the Belgian way of spelling Antwerp so this was clearly a little souvenir clog which has been used in the same way as a concealed shoe.

South Yorkshire

At **Birthwaite Hall** farm a large daisy wheel was spotted on a window jamb in the bothy above the stables. It has a double ring around it. Reported in June 2017 edition of *Yorkshire Vernacular Buildings Study Group newsletter.*

A dried brown rat, thought to date to the nineteenth century, was kept in a bookcase at the Council's Finance Department, Nether Hall, **Doncaster**, but it was disposed of.

A slender narrow-bodied vial was discovered in **Green Moor**. It was dated from around 1780–1790, was 3-5/8 inches high, of English manufacture in pale green glass. It was found during restoration on an old building in Green Moor, a small settlement in South Yorkshire. 'I believe the vial was discovered in a small niche in the chimney breast whilst stripping back old plaster. As far as I know there was nothing in the bottle when it was found'. Reported in June 2004.

An adult's shoe and another smaller shoe, thought to date from the eighteenth century or earlier, were found behind a ground floor fireplace in Manor Road, **Hatfield**.

It is reported that a dried cat was discovered in a public house in **Mexborough** during demolition.

A child's shoe was found in a party wall of a cottage of 1800, in the **Sheffield** area.

A horse's leather blinker was found in a wall in the **Sheffield** area.

A woman's shoe was found in a wall in two pieces in the **Sheffield** area.

In June 2004 the following was reported by e-mail: 'Just to let you know that the Crown Inn on Chesterfield Rd. & Albert Rd. **Sheffield** have a child's shoe on display found above the hearth when the pub was renovated'.

In the Main Street, **Sprotborough**, a child's boot dating to the eighteenth century or earlier was discovered behind a stud partition wall.

A dried black rat, known to predate 1770, was found behind an Adam style fireplace at Finkle Street, **Thorne**.

It is reported that a dried hare was discovered at **Thorne**.

At in St Mary's Mews, **Tickhill**, a variety of marks can be found in the cottage and on a stone at the threshold there is a VV mark. Reported in November 2014.

The Church of All Saints, **Wath upon Dearne**, had a large quantity of shoe outlines recorded on the roof.

A group of leather shoes was found at Harley Hall, **Wentworth**. They are thought to date from the eighteenth or nineteenth century and feature in 'Fine South Yorkshire Timber Framed Houses', *Yorkshire Archaeological Journal*, 1989, 59: 65.

Staffordshire

In the Priory of St Thomas at **Baswich**, a daisy wheel mark can be found in an undercroft with the careful use of a torch. The priory had been rebuilt as a farm in the seventeenth century.

At a cottage in Hazle's Cross, **Kingsley**, four nineteenth-century shoes were discovered by the fireplace/chimney.

A nineteenth-century boot was discovered hidden in the wall of a **Leek** pub, the Sea Lion in Russell Street. Reported on 3 February 1988, in *Post and Times*, p. 5.

Jeremy Harte reported in March 2006: 'My miscellaneous reading has uncovered a note from W. Wells Bladen, "Notes on the folklore of North Staffordshire, chiefly collected at **Stone**", *Staffordshire Field Club* 35 (1900-1) pp133-85 – p148, "The hard clay floor of an old farmhouse in Leekfrith being dug up, an inverted glass bottle was found buried, full of dark water, in which were about nine pins curiously bent. The worthy farmer supposed this was a charm for witchcraft"'.

A concealed shoe was discovered beneath the eaves of a little privy outbuilding at Boosley Grange near **Longnor**. Reported by Andy Bentham in December 2017.

A dried cat has been reported to me by John Billingsley in November 2005. The e-mail reads: 'Was talking to a lady, a Mrs Trodd, the other day on the phone – by chance she had mentioned a mummified cat to a friend. Story: in 1984, doing renovation in attic of 1629 house (The Cottage, **Offley Brook**, near Eccleshall, Staffs), a mummified cat was found. Not knowing of the tradition at the time, they thought ugh and threw it away – but haven't had any particular bad luck!'

It is reported that a witch-bottle has been discovered on the site of the former Turk's Head Inn (now a car park), Tipping Street, **Stafford**. Reported in September 2009 and seen online in *Birmingham Mail*, 10 October 2009.

The site of the burial of a headless horse was discovered during a new development for **Stafford College**, as reported on the BBC News website on 19 November 2003. This is a medieval find and experts are puzzled as to why a horse might be buried instead of its hide and bones used, let alone that it has no head.

A silver spoon was found concealed in the plaster of one of the timber framed walls of Ford Green Hall, **Smallthorne**, Stoke-on-Trent.

It is reputed that a dried cat was found in **Tamworth**. From Pennick 1995. This find is also reported in Howard 1951.

Suffolk

At Bridge Farm, **Alpheton**, it is reported that there is a daisy inscribed on the mantel beam.

In a farmhouse at **Ashfield** a group of shoes were found. They belong to a man, woman and possibly children and were found caked in clay between the boards of the ceiling of a downstairs room and the floor above. They are thought to date to the eighteenth century.

Protection marks were reported at a barn in Station Road, **Bacton**, Stowmarket, in June 2011. The owner thinks the barn dates from around 1800. The marks are somewhat confused and include a possible VV.

At **Barton Mills** a 'very beautiful and unusual' witch-bottle was found up the chimney of a Wealden House dating to 1500.

In a seventeenth century house in **Beccles**, it is reported that a mummified cat was discovered in April 1995. The cat was apparently sitting in a roof space directly above a window and had its jaws open. Mentioned in Sieveking 1999.

At a property in Northgate, **Beccles**, a concealed shoe was found. This was reported in July 2007 as follows: 'the shoe recently found at the rear of [a property in] Northgate during the repair and reconstruction of a 17th century wall. The leather shoe with 7 lace holes and wooden sole has some decorative stitching and because of its size is believed to be a ladies shoe. The shoe was found in a vertical position close to the floor and victorian cobbles. Now that it has "dried out" and been photographed, we propose to rebury it during construction of the adjacent "bin store"'.

At Bedfield Hall, **Bedfield**, circular protective marks can be found in the seventeenth-century plaster ceiling. Marks can also be found at the north end of the seventeenth-century attic floor, over the kitchen chamber. From Easton 1999. Timothy Easton has informed me about many more marks, objects and animal remains found in this property.

At a cottage in High Street, **Bildeston**, Suffolk, many items were discovered, notably a pair of child's soft leather breeches with a silver button fastening. The owner is quoted in a newspaper article: 'There was a hole in the plaster work by the fireplace upstairs … It had been boarded over and that's where I found them. I think they'd been put by the fire to dry and slipped down the back'. The article in the newspaper also relates to a ghost story. From Withers 1998.

It is reported that concealed shoes have been found in the village of **Bramfield**.

At **Bramford**, a bellarmine was found inverted beneath the hearth of a property in The Street. It contained a handful of red dust but tests showed that it once contained urine. A similar large bottle, but without a medallion, broken but complete, was found with it but was thrown away. From Bunn 1982.

During repair work to Bungay House, Earsham Street, **Bungay**, in the 1930s, the contractors discovered horse skulls lying under the floorboards. On lifting two of the floorboards, 'beneath the joists were rows of horse skulls, laid with great regularity, the incisor teeth of each resting on a square of oak or stone … The (floor) boards, which were of red pine, rested immediately upon the skulls'. The room contained up to forty horse skulls, each 'carefully prepared and boiled, and … placed in position with great care and accuracy'. The adjoining house also revealed several horse skulls under the floor but these have been removed. From Armitage 1989b. Also mentioned in Pennick 1986. Ivan Bunn describes this one as 'A large number of horses skulls found beneath the floor-boards of two houses (formerly one house dating from the 1620s). The skulls had been carefully placed and firmly fixed, each having its incisor teeth resting on a square of stone or oak'. Bunn quotes his source as Mann 1934: 253–55.

A witch-bottle was found under the floor of a seventeenth-century house in Looms Lane, **Bury St Edmunds** when it was demolished for road widening. The rusted remains of iron objects, perhaps nails, were found in the neck of the bottle.

In 1975 a bellarmine was found on the site of old houses, **Cornhill**, close to the site of the Bell Inn, Bury St Edmunds. From Bunn 1982.

A dried cat hangs from the ceiling of The Nutshell public house in **Bury St Edmunds**. Below it, on a string, is a dried mouse and nearby a dried rat also. From Pennick 1995. Also mentioned in Sieveking 1999. Alan Murdie suggests that this cat originally came from a pub in St John's Street where it was found in the walls many years ago. In September 1982 it was apparently stolen but was returned to the pub six weeks later.

A horse or cow pelvis was discovered embedded in a wall next to a doorway at the Angel Hotel, **Bury St Edmunds**. The wall probably dates to the eighteenth or nineteenth century.

A witch-bottle and two halves of bottles were found by self-employed builder, Ron West, during work on the old (and now closed) Coach and Horses pub, Honey Hill in **Bury St Edmunds**. These were found above a door and the relics went to Moyses Hall Museum.

Two witch-bottles were discovered beneath the Duke's Head in **Coddenham** dating to the seventeenth century. The first dated from the second half of the seventeenth century and was found in the garden. The second bottle was found buried on its side some three feet under the Tap-room hearth. When opened, a number of blackened pins fell out. From Bunn 1982.

At a property in **Copdock**, the hoof and part of the leg of a sheep or goat was found with some hide still attached. A wand, length 35.6cm, was also discovered. It is thought to have been made with elder wood and is cut and notched along its length.

In **Cratfield**, a seventeenth-century bellarmine was discovered in 1972 containing iron nails, fifty bronze pins and some hair.

At Garden Cottage in **Darsham**, a glass seventeenth-century bellarmine witch-bottle was discovered lying on its side near the threshold of the cottage during building operations. The contents of the bottle were thrown away but one nail was removed.

In 24 Gracechurch Street, **Debenham**, a wooden wand and the wishbone of a goose were found. The wand is 22.1cm long and is thought to be made of hazel and, like the Copdock example, is cut and notched along its length.

The chimney lintel of Camp Green Farm, **Debenham**, dated 1592, has an array of ritual marks along it. There is also a double-sided handwritten text pasted onto the beam. This is thought be date from the early seventeenth century. From Easton 1999.

A bellarmine witch-bottle was found under the floor of a sixteenth-century house in **Debenham**. The bottle had a clay bung set with brass pins (some bent) which was found in the neck. It was thrown away by the builder and only the neck could be retrieved. Timothy Easton mentions this in his article (1983: 29): 'a bellarmine jar, the neck of which had been stopped up with mud and many bent silver pins, found a few years ago buried under the threshold of no 39 Gracechurch Street, Debenham'.

At 3 Gracechurch Street, **Debenham**, a dried cat was found under the seventeenth-century attic floorboard near a sixteenth-century chimney. It was found in early 1980 and is now in Timothy Easton's collection, on loan to the Moyses Hall Museum. From Easton 1983.

At Sexton's Cottage, **Debenham**, (sixteenth-century) protection marks can be found on a fireplace lintel. From Easton 1999.

A partially glazed, saggy based medieval pot was found in the Merchant's House, 24 Gracechurch Street, **Debenham**. It contained bones (including jawbones and horn cores) from various food species: sheep, ox, pig, hare, mallard, chicken and pheasant have been identified. The tip of a slate pencil was also discovered. All this was found in the foundations of a former demolished building under a late fourteenth-century house and shop. The pot dates from the twelfth/thirteenth century and the foundations may be the earlier second church mentioned in the Domesday book. Thanks to Timothy Easton for clarifying the precise location and dating sequence of this building.

In **Debenham**, it is said that three dried kittens were found in a brick box two feet square situated next to the chimney. From Pennick 1995.

At **Eyke**, a bellarmine was found dating to the second half of the seventeenth century. The bottle was found buried under the hearth during the demolition of church cottages. The contents were missing but tests show that it had once contained urine. From Bunn 1982. This bottle is also reported in Smedley, Owles and Paulsen 1964–1966.

Two dried cats were found in the roof space of a row of cottages in **Fakenham Magna** during conversion in 1972. Additionally, a cat and kittens were found in the wall space of the same building and are now in Thetford Museum. These cats were reported in a local paper ('"Black Magic" Cats Scare Workmen', *Bury Free Press*, 18 August 1972 – on file) and the house is named Park House which is on the Euston Estate. The house is large and timber-framed and has grown in at least four stages from the sixteenth to the eighteenth century. Article '"Black Magic" Cats Scare Workmen', *Bury Free Press*, Friday 18 August 1972 – on file. Ivan Bunn adds, 'Two well preserved, mummified cats were discovered in the attic of this 400 years old house. They have never been removed and are still in-situ'. He cites the source as *Thetford and Watton Times*, 10 October 1965.

In a house at **Flixton** which was built in the late seventeenth century, a number of objects were discovered in 1977 when the owner opened up a cavity in the side of the stack. The objects are described by the owner as: 'A small shoe 120mm long. A very thin piece of foot shaped leather 90mm long. A very worn bone handled knife 180mm long. A knife blade and shaft with no handle 120mm long. A few pieces of clay pipe. A few bone buttons. A few scraps of paper, one mentions: – God, Christ, Hell, flames, wrath. Another is in old printed script with the long s, and includes: – oppofition agasinft Poperie – fires of Purgatorie – originall finne and inftificat – the Councell of Trent. These fragments of paper were screwed up and are fragile so not easy to examine. There were some small animal bones'.

In **Halesworth**, a seventeenth-century bellarmine used as a witch-bottle was found. It was said to contain dolls and pins. This was reported in 1972, and the information apparently came from Norwich Castle Museum.

In **Halesworth**, at Halesworth Maltings, a dried cat was discovered in the brickwork of one of the ovens used for roasting barley.

In **Halesworth**, a dried cat was discovered at Forbuoys Newsagents in Thoroughfare – this is part of the Guildhall built in 1475. 'The cat was found below some flooring when alterations were being made, but was put back after things were sorted out, in order to ensure that its "good luck" would continue on in the future'. Quoted from a small leaflet, 'Ghosts and Witchcraft', published by Halesworth and District Museum.

At **Haughley**, concealed shoes have been found. This was reported in August 2008 as follows: 'I am restoring a listed 16th century house in Haughley, Suffolk and have discovered 2 odd children's shoes hidden in a small concealed room behind a large chimney'.

At a farmhouse in **Homersfield**, numerous protection marks are recorded 'in most rooms'. Reported in August 2007.

On the lead roof at **Ilkestshall** St Lawrence can be found a wide range of shoe outlines incised into the lead. Most of the outlines are dated, from the sixteenth to the early twentieth century. Reported in *Northern Earth magazine* 90.

A dried cat was discovered at the Golden Lion inn on Cornhill in **Ipswich**.

In 1958 a stoneware bottle (not a bellarmine) marked with horseshoes and dating from the last quarter of the seventeenth century was unearthed from beneath the floor level of a house near the corner of Pottery Street and Arthur Street, **Ipswich**. The houses had been destroyed prior to the Second World War and the exact location of them is not known, but it was probably number 45 or 47 Pottery Street. The bottle was complete but with one side broken away to reveal its contents which included a piece of felt (in several fragments) but originally sewn into a heart shape, into which six or seven brass pins were stuck. A piece of light brown human hair, more than forty iron nails, a two-pronged table fork, more than forty small fragments of glass, twenty-four brass studs and the fragments of several wooden spills (possibly sulphur matches) were also found. The neck had been firmly plugged with clay and tests showed that the bottle had once contained urine. From Bunn 1982. This find is also reported in depth in Merrifield and Smedley 1958–1960 (which includes excellent photographs). There are also very good photographs on pp. 169 and 170 of Merrifield 1987.

During the restoration of Dover House at **Ixworth**, a bellarmine was discovered buried just outside the south-west door of the house. It contained five or six large nails and had once contained urine. From Bunn 1982. This bottle is also reported in Smedley, Owles and Paulsen 1964–1966. There is a good photograph of the bottle in the article. Ivan Bunn adds that this bottle appears in Evans 1966 and also in Coleman 1963.

Ivan Bunn reports the following: 'Location: Suffolk County Council Teacher Training Centre, **Kelsale** ... A mummified cat discovered in this ?16th century timber-framed building is displayed here'.

A bellarmine witch-bottle, made in Frechen in 1620–1675, 205cm in height, with a stylised face mask – with a star on the forehead and foliage in the mouth – and a petalled flower medallion, was found at Holywell Row, **Lakeheath**, Suffolk. It has original cork and contained a 'black gunge'. Thanks to Alex Wright who supplied this information based on bottles in his collection. Reported via e-mail on 30 March 2016 and published in Wright 2011.

In **Lavenham Guildhall** it is reported that a dried cat was found walled up. The cat is now on display there.

In **Lavenham** a dried rat was discovered in the roof space of Old Priory, preserved there. From Pennick 1995.

Laxfield Church has the outlines of shoes cut directly into the lead on its roof, probably dating from the late eighteenth or early nineteenth century.

Timothy Easton reports that two bonnets have been found in **Laxfield**.

In 1967 a seventeenth-century bellarmine was found buried on its side below the hearth of an unspecified cottage at **Needham Market**. Urine tests were positive. From Bunn 1982.

In the Rectory at **Norton** near Bury St Edmunds there is a VV mark which has a large crack in the timber showing that it must have been there before the crack. This was reported in April 2012 as follows: 'Attached is a photo of what appears to be a Ritual Mark on an oak beam above the fireplace in my kitchen. The building dates from the 15th Century and the marks were clearly made before the large crack opened up. The main symbol resembles a "W", and there is also a mark resembling a lower-case "h" to its right. The building is a former rectory in the village of Norton near Bury St Edmunds in Suffolk. The house is famous for being the first recorded Private Madhouse in Britain. It functioned as a madhouse during the Civil War period when the Reverend John Ashburne was the incumbent. Unfortunately, he was murdered by one of his own mad inmates on 1st August 1661'.

Two phials have been found in **Pakenham** Water Mill. This was reported in January 2009 as follows: 'Two small glass bottles, quite similar to the ones from Pershore pictured on your website, were found under the floorboards of an upstairs room during restoration work in the miller's house attached to Pakenham Water Mill, Suffolk. One contained dust and what might be the dried remains of a cork. Parts of the house date from the 17th century but the bottles were thought more likely to be 19th century (by the local museum in Bury St Edmunds). From the information on your site and others it seems likely that they are witch bottles. They will be going on display in the millers house, which is open to the public'.

A bellarmine was found in a garden in **Reydon** – presumed to be a witch-bottle.

It is reported that a witch-bottle was found in the village of **Risby** in the 1970s and was displayed in the front room of a private house.

At a house in **Rishangles**, a room was protected by two dried cats and on a chimney beam are three 'spectacular' marks.

A complete bellarmine was found at Town Farm near **Southwold**.

A witch-bottle thought to have come from the village of **Stoke** was found on a rubbish tip in Ipswich. The finder threw away the contents but the tine of a rake was jammed inside. Urine tests were positive. From Bunn 1982. This bottle is also reported in Smedley, Owles and Paulsen 1964–1966.

In **Stoke-by-Nayland**, a sixteenth-century woman's shoe was discovered behind plaster in Thorington Hall. Also, three interlacing circles are to be found on the third newel from the bottom of the timber staircase, dating to the mid-seventeenth century. From Underwood 1986: 172.

A silver spoon was discovered in Combs Ford, **Stowmarket**, thought to date to the seventeenth century. It is described as having been deliberately hidden. From Emery, Warner and Pearson 1990: 137.

In Church Street, **Stowmarket**, a bellarmine was discovered during alterations to an unspecified house. It was buried upside down close to the hearth and contained about fifty nails, most of which were square headed cut nails. Roughly three dozen round headed brass pins, all deliberately bent, were also found along with the tine of a rake and a mass of fused metal. Tests showed that it once contained urine. From Bunn 1982. This bottle is also reported in Smedley, Owles and Paulsen 1964–1966.

At a property in Ipswich Street, **Stowmarket**, three odd shoes dating between 1750–1770, some sixteenth-century Delftware and some nineteenth-century china were discovered in a wattle and daub wall.

A bellarmine was found buried inverted beneath the hearth of an old cottage in **Stradbroke**. It had been buried upside down and its contents are report to have included thorns. Tests for urine have proved positive. From Bunn 1982. This bottle was originally reported in Merrifield 1954. This bottle is also reported in Smedley, Owles and Paulsen 1964–1966.

At a farm in **Stradbroke**, it is reported that there are many protection marks on the beams in the property; also, a strange stone was discovered. 'This week I have had some horse hair plaster fall off the ceiling in a downstairs room so I decided to pull it all down, on the top of one of the beams was a stone bigger than my fist which must have been placed there when the house was built, it too has some strange marks on it'. Reported in March 2010.

In **Stratford St Mary**, a seventeenth-century salt-glazed witch-bottle, dating to around 1620, was discovered under the hearth of an old house during renovation. The bottle contained bunches of blackthorn and nails. Bunn states that the bottle was found under an old cottage called Goose Acre (formerly the Shoulder of Mutton Inn). Tests showed that it once contained urine. From Bunn 1982.

Daisy wheels and burn marks have been found at a house in Roost End, **Sturmer**, Haverhill.

A dried cat was discovered in the Mill Hotel in **Sudbury**. The find was featured in the *Hong Kong Standard* in November 1995. A builder reported (in the feature) that 'In my time, I've discovered about a dozen in various houses in the area. I always put them back'. Ivan Bunn gives a more complete account, including the fact that the building was formerly known as the Old Watermill: 'A well-preserved mummified cat with its back legs tied together was discovered in the roof space when the mill was being reconstructed. The building is over 300 years old. The cat was removed and afterwards all sorts of bad luck dogged the reconstruction. Eventually the owners, assisted by the local vicar, re-buried the body in the building together with a note of apology'. Bunn quotes the source as *The Sunday People*, 9 November 1971 which includes photographs. Timothy Easton says this cat is still in the building, behind glass.

At a house on The Green at **Tostock**, an eighteenth-century man's shoe was found along with a handbill advertising a lecture by a doctor, a pillbox and several other papers all in a thatch.

At a farm in **Ubbeston**, a group of four shoes was found bricked up in a chimney. They comprised one man's, one woman's and two children's shoes. They are described as well made and from the seventeenth century.

The discovery of a witch-bottle at **Weybread** was reported in October 2012 as follows: 'I recently uncovered a Bartmann jug less its handle whilst undertaking the an excavation at Weybread, in Suffolk on a Second World War USAAF aircraft scrapping site, there was a multitude of pottery & glassware used as infill for the huge pits the Air Force used to dispose of junk airplane parts.

It has a relief of a bearded man below the neck & an embossed seal. Mine still had the cork & was full of very pungent black fluid which I decanted, I was careful enough to strain the contents which comprised of what appears to be human hair, bent pins & blocks of yellow sulphur'.

At Barley House Farm in **Winston**, a hoard of eighteenth-century miscellanea was found. It comprised twenty leather shoes (eighteenth-century) and one spur guard, three wooden tally sticks (thought to be clog almanacs), two mummified kittens which were less than two or three months old, part of a part-mummified rat, one wing bone of a goose or swan, several bones of a sucking pig, one base of a small glass bottle and assorted fragments of leather and cloth, which have been identified as coming from breeches and a waistcoat; the bowl of a clay pipe was also found (seventeenth-century). This find was also written up in Easton 1983, with illustrations, and again with illustrations in Oliver 1997. Ivan Bunn also reports this information. Apparently, this find was reported in the *Eastern Daily Press* of 29 August 1984. There are illustrations on file.

Protection marks can be found over the hall fireplace at Green Farm, **Winston**. There is an illustration on file. From Easton 1999.

Surrey

At **Charlton Village**, near Littleton, a bellarmine witch-bottle was found. This was reported in June 2016 as follows: 'I purchased a Bellarmine bottle on ebay earlier this year which may be of interest to you. The original listing stated that it had been found "behind a fireplace around thirty years ago" by the lister's builder husband, along with an iron fire-back dated 1631. Further enquiry showed that it came from "an old outhouse" that originally formed part of some cottages demolished to make way for the Queen Mary reservoir at Charlton village, near Littleton in old Middlesex (now modern administrative Surrey). The cottages lay to the rear of what is now Walnut Tree Road off Charlton Road at the eastern edge of the reservoir. I had an opportunity to speak to the vendor's husband, and he had not found anything within the bottle – though he was aware of the significance of my asking. The Bellarmine itself looks to have been affected by heat, which has damaged the surface in places – though whether this happened in the kiln or later is unclear. The handle has also been repaired – though not by the vendor. Though not apparently containing anything that would suggest that this WAS a witch bottle, I thought it worth bringing to your attention because of its position "behind a fireplace", and also the apparent association with a dated fire-back'.

Several shoes and other bits and pieces were found in a mini midden at Hyde Farm, **Churt**, Surrey. This is the place that featured on *At Home with the Georgians* on BBC2, 2010.

Two women's overshoes were found in the roof of a shop in **Cobham,** now in Weybridge Museum.

A nineteenth-century lady's shoe was found in a pub in **Croydon.**

A bellarmine witch-bottle dating from the third quarter of the seventeenth-century and carrying the arms of Amsterdam was found behind a fireplace at a cottage in **East Clandon**. It is said to have contained a charred mess.

Four boy's shoes, two adult and one woman's shoe were found behind the fireplace at a property in West End, **Esher**. They have been dated to 1810–1830.

At **Godalming,** a shoe was found tucked under the eaves in a cottage.

In **Guildford**, a late seventeenth-century man's shoe and a sixteenth-century child's shoe were found in the filling of a wall at the Royal Grammar School.

Three shoes, one a child's, were discovered in **Guildford**, provenance unknown.

An early eighteenth-century clog and a seventeenth/eighteenth-century child's shoe were found in a property in Joseph Road, **Guildford**.

A witch-bottle was found buried in the cellar floor of a house just north of **Leatherhead** in Surrey. Reported in September 2006.

Three shoes were found concealed in the bedroom wall of a seventeenth-century house at **Leith Hill.**

The skeleton of a cat was found in a Tudor house in **Milford**. From Pennick 1995. Merrifield states that the cat was discovered lodged beneath one of the massive roof-timbers of this house which was extended in the seventeenth century. From Merrifield 1987: 131.

At Tanhurst (Tanhouse Farm) in **Newdigate**, thirteen shoes were found behind the staircase. They have been dated to the early nineteenth century. There is some debate about whether these constitute a concealed find as a cobbler previously worked there.

A report from December 2005 stated: 'I live in **Newdigate** in Surrey, not far from the Sussex border. The original part of our cottage dates from 1580 and there is a chimney and large fireplace added we believe in the early 1600s. The lintel above the fireplace has a really nice overlapping double V and two vertical lines just to the right of this. They look very similar to those in Timothy Easton's article from a few years ago. Haven't found any hidden bottles or dead cats yet I'm afraid'.

At **Ockham**, a late nineteenth-century child's canvas and leather shoe was found in a cottage in Ockham Park.

At the Old School Public House, **Ockley**, two shoes were found in the roof, one apparently from the eighteenth century (thanks to June Swann) and the other – a boot – from the nineteenth century. Reported in June 2017.

In **Puttenham**, a mid-eighteenth-century shoe was found in the attic at a property on The Street. It was a lady's shoe, hidden away on a beam in the attic. From *Surrey Advertiser*, 31 August 1974.

Four or five shoes, from the late seventeenth to the early eighteenth century, were found under the staircase at a property in Copse Road, **Redhill**.

In **Reigate**, two shoes (1700–1750) – one male and one female – were discovered at a property in the High Street in a building dated around c.1600. They were both found on the first floor behind a wall. From the files of Janet Pennington.

In **Reigate**, a bellarmine witch-bottle of c.1600 was found intact, upturned but empty within the crosswing of the Old Vicarage, in Church Street. The building was demolished in 1847 and seems to have been built around 1200.

In **Reigate**, a witch-bottle was discovered in London Road. A small piece was published in the Bulletin of the *Surrey Archaeology Society* (date unclear). It was described as 'A glass wine bottle, deposited c1700 (perhaps as late as 1750), corked and containing liquid and nine bent pins. This was upturned and came from a disturbance adjacent to the chalk floor of a 17th century building excavated at 12–14 London Road in 1993'. Dr Alan Massey of Loughborough University privately published a report (on file) and also published, with T. Edmonds, an article 'The Reigate Witch-Bottle' (2000), in which a thorough chemical analysis of the contents of the bottle is presented. The bottle is referred to in the 'Radicals' Kelly 2000. A small piece appeared in *The Times* on 24 March 1999, p. 21, concerning this bottle, written by Alan Massey. Responses appeared in *The Times* on 29 March 1999, p. 21.

In January 2006, Peter Burgess reported to me that he had been discovering VV marks in chalk mines in Surrey, presumably the **Reigate Mines**. Having seen the VV marks described from Goatchurch Cavern, he said, 'I have become aware of very similar marks, in chalk, on the walls of ancient underground quarry workings in Surrey, and although research is in its early stage (we still need to record location and style of all the marks we have found), I thought you might like to be aware of what we have found. The workings are very extensive, and we believe they were active from at least the 12th century until the early 18th century. From what little evidence we have, we believe the area where the ritual protection marks have been found dates from some time in the 16th century, or these workings at least existed at that time, but may of course have been older'.

A dried cat was discovered at a property in High Street, **Staines**. It is described as having its innards removed and being found in a running position.

In April 2001 a report of the finding of a wooden doll from **Tilford** came in two messages as follows: 'I was clearing out this old house for a friend of my and I found this doll it was laying face down under a floorboard that my dad happened to lift up I wondered if you could tell me what this is it's like a very old wooden doll it looked pretty strange. The doll had no hair when I found and it as it looked like the hair had been burned off because the head had like black marks all over it, it was in an old house under the floorboard in Tilford I didn't find anything else but the doll had very fade like knife marks all over it it does look like a very old wooden doll'.

Two child's shoes were found in the wall of a cottage at **Wonersh**, probably dating from the late nineteenth century.

A brown glazed jug of the eighteenth century was discovered under the hearth of a house in **Wonersh**. It contained bits of nails, pins and some non-local red gravel. The jug lay on its side half a metre below the hearth stone. From Merrifield 1987: 174.

Warwickshire

A concealed candlestick and dried cat were discovered at **Henley-in-Arden**. This was reported in January 2016 as follows: 'I wonder if you can help with my research into what I believe to be a 16th C. candle stick. It was found by my father alongside a mummified cat in a chimney niche of a 16th C. cottage he and his cousin were renovating in Henley in Arden during the late 1960's. When found the base had been separated from the cup which my father later soldered together again. Sadly both my father & his cousin are no longer with us so I have only got the sketchy info that I have included which I gleaned from my mother. I have attached a couple of photos for you to look at. It has been constructed from stamped (what I believe to be) latten sheet as it has not tarnished to any noticeable degree as brass would have done. What I would like to learn is if this is the kind of item that would be hidden as a charm and also is the fact that it was broken relevant? Anything else that you might be able to tell me would be much appreciated. Many thanks, Ed Andrews'.

At a cottage in Station Road, **Salford Priors**, a book, patten and shoe were discovered in the roof space behind a plaster panel. A fire had occurred in this thatch cottage many years before but the former owner had retained the objects which were discovered at that time. It was, therefore, surprising to the current owner when this former owner turned up with a box of artefacts wishing them to be reunited with their home. The patten is thought to date from the mid-nineteenth century and the other objects from the mid-sixteenth century.

Many objects have been discovered in a farmhouse in **Wormleighton**. Peter Davidson reported on a postcard that claimed the house 'had the lot: daisy wheels and pentagrams over all windows and fireplaces and witch bottles under floor and poltergeist'.

West Midlands

Staff at Tamworth Castle Museum recall a dried cat which once resided in a case inside the Curzon Street, **Birmingham** former Post Office classical building which is on the site of the new Millennium Point Experience in Birmingham.

In August 2001 the following dried cat was reported: 'The old West Midlands Police station at Hay Mills in **Birmingham** is now a pub, "The Old Bill and Bull". It was built in Victorian times and was originally in Worcestershire (the county boundary changed). It was taken over by Birmingham City Police at the turn of the century (1900's). It was closed as a police station in the 1980's and turned into a pub. When the builders were stripping out the old cells, a dried mummified cat was found under one of the built in cell beds! I know because I saw it'.

A dried cat and bird were found at Hay Hall, Tyseley, **Birmingham**. The animals were set up facing each other in a square cavity. From Pennick 1995. This find is also reported in Howard 1951.

A pair of skates thought to date to around 1890 were found under the floorboards of a house in **Brockmoor**. From Dyas 1993.

At **Cradley Heath**, a pair of old boots was discovered beneath floorboards. From Dyas 1993.

It is reported that a dried cat was found at The Lad in the Lane public house, **Erdington**.

A find of bones was reported in **Sedgeley** in 1860. This was reported in March 2004: 'An incident came up on the Sedgley list that was recorded in the *Birmingham Daily Post*, 31 August 1860: "a quantity of bones buried underneath the hearthstone in a cavity formed by an arch of house-top tiles and mortar", during the demolition of a pub in Sedgley High Street called the Pig and Whistle. At first, it was thought that the bones were human, although there wasn't enough to make up a complete human skeleton. The following week, the Sedgley doctor (J. M. Ballenden) wrote to the Post explaining that the bones certainly weren't human. The quotation posted (from a collection of news-cuttings) didn't say if Ballenden had an opinion about what animal the bones belonged to. As it was the hearth, perhaps it's an example of a cat being used to prevent destructive fire'.

At the Talbot Hotel, **Stourbridge**, during work to a small bridge building within the hotel a number of finds were discovered. These included bone combs, a corset and a shoe – all apparently from the nineteenth century.

A child's preserved arm and a Cromwellian sword were both found in the attic of the White Hart Inn, **Walsall**. The arm was preserved in formaldehyde and is probably a nineteenth-century medical specimen.

During conservation work in May 2003 at Ditchfield's bakery, Ablewell Street, **Walsall**, a number of items were discovered under floorboards. The objects were found between floor joists close to the hearth on the second floor of this Georgian building. These were a child's shoe (dated to c.1850), a wooden egg cup and a wooden spool. These items are all in Walsall Museum.

A concealed shoe and a silver spoon were discovered at house in **Wythall**. The house is thought to date from around 1800. The correspondent reported in November 2012 as follows: 'Just over 17 months ago we purchased an old cottage on Alcester Road. We have just had some work done which involved having a small part of a chimney removed, as the builder was taking part of what looked like an old stove built into the chimney he found a small child's shoe and a silver spoon hidden in the wall of the stove, the shoe looks like a Victorian one black hard leather and very small, the spoon is solid silver and looks as though it has a letter H on it. Is there any significance to them being in the wall and what should we do with them as friend's keep telling us to put them back into another wall. The cottage is some 212 years old so we would really like to know if this means something'.

West Sussex

At a cottage in Hog Lane, **Amberley**, some marks were discovered on the mantle beam: a vertical line with three lines crossing through it, an 'R' letter and a possible Christogram.

At a cottage in Botolphs Road, **Botolphs**, a small lady's kid leather glove, pieces of material including a lady's cuff, a collar with lacework, a waistband, a piece of brown smock material, hair pins, coins, marbles, beads, wallpaper pieces, the top of Monkey soap box label were all found under floorboards above the original entrance door to the cottage. In another area further north in the room under floorboards a collection of winkle shells, a flint and several partially burnt thin wooden spills were found. From the files of Janet Pennington.

At Annington, **Botolphs**, a cat's skull was found beneath the floorboards. From the files of Janet Pennington.

At a property in Broadwater Street East, **Broadwater**, several objects, including many nuts, were discovered in one place directly above the front door. From the files of Janet Pennington.

A witch-bottle was reported to have been discovered in August 2004 at St Mary's Hospital Almshouses in **Chichester**. The bottle was discovered buried in the corner, near the north door. It is a large pot dating from the 1680s and thought to have been locally made. The details here were extracted from a newspaper article and reported to me in August 2004.

A Fulham type Bellarmine was found in association with a hearth in East Street, **Chichester**, during a watching brief in 1998.

At the Crown Inn, **Chichester**, the bones of a hand were found 'between the floorboards'. From the files of Janet Pennington.

A witch-bottle was discovered in **Church Norton**. The details were reported in July 2011 as follows: 'Whilst renovating an old thatch cottaged in Church Norton, Selsey, West Sussex, about 25-30 years ago. I found a stone bottle, filled with coloured glass chips. I found it under the fireplace, whilst lowering the floor. Unfortunately I discarded the contents, but have kept the bottle. I attach a couple of photo's, as you will see, it looks like the bottle originally had some sort of handle. Initially I was going to throw this away, but decided it looked interesting so kept it'.

In **Cowfold**, a stone roofer found a pig/sheep's jaw bone near the chimney of a house. From the files of Janet Pennington.

At Droke Farm, **East Dean**, a late seventeenth-century pot was discovered beneath the inglenook fireplace. A child's shoe dating to the 1880s and a rabbit's foot were also discovered in the fireplace here. From Magliton 1992, 1993.

The **East Grinstead** Museum *Compass* (no 7, Spring 2002) includes notes on footwear and a doll concealed in local buildings for superstitious reasons. From Leppard 2002.

The sole of a child's shoe was found in the Crown Inn at **East Grinstead**. From the files of Janet Pennington.

An old boot was found at a farm in **Fernhurst**. From the files of Janet Pennington.

Two dried cats were discovered in the chimney of a house in **Henfield** in the nineteenth century. From the files of Janet Pennington.

A dried cat was found with a bird beneath the attic floor (second-floor level) of Henfield Workhouse, **Henfield** (1730). They were found underneath the place where the paupers slept. From the files of Janet Pennington.

A concealed shoe was discovered at a farm in **Horsham**, behind panelling in the attic, thought to date to 1830–1880.

Jason Semmens reports a shoe from **Horsham** as follows: 'There are some builders currently working at a property in Causeway, Horsham – just a few doors down from the museum; they are renovating the building and removing some of the later structures and wallpaper added since the 1960s (the wallpaper was used liberally to cover many original features – the front hall and stairs are particularly attractive). The original "core" of the building is medieval, and subsequently added to to take it out to the street in the sixteenth or seventeenth century. There are also eighteenth century additions towards the rear. I'm attaching some images of the leather shoe the builder came into the museum with on Friday 4 October 2013, having discovered it earlier that day (so far as I know). It looks to me to be of late eighteenth/early nineteenth century date. The builder reckoned that the chimney it was pushed up against dated from the late eighteenth century. The shoe was found lodged between the chimney and a lathe and plaster wall (behind the wall) so that it is hardly likely to have got there by accident. The view I had of it was from the opposing wall. Unfortunately they had demolished the chimney stack by the time I got there, but you can see in the photograph the back of the lathe & plaster wall and the remains of the chimney'. Reported in October 2013.

A doll was found under the floorboards at Glaysher's Shop in **Horsham** when the building was dismantled and moved to Singleton Museum.

A dried cat was discovered at a farm near **Horsham**.

In the *Sussex County Magazine*, vol. 8, no. 4 (April 1934), there are pictures of a pair of lady's shoes, dated from the reign of Charles II, found 'in an old house at **Horsham**'. From the files of Janet Pennington.

At Hunston Manor, **Hunston** near Chichester, a Fulham type Bellarmine was found during the renovation of an inglenook fireplace.

At a property in **Hurstpierpoint**, six leather shoes – one small child's shoe, four adult's shoes and one other – were found. From the files of Janet Pennington.

A bellarmine witch-bottle is reported to have been found at Turks Croft, **Ifield**, Crawley. The bottle was discovered upright about two feet below a hearth. From Pennington 1992.

At Sharpenhurst, **Itchingfield,** a worn child's shoe was discovered on the first floor within the chimney. The house dates from c.1425 and the chimney was inserted in around 1595. From the files of Janet Pennington.

At **Lancing College,** two clay pipes were found behind the panelling in Great School which was built in 1882. The carpenters who found them replaced them with a tobacco tin and a coin when they made their own late twentieth-century deposit in the 1990s. From the files of Janet Pennington.

A witch-bottle was found at **Michelham Priory.** The bottle is said to have been buried in a wall in the western range that was still standing in 1667. It is described as a Holmes Type VIII. The jug was sealed at the top with clay and contained water, clay and gravel. It was washed out before the contents were examined in a laboratory. The bottle contained pins and possibly an effigy. A photograph of the bottle and full commentary can be found in Bellam 1990. Janet Pennington states in a later article that a number of pins and other matter were discovered in the bottle which were sent away for analysis. From Pennington 1992.

In Coppett Hold, Edinburgh Square, **Midhurst,** a pair of women's boots and one tie shoes from 1810–1820s was discovered. From the files of Janet Pennington.

At The Wheatsheaf, Rumbolds Hill, **Midhurst,** a youth's buckle shoe dating to 1775 was discovered. From the files of Janet Pennington.

A bellarmine was discovered bricked into a wall at Old Place, **Pulborough** in the 1960s. From Pennington 1992.

A glass medicine bottle and a bellarmine were found together in the rubble of a hearth at The Old House, **Pulborough.** From Pennington 1992.

In **Rudgwick,** a builder is reported to have found several bellarmines under hearths when re-laying them. From Pennington 1992.

At a cottage in West Street, **Selsey,** four pairs of socks were found wrapped in sacking under the floor near the hearth. A collar, possibly a dog collar, was also discovered with the socks. Sometime earlier in the house a dried cockerel was also discovered bricked in by the chimney breast over the staircase during renovations. The cockerel still had many of its white feathers. Its head was bent round over its shoulder which was interpreted as meaning that the cockerel had been concealed alive. It was re-concealed within the chimney breast after discovery. Reported in July 2002.

At a property in **Southwick**, a collection of objects was found under the hearth. These included oyster shells, pottery and clay pipes. A fork with a split bone handle 'fell down the chimney' here and two coins dating 1753/5 and 1806 (pennies) were also found. A separate find was made here of a broken wine glass and part of a boar's upper mandibles with the front part of its skull and tusks tucked into the wine bottle. The front part of the boar's skull was found together with a newspaper dating from 1782, but the broken wine glass was dated to about forty to fifty years earlier. This was found behind panelling in the 'parlour' on the top of the flint rubble wall. These were mortared into the top of a very thick flint rubble wall. From the files of Janet Pennington.

At a property in High Street, **Steyning**, animal bones were found in the east wall, ground floor, amongst the wattle and daub. From the files of Janet Pennington.

In another property in High Street, **Steyning**, three children's shoes dating from between the 1780 and 1790s were found in the roof in 1981. From the files of Janet Pennington.

At a house in Newham Lane, **Steyning**, two pairs of Cromwellian shoes were discovered during alterations in 1899. From the files of Janet Pennington.

In Church Street, **Steyning**, two shoes were found in the eaves of a property. From the files of Janet Pennington.

In High Street, **Steyning**, a child's shoe and leather bottle were discovered under floorboards. From the files of Janet Pennington.

At yet another property in High Street, **Steyning**, a shoe was discovered at the side of the chimney. This may be a man's buckle shoe, possibly from 1720–1760. From the files of Janet Pennington.

At The Old Dairy, High Street, **Steyning**, two cats have been seen 'bricked up into the wall'. From the files of Janet Pennington.

A late nineteenth-century shoe was discovered at the bottom of a well behind the old dairy, **Steyning**. From the files of Janet Pennington.

A large collection of objects was found beneath the floor of a cottage in High Street, **Steyning**. This included hair pins, clay pipe stems and bowls, copper coins, lead shot, and some bones. From the files of Janet Pennington.

A 'Cavalier's' hat was found walled up in a cupboard at Milstones and a small child's shoe was found in the chimney here too, in **Steyning**. From the files of Janet Pennington.

The skeleton of a cat with a rat in its mouth was found in a house at **Steyning**. This was reported in *The Times* of 6 September 1790. From Pennick 1995.

At a property in the High Street, **Upper Beeding**, two shoes were discovered and a doll was found near the hearth (blackened in parts). The shoes were dated to the first half of the eighteenth century. The doll remains near the hearth and the shoes were re-deposited in a special place made for them by the carpenter under the attic floorboards. From the files of Janet Pennington.

One pair and two single children's seventeenth-century shoes were found under the bottom of a staircase in **Upper Beeding**. From the files of Janet Pennington.

The sole of a child's shoe was discovered behind an old cupboard at a property in **Upper Beeding**. From the files of Janet Pennington.

West Yorkshire

A witch-pot was found in **Addingham** Churchyard, apparently similar to the one found at Overgate Croft (below). A slide of it exists in an aisle window of the church.

A witch-pot was found at Fur Cottage, Church Lane, **Addingham**, which has been dated to 1670. The pot was found beneath the present flagged floor. Plaits of corn were found on the hearth here too.

Longley Old Hall, **Almondbury** is reputed to have many protection marks inside it. Reported in March 2008.

The Great House at **Colden** has 'M's on the front doorway and 'W' just inside the wing fireplace. From Armstrong 1998.

At a property in Brunswick Street, **Dewsbury**, a child's boot was discovered. It is described as leather, low heel, high back and front, originally elastic sided, thought to date to the 1870s. This example was found under the floorboards of the house.

It is reported that a witch-pot was found at **Embsay**.

At Hill End Farm, **Harden**, a written charm was discovered in the wall. It is thought to date from 1750 and is written on a single sheet of paper.

The charm was reported in the *Yorkshire Observer* of 15 November 1944. A photograph of the charm appears in the article (on file). The charm reads as follows: 'Good X Lord X Jesus X Thy power is above all powers that is Good X Lord X grant that Thy powers may overcome all powers that is Evil. Good X Lord X Bless Thee Samuel Lund from all Evil Spirits, from witchcraft and fore-speaking and blasting and cramps x all diseases whatsoever in the name of the Father, and of the Son, and of the Holy Ghost Bless Thee Samuel Lund be Thou whole and guarded by the Angels God X Fiat X Fiat X Fiat'.

A pair of clogs were found behind panelling by the front door of a cottage in Wadsworth, **Hebden Bridge.** Reported by John Billingsley in February 2002.

It is reported that a dried cat was discovered at the base of the ruins of the church of St Thomas a Becket, **Heptonstall**, after a destructive storm in 1847. From Pennick 1995.

It is reported that in **Horsforth** two concealed shoes were recovered from the thresholds of local shops.

At Moldgreen, **Huddersfield**, the bowl and part of stem of a large pewter spoon and a leather sole from a child's shoe (both thought to be mid-nineteenth century) were discovered concealed in a house.

In the barn at West Moor House, Middleton, **Ilkley,** 'a boskin post is inscribed with at least five circles with a central hole, as well as an eight-point simple star and a six-point star with lines top and bottom, and initials R M and a date 1906. Is it coincidence that R and M are often paired in East Anglia as a protective symbol?' The barn was re-built in 1906 using old timbers. From Armstrong 1998.

At Broad Bottom, **Mytholmroyd**, there are scratched V protection marks. From Armstrong 1998. A shoe is reported to have come from one of the chimneys at the same place. Reported by John Billingsley in February 2003.

At Marsh Hall, **Northowram** (1626), there is a marked 'W' on the polished stone lintel centre of the wing fireplace. From Armstrong 1998.

An unusual witch-bottle is reported from a farm near **Ogden** which is near Halifax. Kai Roberts reported in December 2011 as follows: 'An acquaintance in the pub told me of the item, which had been discovered on his parents' farm in his youth and had been bequeathed to him following his mother's death last year. I recently took some photographs of it and I've attached a few of the pictures for you to look at.

The bottle was discovered at a farm near Ogden near Halifax (a Grade 2 listed building) sometime around 1975, beneath the doorstep of a C19th outdoor toilet which stood next to the east wing of the house before it was demolished to make way for a modern extension (if you look on the aerial photo, you can just make out where the extension attaches to the house). Stupidly I neglected to take the exact dimensions of the jar itself, although I would estimate it to be approximately 12 inches tall, with a diameter of about 7 inches at its widest point. It's earthenware with a very basic glaze, probably of local origin given that there was a major pottery barely a mile from where it was found. The neck is broken at the top and I'm told it was like that when it was found. Inside, there was apparently some sludge when it was discovered (possibly including urine?) and two figurines, both about 5-6 inches tall. They're probably made from clay, although they're too fragile to move from their box so I couldn't examine them properly. The material is very fine (probably clay of some sort) and they're hollow. It's impossible to tell whether they're meant to be male or female.

Given the date of the privy and how close it was to the surface, it seems unlikely that it's older than the C19th (unless there was an older byre on the site and it was replaced in the new building), but its purpose is more puzzling. It's not the most obvious place to require protection from witchery and given the effigies, I wondered if it might've been intended to create maleficium rather than repel it. Or perhaps given their number, it was intended as a love charm'.

A concealed shoe was found in a building at **Otley**.

In Carlton Street, **Otley**, builders found four pairs of mid-nineteenth-century shoes and an assortment of odd clogs and shoes. They were found in the bedroom chimney breast. This discovery is reported in the *Wharfe Valley Times*, December 1983.

A child's shoe was found concealed in the ceiling during alterations to a bookshop in Beech Hill, **Otley** in 1978.

At **Ovendon Wood**, Halifax, during work on the site of Samuel Webster and Wilson's brewery where a house known as Long Can is being restored, many items were found together. These include a top hat, boots, shoes and other items. They were all found beneath an old fireplace. This find is reported in *The Yorkshire Post*, 3 September 1986.

A witch-pot was found at **Overgate Croft**, described as reddish brown, bulbous pot, narrow necked, glazed inside, half glazed around neck. This was found buried upside down in a house doorway. It contained bits of hair and rusty nails and is still at its original home – aged possibly seventeenth century.

In a seventeenth-century house in **Oxenhope** near Keighly, a group of finds was discovered while a chimney was being moved. The work revealed a blocked-up spice cupboard with a carved oak door which contained many 'worn out bits' including buttons, knitting needles, bobbins, knives, spoons, shoes, pattens and clog leather. It is thought these items were reburied. In addition, it is reported that two scarfed pine beams of the housebody have revealed traces of circles with central holes and scratched A's, V's and W's. From Armstrong 1998.

A dried cat is said to exist in a cottage in **Rastrick**. The correspondent reported in February 2004 as follows: 'I live in Dewsbury, West Yorkshire, I am a carpet cleaner. Today 24th Feb 2004 I cleaned some property in Rastrick, West Yorkshire, I saw on the wall a plaque telling the story about dried cats. When I had finished the job I rang my client telling that I had finished and also mentioned the plaque about the dried cat, he asked if I had removed the plaque from the wall, I answered no, why? He told me to do so and I would see the so said Dried Cat. I then left and travelled home approx' 100 yards from home my vehicle skidded on ice on the road and I collided with a very well built stone wall!!!!! Have you heard of any other such happening after someone has seen a DRIED CAT???'

At a property in **Shepley** near Huddersfield, three objects were found together behind a beam over the window in a first floor bedroom. These comprised a child's shoe (thought to date from the late nineteenth century), very worn and patched, a wooden 'pot' from the game of Knur and Spel, and a wooden Yarn cop. The shoe had a letter or note inside it which disintegrated when touched. The house appears to date from 1810–1820 but has many additions and alterations.

At Shibden Hall, **Shibden**, a shoe was discovered which is thought to have belonged to a member of the Waterhouse family who lived there between 1522 and 1612.

At Crow Trees, **Silsden**, the ends of the scarfed beams are inscribed with hex circle ritual marks, V shaped scratches and later date initials and grafitti. From Armstrong 1998.

Shoes were found when a fireplace was altered at a farm on **Silsden Moor**.

A single child's shoe dating to 1723 was discovered built into the wall of an extension just beneath a window at a property in Lingards, **Slaithwaite**. It was found with a cow horn.

At a cottage in Netherend Road, Hilltop, **Slaithwaite**, a written charm was discovered behind a door panel – this was reported in the *Colne Valley Chronicle* of 20 January 1984 as 'Spirits Mystery in Door Charm'. An extract from the paper and copies of the charm are on file.

At Peel House, **Warley**, near Halifax, a concealed shoe was discovered – this was reported in a local paper.

Wiltshire

Daisy wheels are reported on the inner doorpost at **Borbach Chantry**, West Dean, Salisbury. Reported by Rebecca Ireland from the Churches Conservation Trust in June 2012.

Two VV's have been found on the brickwork of a house in **Bratton**, Wiltshire, from around 1650. Reported in August 2008.

A small bottle said to have contained human blood was found within the wall of **Brinkworth**'s Primitive Methodist Chapel. This was reported in two 1925 editions of the *North Wilts Herald*, 24 April and 1 May, under the title 'A Unique Relic of Ancient Superstition', quoted in *Wilshire Archaeological Magazine* 43 (1925–1927), p. 381.

In a garden at **Broughton Gifford**, an irregularly shaped piece of stone with a roughly pecked human face (possibly recent or Romano-Celtic) was found on the rockery. It is thought that it may have been deliberately placed there to frighten away evil spirits.

At a cottage in **Chilmark**, there are many marks on the stone some of which are Marian marks. Reported in September 2009.

At the Corn Exchange building in **Devizes**, a brass model of ears of wheat with leaves at the base and a screw thread (pole head?) was found buried in the foundations, thought to date from the late eighteenth or early nineteenth century.

At Porch House, Potterne, **Devizes** (built 1470), a dried chicken was found in the great chimney in 1874. From Pennick 1995. This find is also mentioned in Merrifield 1969.

It is reported that a dried cat was discovered within the walls of St Mary's Church, **Devizes**. From Girvan 1997: 26.

The skull of a deer is reported to have been found in the wall of a house in Long Street, **Devizes**. From Girvan 1997: 26.

An old shoe was found having been deliberately built into a wall at 52 Long Street, **Devizes**. From Girvan 1997: 26.

A report by F.K. Annable in *Folklore* 66 (1955), p. 304 describes a find of 'Four shoes, one of late seventeenth-century date, the other three, of which one had belonged to a child in arms being early nineteenth century. There were also fragments of two pottery bowls, and a third, though also broken was complete, the three dating respectively to late seventeenth, late eighteenth, and mid nineteenth centuries. Finally to complete the deposit were fragments of an eighteenth-century clay pipe, a wine glass stem, late eighteenth-century, a small iron file, broken at the tip, and the remains of what looks like a hat box along with a small length of corduroy cloth. This group was discovered in an old cottage which once formed part of a very interesting house (timber framed), dating back to the fifteenth century, and now known as No 8 Monday Market Street [**Devizes**]. It was found by the present owner sealed up between the roof and upper ceiling, during recent renovations in the upper part of the cottage'.

In June 2007 the following report arrived: 'I have just had the front of my house painted during which it was necessary to cut back a clematis covering the front porch. This revealed the bottom end of a glass bottle immediately beneath the ridge tile at the apex of the gable. The house is only 27 years old, yet I wonder whether this is a modern example of a "Witch Bottle" or simply a Wiltshire/rural building tradition'. The property was in **Edington**, near Westbury.

At **Lacock Abbey**, it is reported that daisy wheel ritual marks occur in the infirmary passage (mid-thirteenth century) which are incomplete. From *Mosaic* 1994.

In **Market Lavington**, a dried cat and rat were discovered in the roof of a workshop which was formerly a malt house.

In **Market Lavinton**, two pairs of sack bottles were found in two different houses. In one house they were found either side of the fireplace and in another house they were found built into the wall.

In **Market Lavington**, four worn out children's boots have been found in roofs in the village.

One of the oldest cottages in Northbrook, **Market Lavington**, has many protection marks, reported in December 2012.

A child's leather shoe was found beneath the floorboards of an old cottage in **Marlborough**, thought to date from the eighteenth century.

A carved chalk head 12cm high was discovered in a garden in **Melksham**, thought to date from the seventeenth or eighteenth century.

A rat skull with a snake's body, originally said to have been joined, were found in a wall cavity of a barn built in 1720 near **Melksham**.

A silver coloured metal disc engraved with a number square and with non-standard English words, perhaps incorporating names of demons, angels or elementals, was found in a leather bag in a cottage in **Oaksey**. It is thought that it may have been used by a witch.

Devizes Museum has an odd pair of a man's and lady's single shoes which were found in a hour in **Potterne**. Reported in Girvan 1997: 26.

It is reported that a concealed shoe exists at the Haunch of Venison public house in **Salisbury**. It is also reported that a severed hand and playing card were discovered inside an old baking oven revealed during rebuilding work. Some speculate that this may be linked with the ghostly footsteps of someone staggering around. This is cited in Playfair 1985: 226.

Two well preserved shoes from the early modern period were discovered in the attic of the Bishops Palace in **Salisbury**. The shoes do not match and one may be up to a century older than the other. They were found with a number of oyster shells.

Reported by Katy Jordan, folklorist, concerning **Salisbury Cathedral**: 'A charming explanation of the preservation of the spire was afforded in 1762, by the discovery, during some repairs at the top, of a leaden box containing a bit of woven stuff. This is supposed to be a fragment of the Virgin's robe, and by its miraculous virtue to have kept this beautiful fabric, erected to her name, safe from all perils. It was put back in the place it was found in'. Extract from Noyes 1913: 84.

In St Thomas' Church, **Salisbury**, a dried cat and rat were found – these have not been dated.

A dried cat and rat were found in an unspecified building in **Salisbury**. This find is also reported in Howard 1951.

At **Seend,** a clear glass phial was discovered which originally had a bone in it. It was thought to be possibly a witch-bottle dating to the eighteenth century.

Alyson Gilbert-Smith reported that a daisy wheel was found on a bressumer beam over the inglenook fireplace in a house in **Spirthill** near Calne. Reported by e-mail in January 2001.

In St Margaret's Church, **Stratton St Margaret**, there are some possible protection marks in the porch and on a Victorian window sill. Reported in March 2002.

From Dr Andrew Reynolds, Institute of Archaeology, University College London, comes this report of a Wiltshire horse skull: 'There is indeed the burial of a horse skull, pelvis and back legs in a small, well-cut rectangular pit from **Yatesbury**, Wiltshire. You are welcome to include this find in your research. The burial deposit is dated by sherds of unabraded pottery of the 17th century at present, although our pottery person will be checking this in the next month or so'.

Worcestershire

A lady's shoe was found concealed in the roof of a house in **Alvechurch**, thought to date to the 1790s.

In a cottage at **Bayton** near Kidderminster, a collection of items was discovered. The house dates to 1510 and is timber-framed. A shoe dating from the 1880s/1890s was discovered in a concealed cavity in the roof along with an old basket. Also found in the house was a wooden knitting needle, some old playing cards and a William III crown or half crown. The owner of the cottage has concealed many things of his own about the house 'for fun' and after discussion with me about contents is putting his own witch-bottle into an outbuilding.

A lady's shoe of the Tudor period was found in Tickenhill House, **Bewdley** in 1880. Reported in Fraser 1949: 23.

A door from a house near **Bewdley** has many circle marks on it. Reported in September 2017.

In **Bredon Church** porch, some carved shoe marks can be found on a stone bench on the east wall.

In **Broadwas-on-Teme**, there is a daisy wheel in a barn. The timber was re-used from the demolished solar east wing of a nearby farmhouse. Reported in September 2017.

At a barn next to **Broadway Tower**, a series of marks have been found near the entrance. 'There is an obvious, if faded daisy wheel, possibly some "Ms" maybe a cross and what looks to be a crop tally. Both myself and the owner would be happy to have your insight, they would also be happy to have them in your database. I have other photos in different lights if you would like them'. Reported in January 2017.

A concealed shoe was discovered in a cottage in **Clevelode** after it fell down and hit the correspondent on the head during restoration work.

A dried cat was discovered above the stable block between two lath and plaster panels in **Croome Court**. This was reported to me Dave Parker, a former builder. He said the cat was in a lathe and plaster partition wall above stables, three to four feet off the ground on top of a noggin (beam) in the partition. The cat was lying down (tabby or tortoiseshell originally) and was totally covered in fur. This area was the living accommodation for stable staff, built in the 1750s.

In Bullocks Café in the High Street, **Droitwich**, a doll was discovered in the rafters which workmen refused to touch. This was reported in the *Evening News* (1999).

At Puddleford Farm near **Eastham**, some Marian marks were found in the porch: M M R (Maria Maria Regina). There is an image of the rubbing on file. Reporting the find in September 2017, correspondent Adam Heath said many more marks could be found at the property.

A dried cat was discovered in a cottage in New Road, **Eckington**. The building is a sixteenth-century black and white cottage and the animal was discovered during re-thatching in early 2003.

The **Evesham Abbey** site comprises the tower, cloister arch, All Saints and St Lawrence's. St Lawrence's does not have any visible marks other than mason's marks. All Saints has a collection of large daisy wheels inside the porch and a possible mesh pattern. In a side chapel there is also a Marian mark and two large graffito heads. As a side-note there is also a horned Moses inside the church. The cloister arch has a deeply engraved W on it. The tower inside the passageway has a collection of W's and on the other side a large circle mark, which may be a consecration mark.

A concealed shoe was discovered at a farm in **Lower Broadheath**. The shoe was found when structural work revealed a large hidden inglenook fireplace completely intact with the ashes of the last fire in-situ. The shoe was discovered deep in the flue with the toe turned up 'as if to form some kind of container'. The shoe is believed to have been worn by a youth and is thought to date to between 1805 and 1820.

Chicken bones were discovered built into a cottage wall in **Lower Moor** – the house was not built earlier than the eighteenth century. Dave, the builder, said, 'Working in cottage in Lower Moor in early 80s. Brick cottage, around 150 years old. Stripped plaster off inglenook fireplace and discovered loose brick. They found chicken skull and leg bones (rib-cage missing)'. Dave also reported a bit of builder's folklore which is that 'if you take a roof off a house the spirits are let out. It gets rid of all the spirits'.

A modern example of a concealed pair of shoes from **Malvern** was reported to me in December 2000. The correspondent writes: 'Well, fraid I was too late as the wall is now completed so only managed a photo of the completed wall at the place in which the shoes are concealed. They were my dad's 1st pair of shoes that his mum had kept, so they would be about 65 years old. She gave them to him a few months ago and well he was doing some building and they are now in this Malvern garden wall'.

In **North Littleton,** two very old leather shoes were found in the roof of a sixteenth-century cottage. One shoe has something tucked inside it but it is difficult to access it as the leather has dried and is very hard.

At Newlands, **Pershore**, two phials containing husks of wheat and a brown residue, three children's shoes and several toys were discovered behind a fireplace. They are thought to date from the mid-nineteenth century.

A dried cat was reported to have been found in 1958 above a grocer's shop which comprised 7 and 8 High Street, **Stourport**. The cat was found above the ceiling on the ground floor of this eighteenth-century shop. This was reported to me in January 2002. The shop was the correspondent's grandfather's and then his father's, called A J Lewis & Son.

A builder reported a strange chicken bone charm with pieces of leather attached to it which was discovered in a wall in **Tenbury Wells**.

A pair of clogs were found behind a false wall during building restoration in the 1960s at a seventeenth-century farmhouse in **Wick**. On display at Pershore Heritage Centre.

In the Crown Hotel in **Worcester** (now Crown Passage and pub), a well-made baby's shoe was discovered on the first floor under the floorboards near the fireplace. A dried rat was also found in the building which is thought to date to the eighteenth century.

A bellarmine bottle was discovered during excavations at Sidbury in **Worcester**. Subsequent enquiries have shown that it was found in a pit adjacent to horse remains at the rear of a house. From Morris 1980.

In Alfred Taylor House, 43–49 St Johns, **Worcester**, dating from 1500, some interesting objects were discovered. An extract from 'The Medieval Hall House That Defies Destruction' by Gladys Keithley has been published as a photocopy and states; 'But behind the early twentieth century fireplace, among the brick rubble in the damaged ancient stone fireplace was found an old wooden doll. This is probably early twentieth century. It may be a witch-doll. Its face, square, like the old wood Betsy dolls of Victoriana, is masked in plaster. Its foot is peg-like and etched with a pattern of claws. Its black chest is faintly marked with a drawing of a goat's head. On the back is a light patch where paper has covered it. On this patch, is faded ink where the words "help me to –" but these words have faced from exposure'. The current whereabouts of the doll are unknown.

A dried cat and kittens were discovered at the Reindeer Inn, **Worcester**. The animals were believed to have been placed there, or at least ended up there, in 1740. From Pennick 1995.

Wales

Listed by alphabetical order of place name

At St Baruch's Well, **Barry Island**, a bottle of nineteenth-century date was found. From Merrifield 1955.

Linda Hall reports that at 'Penpont, near **Brecon** – amazing huge staircase in the centre of a much later house. Daisy wheel on bottom newel post, partly under the moulded cap so clearly made at the time of construction and not added later'. Reported in August 2013.

A reference to a charm from **Carno** in Powys was received in May 2012. He said: 'Please find enclosed the charm letter. This was written for my great grandfather, John Thomas who lived on a farm called Craigfryn in Carno Montgomeryshire. He had lost all his horses and believed he had been "witched". It was found in a sealed bottle in their attic a good few years ago'.

At **Cascob Church**, Radnorshire, a seventeenth-century abracadabra charm was discovered.

A charm was discovered at Ty Gwyn, Fron-isaf, **Chirk**, Denbighshire. The charm was discovered folded into a long spill and then folded again into a pentagon and pushed into a wide crack in the main beam in the kitchen living room. It is thought to date from the nineteenth century and a full transcription can be found in Owen 1960.

At a chapel in **Cilfynnydd** in South Wales, the following account was received in September 2009: 'My most significant lost find of those days was in a chapel in Cilfynnydd in South Wales. It was built into the hill side and so the basement room was shallower than the rest. At the back was an alcove bookcase. 12 ft high by about 8 ft wide and 18 inches deep and full of dry rot. When it was pulled apart it revealed a bricked up archway about 4ft high and in front of it in a depression in the brickwork directly behind the bookcase was a witches bottle (blue glass, corked with some things bobbing in fluid inside), 2 rodent skulls and some bent floor board clouts. Attached to the back of the dresser were two pieces of paper about A4 in size with very rough hand writing, not any language I knew but a similar circle design to the one Des used. The foreman threw the bottle and papers straight into a barrel fire going outside, stamped on the skulls crushing them to dust, cursed such "bullshit" and ordered us to get on. We shuttered the wall, as planned before the find, and filled it with concrete to shore up the upper levels'.

At **Cilgerran**, near Cardigan, a dried bat, a shoe, several small bottles and a small animal skull have been found. The dried bat was found beneath a window lintel in the main house and the bottles and skull found in outbuildings. Reported in May 2002.

Two horse skulls were found placed beneath the floorboards in the corner of a room in a seventeenth-century house in **Clwyd**. From Merrifield 1987: 124.

A concealed shoe and witch-bottle were discovered in a house at the foot of the Preseli Hills near **Crosswell**. This was reported in January 2008 as follows: 'Thought you might like to see the attached pictures of a shoe found during the course of taking down an unstable wall at our farmhouse in North Pembrokeshire. It was found with or near (impossible to be precise as the wall came down with the aid of a JCB ...) a stoppered glass bottle two thirds filled with a pale yellowish liquid which we did not open, and a large horseshoe. The house has a granary/

cart-shed built in line with the north gable end. The wall we took down was the rear wall of a lean to constructed against the granary/cart-shed, probably used for dairying. The "back" door (although it's actually at the side) is accessed via this lean to'.

The most amazing daisy wheel covered ceiling was discovered in **Conwy**. Reported in November 2015.

At **Cowbridge**, south Wales, a jawbone, possible belonging to a horse, has been found in the wall of a cottage. This was reported in February 2010 as follows: 'My fiancé and I are currently renovating a flat we have bought in a converted Manor near Cowbridge, South Wales. Although most of the house is mostly Victorian, the core is Tudor, or possibly Medieval, this is where we are. We have uncovered an extremely old doorway with sections of rubblestone walls extending out from it. Whilst removing the old lime plaster so as to expose the stone, we found one of the stones to be loose so pulled it out exposing a void behind it, naturally we just had to look. Inside was a large piece of animal lower jawbone totally clean of mortar, so it wasn't accidentally mixed in, it has to have been intentionally placed there. We have not had it positively identified yet, but it's too big for dog, and probably too big for sheep, I can only assume it's horse or at least pony. I'd never heard of this before, thanks for putting this page on the web, otherwise I'd still be wondering about it'.

A concealed shoe from **Dolwyddelan** was found in the remains of a sixteenth-century chimney. Reported in March 2007.

At a house in the **Elan Valley**, a rare clog was discovered dating to 1820–1840s (thanks to June Swann for this). The owner mentioned that other objects were found with the clog but she cannot remember what they were.

At a house near **Ffestiniog**, there are reputed to be protection marks. Reported in May 2009.

A charm was discovered at Nantyr, **Glyn Ceiriog**. This was mentioned in Owen 1960.

Linda Hall reports burn marks and incised lines from Howell's House, **Grosmont**.

At Lygan-y-Wern, **Halkyn**, two horse skulls (one bleached) were discovered beneath floorboards during restoration work. Reported in Gwyndaf and Gruffydd 1985. These skulls were found in 1965, accession number 65/525/2.

At **Llancaiach Fawr Manor** in the Rhymney Valley (South Wales), a dried cat, several shoes, animal material and many burn marks have been found (see the case studies in Part II).

It is reported that horse skulls were discovered embedded in the choir stalls of **Llandaff Cathedral**. From Pennick 1986.

At a cottage in Gasworks Lane, **Llandovery**, Carmarthenshire, three bone-handled penknives have been found wrapped in cloth in two findspots, both in bedroom chimneys. Reported in May 2002.

At Pen-y-garnedd, near **Llanfyllin**, Montgomeryshire, a written charm came to light. Full transcription and notes are provided in Owen 1959: 253–54.

At a house in Bethesda Bach, **Llanwnda**, Caernarfon, an old shoe was discovered inside an oven. The correspondent described the find in May 2002 as follows: 'I have a lovely old seventeenth century or older, farm cottage, on excavating a spiral staircase we stumbled upon a sealed oven, brick lined the slipper was inside. Probably older than the oven which when built meant the spiral staircase could not be used, and a wooden one had been built. We also have the tombstone of a Solomon Parry, which was found under the kitchen floor, and I know he lived in the house in the seventeenth century, so if we excavate the kitchen floor it could be interesting!!I hope this is of interest'.

At a 1780 house in **Llanrwst** in the Conwy Valley, a shoe last was discovered in the roof along with several bottles. The correspondent said: 'Last found under roofing over chimney. Bottles all 19th Century except one, the interesting one. Again, found lying under the roofing over the chimney. The interesting thing about it is its date – 1950's medicine bottle'.

At **Lledrod**, Dyfed, three horse skulls were discovered. Reported in Gwyndaf and Gruffydd 1985.

A report was received in September 2006 about the discovery of some bones: 'We have recently converted an old stables building and found a collection of bones under one corner of the outside walls – including jaw bones of various sizes. I had heard locally that it was traditional to bury bones under the corners of barns while building'. The property is near **Machynlleth**.

Jeremy Harte informed me of the following in August 2002: 'I note that in the *Countryman* 64 (1965) p208, E. Emrys Jones writes "When an old cottage was demolished in **Merioneth**, various charms, including scraps of food, bones, hair and the remains of some plants, were found on top of the wall under the roof"'.

At a cottage called Gelli Iago, **Nant Gwynant**, in Snowdonia, over 100 concealed shoes were found. This property belongs to the National Trust. The story was reported on the BBC News website on 24 September 2010; the shoes were hidden 'under a fireplace' apparently and are Victorian, though the cottage dates from the seventeenth century.

A child's boot was discovered beneath floorboards in a cottage in **Narberth**, reported in August 2011: 'I am attaching a photo of a child's boot that was found by a builder friend of mine under the floorboards of a house in Narberth, Pembrokeshire. I am an artist and he has lent it to me to use to make a cast for some glass work I am researching, and I am interested to find out more about it. The boot is about 15cms long and is obviously a child's boot, as you can see, it is well worn'.

At **Newchurch** in Powys, beneath the floorboards of a nineteenth-century nonconformist chapel a large bone from a cow or bullock was found.

Newport Museum has a dried cat in its collection.

A dried cat was found wrapped in a shroud of reeds under the floor of **Newton House** in Carmarthenshire. From Brooks 2000.

At Penrhos Bradwen Farm, **Penrhos**, Holyhead, a Buckley pot was discovered which contained the bones of a frog, together with its dried skin which was pierced by about forty pins. The pot was covered by a crude slate on which was scratched 'Nanny Roberts'. This is described by the authors of the article reporting it as a practice of bewitchment. The pot was found in an old earthen bank on the farm. From Gruffydd 1981.

In the 1970s a pile of old boots and shoes were found beneath stairs at a seventeenth-century farmhouse on the **Rhiwlas** estate about a mile north-east of Bala in the old county of Mereioneth. The staircase was not original and is thought to be within 200 years old of the time of writing. Reported in October 2001. June Swann dated the boots to the 1860s/1870s.

An account was received of some apparently very recent 'witch-bottles' that have been tied to trees near a property in the **Rhondda**. The correspondent sent me one of the bottles which I still have – it appears to have grey mud or silt inside.

A possible witch-bottle was discovered inside an exterior wall at St Mary's Parish Church, **Risca**, Newport, Gwent. This small bottle appeared to have mud inside it. It was sent to Dr Alan Massey for analysis.

At a house in **Ruthin**, the following interesting objects, found during renovation work, were reported in October 2002: 'I was working as site foreman on the renovation of a sixteenth century timber framed building. The house is located on the outskirts of Ruthin in north Wales... Having located the original positions of the front and back doors, we began turning back into doorways, the stone flags which were outside the doors were lifted and revealed two very small riding spurs. They were made of brass and they were that small I doubt if they would have fitted a child of more than two years old. One had been placed outside the back door, and one at the front, but also at the front to the right-hand side, I found a brass disc about the size of an old shilling, it was plain with nothing on it. I wondered at the time if the original owner had placed a gold coin in the mortice where it was found, but had been stolen and replaced with the brass by, one of the Joiners working on the building at the time. I think that I've heard somewhere, that a coin hidden by the entrance to a house brings the owner good luck and fortune, I may be wrong'.

At a farm called Pentrynant near **Sarn** in Montgomeryshire, a nineteenth-century written charm was discovered in a stoneware bottle. A full analysis can be found in Merrifield 1955.

At a cottage in **St David's**, Pembrokeshire, which is currently a B&B, a horse skull is on display in a case which was allegedly discovered in foundations during renovations. Reported in February 2017.

At **Tretower Court**, near Brecon, the wall at the high end has circular protective marks on it. From Easton 1999.

A cat was found during the demolition of the wall of a seventeenth-century inn at **Usk**, Monmouthshire. The cat was found lying on its side in a natural position. This find is reported in Howard 1951.

A written charm in a bottle was discovered at a farm known as Trefnant Hall near **Welshpool**. The correspondent reported this to me in June 2011 as follows: 'CHARM in BOTTLE: I remember as a child in Welshpool, Montgomeryshire, visiting a farm in the hills and being told by the farmer (who produced the bottle) that there was a charm in the bottle to keep Satan away, and that the demon who had been troubling the farm was now under a stone in the farmyard. I dimly remember a tall stone there, but last year or so ago I went up to the farm house to see if the stone was still there and drove round the farmhouse, but there was nothing resembling the stone there. If it had been a small standing stone it has gone. He let me hold the bottle. His name was Mr Humphreys, and the name of the farm was Trefnant (Trefnant Hall) – which is one of the estate farms belonging now (and very likely then) to the Powis Castle estate, now owned by the National Trust. This would have been in the 1950s'.

At Allt y Rhiw, **Wern Ddu**, near Oswestry, a Buckley pot was discovered at the base of an ancient yew tree. The pot was discovered a quarter full of lead and had clearly been buried for a reason. The owners of the house believed that the pot had been placed there to ward off evil. Reported in Gwyndaf and Gruffydd 1985.

In June 2017 a correspondent reported that she purchased a box from a junk shop in Rossett near **Wrexham** which has a daisy wheel on it and saltire cross patterns all around it.

Scotland

Listed by alphabetical order of place name

An apparent witch-bottle or jar was discovered at **Abbottsford**, described as a small jar containing a lump of dried clay, held together by what seemed to be human hair. Walter Scott described it thus: 'In a remote part of the Highlands, an ignorant and malignant woman seems really to have meditated the destruction of her neighbour's property, by placing in a cowhouse, or byre, as we call it, a pot of baked clay, containing locks of hair, parings of nails, and other trumpery. This precious spell was discovered, the design conjectured, and the witch would have been torn to pieces, had not a high-spirited and excellent lady in the neighbourhood gathered some of her people, (thought these were not very fond of the service,) and by main force taken the unfortunate creature out of the hands of the populace. The formidable spell is now in my possession'. A later quote describes how the farmer felt that this spell was responsible for the deaths of some of his animals. From Parsons 1964.

In 2002 the *Aberdeen Independent* reported the following find of concealed pottery from Kings College Chapel, **Aberdeen**: 'Masons at Kings College Chapel have discovered pots dating back to between the 14th and 16th centuries, writes Jonathan Hansmann. Four broken pottery jugs were found carefully placed behind the stones while the west wall of the Chapel was being re-pointed. The pots had been set on their sides, their rims and handles removed, with the bases pointing in towards the interior of the wall. They had clearly been hidden deliberately, as elsewhere in the building gaps in the joints had been filled with chips of slates. Archaeologists and historians are puzzled as to why the jugs were there. They are also wondering if similar examples have been found elsewhere, as pots in walls are unusual but not unknown. Dr Jane Geddes, senior lecturer in art history at Aberdeen University said: "Our pots are not sealed and were found halfway up the wall in the King's College Chapel. It may be significant that they are at the same level as the three heraldic plaques. We are interested in finding out what the jars were used for – could it be that the jars were used as handy paint pots for painting the heraldry? Although there were no traces of paint found on the pots"'.

Some apparent ritual marks and other deposits, including a rag doll and scrumpled up pages from an eighteenth-century bible, have been found at a property on Shore Street, **Anstruther**, Fife. This was reported in November 2002 as follows: 'Essentially, there is a monogram and some carvings on an oak beam located above a fireplace in the house and a load of "spiritual deposits" have been found concealed throughout the house, bricked up in the walls. These "deposits" contain a range of deposited household items. An old, hand-made rag doll has also been found concealed in the building along with various scrumpled up pages from an 18th century bible.

Consequently, I just wondered whether this monogram on the Anstruther house's fireplace lintel could be a Virgin Mary apotropaic mark that might stand for AMB K ... maybe Ave Marie Beate (Hail Blessed Mary)'.

A Scotsman reported the following concerning **Ballater**, Royal Deeside, to Ian Evans by e-mail who then reported it to me in September 2005: 'Having come from Scotland, my parents house in the north eastern highlands was built in 1873. The grounds of the house were surrounded by rowan (or rodden) trees as well as each corner of the main walls. This was to ward off witches and bad omen. We opened the floorboards of the study many years ago and found a pair of black gloves, a shoe and a top hat. They were placed on top off each other. We were told that this was to illustrate that the house was a place of celebration and good fortune. The pantry, which is situated below the staircase, also had a scattering of children's toys. Your idea of innocence is correct.

My Mother's great uncle who lived in Darwin, placed willow branches underneath his floorboards whilst building it. This is another wood that was used to protect your soul from witches. Witches, were hung from rowan or willow trees'. He continued: 'My Parents house is in Ballater, Royal Deeside, Scotland – about 70km east of Aberdeen in the north-east of the country. I have no idea where the house is situated in Darwin. I forgot to mention that items were placed in hidden places of the house every time a new house owner moved in, not just when the house was built. I have spoken to my mother and she has said that she placed a flute and childrens toys from her childhood beneath the floorboards when we moved into the house in 1979'.

At **Culross Palace**, Fife, 'There are marks over a fireplace in Culross Palace, Fife. This is an NTS property. There are circles, concentric circles and daisy wheels'. Reported in October 2005.

A heart stuck with pins was discovered in the floor rubbish of a house in **Dalkeith**. A woman aged over eighty 'recollected, in her youth, a bad disease having got amongst the cattle in that quarter, and particularly among those kept in the house in question; and that she knew that it was then the practice, when such calamities befell their cattle, for the country people to take the heart of a calf, as a representative for the heart of the witch by whose malice their cattle were visited, and to place it on a spit before the fire, sticking in a pin at every turn, until it was completely roasted, by which the witch was subjected to a simultaneous operation of proportional severity in her own bosom... The heart thus prepared was secretly deposited near the cattle; and no doubt the one in question had been of that description'. From Parsons 1964.

Staff at Wolverhampton Art Gallery and Museum reported that dried cats can be seen at **Comlongon Castle** near Dumfries.

Phil Rogers reported the following finds from a flat at 11 Windsor Street in **Dundee**: 'I lived for 5 years in an attic flat in Dundee. Having access to the roof space (which was small, due to it having a flat roof) I was surprised to find a length of red wool knotted around an iron nail. There is a Scots saying "Red thread, Lammer bead, all put witches to their speed", or something like that – and this could be part of the significance of the item. The building was built in the 1850's and I felt that the item had been there for as long as the building'.

It is reported that horse skulls were discovered concealed in the pulpit of **Edinburgh** meeting house. From Pennick 1986.

An American correspondent related the following tale to me in September 2000: 'I was born and raised in the Southern Appalachians in the state of Virginia. The area was predominantly settled by English, Scottish, Irish and Welsh immigrants. They brought many of their folk beliefs along with them. As a result there are a lot of folk beliefs and types of folk magic present in that area which are variants of old European practices. I grew up hearing scads of stories about ghost hounds, hauntings, animals with angel vision etc.

Anyway, with regards to horse heads … I was on holiday in Scotland about a year and a half ago. While in **Edinburgh** I learned about some historical tours of older parts of the city and decided to look into it. At that time considerable archaeological work was being done within the old North Bridge (perhaps the South section as well.) The bridge was hollow and vaulted and in centuries past a bustling business had developed within. Actually, there were quite a few business – everything from prostitution to cobbling in fact. The tour guide informed us that one of the more interesting finds had been a horse skull. At that time they were not certain if it had been from a draft animal in the bridge or from a tannery (which would have used the brains I expect). Another possibility that was being explored was whether or not it had occult or magical connections'.

A human arm bone has been found in the roof of St Giles Church in **Edinburgh**. The local newspaper speculated at great length as to whether this could be the arm of the patron saint and if so why was it not inside a reliquary. Local pathologists said it was definitely a very old bone but could not say much beyond that. Reported in November 2002.

At **Kilbirnie**, a report of a Marian carved stone was received as follows: 'When exploring Kilbirnie Palace I noticed this odd insertion of two sections of red sandstone Gothic lettering. The first word reads "Maria" and the second has yet to be deciphered. Several associates have suggested that it may be an apotropaic device due to its position in the chimney flue. It would have been hidden by the fireplace canopy or hood so that disapproving eyes would not see it in the John Knox era. The red sandstone contrasts with the white stonework of the keep. It has been proposed that the lettering could have come from Kilwinning Abbey following its destruction by the Earl of Glencairn and others'. Reported in March 2016.

Concealed shoes were found in **Lochgoilhead** in Argyll and Bute. This was reported in December 2012 as follows: 'I'm a joiner and doing a farmhouse renovation in the Lochgoilhead area of Scotland in Argyll and Bute. I have recently found shoes under the floorboards of the attic space of the house. They are a mix of child's shoes with laces and green/ gold eyelets. Men's shoes with iron nails on the sole. Also found were baby shoes and clogs. It probably amounts to 12 pairs all in. I found them all in the one area, under the floor boards in the attic, underneath the parti wall between the farmhouse and the barn which backs onto it. The barn dates to at least 1840 with the farm house having been built onto the side at a later date, although still Victorian. I came across your page whilst trying to find out why they were there. Thought you would like to know about the find as you say it goes largely unreported'.

A polished stone axe (thunderstone) was appropriated for use as a charm in a building at **Onich**, Argyllshire in 1750. From Penney 1976.

A concealed shoe and some bottles have been reported from **Orkney**: 'Today a small outhouse attached to an old hen house was being rebuilt and an old shoe was found in the foundations, together with a lot of small bottles. The builder said it looked as if they all been deliberately put into a hole. The outhouse might have been a privy but more likely a store for animal feed. The walls up here in Orkney are of rubble construction and very thick indeed. The main cottage was built in 1896 and the outbuildings, many of which are dated, are mostly 10–15 years later'. Reported in October 2007.

An unusual piece of wood shaped liked a webbed foot was found behind the lathe and plaster of an eighteenth-century attic room in **Orkney**. It is crudely carved, around 13 inches in length and has four pointed toes at the wider end and then tapers down towards the other end.

In the valley of Tingwall, near **Scalloway**, Shetland, a polished stone axe was formerly kept as a 'thunderbolt'. From Penney 1976.

USA

Listed in alphabetical order of state

Medicine bottles found above thresholds in **Arkansas** were reported in May 2002: 'My great-niece was observing as a carpenter dismantled the home of her husband's childhood. It was a two-story house built some- time around the turn of the century (1890s to early 1900s) in what was then "Indian Territory" in Northwest Arkansas (USA) near Oklahoma

Indian Territory. As the gentleman began the dismantling, it was noted that OVER EVERY DOOR was a "medicine bottle". These bottles were all of the type which was used to contain medicine in the early days of "drug stores". One even still had congealed medication in it and "directions" on the bottle which were readable. Our question ... what could have been the significance of all those bottles and their placement over EVERY DOOR. I have a very vivid imagination and I personally believe they could have had something to do with protection for the house and its occupants, or just "good medicine" for the home. Other suggestions have been a builder who indulged in drinking "spirits" while on the job and that was his disposal method. I do not believe this. I was reared in that area of the United States, and I know that most of the distillers used either canning jars or stoneware jugs for their product'.

A dried cat was found in Bakersfield, **California**, reported in December 2006. Someone attempted to sell me the cat. He said: 'my uncle bought a house in Bakersfield, California and while he was replacing the floor he found it. It seemed as though it was trapped, so we were fortunate enough to have found it'.

A report of a dried cat from **California** was received in May 2002: 'While helping a friend in Berkeley, California, recently in jacking up the foundation of his 90-year old house, we came across a dried cat which had been placed in a small hollow inside the foundation. We assumed that it had crept into the hollow and had died there, but what made me wonder about it was that the cat looked as though it had been *propped* there, in a standing position against the back of the niche, and even with a front paw stretched out as if to scratch someone, and with the teeth bared. I wondered about whether rigor mortis could actually do that. We weren't sure what to do with it, but my friend said he would probably put it back into the foundation after the repairs were done. "After all – maybe he's been protecting the house all these years", my friend mused. I do know that my friend's house was constructed around 1910 by immigrant Finnish farmers. I don't know anything about what superstitions that may have arrived here with the Finnish builders, but I thought that you might like to hear of this'.

In Connecticut, a shoe and phials were found, as reported in March 2004: 'I found your website (very informative) and wondered if you would interpret the attached photos of what I believe to be a "concealed shoe". The shoe was discovered by previous owners of the house ... but little information as to the purpose or nature of the shoe was passed on to us when we bought the house fourteen years ago. The shoe is lodged between the boarding of a wall cupboard and the center chimney stack. Only the toe area of the shoe is visible. In the attached photo you are looking between two boards where a casement moulding for the door to the cupboard had been removed at one time. You are looking toward the stone chimney stack. It is likely that the shoe was discovered by the previous owner at the time that an electrical outlet was wired (box visible in photo). The house is a New England (CT River Valley) embankment center chimney colonial – circa 1720. In reading your website and some others regarding concealed items, some other possible notable caches have been found be me over the past 14 years. There are corn cobs in the boxed overhangs of the cantilevered girts at the roofline (mostly in the north-east corner of the house), also I have found a few (what I thought were medicinal) early phials in the same boxed overhangs on the south side of the house (center over the entrance door). In an early interior room on the first level I removed an early makeshift ceiling and wall and found numerous bones; what looked like animal bones of some sort. I kept these bones and can photograph them. Also behind the wall I found a broken bottle (I believe I may have kept this as well). An odd thought I had at the time was that these items had to have been encased at the time of the construction of the room as the ceiling boards and wall boards were attached to structural members. I never thought although of these items as concealed with intention for a specific purpose of any kind'.

A concealed shoe and small phial were found in **Connecticut**, as reported in January 2001: 'I live in a house built in Suffield, Connecticut in the 1790s or so and recently we found a small shoe (that of a baby or small child) and a glass vial concealed in the wall of our salt box home. We put them back in the wall'.

Concealed shoes were recovered from a fireplace in **Connecticut**, reported in September 2000: 'I write this from Ridgefield, CT, USA. In 1962 we bought the old house here in Ridgefield from which I am emailing you. At some point during the restoration – rather early on as I remember it – and admittedly my memory is somewhat sketchy after all these years – one and I think I remember, two shoes were found in the chimney, perhaps in the ashpit, or perhaps within the construction of the chimney. I vividly remember one shoe, which was actually a slipper, like a man's carpet slipper, except that it was obviously a cut-down boot, much mended. The other shoe was less memorable and of course very "wizened" by age'.

A report of horse skulls found under floors in **Illinois** was received in December 2000: 'Cahokia Courthouse State Historic Site. In one of our houses we have discovered four horse skulls concealed under the floors and one was found in a cavity next to the fireplace. The house with the four skulls was built from 1807–1810, it is known as the Jarrot Mansion, and is located in Cahokia, Illinois. The French settle in the Cahokia area in 1699 and the community is named after the Cahokia Native Americans. Nichols Jarrot, the man which had the mansion built, came from France and settled in the Cahokia area. He was a Judge, fur trader, and land speculator. He was very wealthy. The Jarrot Mansion's architecture is known as "Federalist" style. Nichols Jarrot was living in a vertical log house known as post-on-sill, but then he had this "Federalist" style building built because he liked this type of architecture, which he first saw in Baltimore, Maryland. The point I would like to make is that this is a wealthy French American having English Americans build this "Federalist" structure'.

This report was received in February 2003: 'At a property in Nobleboro, **Maine** a total of three shoes were revealed, and one piece of fabric. Two shoes and the fabric were found in the vicinity of the South-west corner of a ground floor wall. The house was built around 1800 and I would guess the shoes are contemporaneous – what I would call a low Oxford, in rather small sizes (women's or older children, perhaps), very flat heel, pegged soles. The shoes were black when I found them, and appeared to have been always this color. The fabric was black hand-woven woolen, torn edges, roughly square in shape, measuring about 10' square. The fabric showed a felled seam. The third shoe was found in the vicinity of the center of the house. When the house was built, it had had a large center chimney, which would have had hearths in several rooms. The shoe was probably located under a hearth. When the house was renovated, probably around 1900, this center chimney was removed, and the shoe remained in some underlying rocks and rubble. This area was settled by Scots and English'.

In **Maryland**, horse skulls were found, as reported in April 2011: 'We found about 28 horse skulls in a 1770 three story house. They were placed in the floor joists between the 1st and 2nd floors. It was a very exciting find and I googled the find and found your information. We are taking that house down and building a new home. We plan to place a few of those skulls in our new home … carrying on the tradition and hopefully the protection! The 1770 house is located in the Kent County, Upper Eastern Shore of Maryland'.

Many marks have been found at a property in Burndean, Newton, **Massachusetts**. These include a large mesh mark in the attic. Reported in December 2014.

Concealed shoes were found in Fairbanks House in **Massachusetts**, as reported in October 2006: 'four concealed shoes that were found in the Fairbanks House (thought to be the oldest standing timber-framed building in the United States; first portion built circa 1641, later additions built circa 1780–1800). The shoes are currently identified as a pair of 18th-century men's shoes found in a ceiling, and two unmatched women's shoes dated to the late 18th or early 19th centuries, found next to the chimney. The shoes could well be associated with periods of remodeling, as the dates as far as we know them at the moment could easily coincide with the period(s) when the additions were built'.

A dried cat found in **Massachusetts** was reported in May 2002: 'I live in Shutesbury, Massachusetts, USA, in a house built in 1848. During renovations last year, the builders discovered a dried cat beneath the floorboards. I call it "Desi", the dessicated cat. I thought this was interesting, as I had seen mummified cats in the UK, both in the Shaftesbury museum described in the website and in another small museum (I think at Woodstock but I am not certain). Both displays stated that dried cats were placed in thatched roofs to repel vermin. Recently, I was discussing old houses with the owner of a house similar to mine (in the same town). He told me that he had done extensive work to his house some years before, and found a dried cat under the floorboards. It was all the more interesting in that his cat was in the same location as the one in my house'.

A report of shoes found in **Massachusetts** was received in February 2007: 'I have in my possession several pairs of antique shoes which were found concealed within the central chimney of a 1755 "hall and parlor" town-house in Northampton, Massachusetts'.

In Marshfield, **Massachusetts**, the discovery of protection marks and concealed knife was reported in August 2008: 'I am trying to figure out the history of my house. It is situated in Marshfield, Massachusetts in Plymouth county and listed as being built about 1830. Anyway, in my investigations I have discovered what looks like a "daisy mark" on the entry post to the right of the original front door. Also, in the attic I have found a small concealed knife hidden in a notched beam under the end window'.

Seven shoes were recovered from beneath floorboards in a property on 11th Avenue, Minneapolis, **Minnesota**, as well as bottles and a pattern that looks like a daisy wheel. Reported in July 2017.

A shoe find from Northfield, **Minnesota**, was reported in September 2006: 'The house that I live in dates from 1913, but I've just moved in this summer. We're in the midst of renovations, and yesterday, my husband found a woman's shoe covered by a newspaper (in Norwegian) dated April 22, 1915. I found this quite exciting, especially since the shoe is of a charming design and apparently my size. The shoe is a woman's leather shoe with 3 button closures, a nailed stacked heel, and a small leather bow toward the front of the shoe. The shoe was patched at least once, and a hole is worn through the bottom of the shoe under the ball of the foot. I took a few pictures with my digital camera before replacing the shoe in its original location (near the NW corner of the house). If you have any interest, I'd be happy to send you a couple photos of the shoe'.

A child's concealed shoe and an inkwell were discovered in 2004 in Argyll, **Missouri**. 'My husband and I were remodeling a room in our home in 2004 when we found a child's shoe and an ink well. They were found in what was originally an exterior wall. I don't know the exact date the home was built, but it would have been sometime between 1914 and 1922'.

A cache of objects found in **Nevada** was reported in May 2002: 'I am finishing up my dissertation on an archaeological site in Virginia City, Nevada and have realized I likely have a ritual deposit. I would like any insight you have into the collection and would be happy to share all information about the find. First a little site background … the home was a small cottage sized dwelling approximately 10 feet by 10 feet. It was located in a fairly dense neighborhood next to Chinatown and the entertainment/red light district … basically, an international working class community. Most of the immigrants were either from England, Ireland, and Germany. The home was likely built in the 1860s. It was a rental home that was rented by a dressmaker in 1873 and the British immigrant family in 1875. In October 1875 the home burned … as did most of Virginia City. During our excavation we encountered a nice dark lens of ash as well as fragments from floorboards representing 1875. As we dug through the floor and into the builders trench we came upon a cache of complete items. It was against a trench in the northern portion of the home. There was a man's 10 1/2' leather, pull on work boot; a suede leather hat; a wine bottle partially inverted; an iron padlock with a brass heart shaped escutcheon; and a piece of thin leather (possibly from a woman's boot/ shoe) that had vertical score marks across the leather fragment. There was a Florida water bottle in there as well that was probably complete before the pick hit it. There were other smaller fragments of glass but it seems those fragments were part of the soil matrix inadvertently kicked or swept in'.

Shoe and bottle finds from a 1760s Dutch Colonial **New Hampshire** building were reported in August 2006: 'Sometime about 1965 my parents were in the process of renovating the upstairs of a "circa 1760's Dutch Colonial". In the process we found some loose boards at the end of the eaves this opened up to a "tunnel" that went the length of the house. Inspection with a flashlight revealed some objects about mid-point, well not wanting to lose me my father tied a rope around my ankle just in case I got stuck I then proceeded to crawl in to retrieve the objects. What we recovered was one shoe, a child's I believe and some hand blown bottles that at the time held this tarry substance. The shoe was very worn and had wooden pegs in its construction there was a place for a buckle also. The bottles were very fragile and one broke in the I now realize unfortunate cleaning process. All items were found where the original front entrance had been before later renovations. The bottles are eight inches in height with long necks'.

A concealed shoe was recovered from a hollow in a wall in **New Hampshire**, as reported in September 2000: 'My mother's house in Manchester, New Hampshire, U.S.A. was built, we always assumed, in the 1860's–70's. During a recent renovation of the fieldstone-walled cellar, an old clay pipe turned up in the earthen floor that made up the northern corner. A window in this area (that had been used as a coal chute in the early twentieth century) had a hollow area within the wall, and in it, the workman found an old shoe – a "high button" woman's shoe, smallish and without laces, black and apparently worn. It had been carefully placed, wrapped in old paper within the wall'.

The discovery of mass cards and infant clothing was made in an attic in **New Jersey**, as reported in August 2000: 'I don't know if this will help you. It may not be what you're looking for but … several years ago my friends lived in a house in East Rutherford, New Jersey. They decided to renovate the attic so that they could rent out the rooms on the second floor. When they went into the attic they had found mass cards (small prayercards usually given out at funeral masses as remembrances of the deceased) hanging on strings from the ceiling. Weird but … Anyway, they pulled up the flooring also and found a layer of old infant clothing under the floor boards'.

A dried cat was found under a barn in upstate **New York**, as reported in September 2008: 'This cat was found under a very old barn floor. The barn was located in upstate New York. I was amazed at how well preserved it is'.

A shoe, last, purse and spoon were found together beneath floorboards in **New York** state, as reported in August 2001: 'Gomez Mill House is the oldest house in Orange County, New York. The first floor base was built in 1714. The second owner, added the second story and attic in 1772. We are in the middle of a restoration program funded partially by NY State. Part of the project was removing the second story bathroom circa 1975. When we removed the bathroom and the built up floor, we returned to the 1772 floor. In replacing the floor boards, we found in the adjacent wall, a child's shoe, a "last", a purse and a spoon. Now, this cache would be right above the front door on the second floor'.

Concealed shoes were found in **New York** State, as reported in March 2002: 'I live in a town named Monroe which is approximately 50 miles north and west of New York City. During the course of recent renovations (March 2002) of the old house in which we currently live, a total of eight old shoes were found in a wall of the original structure. A friend and fellow history buff referred us to your website for further research on the meaning and significance of this discovery. This email in being sent in accordance with your advice regarding pertinent facts relevant to this type of find. The shoes were found in the oldest part of the current structure which we believe pre-dates 1800'.

A concealed shoe was recovered from house in **New York** State, as reported in April 2002: 'Found in wall near window as we were re-roofing our 1750ish house in Highland Mills, NY, USA. Can send photos; shoe has been re-concealed. Probably a child's or woman's shoe, well worn. Ours was a Quaker farmhouse as were several others in this area where concealed shoes have been found. Is there any significance to the Quaker connection?' June Swann dated the shoe to the 1860s.

In **New York** State, the discovery of a shoe and other items was reported in February 2006: 'My husband and I bought a 1733 (may date to 1703) stone house in Ulster County, New York (an old Dutch settlement area) and the workmen restoring one of the hearths pulled 3 different shoes (leather soles) out (along with wooden tools, lots of old fabric and, buttons, nails, etc.)'.

A shoe and bottles were found in **North Carolina**, as reported in January 2003: 'I found an old shoe on the chimney ledge in that kitchen, inside of a wall along with old medicine and flavoring bottles, which have been researched and dated to the late 1800's. The single shoe is very worn, but still intact. It has home made shoe laces, twisted of thin twine and was probably very fashionable in that time period. The sole of this shoe is worn completely through and had been repaired many times'.

A dried cat was found during the installation of an air condition system at Fairport Lighthouse, **Ohio**. Reported in November 2017.

The discovery of Marian marks from a 1715 **Pennsylvania** house in Lancaster was reported in November 2010: 'Attached are photos of possible ritual marks in a 1715 house located in Lancaster, PA. We do have many roman numerals marked in the timbers for construction purposes, but we are not familiar with the marks I am attaching to this email. Please note these marks are in the interior attic opposite the window and opposite of the fireplace. All are located on the top timbers of the structure'. Several VV marks.

Owl claws were found inside a window jamb in **Pennsylvania**, as reported in January 2002: 'Just found out about a new case of ritual concealment. Up in Pennsylvania, people restoring a house (18th century I think) found owl claws concealed inside the window jambs. I think they were between the window frame and the wall, inside a hollowed out area'.

Marian marks were found in the Dritt House, built in the mid-eighteenth century, in **Pennsylvania**, as reported in October 2000. There are clear VV symbols.

A cat and bottles were find in **Pennsylvania**, as reported in September 2002: 'I have just moved to Pennsylvania (USA), and the owners of the Victorian house I am living in apparently found a mummified cat under the foundation of their house. Have you heard of any other occurrences of placing dried cats in Victorian houses in the US? I was unaware that this tradition "carried on" into the US from England. The house was built in 1882. The cat was in very good condition as far as dead dried cats are concerned. It was found under the back porch, under what would have been the original door leading out to the porch, which has now been walled up and a new door has been added. There were nine bottles found with the cat. Three were bottles from the Hires Carbonated Beverage company. One of the three had "Hires Carbonated Beverages" on the front of the bottle, and the other two, obviously older, only had

"Hires 17" on the bottom of the bottle. There was also a brown bottle with the words "Hoster Col, O." on the front of the bottle. A small milk bottle was found that said "Rock Farms, Bellefonte, PA" and had a five pointed star in the middle of the logo. Another bottle, mason-type in shape, had "PAT July 11, 1893 JVC Co." on the bottom of it. The other three bottles had no writing of any sort on them'.

The discovery of a cat in Warren Center, **Pennsylvania**, was reported in March 2006: 'We bought a house back in November of 2004 in Warren Center, Pennsylvania. We checked records and things before and found that the house was built in the 1840's. We now have been living in the house for a little over a year and recently started some renovations. While one of the people were in the attic they found a dead dried up old cat. We were all amazed and quite repulsed by this find. The cat was found underneath the blown in insulation so we figure it must have been there before. We found it very odd that the cat is completely undisturbed, no animals or bugs tried to eat it all, the entire cat is still in one large piece. At first I was completely amazed that no one in the house would have heard this poor cat scratching or meowing as I am sure it made quite a racket if it got caught up there and was starving to death. Not to mention, once it died, it had to have smelled terrible and it definitely would have smelled up the rooms it was above and yet no one looked for the source of the smell??? it wasn't difficult to find as it was very close to the only entrance crawl hole to the attic. Now after seeing your site and others with the same type of info, I am wondering if this maybe why I had a dried cat in my attic. Have you heard of these types of things happening in the US??? I am also wondering if you know of any museums that would be interested in having my cat for display as I have it in a box??? Thank you for having this site and I hope to hear from you as I am very interested in this'.

A concealed shoe was recovered from a property in **Tennessee**, as reported in August 2001: 'My brother-in-law was given the shoe by his aunt prior to her death in 1969 … it was removed from a wall in a house built in Civil War times in Commerce. The house was being remodelled in the early 1920's when the shoe was discovered. The house was located near a church and cemetery on a road near Commerce, TN. The exact wall seems to be unknowable since it was not recorded. The shoe was not cleaned and was packed away and has remained packed away or under a display bell only intermittently since that time'.

A concealed shoe was found in a wall in **Utah**, as reported in December 2001: 'we had a case here at the state historic preservation office involving a concealed shoe in a wall. A few weeks ago a woman came in with a brick from a partially demolished interior adobe brick wall (adobe sun-baked clay bricks) was perhaps the most common building material in Utah from the mid-to-late 19th century. In this brick was a partially protruding shoe. She found this curious and wanted our take on it. I spoke with the owner of the house from which this came and she said that it was located in an interior wall at the north side of the house. I'm not sure if that has any significance. The house is quite small, a late-Victorian-era cottage in Salt Lake City, built ca.1905. We have no history of the building's occupants, so I don't know the background of whomever built the house'.

A discovery of shoes in **Vermont** was reported in September 2006: 'My husband was crawling around in the attic of our 1823 farmhouse and found 2 very old, leather shoes in a broken clay bowl. I can send a picture if that would help give you some idea of the age. The home has been in our family for generations and we plan to move back there when we finish renovating it. The shoes both look like they fit the right foot and one had been resoled. One is larger than the other and likely not for the same person. They have straight soles, in that they are not particularly shaped for right or left feet'.

A shoe found in **Vermont** was reported in February 2003: 'In South Ryegate, Vermont a child's side button shoe was found in the crawl space behind the kneewall in the second floor (south side of the house). The house was built in the mid 19th century, I believe. This part of Vermont was widely settled & inhabited by the Scots. I have met elderly people in the area who remember from their childhoods older folks speaking Gaelic'.

A bottle containing pebbles was found in **Virginia**, as reported in February 2001: 'We are currently excavating the site of James Fort. This is the settlement from 1607 in Virginia that brought John Smith and Pocahontas to the level of Historical Icons in this part of the world. The early structures at Jamestown are earth-fast and therefore do not leave much of a foot print for the archaeologists. Buried upright in the clay floor along the projected wall of a structure dating to circa 1610 we found a glass case bottle filled with small quartzite pebbles. There is no clear proof of this being in the threshold of the building due to the lack of architectural remains, however it is in an ideal position for a lobby entrance floor plan. This bottle was a fancier type capped with a pewter lid and would have been a valuable object in 1610 Virginia. This building was built into the perimeter of the fort so not only was it the entrance to the building but it was an entrance to the entire settlement, not the primary entrance though'.

Shoes and other objects found in Salville, **Virginia**, were reported in April 2004: 'I am restoring a house built between 1897-1904. when we removed the walls next to the front door we found shoes, garments, umbrellas, bottles, letters, shoe polish tins and various other items. We are going to put them back. The house is in Salville, Virginia, USA. We believe the original owner probably came here from England.
1. Blue square bottle
2. clear square bottle w/ white powder in it
3. clear bottle w/ poison label
4. wooden bottle – all bottles are corked
5. beer bottles
6. wallpaper
7. ladies corset w/ buttons and pintucks
8. leather covered box, believe to have contained a razor strap
9. ladies jacket
10. white bow tie, think it is a ladies tie
11. American Humor pamphlet
The other papers are parts of letters, baggage tickets and other paper items.
What should I do with these things? think I am going to put shoes and clothing back in wall'.

In March 2010, a report was received of a large number of bottles discovered within walls in **Washington** State: 'Hi my name is Gary, I had found over a 100 bottles in the walls while remodelling not much value but really weird. So in detail they were hanging from a wire maybe 2 on one wire or 6 on one, several wires not a big wall dividing the duplex in half it was all original fur on both sides so they put them in the wall when it was built in 1919 in Snoqualmie, Washington USA. My friend told me about witch bottles and so I am trying to investigate'.

⁘ References

Abbey, A. 2010. *Concealed Within – Purposefully Concealed Artefacts and their Cultural Context*, unpublished MA thesis, 27 August 2010.

Allan, J. 1983. 'Some Post-Medieval Documentary Evidence for the Trade in Ceramics', in P. Davey and R. Hodges (eds), *Ceramics and Trade – The Production and Distribution of Later Medieval Pottery in North-west Europe*. Sheffield: University of Sheffield, 37–45.

Allen, D. 1991. 'Four Bellarmine Stoneware "Witch-bottles" from Abbotts Ann, Hampshire', in E. Lewis (ed.), *Custom and Ceramics*. Wickham: APE, 147–56.

Anderson, M.D. 1971. *History and Imagery in British Churches*. London.

Armitage, P. L. 1989a. 'The Use of Animal Bones as Building Material in Post-Medieval Britain', in D. Serjeantson and T. Waldron (eds), *Diet and Crafts in Towns – The Evidence of Animal Remains from the Roman to Post-Medieval Periods*. BAR British Series 199, 147–60.

_____. 1989b. 'Gazeteer of Sites with Animal Bones Used as Building Material', in D. Serjeantson and T. Waldron (eds), *Diet and Crafts in Towns – The Evidence of Animal Remains from the Roman to Post-Medieval Periods*. BAR British Series 199, 201–23.

Armstrong, A. 1998. 'Protective Markings in Yorkshire Buildings', *Journal of the Yorkshire Vernacular Buildings Group* 82–84.

Atzbach, R. 2000. 'Medieval and Postmedieval Turning Shoes from Kempten (Allgäu), Germany: New Aspects of Shoemaker Technique at about 1500', in I. Planka (ed.), *Shoes in History 2000: The Collection of Lectures of the 3rd International Conference in Zlín, 25th–27th October 2000* (Zlín 2001), 184–194.

Ávido, D. 2013. 'A Case of Deliberately Concealed Objects from Argentina (Province of Buenos Aires, 19th century)', *The Post Hole* 32: 6–13.

Baldwin, G. 1992. *More Ghosts of the Isle of Wight*. Published privately, 7.

Barba, P.A. 1954. *Pennsylvania German Tombstones*. Allentown: The Pennsylvania German Folklore Society.

Bellam, J. 1990. 'The Bellarmine Witch-bottle and its Contents', *Sussex Archaeological Collections* 128: 254–56.

Billingsley, J. 2014. 'Footprints in Lead Roofs', *FLS News – The Newsletter of the Folklore Society* 72 (February): 8–9.

_____. 2017. 'The Head that Works for You: Apotropaic *vs* Show', in J. Billingsley, J. Harte and B. Hoggard (eds). *Hidden Charms 2016: Proceedings*. Hebden Bridge: Northern Earth, 52–59.

Binding, C. 2015. 'Summary of Graffiti and Ritual Protection Marks on the Sarcophagus of Bishop John Harewell in Wells Cathedral, Somerset', privately published.

Binding, C. and L. Wilson. 2004. 'Ritual Protection Marks in Goatchurch Cavern, Burrinton Combe, North Somerset', *Proceedings of the University of Bristol Spelaeological Society* 23(2): 119–33.

_____. 2010. 'Ritual Protection Marks in Wookey Hole and Long Hole, Somerset', *Proceedings of the University of Bristol Spelaeological Society* 25(1): 47–73.

Birmingham Mail, 2009, 10 October.

Blagrave, J. 1671. *Astrological Practice of Physick*. London. Quoted in R. Merrifield, 1954, 'The Use of Bellarmines as Witch-Bottles', *Guildhall Miscellany* 3, offprint.

Blaising, J.M. 2016. 'Archéologie de quelques pratiques apotropaïques entre Lorraine et Luxembourg', *Renaissance du Vieux Metz et des Pays Lorrains*, Bulletin no 181 (October): 32–40.

_____. 2017. 'Archéologie des pratiques apotropaïques entre Lorraine et Luxembourg', in C. Bis-Worch and C. Theune (eds), *Religion, Cults & Rituals in the Medieval Rural Environment*. Leiden: Sidestone Press, 347–56.

Bonner, D. 1994. *Archaeological Investigations at All Saints Church, Loughton, Milton Keynes*. Buckinghamshire County Museum Archaeological Service, County Museum Technical Centre.

Brendan, E. 1985. 'Good Luck "Treasure"', *Period Home* 6 (9): 10.

Brooke, I. 1972. *Footwear – A Short History of European and American Shoes*. London: Pitman.

Brooks, E. 2000. 'Watch Your Step', *The National Trust Magazine*, 91 (Autumn): 66–68.

Brunskill, R.W. 1992. *Traditional Buildings of Britain – An Introduction to Vernacular Architecture*, no imprint.

Buchanan, R.H. 1956. 'A Buried Hose Skull', *Ulster Folklife* 2: 60–61.

Bunn, I.A.W. 1982. '"A Devil's Shield": Notes on Suffolk Witch-Bottles', *Lantern* 39 (Autumn): 3–7.

Cambridge Evening News. 1979. 'Witchcraft in the Pub!', 25 May, 26.

Cambridge Weekly News, 23 April 1981.

Carmarthen Journal. 2000. 'Mummified Cat Unearthed', 27 September, 7.

Cawte, E.C. 1978. *Ritual Animal Disguise*. Ipswich: The Folklore Society.

Champion, M. 2014. 'The Graffiti Inscriptions of St Mary's Church, Troston', *Proceedings of the Suffolk Institute for Archaeology* 43(2).

_____. 2015. *Medieval Graffiti: The Lost Voice of England's Churches*. London: Ebury Press.

Charleston, R.J. 1984. *English Glass and the Glass used in England, 400–1940*. London: George Allen & Unwin.

Clarke, H. and A. Carter. 1977. *Excavations in Kings Lynn 1963–1970*, Society for Medieval Archaeology, Monograph series, no 7.

Cobban, J.L. 2011. *The Lure of the Lancashire Witches*. Lancaster: Palatine Book.

Coleman, S. 1963. 'A Wealden House at Ixworth', *Proceedings of the Suffolk Institute of Archaeology* XXIX, part 3.

Collins, A. 1985. 'The Guardian Dog of Leigh', *Earthquest News*,1 (13): 9–18.

_____. 2003. 'The Devil in Essex – Folk Magic in a English Village', *Cauldron*, 108: 28–33.

Colm. 2015. 'Buried Horse Skulls: Folklore and Superstition in Early Modern Ireland', retrieved 11 December 2016 from http://irisharchaeology.ie/2015/02/buried-horse-skulls-folklore-and-superstition-in-early-modern-ireland/.

Colne Valley Chronicle. 1984. 'Spirits Mystery in Door Charm', 20 January.

Costello, J. 2014. 'Tracing the Footsteps of Ritual: Concealed Footwear in America', in C. Fennell and C. Manning (eds), *Manifestations of Magic: The Archaeology and Material Culture of Folk Religion*, a special edition of *Historical Archaeology*, 48 (3): 35–51.

Cornish and Devon Post, 6 October 1928.

Cornwall, I.W. 1956. *Bones for the Archaeologist*. London: Phoenix.

Country Life, 1955, 1682.

Coxhead, J.R.W. 1959. *Devon Traditions and Fairy Tales*. Exmouth: Raleigh Press.

Darwood, A. and A. Sherriff. 2003. 'Apotropaic Markings and Spiritual Middens found in a House at 21 Shore Street, Anstruther, Fife', *Tayside and Fife Archaeological Journal*, 9: 124–28.

Davies, O. 1999a. *A People Bewitched – Witchcraft and Magic in Nineteenth-Century Somerset*, privately published.

_____. 1999b. *Witchcraft, Magic and Culture 1736–1951*. Manchester: Manchester University Press.

Dean, J. and N. Hill. 2014. 'Burn Marks on Buildings: Accidental or Deliberate', in *Vernacular Architecture*, 45: 1–15.

de Somer, R. 2003. 'Is there a cat in the house', *Northern Earth* 95 (Autumn): 7–11.

Devon and Cornwall Notes and Queries, 11, 1921, 288.

Dixon-Smith, D. 1990. 'Concealed Shoes', *Archaeological Leather Group Newsletter*, 6 (Spring).

Dodds, G. 1870. 'The Translation of an Ancient Formula of Magical Exorcism, Written in Cipher', *The Reliquary* X: 129–38.

Donmoyer, P. 2013. *Hex Signs – Myth and Meaning in Pennsylvania Dutch Barn Stars*. A publication of the Pennsylvania German Cultural Heritage Center at Kutztown University of Pennsylvania.

_____. 2014. 'The Concealment of Written Blessings in Pennsylvania Barns', in C. Fennell and Manning (eds), *Manifestations of Magic: The Archaeology and Material Culture of Folk Religion*, a special edition of *Historical Archaeology*, 48 (3): 179–95.

Dorset Evening Echo, 30 April 1987.

Duffy, E, 1992. *The Stripping of the Altars – Traditional Religion in England 1400–1580*. New Haven, CT and London.

Dundee Courier. 1995. 'Walls Reveal Cult Find', 26 June.

Dutt, W.A. 1905. *Homeland Handbook No 41 – Kings Lynn and its Surroundings*, Thew and Son.

Dyas, E. 1993. 'Shoe-Burials – to Ward-Off Witches and Evil Spirits!', *Bugle Annual*, 50.

Eastern Daily Press 1963, 27 February.

Easton, T. 1983. 'Shoes and Other Objects of Superstition found in the Debenham Area', *Suffolk Local History Review and Newsletter* (September): 28–29.

_____. 1997. 'Spiritual Middens', in Paul Oliver (ed.), *The Encyclopedia of Vernacular Architecture of the World*. Cambridge: Cambridge University Press, 568.

_____. 1999. 'Ritual Marks on Historic Timber', *Weald and Downland Open Air Museum Magazine*, Spring, 22–30.

_____. 2011. 'Candle Powers', *Cornerstone* 32(4): 56–60.

_____. 2012. 'Burning Issues', *SPAB Magazine* (Winter): 44–47.

_____. 2013. 'Plumbing the Spiritual World', *SPAB Magazine* (Winter): 40–47.

_____. 2014a. 'Portals of Protection', *SPAB Magazine* (Winter): 53–57.

_____. 2014b. 'Four Spiritual Middens in Mid Suffolk, England, ca 1650–1850', in C. Fennell and C. Manning (eds), *Manifestations of Magic: The Archaeology and Material Culture of Folk Religion*, a special edition of *Historical Archaeology*, 48 (3): 10–34.

_____. 2018. 'Sixteenth Century Belief in Witchcraft: A Comment on the Previous Article by Martin Higgins', *Vernacular Architecture Group – Newsletter*, 75 (July): 26–27.

Eastop, D. 2001. 'Garments Deliberately Concealed in Buildings', in R. Wallis and K. Lymer (eds), *A Permeability of Boundaries? New Approaches to the Archaeology Art, Religion and Folklore*. Oxford: BAR International Series S936, British Archaeological Reports, 79–83.

Ellis, B. 1993. *Halkyn Mountain Communities in Times Past*. Countryside News.

Emery, N., J. Warner and A. Pearson. 1990. 'Causeway House, Northumberland', *Archaeologia Aeliana*, 4th series, Vol XVIII.

Evans, G.E. 1966. *The Pattern under the Plough*. London: Faber & Faber.

Evans, I. 2010. 'Touching Magic – Deliberately Concealed Objects in Old Australian Houses and Buildings', PhD Thesis, University of Newcastle, NSW.

_____. 2011. 'Ritual Marks & Magic', *Trust News Australia* (May): 20–21.

_____. 2015. 'Defence Against the Devil – Apotropaic Marks in Australia', accessed via Academia.edu on 23 April 2017.

_____. 2016. 'House Magic Marks Discovered in Queensland', accessed via Academia.edu on 23 April 2017.

Farley, M. 1978. 'A Witch-Bottle from Winslow', *Records of Bucks* XX (part 4): 635–36.

Fearn, A. 2017. 'A Light in the Darkness – the Taper Burns of Donington le Heath Manor House', *Peregrinations: Journal of Medieval Art and Architecture* 6 (1): 92–118.

Fletcher, E. 2005. *Leaden Tokens & Tallies – Roman to Victorian*. Essex: Greenlight Publishing.

Foley, R. and K. Foley. 1991. 'Bryant's Surprise', *Old House Journal* 19 (3): 49–50.

Folklore. 1938. 'Thunderbolts', 49 (XL): 48–49.

Fraser, M. 1949. *Companion into Worcestershire*. Methuen.

Gaimster, D. 1997. *German Stoneware 1200–1900*. London: British Museum.

Garrad, L.S. 1989. 'Additional Examples of Possible House Charms in the Isle of Man', *Folklore* 100 (1): 110.

Girvan, J. 1997. *Ghosts of Devizes: Casebook II*, privately published.

Glanvil, J. 1681. *Sadducismus Triumphatus*, 205–208. Quoted in R. Merrifield, 1954, 'The Use of Bellarmines as Witch-Bottles', *Guildhall Miscellany* 3, off-print.

Golding-Bird, G. 1933. *East Grinstead and its Parish Church*, 11.

Gooley, V. 1993. 'Skull of Horse Discovered under Floorboards of County Pub', *Hereford Times*, 8 July 1993.

Grant, I.F. and H. Cheape. 1987. *Periods in Highland History*. London: Shepheard-Walwyn.

Green, C. 1999. *John Dwight's Fulham Pottery – Excavations 1971–79*. London: English Heritage.

Gruffydd, E. 1981. 'A Buckley Pot Used in Witchcraft', *Buckley* 6: 42.

Guilding, J.M. (ed). 1892. *Reading Records – The Diary of the Corporation*, London, V2, 311–12.

Gutch, E. 1901. *Examples of Printed Folklore Concerning the North Riding of Yorkshire, York and the Ainsty*. London: Folklore Society.

Gwyndaf, R. and E. Gruffydd. 1985. 'A Buckley Pot Used as a Charm', *Buckley* 10: 14–16.

Hall, L. 2003. 'Fixtures and Fittings', in E. Roberts (ed.), *Hampshire Houses 1250–1700*. Hampshire County Council, 63–124.

Harte, J. 2017. 'Luck and Dread: How Household Curiosities become Ritual Protectors', in J. Billingsley, J. Harte and B. Hoggard (eds), *Hidden Charms 2016: Proceedings*. Hebden Bridge: Northern Earth, 24–31.

Hartland, E.S. 1897. 'On an Inscribed Leaden Tablet found at Dymock, in Gloucestershire', *Reliquary and Illustrated Archaeologist*, New Series III: 140–50.

Hayes, R.H. and J.G. Rutter. 1972. *Cruck Framed Buildings in Ryedale & Eskdale*. Scarborough: Scarborough and District Archaeological Society.

Hayhurst, Y. 1989. 'A Recent Find of a Horse Skull in a House at Ballaugh, Isle of Man', *Folklore* 100(1): 105–107.

Henderson, L. and E.J. Cowan. 2001. *Scottish Fairy Belief*. Scotland: Tuckwell Press.

Henderson, P. 1983. 'Life at the Top', *Country Life* 3 (1): 6–9.

Hereford Times. 1987. 'Strange Discovery', 26 February.

Herts and Essex Observer, 11 November 1999, 24.

Hoggard, B. 2001. 'Home's Hidden Charms', *SPAB News* 22(3): 18–21.

———. 2004. 'The Archaeology of Counter-Witchcraft and Popular Magic', in O. Davies and W. Blécourt. *Beyond the Witch-Trials*. Manchester: Manchester University Press, pp. 167–86.

———. 2016a. 'Witch-Bottles: Their Contents, Contexts and Uses', in R. Hutton (ed.), *Physical Evidence for Ritual Acts, Sorcery and Witchcraft in Christian Britain – A Feeling for Magic*. Basingstoke: Palgrave, pp. 91–105.

_____. 2016b. 'Concealed Animals', in R. Hutton (ed.), *Physical Evidence for Ritual Acts, Sorcery and Witchcraft in Christian Britain – A Feeling for Magic*. Basingstoke: Palgrave, pp. 106–17.

_____. 2016c. 'Threshold Guardians', in A. Hulubas and I. Repciuc (eds), *Riturile de trecere în actualitate: The Rites of Passage Time After Time*. Editura Universităţii 'Alexandru Ioan Cuza' Iaşi, pp. 333–49.

_____. 2016d. 'Witch-Bottles: Message in a Bottle', *The Society for the Protection of Ancient Buildings Magazine* (Spring): 45–47.

_____. 2017a. 'Introduction', in J. Billingsley, J. Harte and B. Hoggard (eds), *Hidden Charms 2016: Proceedings*. Hebden Bridge: Northern Earth, pp. 3–4.

_____. 2017b. 'Evidence of Unseen Forces: Apotropaic Objects on the Threshold of Materiality', in J. Billingsley, J. Harte and B. Hoggard (eds), *Hidden Charms 2016: Proceedings*. Hebden Bridge: Northern Earth, pp. 5–13.

Hoggard, B. and A. Jessup. 2017. 'Llancaiach Fawr Manor: Fortified Against Evil', *The Society for the Protection of Ancient Buildings Magazine* (Autumn): 51–55.

Holmes, M.R. 1950. 'The So-Called "Bellarmine" Mask on Imported Rhenish Stoneware', *Antiquaries Journal* XXXI: 173–79.

Hooper, B. 1988. 'Ritual and Magic in Manuden', *Essex Journal* 23 (1): 3–4.

_____. 1989. 'A Shoe for the Devil', *Essex Countryside* 37 (395), December: 22–23.

Howard, M. 1951. 'Dried Cats', *Man – A Monthly Record of Anthropological Science*, LI (252): 149–51.

Huber, G.D. 2017. *The Historic Barns of South-Eastern Pennsylvania – Architecture and Preservation, Built 1750–1900*. Atglen, PA: Schiffer.

Hukantaival, S. 2009. 'Horse Skulls and Alder-Horse: The Horse as a Depositional Sacrifice in Buildings', in A. Bliujienè (ed.), *The Horse and Man in European Antiquity: Worldview, Burial Rites and Military and Everyday Life*, Archaeologia Baltica 11, Klaipèda: Klaipèda University Press, 350–56.

_____. 2015. 'Frogs in Miniature Coffins from Churches in Finland: Folk Magic in Christian Holy Places', *MIRATOR* 16 (1): 192–220.

_____. 2016, '"For a Witch Cannot Cross Such a Threshold!" – Building Concealment Traditions in Finland c. 1200–1950', *Archaeologia Medii Aevi Finlandiae XXIII Suomen keskiajan arkeologian seura – Sällskapet för medeltidsarkeologi I Finland*, Turku.

_____. 2017. 'Same Mental Idea, Different Manifestation? Hidden Charms in Finland and the British Isles', in J. Billingsley, J. Harte and B. Hoggard (eds), *Hidden Charms 2016: Proceedings*. Hebden Bridge: Northern Earth, pp. 14–23.

Hulubaş, A. 2018. 'A View on Active Construction Rites from Romania', at the *Hidden Charms 2* conference, 21 April, Salisbury. Publication pending.

Irvine, W.F. and N.F. McMillan. 1969. 'A Foundation Sacrifice at Birkenhead Priory', *Antiquity* 43 (169): 56–57.

Jewitt, L. 1870. 'Note on a Curious Love Charm', *The Reliquary* X: 139.

Johnson, N. 1994. 'Circle and Floret Designs'. *Mosaic – National Trust Archaeological Newsletter* (Winter): 2.

Kelly, P, 2000, 'Radicals', *Chemistry in Britain*, February, 56.

Keverne, R. 1947. *Tales of Old Inns*. London; Collins.

Kittredge, G.L. 1928. *Witchcraft in Old and New England*. Cambridge, MA: Harvard University Press, 102.

Lang, J.B. 1969. 'Charming of Cattle', *Proceedings of the Dorset Natural Historical & Archaeological Society*, 91: 222–23.

Lecouteux, C. 2000 (2013 English Translation). *The Tradition of Household Spirits – Ancestral Lore and Practices*. Paris.

Le Pard, G. 2008. 'An Unusual Cat Burial from Charmouth', *Proceedings of the Dorset Natural History and Archaeology Society*, 129: 181–82.

Leppard, M.J. 2002. 'Ritual Protection', *East Grinstead Museum Compass*, 8 (Summer).

Lewis, H. 2010. 'From Prehistoric to Urban. Shoreditch: Excavations at Holywell Priory, Holywell Lane, London EC2', *London Archaeologist*, 12 (9), Summer: 249–54.

Lewis, J. 1973. *Heath Robinson – Artist and Comic Genius*. London.

Mackay, A. 1991. 'Northampton Museums Concealed Shoe Index'. Northampton Museum, 16 April.

Magilton, J. 1992. 'An East Dean Mystery', *Chichester and District Archaeology*: 70–71.

_____. 1993. 'An East Dean Mystery Resolved', *Chichester and District Archaeology*, 37–38.

Mallory, J. and F. McCormick. 1984, 'Horse Skulls at Bay Farm Cottage, Carnlough', *The Glynns – Journal of the Glens of Antrim Historical Society*, 12: 50–53.

Manchester Evening News, 2007, 29 August.

Mann, E. 1934. *Old Bungay*, London.

Manninen, M. 2015. *Artifacts of the Flower of Life*, downloaded from Academia.edu on 18 August 2017.

Manning, C. 2012. *Homemade Magic: Concealed Deposits in Architectural Contexts in the Eastern United States*. Unpublished PhD Thesis, Ball State University.

_____. 2014. 'The Material Culture of Ritual Concealments in the United States', in C. Fennell and C. Manning (eds), *Manifestations of Magic: The Archaeology and Material Culture of Folk Religion*, a special edition of *Historical Archaeology*, 48 (3): 52–83.

Marks, R, 2002. 'A Late Medieval Pilgrimage Cult: Master John Schorn of North Marston and Windsor', in S. Brown (ed.), *Windsor – Medieval Archaeology, Art and Architecture of the Thames Valley*. Leeds: British Archaeological Association.

Massey, A. 2017. *Witch Bottle Magic*, privately published monograph.

Massey, A. and T. Clough. 2015. 'A Witch-Bottle from Exton, Rutland', *Rutland Record – Journal of the Rutland Local History and Record Society* 35: 209–12.

Massey, A. and T. Edmonds. 2000. 'The Reigate Witch Bottle', *Current Archaeology* 169: 34–36.

Massey, A., R.M. Smith and T.A.D. Smith. 2003. 'A Witch Bottle from Dorset', *Education in Chemistry* (July): 97–100.

Mather, C. 1691. *Late Memorable Providences*, quoted in G.L. Kittredge, 1928, *Witchcraft in Old and New England*, Cambridge, MA: Harvard, University Press, 102.

Mather, I. 1694. *An Essay for the Recording of Illustrious Providences: Wherein, an Account Is Given of Many Remarkable and Very Memorable Events, Which Have Happened in This Last Age; Especially in New-England*. Boston, MA: Samuel Green.

Meeson, B. 2005. 'Ritual Marks and Graffiti: Curiosities or Meaningful Symbols?', *Vernacular Architecture* 36: 41–48.

Merrifield, R. 1954. 'The Use of Bellarmines as Witch-Bottles', *Guildhall Miscellany* 3, offprint.

———. 1955. 'A Charm Against Witchcraft', *Country Life*, 23 June, 1612–13.

———. 1969. 'Folklore in London Archaeology', *London Archaeologist* 2 (5): 99–104.

———. 1987. *The Archaeology of Ritual and Magic*. London: Batsford.

Merrifield, R. and Norman Smedley. 1958–1960. 'Two Witch-Bottles from Suffolk', *Proceedings of the Suffolk Institute of Archaeology*, XXVIII.

Moad, M. 1976. 'The Old Vicarage, Upchurch and the Discovery of Leather Shoes', *Kent Archaeological Review* (Autumn): 110–12.

Montembault, V. 2005. 'Postmedieval Shoes Concealed in a Barn at Saint-Benoît du Sault', in I. Ericsson and R. Atzbach (eds), *Depotfunde aus Gebäuden in Zentraleuropa*. Berlin: scrîpvaz-Verlag, pp. 31–33.

Morris, E. 1980. 'Medieval and Post Medieval Pottery in Worcester – A Type Series', *Transactions of the Worcestershire Archaeological Society*, 3rd series, 7: 248.

Morton, E. and M. Maddison. 2017. 'Burn Marks on Furniture: Their Dating and Relationship to Building Timbers', *Vernacular Architecture Group – Newsletter* 73 (August): 22–25.

Mosaic - the National Trust Archaeology Newsletter. 1994. Summer: 25.

Nattrass, M. 1962. 'Witch-posts', *Gwerin* 3 (5) June: 254–67.

News of the World, 14 April 1985.

Nielsen, I. 2017. 'Building Sacrifices and Magical Protection', in C. Bis-Worch and C. Theune (eds), *Religion, Cults & Rituals in the Medieval Rural Environment*. London: Sidestone Press, 325–36.

North Wilts Herald, 1925, 24 April and 1 May,

Noyes, E. 1913. *Salisbury Plain: Its Stones, Cathedral, City, Villages and Folk*. London: Dent.

O'Connor, T. 2000. *The Archaeology of Animal Bones, Sutton*. Gloucestershire.

Ó Danachair, C. 1970. 'The Luck of the House', in *Studies in Folklore Presented to Emyr Estyn Evans*, Ulster Folk Museum, 22.

Ó Súilleabháin, S. 1945. 'Foundation Sacrifices', *Journal of the Royal Society of Antiquaries of Ireland*, 75: 49–50.

Oliver, P. (ed.). 1997. *The Encyclopedia of Vernacular Architecture of the World*. Cambridge: Cambridge University Press.

Owen, T.M. 1959. *Welsh Folk Customs*. Cardiff: National Museum of Wales.

———. 1960. 'A Charm from Chirk', *Transactions of Denbighshire Historical Society*, 9.

Page, R.I. 1971. 'How Long Did the Scandinavian Language Survive in England? The Epigraphical Evidence', in R.I. Page, *Runes and Runic Inscriptions*. Woodbridge: Boydell Press, 181–96.

Palmer, Roy. 1992. *The Folklore of Hereford and Worcester*. Herefordshire: Logaston Press.

Pantin, W.A. 1961. 'Medieval Inns', in E.M. Jope (ed.), *Studies in Building History – Essays in Recognition of the Work of B H St. J O'Neil*. Odhams Press Ltd, 166–91.

Parker, R. 1976. *The Common Stream: Foxton*. London.

Parsons, C.O. 1964. *Witchcraft and Demonology in Scott's Fiction*. Oliver and Boyd, 137-8.

Patterson, S. 2017. 'The Strange Tale of the Discovery of a Curse in West Cornwall', a lecture presented at *Museum of Witchcraft & Magic Cursing Conference 2017*, Boscastle, Cornwall.

Paynter, W.H. 1929. 'The Evil Eye', *Cornish Times*, 23 August, 2.

_____. 2016. *Cornish Witchcraft – The Confessions of a Westcountry Witch-Finder*. Liskeard, privately published with foreword by Jason Semmens.

Penney, S.H. 1976. 'Axes Arrowheads and other Antiquities in Irish Folklore', *Ulster Folklife* 22: 70–75.

Pennick, N. 1986. *Skulls, Cats and Witch-bottles*, privately published.

_____. 1995. *Mummified Cats*, privately published.

Pennington, J. 1992. 'Bellarmines and Witch-Bottles in Sussex', *Sussex Archaeological Collections* 130: 242.

Perkins, A. and Armine Edmonds. 1999. *The Book of Sonning*, revised edition, Buckingham: Baron Books.

Pitt, F. 1997. 'Builders, Bakers and Madhouses: Some Recent Information from the *Concealed Shoe Index*', a report on a lecture at the Archaeological Leather Group AGM in September 1997 contained in 'Hidden Shoes and Concealed Beliefs', *Archaeological Leather Group Newsletter*, February 1998.

Playfair, G.L. 1985. *The Haunted Pub Guide*, Guild Publishing, 75.

Pleasant, J. 1995. 'Strange Curse of the Feline Mummy', *Hong Kong Standard*, November.

Porter, Enid. 1969. *Cambridgeshire Folklore and Customs*. London.

Pritchard, V. 1967. *English Medieval Graffiti*. Cambridge: Cambridge University Press.

Proceedings of the Dorset Natural History and Archaeological Society 74, 1952, 110.

Proceedings of the Dorset Natural History and Archaeological Society 117, 1995, 142.

Radford, E. and M.A. Radford. 1961. Edited and revised by C. Hole, *The Encyclopedia of Superstitions*, Helicon Edition, 1980.

Report and Transactions of the Devonshire Association for the Advancement of Science, Literature and Art 103, 1971, 266.

Report and Transactions of the Devonshire Association for the Advancement of Science, Literature and Art 110, 1978, 214.

Rhea, N. 2011. 'Blessed Houses Marked with an X', *Darlington & Stockton Times*, 1 April.

_____. 2014. 'Witch-posts Reinterpreted', *FLS News – The Newsletter of the Folklore Society* 73 (June): 13–15.

Richard, J.D. 1993. *The Bedern Foundry*, The Archaeology of York series (ed. P Addyman), York.

Rodwell, K. and I. Friel. 2004. 'Acton Court: The Evolution of an Early Tudor Courtier's House', extract of report, English Heritage, London.

Rushen, J. 1984. 'Folklore and Witchcraft in Tudor and Stuart England', *Popular Archaeology* (April): 33–36.

———. 1985. 'Hidden Secrets of Old Houses', *The Period Home* 1(6): 11–13.

Rye, W.B. 1865. *England as Seen by Foreigners in the Days of Elizabeth and James the First*. London.

Sandklef, A. 1949. 'Singing Flails: a Study in Threshing-floor Constructions, Flail Threshing Traditions and the Magic Guarding of the House', *F F Communications* LVI (136).

Schad, P. 2005. 'Tiermumien aus Depotfunden im Landkreis Ludwigsburg – Relikte frühneuzeitlicher Magievorstellung?', in I. Ericsson and R. Atzbach, *Depotfunde aus Gebäuden in Zentraleuropa*. Berlin: scrîpvaz-Verlag, pp. 151–61.

Scharfenberger, G.P. 2009. 'Upon this Rock: Salvage Archaeology at the Early-Eighteenth-Century Baptist Holmdel Baptist Church', *Historical Archaeology* 43 (1): 12–29.

Semmens, J. 2000. 'The Usage of Witch-Bottles and Apotropaic Charms in Cornwall', *Old Cornwall* 12 (6): 25–30.

———. 2017. 'Cunning-folk and the Protection of Property: The View from the Westcountry', in J. Billingsley, J. Harte and B. Hoggard (eds), *Hidden Charms 2016: Proceedings*. Hebden Bridge: Northern Earth.

Sheehan, J. 1990. 'A Seventeenth Century Dried Cat from Ennis Friary, Co. Clare', *North Munster Antiquarian Journal* XXXII: 64–68.

Sieveking, P. 1999. 'Death is Kept at Bay by the Skull of a Cow', *Sunday Telegraph*, 12 September 1999.

Smedley, N., E. Owles and F.R. Paulsen. 1964–1966. 'More Suffolk Witch-Bottles', *Proceedings of the Suffolk Institute of Archaeology* XXX: 88–93.

Smith, L. 1997. 'Compass, Cut Circle and Daisy Wheel', *The Mortice and Tenon*, 5.

———. 2007. 'A Three-Dimensional, Timber-Framed Encyclopaedia of Geometrical Carpentry Design', *Vernacular Architecture* 38: 35–47.

Søvsø, M. 2017. 'Votive Offerings in Buildings from Rural Settlements', in C. Bis-Worch and C. Theune (eds), *Religion, Cults & Rituals in the Medieval Rural Environment*. Leiden: Sidestone Press, 337–46.

Stenning, D.F. 1989. 'Early Brick Chimney Stacks', *Essex Archaeology and History* 20: 92–102.

Stevens, J. 1977. *Old Jersey Houses and Those Who Lived in Them*. Chicester: The History Press.

Stewart, R.J. 1990. *Robert Kirk: Walker Between Worlds – A New Edition of the Secret Commonwealth of Elves, Fauns and Fairies*. Dorset.

Stockton, J. 1981. *Victorian Bottles – A Collectors Guide to Yesterday's Empties*. London: David & Charles.

Streeten, A.D.F. 1976. 'A Bellarmine Bottle from Hook Green, Lamberhurst', *Archaeologia Cantiana* XCII: 227–28.

Swann, J. 1969. 'Shoes Concealed in Buildings', *Journal of Northampton Art Gallery and Museum*, 6 December: 8–21.

———. 1982. *Shoes*. London: Batsford.

_____. 1996. 'Concealed Shoes in Buildings', *Costume Society Journal* 30: 56–69.

_____. 1997. 'Shoes Concealed in Buildings', a report on a lecture at the Archaeological Leather Group AGM in September 1997, in 'Concealed Shoes and Concealed Beliefs', *Archaeological Leather Group Newsletter*, February 1998.

_____. 2005. 'Interpreting Concealed Shoes and Associated Finds', in I. Ericsson and R. Atzbach, *Depotfunde aus Gebäuden in Zentraleuropa*. Berlin: scrîpvaz-Verlag, 115–19.

Taylor, A. 1902. *The Ancient Crosses of Lancashire: The Hundred of West Derby*.

Tester, P.J. 1978. 'Excavations on the site of Leeds Priory II', *Archaeologia Cantiana* XCIV: 82.

The Local de. 2010. '300 Year Old Shoes found in Castle Wall during Restoration', 5 November 2010.

The Bedforshire Advertiser. 1903. 21 August.

The Sunday People, 1971, 9 November.

The Times, 1954, 'Witchcraft in Stuart Times', 14 February 1954, 8.

The Times, 1954, 19 March, 3.

The Times, 1999, 24 March, 21.

The Times, 1999 29 March, 21.

The Yorkshire Observer. 1944. 'Witchcraft: Story of a Charm', 2.

Thetford and Watton Times, 1965, 10 October.

Thomas, K. 1971. *Religion and the Decline of Magic*. London.

Tilley, E.W. 1965. 'A Witch-Bottle from Gravesend', *Archaeologia Cantiana* LXXX: 252–56.

Tolhurst, P. 2018. *This Hollow Land – Aspects of Norfolk Folklore*. Norwich.

Trumbull, H.C. 1896. *The Threshold Covenant*. Edinburgh.

Underwood, P. 1986. *This Haunted Isle: The Ghosts and Legends of Britain's Historic Buildings*. Javelin Books.

Vandenbeusch, M. and D. Antoine. 2015. 'Under Saint Michael's Protection: A Tattoo from Christian Nubia', *Journal of the Canadian Centre for Epigraphic Documents* 1: 15–19.

Van Gennep, A. 1960. *The Rites of Passage*. Chicago: University of Chicago Press.

Vernacular Architecture Group Newsletter 67, July 2014, 15.

Vernot, N. 2014. *Le cœur en Franche-Comté à l'époque moderne: iconographie et symbolique*, doctoral thesis in History, Paris, 4 vol.

H.L. Verry, *Manuden (Essex) Annals of the parish Church of Saint Mary the Virgin Since Ad 1143*, privately published in 1978, 13–14.

Walker, J. 1987. 'A Witch Bottle from Hellington', *Norfolk Archaeology* 40: 113–14.

Waring, E. 1977. *Ghosts and Legends of the Dorset Countryside*. Tisbury: Compton Press.

Wells Bladen, W. 1900–1901. 'Notes on the Folklore of North Staffordshire, Chiefly Collected at Stone', *Staffordshire Field Club* 35: 133–85.

Western Morning News, 12 October 2003, 'Renovations Reveal Link to Witchcraft'.

Wharfe Valley Times, 1983, December.

Wheeler, W. 2017. 'Magical Dwelling: Apotropaic Building Practices in the New World Dutch Cultural Hearth', in C. Bis-Worch and C. Theune (eds),

Religion, Cults & Rituals in the Medieval Rural Environment. Leiden: Sidestone Press, 373–96.

Wiliam, E. 2000. 'Concealed Hose Skulls – Testimony and Message', in *From Corrib to Cultra – Folklife Essays in Honour of Alan Gailey.* Belfast: QUB, 136–49.

Williams, D.J. 1998. '1.3 Post-medieval Ritual Deposits at 17 and 19 Whitecross Street, Barton-on-Humber', in *The Anglo-Saxon Cemetery at Castledyke.* Sheffield, 4–6.

Wilson, L. 2017. '"By Midnight, By Moonlight": Ritual Protection Marks in Caves Beneath the Mendip Hills, Somerset', in J. Billingsley, J. Harte and B. Hoggard (eds), *Hidden Charms 2016: Proceedings.* Hebden Bridge: Northern Earth, 41–51.

Wilshire Archaeological Magazine (1925-1927), 43, 381.

Winzar, P. 1995. 'Witchcraft Counter Spells in Charing', *Archaeologia Cantiana* CXV: 23–28.

Withers, A. 1998. 'History Revealed under the Floor', *East Anglian Daily Times,* 15 December.

Wright, A. 2009. *The Bellarmine and other German Stoneware.* Little Dunham.

_____. 2011. *The Bellarmine and other German Stoneware II.* Little Dunham.

_____. 2016. *The Bellarmine and other German Stoneware III.* Little Dunham.

Wright, J. 2017. 'Cultural Anxieties and Ritual Protection in High-status Early Modern Houses', in J. Billingsley, J. Harte and B. Hoggard (eds), *Hidden Charms 2016: Proceedings.* Hebden Bridge: Northern Earth, 71–81.

Wright, T. 1922. *The Romance of the Shoe – The History of Shoemaking.* London.

Yeatherd, A. 1920. 'A Bellarmine Jug found in Huntingdonshire', *Transactions of the Cambridgeshire & Huntingdonshire Archaeological Society,* Vol IV, part IV, 125–26.

Yorkshire Archaeological Journal, 1989, 'Fine South Yorkshire Timber Framed Houses', 59: 65.

Yorkshire Vernacular Buildings Study Group newsletter, 2017, June.

●● Index

www.ingramcontent.com/pod-product-compliance
Lightning Source LLC
Chambersburg PA
CBHW070903030426
42336CB00014BA/2304